LeRoi Smith

MONEY-SAVERS' DO-IT-YOURSELF CAR REPAIR

MACMILLAN PUBLISHING CO., INC.

New York

COLLIER MACMILLAN PUBLISHERS

London

ACKNOWLEDGEMENT

The author wishes to thank the numerous companies who have supplied technical drawings for this book, with special thanks to the Mobil Oil Corp. for the loan of their superb cutaway illustrations.

Macmillan Publishing Co., Inc.
866 Third Avenue, New York, N. Y. 10022
Collier-Macmillan Canada Ltd.

Library of Congress Cataloging in Publication Data

Smith, LeRoi Tex.
    Money-savers' do-it-yourself car repair.

    1. Automobiles—Maintenance and repair.   I.   Title.
TL152.S613   629.28'8'22   73-18509
ISBN 0-02-611940-4

First Printing 1975
Printed in the United States of America

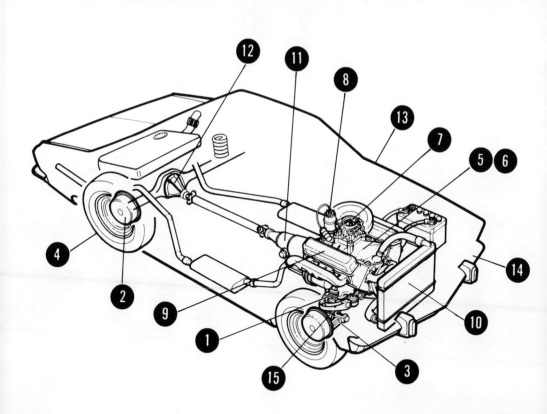

contents

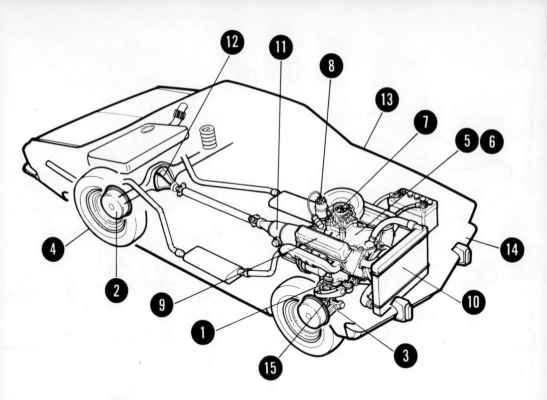

introduction

NEXT TO A HOUSE, an automobile is the largest single purchase the average American makes—and his total lifetime expenditure on automobiles is enormous. The typical family now purchases a new car once every six years, and many families have two or more cars. Suppose a family is accustomed to pay about $5000 for a car, and that prices stay about the same. It is easy to project total investment in private transportation for this family at nearly $75,000 over a driving period of 40 years. During this period the family is likely to own six or 7 new $5000 cars (roughly $35,000); to use $600 worth of gasoline a year ($24,000); to pay an average of $100 a year for insurance ($4000); to spend an average of $50 a year on tires ($2000); and to spend an average of $200 a year on maintenance ($8000).

Of course it is possible to reduce these costs considerably. You can save quite a bit of money—around $10,000—by purchasing cars in the $3500 range instead of the $5000 range. If you can double gasoline mileage, to an average of 20 mpg rather than 10 mpg, you can save another $12,000. If you have relatively light cars, keep your eyes open for sales, and drive properly, you may save as much as 30 percent on tires. You can even save on insurance by shopping for it carefully and maintaining a good driving record.

Finally—and this is the reason for this book—you can save yourself many thousands of dollars in the field of maintenance, whether you economize in other ways or not. I have figured maintenance costs to average about $200 a year, although it can be much more. If your car requires a new engine, or automatic transmission, or suspension components, during the time you own it, the annual maintenance costs are going to average out very high. Much of this expense can be saved if you are willing to do some of your own vehicle repairs and periodic maintenance at home, and if you understand automobiles well enough to catch trouble before it becomes expensive.

Most professional mechanics agree that abuse is the single most important reason why automobiles break down. The modern American car is easily capable of logging 150,000 trouble-free miles on the odometer *if* the owner is careful to keep it in excellent tune, lubricated properly and with the suspension aligned, and if he observes reasonable driving habits.

Once the average American male was expected to be mechanically adept, and he was. Grandfather *had* to know the basic elements of automobile engineering, because there were few repair shops and no extra money to pay the professional mechanic.

But the situation has changed. Grandfather's cars were simple; all that was usually needed to repair a Model T was a normal intelligence quotient, a pair of pliers, and some baling wire. The modern car, with all its engineering sophistication aimed at more comfortable driving, is far removed from the Model T in terms of complexity, even though only a few basic tools are needed for home repairs. And while automobiles have become more complex, more and more men and women have steered away from mechanics of any kind. This is evident in the leaping increase in repair calls for home appliances, most of which are really quite simple to anyone willing to disassemble the chrome and enamel exteriors. The automotive industry as a whole has begun to feel the severe shortage of qualified mechanics, and is currently trying to attract young people to this field as a career. (An interesting statistic: automobile dealerships account for only about 20 percent of service dollars; gasoline stations and private garages get the rest.)

But you still don't need more than an average intelligence, and learning to do your own home automotive repairs, at least those more routine jobs, is more a question of determination than of specialized training. This is especially true on modern cars, where repair means remove-and-replace, rather than remove-and-fix as on older cars. These days it is less expensive to remove a starter and trade it for a rebuilt version than to try to rebuild it yourself. But at the same time, if you can trace the trouble to a faulty wiring connection, you can keep your starter and save both money and effort.

We'll be going into all parts of the automobile. Occasionally you may feel that you're being told more than you really want to know, but you're apt to find all the information in this book very handy at a later date, when some problem with your car requires more than a simple "tinkering" adjustment. At the same time, space is limited and we can't devote pages to each particular automobile make. Fortunately, things mechanical fall into a rather general pattern, a general truth especially applicable to cars. Thus when we speak of a two- or four-barrel carburetor, operation and repair will be similar for nearly all carburetor models and makes. Of course, if you need to know more about some specific car, you can buy a Motor's or Chilton repair manual for that car.

I can offer this iron-clad guarantee: Once you've read through this book and have discovered that a car is really not so much a mystery after all, you've progressed 50 percent of the way to becoming a good mechanic. And that isn't a bad investment, as I pointed out at the beginning of this section. Furthermore, there is something very contagious about repairing automobiles. The doctor or store clerk who starts out tinkering with the family transportation more often than not ends up restoring a Ford Model A. Working on things mechanical becomes a kind of physical relaxation, a nuts-and-bolts elixir that makes the old young, and the young patient. You can repair anything on your own car—if you want to!

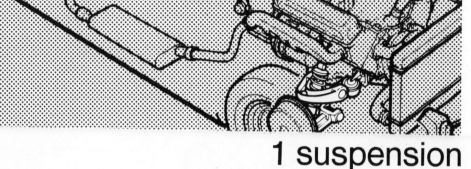

1 suspension

THE ITEMS THAT MAKE UP the suspension of an automobile include axles, A-arms, springs, shock absorbers, limiting devices, sway-control bars, and so on, all connected to the automobile frame. While the design and manufacture of these suspension components involves sophisticated engineering, normal maintenance and repair of them is usually simple. Some suspension problem are among the most complex a mechanic ever faces, but fortunately for the home mechanic, most can be solved with basic tools and only a rudimentary understanding of the engineering principles involved.

Springs and shock absorbers are the most obvious components of a supension system, but the discussion of suspension cannot be limited to only them. Most mechanics tend to talk of the entire front axle assembly as a part of the general suspension system, so we will follow the trend. Thus in discussing front suspension we will be concerned with springs, shocks, front A-arms, ball joints, wheel bearings, and wheel alignment, and how they work together.

If you were to do an in-depth study of automobile engineering, you would find that practically everything to do with the car has been a cut-and-try operation. This kind of trial-and-error engineering is common to practically all technology at early stages, but it continues to a very great degree in automobile manufacturing. The modern automobile suspension is really not a great deal different from that produced nearly a century ago, and in fact many of the heralded "advancements" of today were discovered many, many years past.

There are plenty of problems associated with creating a workable automobile suspension, but the contemporary car is faced with two basic requirements: performance and reliability. That means that most designers are trying to come

1

Assembly of a new Chevrolet frame and suspension. Frame is just a platform; the suspension must do all the work.

There has not been a great change in chassis since the early 1950s as this picture of a 1955 Chevrolet shows. However, engineers "tune" suspension members to wheelbase, tread width, type of tires, weight of car.

up with a car that will handle like a racer, ride super-smooth, and last for-ever. Amazingly, they have come very close to accomplishing this task.

SPRINGS

Since springs in some form or another are really the things that suspend a car, let's look at them first. As a home me-chanic, you may think that nothing possible could go wrong with a spring, and that if it did only a garage could repair it. Actually, you can do most spring work at home, since it is usually just a case of remove and replace rather than repair of the actual spring.

Springs common to the modern car fall into three categories: leaf, coil, and torsion bar. Actually, a coil spring is nothing more that a crooked torsion bar, and if you visualize the cross section movement of a coil spring, you can see how the coil wire is twisting under tor-sion. Generally speaking, the leaf spring is used almost universally at the rear

now, and the coil spring in front. A few cars use coil springs in the rear too, and Chrysler Corporation cars use a straight torsion bar in front. Utility vehicles sometimes use leaf springs at the front in combination with beam axles.

Leaf Springs

About the only thing that can go wrong with a leaf spring is fracture of a leaf, if the unit is only a few years old. However, if a car is subjected to bad weather conditions, serious troubles can develop with the leaf springs.

A leaf spring is composed of several leaves of different lengths. The main leaf will have round eyes rolled at either end, and these eyes connect by some means to the frame. At the center of the spring will be a bolt that holds all leaves together, and somewhere near this centerpoint the spring will attach to the axle with U-bolts. A single spring leaf could be used, and is used on some of the compact GM cars, but this does not allow the spring to be "stacked" or "loaded." The idea in good suspension is

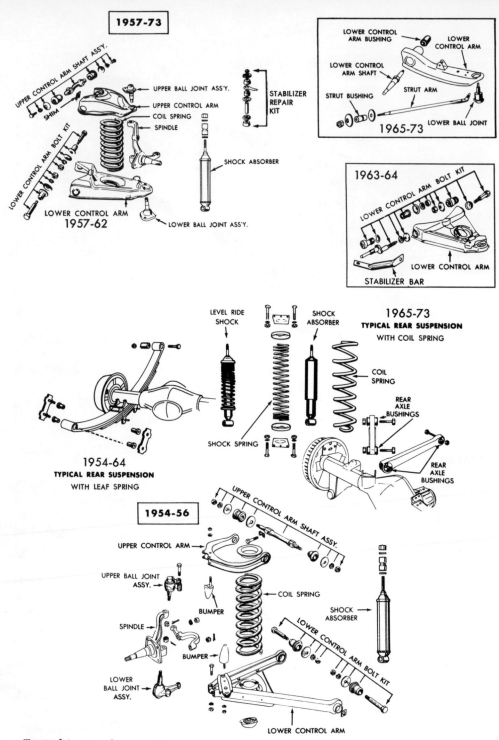

1957-73

UPPER CONTROL ARM SHAFT ASS'Y.

SHIM

UPPER BALL JOINT ASS'Y.

UPPER CONTROL ARM

COIL SPRING

SPINDLE

STABILIZER REPAIR KIT

LOWER CONTROL ARM BOLT KIT

SHOCK ABSORBER

LOWER CONTROL ARM
1957-62

LOWER BALL JOINT ASS'Y.

LOWER CONTROL ARM BUSHING

LOWER CONTROL ARM

LOWER CONTROL ARM SHAFT

STRUT BUSHING

STRUT ARM

LOWER BALL JOINT

1965-73

1963-64

LOWER CONTROL ARM BOLT KIT

LOWER CONTROL ARM

STABILIZER BAR

LEVEL RIDE SHOCK

SHOCK ABSORBER

1965-73
TYPICAL REAR SUSPENSION
WITH COIL SPRING

COIL SPRING

REAR AXLE BUSHINGS

SHOCK SPRING

REAR AXLE BUSHINGS

1954-64
TYPICAL REAR SUSPENSION
WITH LEAF SPRING

1954-56

UPPER CONTROL ARM SHAFT ASS'Y.

UPPER CONTROL ARM

UPPER BALL JOINT ASS'Y.

BUMPER

SPINDLE

BUMPER

LOWER BALL JOINT ASS'Y.

COIL SPRING

SHOCK ABSORBER

LOWER CONTROL ARM BOLT KIT

LOWER CONTROL ARM

Typical front and rear end component parts from Mercury suspensions from 1957–1973. Note use of lighter weight lower control arms for 1965–73 cars. Points of wear would be ball joints and shaft assembly bushings, *springs may sag. Usually there would be little wear of rear end components other than shocks. (Illustration courtesy TRW corporation)*

The average automobile owner almost never considers the vehicle springs for periodic maintenance, yet a spring has a direct effect on how the car handles and rides. As springs age they can and will sag; the same condition is possible from overloading (common to station wagons). If one spring sags more than another, it will effect the front end alignment also. Check the height of the spring by tape measure with the spring installed in the car, replace any spring that has sagged. A temporary cure might be to have a mechanic slightly heat the longer spring, but this should only be considered as an emergency measure. If buying used replacement springs from a wrecking yard, check their unloaded height against the correct measurement as given in a shop manual for that particular car.

for the spring to become increasingly resistant to force as more force is exerted. In this way, a slight bump that moves the spring only a bit will meet little resistance from the spring, but a severe bump will meet greater resistance. Thus the ride can be soft and yet the springs can cope with severe bumps. Spring "stacking" is achieved by making each succeeding leaf shorter. The longer leaf will flex easily until it bends enough to take up the next leaf, at which time it becomes stiffer, and so on.

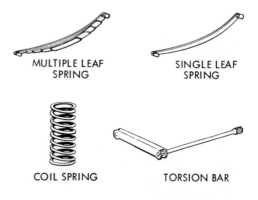

MULTIPLE LEAF SPRING   SINGLE LEAF SPRING

COIL SPRING   TORSION BAR

SUSPENSION SPRINGS

Typical types of springs used in most cars. Single leaf is used on some lightweight GM products, torsion bar is common to Chrysler cars. (Illustration courtesy Monroe Shock Absorbers)

To get a soft ride, some engineers design rear springs that are quite long, especially from the centerbolt to the rear spring end. Such long springs tend to sag. The best remedies for a sagging spring are either to re-arch the spring leaves (which you can have a spring-repair shop do) or to replace the entire spring with a new one. Alternatives include installation of some kind of spring assist, such as Monroe Load-Levelers, or the less desirable air shocks.

Any time you must remove a leaf spring, disconnect the shock absorber at one end first, then jack up the car frame until the spring is fully extended. Place jackstands under the car frame and loosen the spring shackles. Next remove the front spring pivot bolt, and finally remove the U-bolts at the axle. The spring will be heavy.

If you are going to remove the centerbolt and disassemble the spring, which will be necessary if you are going to replace a broken leaf or clean the leaves, always clamp the spring in a sturdy vise, or use a large C-clamp. The centerbolt pulls all the leaves together under tension, and if you loosen it without clamping the spring, the leaves will fly apart.

If the spring is several years old, there will often be a rust build-up between the leaves. Clean the leaves thoroughly with a solvent and wire brush.

Only the tip of each leaf rubs against the next leaf, and this wear spot can become a groove. You can grind the groove smooth, but if a leaf is that far gone it is better to get a replacement. Most modern springs have some kind of rubbing block at the leaf tips. These should be replaced if they are worn or gone; they are inexpensive.

Use the bench vise or large C-clamp to reassemble the spring. Sometimes there will be a bronze bushing in the spring eyes that may need replacement. You can do this at home with a hammer and bushing set, but it is easier to farm this job out to a frame-and-front-end shop.

Coil Springs

A coil spring can sag or it can break. In either case, it must be replaced; there is no clean-up or repair that will help. Also, you may want to substitute heavy-duty springs for those your car came with.

About the only way you can get a front coil spring out of its perch is to remove either the upper or lower A-arm connection at the spindle. Since most modern cars have ball-joint connections at these points the job is a bit easier. Jack up the car and put jackstands under the frame. The front wheel should be several inches off the floor.

Most modern cars locate the front shock absorber inside the coil spring to save space, so the shock must be re-

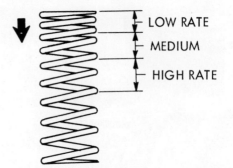

Variable rate coil spring. When coils are wound close together, as at top of spring, the spring deflects easily. As coils become farther apart, spring gets stiffer. Usually the softer section sags (collapses) first, meaning replacement is needed.

moved first. Then place a jack near the outer end of the lower A-arm and put some tension on it. Loosen the ball-joint stud nut. Release some of the jack tension. You may have to pry the ball joint loose (several smart slaps with a hammer on the spindle housing where the ball-joint stud fits will usually free the tapered stud). With the lower A-arm free of the spindle, slowly lower the jack and remove the coil spring.

The coil-spring rear end is a bit more complicated. A coil spring can give a lot of spring movement in a relatively small space, so it will sometimes give a softer ride than a leaf spring, and that is why it is occasionally used in the rear. However, it has the drawback of being flexible in all directions, and thus needs some kind of locator bars to stabilize the rear-end housing. These locators keep the rear end from twisting on the axle centerline, keep the rear-end housing located correctly in the frame (fore/aft alignment), and prevent sideways movement of the rear-end housing.

Coil-spring rear-suspension systems have been used on Buicks for many

Front ends with single strut lower control arm are lightweight but suffer from front collisions. It is important that all rubber insulators in suspension be good to isolate vibrations. The home mechanic can do a great deal of front end work, but if springs are being removed it is advisable to work with caution.

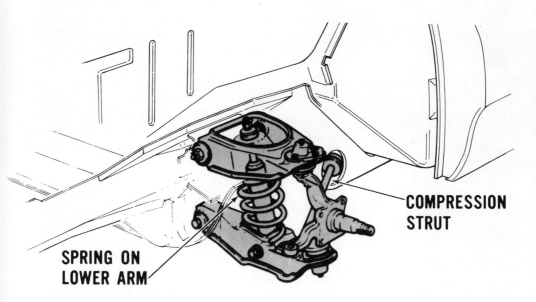

COMPRESSION STRUT

SPRING ON LOWER ARM

This is the most common type of front end. If the coil spring were mounted in a tower above the upper control arm, it would be called a McPherson strut. If ball joints are to be replaced it is necessary to support weight of car either at lower arm or at wheel, depending upon which joint is removed.

 7

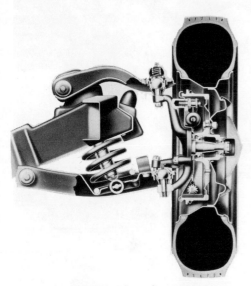

Cutaway of 1955 Chevrolet front suspension, a type that is still in widespread use.

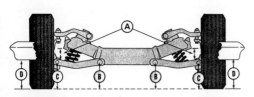

To check for sagging springs, measure dimension A, which is distance between lower control arm and the frame. There should be maximum of ¼-inch difference from one side to the other. Measure dimensions B and C from ground level to center of pivot points. Difference here should be no more than ¼-inch. Make sure bumper is straight and measure distances at D, where the difference should be no more than ⅜-inch. (Illustration courtesy TRW corporation)

years, and have been used periodically on most contemporary automobiles. In 1961, General Motors included coils on their BOP (Buick, Olds, Pontiac) compacts, which meant a great deal of work with locators was necessary, since the original Buick design used a closed

driveshaft to control all but sideways rear end movement. The early Oldsmobile V8s were equipped with coil rear springs which mounted to control-arm locators off the open drive rear end. Many modern cars use two lower control arms that mount at the outer ends of the axle housing and run forward almost parallel with each frame rail. Rather than use a transverse-mounted "track rod" to control sideways movement of the housing, two shorter locators mount near the center of the housing and angle diagonally outward to an attachment at the frame or body structure. These arms prevent axle wrap-up as well as locate the rear end laterally.

You might have to replace one or more of the rubber bushings in these locator ends, but otherwise you would have no need to service them. They are held in place by large bolts, which remove easily, and unless they have been bent by a collision, there is no provision for rear-end alignment at these locators.

Sometimes there is an irritating squeak that comes from the rubber-bushed locator ends, which can be cured by a rubber lubricant. Rear coil springs are often held in place by a bolt; if this bolt comes loose even slightly the rear spring can move on its pad and will produce a hard-to-find squeak or thunk.

Independent Rear Suspensions

Independent rear suspensions are a different breed of cat from the "dead" axle most cars use. The Corvair and Corvette are typical examples of American IRS (independent rear suspension) cars, and neither can be worked on handily by the home mechanic, aside from replacing springs or locating members. The Corvair rear end utilized a special trailing A-arm at first, and this

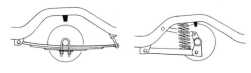

SEMI-ELLIPTIC LEAF SPRING   TRAILING ARM & COIL SPRING

The two most common types of suspension used on production automobiles. Neither is superior for ordinary use, but you should keep a close watch on suspension links for signs of failure.

could be easily replaced, but late-model Corvairs and all Stingray Corvettes have fully adjustable rear ends that must be aligned by a professional. You can save yourself money by doing the labor of parts replacement, but leave the alignment to the garage mechanic.

Rear-End Alignment

About the only ways a rear end can get out of alignment is from a collision or from the locators being loose or wearing excessively. A quick check is to drive the car on dirt or sand in a straight-ahead path for several yards. Inspect the tire tracks. The rear-end tracks should be directly over the front tire tracks, or slightly inside, but perfectly parallel to, the front tracks. If the tracks are not correct, suspect the rear end alignment.

If the car has leaf springs, look at the lower spring clip plate directly under the axle. If the tiebolt or spring centerbolt is not in the clip locating hole, the U-bolts have loosened and allowed the rear end to slip fore or aft slightly. Loosen the U-bolts and move the axle back into position. Check for sideways displacement of the rear end by measuring from the inside face of each backing plate to the frame. If the measurements are off by a half-inch or more, loosen both spring U-bolts and bump the rear end back into place.

Large channel-shaped control arms locate the rear end and help control effects of engine torque/braking torque. Small diameter rod running beneath rear end is *sway bar which can be added to help improve handling of car through corners. Shock absorbers are mounted at an angle to help control sidesway.*

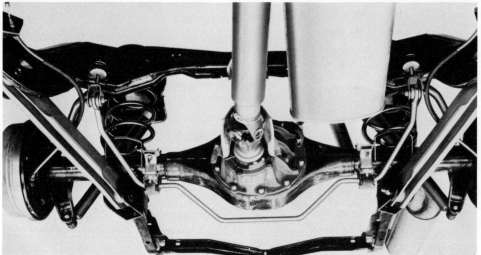

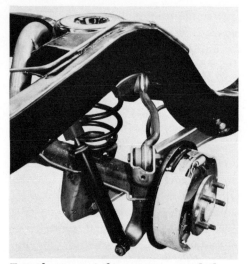

Topside view of the same rear end shows upper control arm. To control torque working on rear end, it is mounted at an angle toward center of car. Keep a close watch on rubber insulators used at ends of control arms.

Air Lift air bags are available with dashboard controls which would be a convenience if the vehicle will do transport work in a city. Such devices can help substitute for sagging springs.

Any misalignment that shows up with a coil-spring rear end can almost always be traced to excessively worn locator arms (rare) or bent arms (not rare).

SHOCK ABSORBERS

Actually the term "shock absorber" is a misnomer; the shock-absorbing action is done by the tires and springs. The British term "damper" is a better description, since that is exactly what the shock absorber does—dampen the action of the spring or springs. When a spring is bent or depressed as in going over a bump, its tendency is not only to return to its original position but to continue past it—in other words to oscillate. On a car with bad shocks you can see this happen; after hitting a bump the car continues to bounce up and down several times, or if you push down on the brake and suddenly release it, the car continues to move up and down. What the shock absorbers actually do is to control this action so that the spring

Air Bags are available as aftermarket items, can be inflated to give a stiffer spring rate (effectively) and to help the car carry extra loads. This unit is to be used in conjunction with leaf springs.

does not move rapidly, and when moved returns only to its normal position.

The usual shock absorber used on all American cars since the early 1950s is the sealed tubular shock commonly referred to as the telescopic or "airplane" type (the system first appeared on aircraft landing gear). There are other types. A very early design, still used on certain kinds of racing cars, operates through friction by means of a series of hardwood biscuits separated by metal mounted on a base and topped by a lever. A through-bolt and spring provides adjustable pressure and therefore

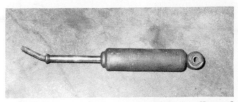

If the shock absorber mounting is allowed to come loose, the shock shaft can be bent, as this one. If the shaft is bent in the actuating area, the shock will rapidly become inoperative. It is imperative to keep all shock mounting bolts and nuts tight.

Always check to see if shock is good by compressing and spreading it in a vertical plane. If the shock absorber body is damaged it will not function properly.

Various types of Monroe shock absorbers, including front load-levelers, rear load-levelers, and the air shock. Note different types of mountings of shocks.

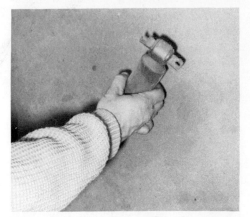

If the shock mounting is allowed to remain loose, it can break over a period of time. A hard jolt to the suspension system can also break a mounting bracket, a break that might go undetected unless periodic inspection is very thorough.

 11

adjustable friction. Still another early design was a round case filled with viscous hydraulic fluid and containing a set of vanes which were attached to a lever outside the case. This was the type used on early Fords and certain other cars. Still in use on certain imported cars and some trucks are the piston-and-lever shocks. These have a case with a piston inside and holes that let fluid pass slowly around the piston as it moves back and forth. The piston is linked to an external lever that moves with the suspension. This type of shock is often rebuildable, generally refillable, and sometimes adjustable either externally or by changing the size of the holes in the case. The main problems with piston-and-lever shocks as far as the manufacturers are concerned are that they are relatively expensive to manufacture and that the linkage from the lever to the independent suspension is cumbersome unless the case is built right into the control arm, which makes things difficult when it comes time to replace the shock. Consequently most car manufacturers have gone to the full tubular shocks for both front and rear suspension.

Very basically, the tubular shock consists of a case inside which slides a piston, as in the lever shock just described, but the piston is much larger and incorporates the valving itself. In certain instances the case is dual-walled and there is also valving in the case, transferring fluid from one chamber to another. The restricted movement of the piston through the fluid, or of the fluid by the piston through the case and valve holes, provides the damping effect. With very few exceptions, all original-equipment shocks are set and sealed by the manufacturer and cannot be either re-

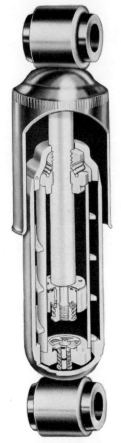

Restrictions on the inside of a shock absorber tubing determine how "stiff" the unit is; when the seals wear the shock will lose this "stiffness." Shocks can determine how a car handles, and can cause unusual front tire wear if they are in poor condition (the shocks, that is).

filled or serviced by anybody other than a rebuilder. The same thing goes for nearly all replacement shocks. There is no adjusting the usual tubular shock absorber; its stiffness and control ratio are set at the factory. (The control ratio is the amount of stiffness exerted by the shock on bump and rebound.)

The average shock is generally referred to as a 70-30, which means that on a somewhat tenuous and not too well-defined scale of 100, 30 percent stiffness

There are several different types of shock absorber mounting methods; this would be the stud type at both ends. It is important that the shock insulator rubbers be snug but not compressed.

is exerted to control bump or initial spring deflection and 70 percent, or more than twice as much, is used for rebound control so that the car settles into the bump against both spring and shock, and rebound is rigidly dampened. Heavy-duty vehicles and racing cars generally use a stiffer setting—a 60-40 or even a 50-50 ratio. This ratio has nothing to do with the overall stiffness or resistance of a given shock absorber, merely its action. Stiffness is governed by the viscosity or thickness of the fluid and by the size of the holes through which it is forced.

Adjustable Shock Absorbers

There are three makes of shocks, or rather types within makes, that can be adjusted, rebuilt, or both. These are all,

as far as the American market is concerned, replacement items; none are factory equipment.

Foremost among these is the justly famous Koni, made in Holland but marketed worldwide. Perhaps its first claim to fame is total, uncompromising quality. Every unit is matched internally to exact tolerances, and all the valving and sealing is metallic; there is no plastic, leather, or rubber on the piston whatever. Quality aside, what made it really well-known is the fact that it can be adjusted exactly over a very wide range from just the soft side of firm to nearly rock-hard when new. Except for competition, very few are set hard to begin with. Tailored individually for the car involved in terms of control ratio, they are generally installed at a softer setting or just on the firm side, and then as time goes on, they can be gradually adjusted to make up for wear or other conditions. Combined with the quality control, this feature makes them good for the lifetime of the car, which more than justifies their initially higher cost. Setting is accomplished on the Koni by disconnecting it and collapsing the shock all the way, then turning the lower half gently until a slight click is felt. Turning one way hardens it and the other way softens it. The adjustment is done inside by a nut that progressively shuts off orifices in the central valving. Another point with the Koni is that it can be rebuilt and even tailored in action by any of the several distribution centers around the country.

Another of the adjustables is the Armstrong, which can be had in both lever and tubular form. In the latter form, combined with an integral coil spring, it is used by most of the finest racing cars in the world. Its great advantage is that it can be adjusted from the outside while mounted on the car, a feature also available on a few models of Koni. There are two forms. One adjusts through ten positions by means of a knob on the side of the shock tube or, in the case of a shock meant to ride inside a front spring, by means of a slotted head in the same place that can be turned with a screwdriver. Another form adjusts from the dash through four positions by means of a remote control unit within the car.

The third adjustable shock is the Gabriel Adjust-O-Matic, which is set, like the Koni, by detaching and collapsing the shock to engage a pawl inside the unit. The Gabriel, however, does not have the infinite adjustment of the Dutch shock but has three positions: soft, medium, and hard. Again the prime purpose is to take up for wear and age, but it can also be used to make the car suitable for different road surfaces or high speeds. It is much more widely available than the other two and less expensive, which offsets its lesser flexibility.

There is also a so-called adjustable type of shock which is air-filled. Adjustment is by bleeding air off for softer settings and adding it from a filling-station hose for harder settings. However, this is not a true shock absorber but rather a helper spring, since it does nothing to dampen the action but merely keeps the springs from bottoming on a bump.

WHEEL BEARINGS

There is considerable work the home mechanic can do on the front suspension relative to ball joints, kingpins, bearings, and even wheel alignment. The first point of wear will likely be the wheel

bearings. To check for bearing wear, or poor adjustment, it is important to use the floor jack properly—otherwise you might confuse ball-joint wear for bearing play. If the spring is above the upper A-arm (McPherson strut design) as on Ford, American Motors, and some Chevrolet cars, the jack should be placed under the lower suspension arm. On cars which have the spring between the A-arms, the jack should be placed under the frame crossmember. This keeps the ball joints in tension and allows only bearing movement.

Tapered Bearings

Since the advent of tapered roller bearings for front wheels, car makers now recommend that the bearings and spindle be lubricated only when brake linings are being replaced or when the wheel and drum is removed for any other reason (see Chapter 15). However, any time the front wheels are off the ground it is advisable to make two quick checks for bearing condition. The first is to rotate the wheel and listen closely for evidence of wear or damage. Worn rollers or galled cups will make a rumbling sound that is easily distinguishable from other wheel noises, such as a normal slight scraping of the brake lining. A dry bearing will squeak. The second check is to grasp the tire at the top and pull back and forth on it. If wheel motion is excessive, it may be worn bearings, although the same symptom is caused by worn ball joints in the front suspension. You can tell which by looking closely to see where the movement is.

The parts of a typical front wheel and axle that will concern you when you're working on bearings are the spindle, the seal, the inner and outer bearing assemblies, the locking nuts and washers, and the dust cap. Some cars may have a static collector installed just ahead of the dust cap.

The important points to remember in lubrication and assembly are that the inner bearing races are designed to creep slightly around the spindle, and therefore the latter should be smooth and lightly coated with lubricant to ensure a slip fit; and that the tapered bearings cannot function satisfactorily if any pressure is exerted upon them by the locking nut, yet the locking nut must be tight enough to prevent excessive end play.

Installation with a torque wrench is best, but if you don't have access to the tool or the torque figures specified by each car make, the following procedure may be safely followed: Tighten the lock nut with an 8- or 10-inch wrench, using enough force to ensure that all parts are properly seated while the wheel is spinning. Back off the lock nut finger-loose, then tighten finger-tight. If the hole in the spindle lines up with a slot in the nut, install the cotter pin. If not, back off to the next slot and install the pin. Finally, clinch the cotter pin and cut off the excess length to ensure that the ends do not interfere with the dust cap or static collector. In some designs a tab-type lock washer is substituted, but the cotter pin is most common.

For lubrication use nothing but an extreme-pressure (EP) lithium-based grease made especially for this purpose. Special packing tools are available for greasing the bearings, but a suitable substitute is to put a quantity of grease in the palm of one hand and work it into the bearing with a rotating motion of the other hand. Before lubrication all parts should be cleaned in kerosene. New lubricant should not be added to

the old, and whenever these parts are lubricated, a new oil seal should be installed. This seal can be seated by hammering gently.

On cars equipped with drum-type brakes, it may be necessary to loosen the brake adjustment before the wheel and drum can be removed as a unit. On cars with disc-type front brakes the caliper assembly dangles on its hose. Hang it on the nearest convenient piece of steering linkage. On front-wheel-drive cars such as the Toronado and Eldorado, the rear-wheel bearings may be removed, lubricated, and replaced in a manner quite similar to that described above.

Ball Bearings

Procedures for removal and greasing of front-wheel ball bearings are the same as for tapered rollers. However, the installation of the bearings is slightly different. Ball bearings must be installed with a slight preload so that the balls and races are brought into proper contact. All kinds of directions have been devised for adjusting front-wheel ball bearings, most of them difficult to understand. Most castellated nuts have only six positions for the cotter key, so even after you get the nut exactly where you want it, you may have to turn it tighter or looser to insert the key.

The main thing to remember on ball bearings is that they must never be adjusted loose. This doesn't mean to put a 3-foot breaker bar on the nut to tighten it. It does mean that there should be zero play, with a slight amount of preload. Ball bearings were a great source of trouble on the cars that used them. Today all cars use tapered rollers, which have eliminated the front-wheel-bearing problems.

There is no tapered roller that will

interchange with the old ball bearings, but there is a trick that can be used to prolong their life. The secret is to use a grease in the wheel bearings that is almost runny. Some chassis lubes are soft and will work fine. If the grease is one of the newer "black" greases with moly in it, so much the better. Never use the old long-fiber wheel-bearing greases that were so stiff. The grease has to be loose enough so that it will run back onto the balls after it is thrown off by the rotation of the wheel. Hard greases will fly off the first time the car gets up to speed, and then the bearing runs dry until it is packed again. Invariably damage will occur.

BALL JOINTS

It must be remembered that ball joints produced by most automobile manufacturers are not as good as the quality replacements (such as those from Moog). The replacements are not cheap, but they should definitely be considered if the originals wear out. Ball joints can and do fail. When this happens, the front end will collapse. Keep a close watch on ball-joint front ends.

To check ball joints, reverse the jacking procedure used for checking the bearings. In both cases, make sure you use jackstands for safety. With the car

Almost any front end shop can show you a broken ball joint like this one. It comes usually from poor lubrication, lack of maintenance by the owner.

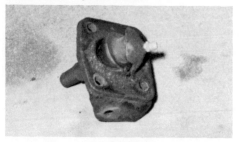

properly jacked for the type of springs involved, two checks are to be made, one for up-and-down play and another for side play.

As the term implies, up-and-down play is checked by firmly grasping the wheel and moving it, or attempting to move it, vertically. In Chrysler products the allowable movement is .050 inch, measured at the lower ball joint. Ford and Mercury (1960-61), Thunderbird (1960), and Lincoln Continental (to 1968) allow .200-inch vertical movement. For General Motors products, consult the service manual for the car and year involved, as the allowable movement varies widely from car to car and year to year. On Ford and Mercury models from 1962 to the present the tolerance is absolute zero. These are all cars with springs between the suspension arms, and all measurements are taken at the lower ball joint.

On cars with springs above the upper suspension arm, the vertical play allowed is also zero, with two exceptions: the 1960-62 Falcon-Comet, in which .200 inch is allowed; and all Chevy II models, in which .093 inch is allowed. These are measured at the upper ball joint. To put it another way, all measurements are taken at the load-carrying joint, since the other arm is free to travel.

The next check is taken in a horizontal or rocking plane, and in this case it's easy: all makes and all models with springs either between the arms or above the arms call for a maximum movement at the tire shoulder of .250 inch. This is quite a lot and should be considered the absolute maximum. One exception is in the Rambler and Javelin, which have no upper ball joint and should have little or no movement, what there is being traceable to the lower ball joint.

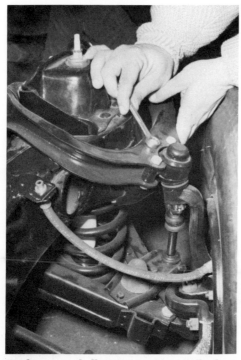

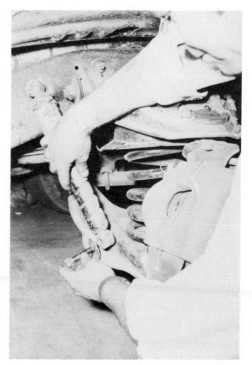

Replacement ball joints are not difficult to install, but they will take time and a floorjack. It is necessary to use the floorjack and jackstands, since the spring will try to throw the A-arms apart if they are not "loaded" when the ball joints are removed. If the original ball joint is riveted, the rivets are broken with a chisel, and the new joints are installed with high-quality bolts and nuts.

Repair of front end ball joints or changing the spring both require unbolting lower ball joint if spring fits between A-arms. Remove the shock absorber first; check bolts for fatigue cracks and bolt holes for enlargement. These problems cause loose shocks that lead to sloppy handling and hard-to-find "klunk."

Place jack under lower A-arm before removing ball joint nut (arrow shows where jack should be.) Use small floor jack only; for safety, do not use smaller hydraulic jack.

Specifics on replacing ball joints on every car are beyond the scope of this book, since the methods both of removal and of attachment vary considerably from car to car, even in a single manufacturer's line. However, certain general remarks are in order. A great number of cars have ball joints that are held to the control arm by a combination of rivets and bolts in varying combinations. When replacement becomes necessary

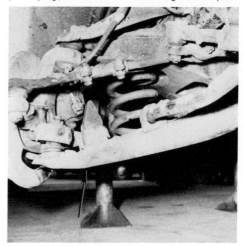

After ball joint is loosened, entire lower A-arm swings free. Tension is now removed from ball joints, spring, and inner A-arm bushings. Do not attempt repairs of these items with spring under compression.

KINGPINS

Kingpin repair and replacement is not so common now that ball joints are used on most passenger cars, but kingpins are still used on many utility vehicles. To check for kingpin play, jack up the car under the axle and grasp the tire at top and bottom. If there is discernible play when the tire is rocked, place your finger where the kingpin touches the axle and feel for movement. If there is excessive movement here, plan on new pins and bushings. But remember that excessive wheel-bearing play can appear to be kingpin slop, so use the finger-feel method.

Most vehicles equipped with kingpins have a kingpin locating bolt, which keeps the pin from working up and down in the boss. Remove this bolt. The pin can then be driven upward from the bottom. Never install new kingpins without installing new bushings in the spindle bosses. These should be carefully inserted and tapped into place

the bolts are removed in the normal way and the rivets must be chiseled off. It is easier if the rivets are drilled first, but avoid drilling through and enlarging the holes. The replacement unit will have special bolts included to take the place of the rivets, and these, not ordinary bolts, must be used. On some Ford products and some GM cars the ball joints are pressed in, and it is inadvisable for these to be replaced anywhere but in a shop equipped with an arbor press to do the job. On Chrysler products the joints are threaded into the control arms, and it is best to consult the service manual for that particular make and model and year of manufacture.

Rigid front axle. The two designs shown here have in general been superseded by the independent front suspension.

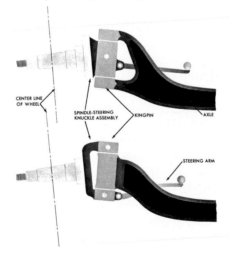

CENTER LINE OF WHEEL

SPINDLE-STEERING KNUCKLE ASSEMBLY — KINGPIN — AXLE

STEERING ARM

with a mallet so that oiling holes in the inserts will align with grease nipples in the spindle boss. Apply a heavy-duty grease to the bushings before tapping the new kingpins into place.

In some cases, special shims are used between a beam axle and the spindle bosses. These are to control excessive up/down movement of the spindle at the kingpin area, and should always be replaced as you found them.

WHEEL ALIGNMENT

Amazingly, front-wheel alignment, a simple matter of adjustment combinations, is a mystery to most car owners. In fact, even many professional mechanics do not understand front-end alignment as well as they should, and consequently good alignment jobs seem difficult to come by. Although the method of adjustment will vary from car to car, the basic adjustments remain constant and even the home mechanic can do some of the alignment work himself. If you live in an area with bad roads, you realize that keeping a front end aligned can run into big money over a year's span.

But never dive into front-wheel alignment until you have very carefully checked out wheel bearings, ball joints, steering linkage (covered in Chapter 3), suspension attachment points, and wheel/tire condition (see Chapter 4). We've explained how to inspect the mechanical parts, so while you have the front end jacked up, check the wheel and tire. Make yourself some kind of static pointer from a nail driven through a wooden slat. Hold this pointer against the middle of the tire tread and rotate the wheel. If the tire is more than $\frac{1}{16}$ inch out of round, you can expect a balance/wear problem. Place the pointer

near the wheel-rim lip and repeat the check for wheel roundness. If the wheel checks round, then the out-of-round tire can be causing severe balance problems and perhaps pull the steering wheel as though the front end were out of alignment.

If the wheel itself is out of round more than $\frac{1}{16}$ inch it should be replaced. With the pointer in the same area on the wheel rim it can be determined if the wheel has "wobble" (sideways movement). This also should not exceed $\frac{1}{16}$ inch. Wheels can be bent just by hitting a bad road break or curb. If the wheel seems to have excess wobble, move the pointer and check for wobble at the lugbolt circle. If the wheel is not seating perfectly on the hub it will indicate wobble. Wheels should really be tightened with a torque wrench, something that is almost never done (see Chapter 4).

You can get a fair idea of front-end condition from the appearance of the tires. If a tire is wearing uniformly on the inside or outside edge, the fault is alignment. But if it has a scalloped wear pattern, the fault is possibly balance.

Alignment Factors

Factors involved in front-end alignment (and in some cases, rear end alignment) are toe-in or toe-out, caster, camber, and kingpin angle. Another factor in front-end alignment is known as the Ackermann, from the term "Ackermann principle," which is that the inside wheel of a car in a turn should cut a sharper angle so that each wheel follows the circumference of the correct circle, the inside wheel scribing a smaller circle than the outside wheel. This is a built-in effect and is a function of the relationship of the steering arms and

 19

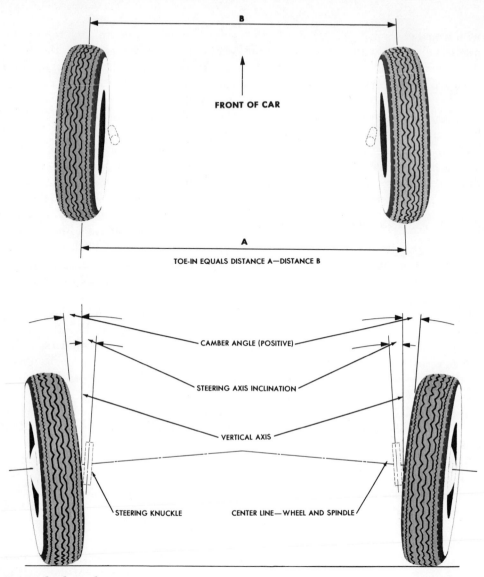

B

FRONT OF CAR

TOE-IN EQUALS DISTANCE A—DISTANCE B

A

CAMBER ANGLE (POSITIVE)

STEERING AXIS INCLINATION

VERTICAL AXIS

STEERING KNUCKLE   CENTER LINE—WHEEL AND SPINDLE

Front-wheel camber.

draglink or tie rod and is not normally adjustable.

Toe-in or *toe-out* describes the relationship of the front wheels to each other when the steering is in a straight-ahead position. In the average car there is a slight toe-in; the front edges of the front wheels are closer together than the rear edges by roughly ⅛ inch. It isn't much, but the effect is to keep all the steering linkage in tension, keeping any slop out of it in the straight-ahead driving position where no cornering forces are present to keep things taut. Toe-out, the opposite effect, is found in the straight ahead position only in certain front-

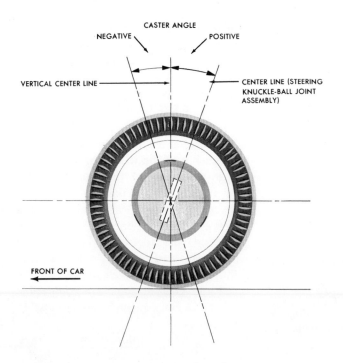

CASTER ANGLE
NEGATIVE   POSITIVE
VERTICAL CENTER LINE   CENTER LINE (STEERING KNUCKLE-BALL JOINT ASSEMBLY)
FRONT OF CAR

Front-wheel caster. Caster is the tilt at the top of the spindle, as viewed from the side. Negative caster is a foward tilt, positive caster is backward tilt. Caster enables the front wheel to maintain a straight-ahead position when moving, and helps it return to this position after a turn.

wheel-drive cars, unless the alignment is faulty. Naturally, because of the Ackerman principle there is toe-out in the turn position.

Caster is the effect formed by the inclination of the top of the kingpin or upper ball joint to the rear, which acts like a furniture caster in keeping the wheels headed in a straight line. In the average passenger car this angle is 1° to 3° off a vertical line. On cars with solid axles it is as much as 7°.

Camber, which is referred to as either negative or positive, is the inclination of the wheels inward or outward at the top; in other words, leaning into or away from the car. Earlier cars, meant for use on high-crowned roads, had quite a bit of positive caster (leaning out) to bring the tires perpendicular to the road surface. More recent cars have little or none, and some of the later high-performance cars have from 1° to 2° of negative camber to aid in corner-

21

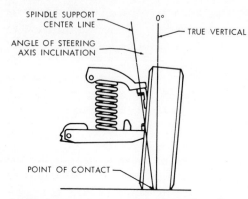

SPINDLE SUPPORT
CENTER LINE

0°

TRUE VERTICAL

ANGLE OF STEERING
AXIS INCLINATION

POINT OF CONTACT

Angle between true vertical and a line through the axis of the ball joints or king pins is known as steering axis inclination. This angle is not adjustable, but can be changed relative to the tire point of contact of wheels with offset different from original or fitted. Purpose of this axis inclination is to aid steering stability and establish a pivot point about which the wheel can be easily turned.

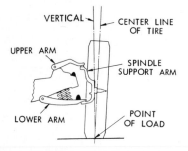

VERTICAL

CENTER LINE
OF TIRE

UPPER ARM

SPINDLE
SUPPORT ARM

LOWER ARM

POINT
OF LOAD

(POSITIVE CAMBER SHOWN)

Camber is the tilt of the wheel at the top from true vertical. Negative camber is a tilt inward, positive camber is tilt to the outside. Camber brings the road contact point of the tire nearly under the point of load and eliminates excessive tire wear.

ing by offsetting the tendency of a tire to roll under in a turning situation. This angularity is the combined total; thus in a car with 1° camber each wheel would be inclined .5°.

Kingpin inclination is the angle of a line drawn through the kingpin and

upper and lower ball joints laterally to the ground. This line should be such that it meets the ground at the center-line or inside edge of the tire at the same point. This angle varies from car to car and has been engineered in accordance with suspension geometry, wheel size, and wheel rim offset, or the relationship of the wheel lugbolt surface to the centerline of the rim. It is this measurement that makes the indiscriminate mixing of wheel sizes and rim offsets a tricky proposition. Casual switching around with different-sized wheels can lead to rapid wheel-bearing failure if care isn't taken to see that the offset and kingpin angle are compatible so that the lines meet or come close to the ground.

The figures mentioned are averages, and you should consult the service manual for your particular car for the exact measurements.

Tire Wear and Alignment

The first place to check for faulty suspension or alignment is the rubber on the front wheels. Discounting odd-ball wear that can come from under- or over-inflation, check to see if the tires or one tire is worn more on one side than the other; if so, then toe-in of one or both is off. If it is only one that is off, it will show in steering on the road; there will be a definite pull to one side or the other. If both are out of adjustment, tire wear and hard steering in either direction will occur. Tire cupping—an undulating, scalloped wear pattern—can be the result of poor shock absorbers, one wheel out of alignment, a bent spindle, or, what is more likely, a combination of these, possibly complicated by loose tie-rod ends, which can be caused by misalignment. As a matter of fact, misalignment can, in time, trigger a whole series of ailments and rapid wear. A car that is kept in alignment—with proper tires, good shock absorbers and periodic lubrication—is practically wearproof; but neglect one item and a chain reaction is the inevitable result.

Toe-in Adjustment

Toe-in settings are easily done with a minimum of equipment—and that can be homemade. The only gauge necessary is a straight piece of wood, such as a 1x1 or even a long piece of lath provided it is straight. Drive two nails into the wood at the exact distance that the front inner edges of the tires of your particular car would be at zero toe-in. Even this isn't needed if you have help and a good steel tape measure.

The first check for misalignment is whether or not the steering wheel is in the straight-ahead position when the car is moving straight ahead. If it is cocked to one side or the other, there is an excellent chance that toe-in is off. Assuming that the wheel has been properly installed in the first place (splined hub only; a keyed hub cannot be installed off-center), the off-center condition will probably be corrected in the alignment process.

Chapter 3 explains the systems of tie rods and drag links. The systems are of two general types. In one, the drag link from the pitman arm connects with an idler in the center, from which relatively long steering links run to the steering arms at the front hub carriers. In the other, the pitman arm attaches to a center link and is matched by an idler arm on the opposite (right) side of the same dimensions as the pitman arm. The center link connects these two arms, and from these arms run short links to each front steering arm on the hub carriers. A variation of this has a drag link from the pitman arm to a point on a heavy center link that connects a pair of idler arms, one at each side, each of which connects to the wheels via short links, as in the second system just described.

What is of importance here are the links that run from the steering arms at the wheels. It makes little or no difference whether their inboard ends attach to a center idler arm, to the pitman and matching idler, or to a pair of idlers. These links have ends that are threaded right-hand on one end and left-hand on the other, so that once the clamps are loosened, they can be turned or twisted. This either lengthens or shortens them, depending on which way they are twisted, which in turn increases or decreases the toe-in of the wheel relative to the centerline of the car.

To proceed with the toe-in adujstments, put the front end of the car on jack stands with the jacks placed so as to load the ball joints—that is, just as for checking wheel bearings. Loosen the clamps at the tie-rod ends and, using equal turns on the tie rods or sleeves, set the required toe-in value. Now check the position of the steering wheel. If it is centered, you're in business and you can tighten the clamps. If not, lengthen one rod and shorten the other exactly the same amount until the wheel is centered at the straight-ahead position, which is to say the "high spot" in the pitman-arm travel.

Camber and Caster Adjustment

Camber and caster settings are really jobs for shops equipped with front-end

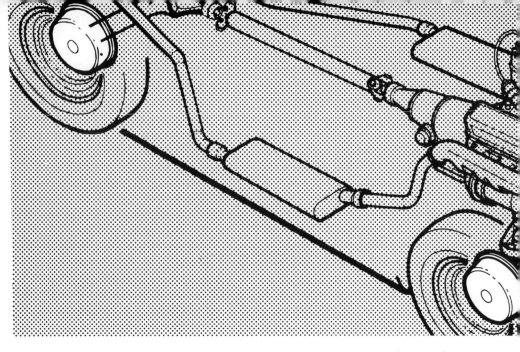

2 brakes

FROM THE VERY START of automobile engineering, it has been realized that brakes are one of the essential components of a car, and certainly brake systems have received their share of engineering concern. The problem is really a simple one: How can you slow and stop a moving vehicle safely, in the least possible amount of time? There have been so many different methods proposed that international patent attorneys are constantly sorting out who is infringing upon whose idea. There aren't many really new ideas presented, though —usually only improvements on basic ideas.

Nearly every part of a vehicle is designed to work under conditions of reduced friction, with the exception of the brakes. The basic scrubbing block mounted to rub against a wagon-wheel rim is a friction device—obviously not too efficient even on a wagon. From the start, car builders found a better form of brake was necessary, and many early experiments included the drum brake in one fashion or another. This was basically the same idea as the scrub brake, but a smaller-diameter "wheel" substituted for the primary wheel, and the scrubbing device was enlarged to have more surface contact with the "wheel," or drum. Most of these early drum brakes were of the external contracting-band type, however, and never proved really satisfactory.

In this design, some form of band was wrapped around the outside perimeter of a drum, and the band's inner face had an asbestos lining of some type. One end of the band was fixed to the rear-end housing, and the movable end was then usually connected to either a cable or rod mechanism that ended up at the driver's foot or hand. Such an external-wrap design will get the job done, of course, but the drawbacks were many. In the first place, if the brakes were used severely, as when going down steep hills, the drum would heat up and expand until it finally came into contact with the band. The driver then had to adjust the bands looser, and then when the drums cooled the bands had too much play and needed readjusting. If the bands got wet, they tended to swell and cause the same problem. Furthermore, external-wrap bands tend to grab, rather than slow smoothly.

The internal expanding brake cured most of these problems, but it has a very distinct disadvantage all its own—fade. In this type of design, two or more brake shoes are mounted inside the rotating drum, affixed in some way to the axle housing. The shoes have some kind of friction material attached to their surface, and expand to touch the drum. They may be expanded by mechanical means, as with rods and levers such as those common on cars up into the 1930s, or by a hydraulic cylinder, as used on all modern cars. Such an expanding-shoe design cures many of the faults of the contracting-shoe design, but the problem of heated drums is still there. As the drum heats in a modern brake, it tends to expand, thus growing away from the inside brake shoes. When a modern car is stopped rapidly from a high speed, the drums "grow" so much in diameter that quite often the brake shoes can no longer make contact. This is called brake fade, and it is one reason disc brakes have become standard equipment on most late-model, high-performance production automobiles.

At first, brakes were applied to the rear axle only, not because it was easier that way (although it certainly was), but because brakes on the steerable front wheels were extremely difficult to balance. One side or the other was always grabbing first, which would pull the vehicle sharply to that direction. In effect, four-wheel brakes in the early days were a very real danger. The first balanced four-wheel brakes appeared with the Phoenix racing cars built in England around 1908. Racing cars used four-wheel brakes off and on thereafter, but it wasn't until the 1920s that American production cars started using the new Bendix four-wheel brakes.

Part of the problem of braking balance is linkage. In a mechanical linkage, there is no way the entire system can adjust to a problem at one corner. Malcolm Lockheed created a hydraulic linkage system that came out on the 1921 Duesenberg racing cars (interestingly, the brakes were external-contracting), based on the knowledge that any pressure exerted at any point on a confined fluid will transmit this pressure throughout the system equally, and in all directions. By 1939, when Ford finally converted from mechanical to hydraulic brakes, all American cars were using the hydraulic principle.

Practically all brakes in use today are either the internal-expanding-shoe drum type or the disc type. They are called upon to do a tremendous job. Brakes fulfill their purpose by converting mechanical energy to heat, which is generated by the friction between the shoe facings and the drum, or the pads and disc in a disc-type brake. The heat, in turn, must be dissipated by the drum or disc to passing air.

If 100 horsepower will accelerate a 3500-pound vehicle to 60 mph in 750 feet, and the brakes are required to stop in 150 feet, the brakes must dissipate five times the torque exerted by the engine, or the equivalent of 500 horsepower. One hard, crash stop from 75 mph in some cars can induce complete "fade"—a condition in which the drum becomes so hot that it expands away from the shoes and renders the brakes completely ineffective until they are cooled for 15 or 20 minutes. Heat dissipation has been, and continues to be, a big factor in brake design.

INTERNAL-EXPANDING BRAKES

Internal-expanding-shoe brakes consist of two or more nonrotating segments, or shoes, faced with a friction material. When the foot pedal is pushed, hydraulic pressure is exerted on the shoes through the wheel brake cylinders, forcing them outward and into contact with the drum. In most cases, the drum is integral with the hub. The wheel is usually fastened directly to the drum and hub. In some cases, especially in many race-car applications, the brake drum may be remote from the hub but still connected through a common shaft. Such drum mountings are usually referred to as being "inboard." No matter where the drum is located, the effect is the same: friction between the fixed shoes and the rotating drum slows the drum. The effectiveness of this action (slowing of the car) is directly dependent on such things as pedal pressure, vehicle weight, car speed, design, and the condition of shoes and drums.

Internal-expanding brake systems also contain one or more hydraulic slave cylinders, one or more brake-shoe anchors, return springs, and a method of adjusting the clearance between the drum and shoes. All of the nonrotating parts are attached to the backing plate, a round plate vertically mounted to the station-ary rear-axle housing or front spindle. In addition to mounting the parts that make up the brake, the backing plates keep the drum and operating mechanism reasonably free from mud, water, dirt, etc. The backing plate also absorbs all of the braking torque. In the simplest designs, the wheel cylinder is bolted at the top of the backing plate so that the axis of the cylinder is almost horizontal. This cylinder has two pistons and seal or cup assemblies that are separated by a light compression spring. The outer ends of the pistons have slots or spherical seats to position the upper ends of the shoes. The bottom ends of the shoes are pivotally mounted by anchor bolts to the bottom of the backing plate. A strong tension spring is attached to both shoes near the top to keep the shoes pulled together, or toward each other and away from the drum, when not in use. Each shoe contacts an adjusting eccentric, the adjustment being necessary because normal wear increases the clearance between friction material on the shoes and the drum. The front hub and drum assemblies are mounted on bearings, and the rears are connected solidly to the rear driving axle.

When the brake pedal is pressed, extra brake fluid enters the wheel cylinder under pressure, forcing the two pistons apart. The hydraulic pressure within the cylinder does the forcing, overcoming the tension-spring pressure. The pistons in turn push the shoes toward the drum. The bottom ends of the shoes pivot about the center of the anchor bolts. When the brake pedal is released, hydraulic pressure in the system drops to nearly zero and the tension or return springs pull the shoes away from the drum.

In the two-shoe design just men-

Hydraulic system. Brake-pedal pressure is transmitted hydraulically to each brake through the master cylinder, connecting lines, and brake or wheel cylinders. Depressing the pedal causes the piston of the master cylinder, which together with the rest of the system is always full of fluid as long as the reservoir contains the required excess quantity, to exert on the fluid a pressure which is distributed throughout the system. Under this pressure, the pistons in the wheel cylinders force the brake shoes against the wheel braking surfaces. When pressure on the pedal is released, the piston in the master cylinder is returned by the spring to its normal or "off" position. This releases the pressure in the remainder of the system, because as soon as the master cylinder pressure drops, the momentary excess pressure in the system opens the line return valve and permits fluid to return to the master cylinder. The wheel-cylinder pistons then retract, the dropping of system pressure enabling the brake-shoe return springs

to become effective and retract the shoes. This action applies in principle to both drum and disc brakes. As a safety measure, some systems have a dual master cylinder, one part supplying the front and the other the rear brakes. Their operation is essentially as described. Such systems also include a spool valve, responsive to pressure differences between front and rear sections, that actuates a dash light as a warning of failure in either section.

The drum brake shown has a self-adjustment feature by which, during brake application while the car is in reverse, excessive movement of a shoe (indicating need for adjustment) causes an adjustment lever to be moved sufficiently to turn a small star wheel on the adjustment screw and thus advance both shoes closer to the drum. As long as the adjustment remains satisfactory, the lever cannot be moved enough to actuate the star wheel and screw. (Courtesy Mobil Oil Corp.)

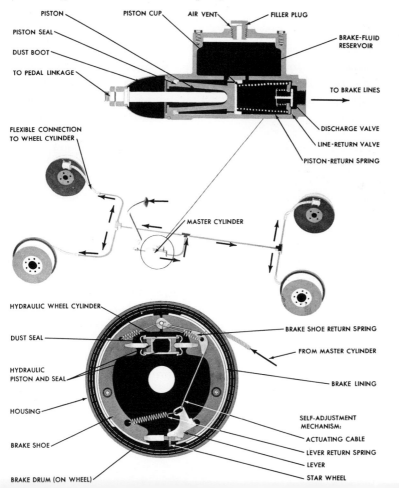

tioned, the shoes are opposite each other and each covers approximately a third of the drum circumference. As the brakes are used over a period of time, the drum and the friction material on the shoes wear, increasing the clearance between them. Thus the need for the adjusting eccentrics.

The Self-Energizing Effect

In automotive brake systems, the shoes that face toward the front of the car are called the primary or leading shoes. The units that face to the rear are called the secondary or trailing shoes. When the car moves forward and the brakes are applied, the friction on the leading shoe is increased, since the shoe tries to lean into the drum. This is called the self-energizing effect. The opposite happens to the trailing shoe, which tries to push away from the drum. When braking in reverse, the secondary shoe becomes self-energizing. This system has been used by Lockheed designs on several cars, including Fords, Mercurys, and some models of Lincoln from 1939 through 1948. The system is simple and dependable.

This self-energizing effect brings up an interesting point: that the effectiveness of the self-energizing shoes is usually about twice that of the trailing shoe. The disadvantage of such a system is extra loading of the wheel bearings when the brakes are used. This loading is directly proportional to the braking-force difference between the primary and secondary shoes, the diameter of the brake drum, and the location of the brake assembly in relation to the bearings. The front shoe is doing more work and will wear faster. To equalize as much as possible the braking forces between the two shoes, the lining on the

leading shoe is shorter and thicker than that on the secondary shoe. In addition, the wheel hydraulic cylinders are usually step-bored, with the piston actuating the secondary slightly larger than that moving the leading shoe.

Rather common on foreign cars and used for some years in the United States by Chrysler Corporation is the two leading-shoe system. This layout takes full advantage of the self-energizing effect in that each shoe is a primary or leading shoe connected at its toe to its own cylinder. The cylinders are located 180 degrees from each other at the top and bottom of the backing plate. The front shoe is operated by the top cylinder, the back shoe by the bottom cylinder. Each shoe then benefits from the self-energizing effect, since it faces the direction of drum rotation. Linings on both shoes are identical. The two cylinders are joined by a common hydraulic line that keeps the cylinder pressures the same. The heel of each shoe is pivotally anchored, but instead of being close together as before, the anchors are diametrically opposed. Adjustments are through eccentrics or ratchets. This arrangement is usually found only on the front brakes in American cars.

The twin-leading-shoe brake takes maximum advantage of the self-energizing effect, which in turn means less pedal pressure and less strain on the front wheel bearings. Its disadvantages are quick heat build-up under extreme or prolonged use, which may mean fade. The tendency to lock or grab is greater if water or dirt happen to get between the shoe and the drum, but this isn't a major problem. Three-leading-shoe and four-leading-shoe designs have been tried but aren't common.

The Bendix Duo-Servo system makes

the frictional force of one shoe apply frictional force to another shoe. In this type of system only one wheel cylinder is used, mounted near the top of the backing plate. The shoes are anchored at the top of the backing plate above the cylinder, and when not in use the shoes are pulled against the anchor by a tension spring. A link between the bottoms of the shoes is necessary, a function performed by an adjusting strut assembly. A tension spring keeps the bottom of the shoes in contact with the strut and also acts as a lock for the adjustment screw.

When the brake pedal is pressed, the shoes expand to the drum. Forward rotation of the drum gives the leading shoe a self-energizing effect. The leading shoe transmits some of this self-energizing effect to the back shoe

through the adjusting assembly, making the back shoe also a leading shoe. However, the back shoe receives more actual pressure than the front shoe, and consequently is susceptible to greater lining wear. Additionally, the back shoe usually has a smaller or shorter lining to help lessen wheel-bearing load. This type of system is desirable because it permits a marked decrease in pedal pressure, and to some extent it is "floating" or "self-centering."

DISC BRAKES

Disc brakes are a different story altogether. They approach the problem of converting energy to heat in a way that is hardly new, but is relatively new to automobiles. In fact, the idea of a disc brake was introduced before 1900, and

This is a typical disc brake, showing how the caliper assembly, consisting of matching halves, fits around the wheel rotor. Each side of the caliper has similar brake-shoe and hydraulic-piston assemblies, usually with a pair of pistons bearing against each shoe. Hydraulic action is the same as that of drum brakes.

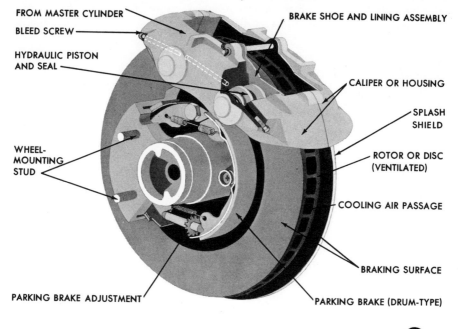

FROM MASTER CYLINDER

BLEED SCREW

HYDRAULIC PISTON AND SEAL

WHEEL-MOUNTING STUD

PARKING BRAKE ADJUSTMENT

BRAKE SHOE AND LINING ASSEMBLY

CALIPER OR HOUSING

SPLASH SHIELD

ROTOR OR DISC (VENTILATED)

COOLING AIR PASSAGE

BRAKING SURFACE

PARKING BRAKE (DRUM-TYPE)

the design has been used off and on in all forms of mechanical apparatus since that time. But only since 1965 has the idea been common to the American automobile scene.

Disc brakes have been used for years by European car builders, based primarily upon the success of road-racing cars using brakes developed by jet aircraft designers. But these are relatively lightweight cars, and the heavy American car hasn't been able to use discs for one engineering reason or another. The primary problem with discs for U.S. cars was cost, but other problems as well kept nagging engineers. Most disc brakes squeaked (they still do), which the average American driver just wouldn't accept. Pedal pressures were high (since cured), and cooling of early designs was not good.

The postwar Crosley used disc brakes, which worked well since this was a very light car. The Chrysler Imperial tried them briefly around 1953. Goodyear was spending a lot of time trying to perfect a brake that would work well on American cars, and by the time of the Detroit "muscle car" of the 1960s, disc brakes could be ordered as options on almost all car makes. Since that time, discs have gone from options to standard equipment on many heavy passenger cars, and they are considered a necessity on camper-hauling pickup trucks.

The disc brake has a circular plate-shaped disc that bolts directly to the hub. This disc may be rather thin (about ⅜ inch thick) on light cars, but on most American cars it is of the vented type and is about 1¼ inches thick. "Vented" means that two thin discs are cast side by side with struts between. Air can then rush through the "inside" of the disc, aiding cooling. The vented disc is imperative on heavy vehicles—say, anything over 3000 pounds gross weight.

Connected to the axle housing (rear) or spindle (front) is a brake caliper. If you cup your hand around a plate edge, you have the same thing. The tighter you squeeze the plate, the harder it is to move that plate in your hand. Sometimes the caliper will have movable friction material, called pucks, on both sides of the disc, and sometimes only the inside puck will move, forcing the disc against the stationary outside puck. If both pucks move, the system is better.

The disc brake can actually have greater friction-material contact in square inches than a drum brake, but usually they don't. Because there is better cooling of the disc and caliper, the disc design needs less area. In demonstrations, the material in a disc brake has actually been heated so hot that it started to burn and melt, yet the system continued to operate! The only way fade can prove detrimental is for the heat to be so great that it causes substantial growth in the caliper, and this is extremely rare.

BRAKE LINKAGES

It has been mentioned that modern brake-actuation systems are dependent on the basic hydraulic principle that any pressure exerted is equal in all directions. Hydraulic brake systems use a specially compounded oil which will not deteriorate the various rubberlike seals and lines in the system. In addition, these hydraulic fluids are relatively incompressible at the pressures and temperatures that occur in an automobile braking system.

In a closed hydraulic system of any

sort, if a cubic inch of fluid in the master cylinder is displaced by the brake pedal, a like amount of fluid must move into the rest of the hydraulic system. In the automobile brake system, the clearance between brake shoes at rest and the drum provide the area for the fluid to be displaced to, in the manner of speaking. Of course, it takes a really tremendous amount of pressure at each brake shoe to stop a two-ton hulk of automobile, an amount of pressure no human could provide if he pushed directly on the master-cylinder piston. Therefore, the laws of leverage are utilized at the brake pedal.

The brake pedal is basically a pendulum with a large foot pad at one end. At or near the other end the pendulum is secured to some portion of the body or frame structure so that it is free to swing fore and aft only. Slightly below (or above, whichever the case may be) this connection is the connection between the pedal arm and the master cylinder via a piston rod. Through leverage, just a small force at the pedal is multiplied to much more pressure at the master cylinder and several thousand pounds of pressure at the wheel cylinders. For example, suppose the brake-pedal arm is 10 inches long from the pivot point to the foot pad. From the center of the pivot point to the center of the bolt attaching master cylinder rod and pedal arm is one inch. The lever advantage is a strong 10 to 1, so 65 pounds of force on the brake pedal will figure out to be 650 pounds at the master-cylinder piston. Now, if the master-cylinder bore is just one inch, the hydraulic line pressure will be the area of the master-cylinder piston (.7854 square inches multiplied by the force applied

to the piston, or 510.5 pounds per square inch.) On cars produced since 1950, the line pressure may vary from 350 psi up (65 pounds initial force), with power brake boosters giving figures often three times greater. The combined mechanical leverage and hydraulic advantage thus forms a ratio of roughly 80 to 1 between the pedal and the brake shoes. So if the driver pushes on the brake pedal with a force of 65 pounds, the radial pressure of the shoes on the drums is 5200 pounds. This example does not take into account that the actual efficiency of such a mechanical and hydraulic linkage is closer to 90 percent than 100. On the other hand, it must be remembered that since most braking systems use at least one leading shoe, the self-energizing effect just about doubles the effect of a nonenergized shoe.

One of the greatest advantages of the hydraulic automobile brake system is that in a fluid system any pressure variation anywhere in the entire system is instantaneous and exactly equal everywhere. If one brake shoe happens to be closer to a drum than all the rest, it will touch the drum first when the brakes are used. But it won't really brake its drum until all the other shoes in the system reach the same point of pressure. It's easy to see, then, that this one property of fluids makes extremely close adjustments in a hydraulic system unnecessary. Another advantage is that there is no lost motion in a hydraulic system and routing of the hydraulic lines is relatively simple. Lines should be clamped every two feet or so, preferably well inside the frame structure out of the way of possible flying rocks and the like.

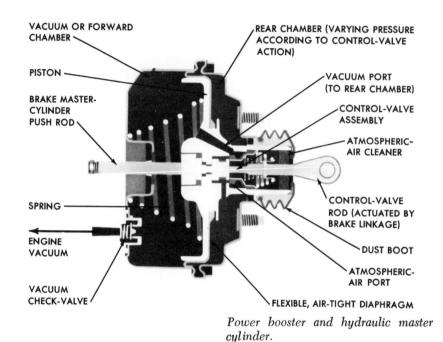

VACUUM OR FORWARD CHAMBER

PISTON

BRAKE MASTER-CYLINDER PUSH ROD

SPRING

ENGINE VACUUM

VACUUM CHECK-VALVE

REAR CHAMBER (VARYING PRESSURE ACCORDING TO CONTROL-VALVE ACTION)

VACUUM PORT (TO REAR CHAMBER)

CONTROL-VALVE ASSEMBLY

ATMOSPHERIC-AIR CLEANER

CONTROL-VALVE ROD (ACTUATED BY BRAKE LINKAGE)

DUST BOOT

ATMOSPHERIC-AIR PORT

FLEXIBLE, AIR-TIGHT DIAPHRAGM

Power booster and hydraulic master cylinder.

The Master Cylinder

The real heart of the hydraulic system is the master cylinder, primarily because all action in the entire system depends upon this one item. Back in the "old" days, many motorists cussed the engineers for attaching the brake mechanism directly to a major frame structure, usually somewhere under the floor. The brake pedals bolted to a part of the frame and connected by a rod to the master cylinder. Inevitably, the master cylinder was hidden away beneath a cross member or such and was most difficult to service. But since the early 1950s it has become virtually universal practice to use "swinging" pedals and firewall-mounted master cylinders. This makes checking the level of the master-cylinder fluid an under-the-hood operation (see Chapter 15). In such installations, the master cylinder usually is integral in one housing with the fluid reservoir. In very recent years, since the widespread use of hydraulic clutch-operating mechanisms, brake master cylinder and clutch master cylinder have been sharing a common reservoir, though in some foreign cars the master cylinder and reservoir are separate.

In a typical American master-cylinder assembly, the cylinder and reservoir housing is made from a close-grain alloyed cast iron. The bore is machined to precise measurements and precision-honed. The cylinder head screws into the end of the housing bore opposite the pedal side. The bore is located below the reservoir, and inside the bore is a piston, usually made of aluminum alloy or brass. This piston has a primary and a secondary seal (or cup). The primary seal acts to keep fluid from leaking from the pressure side of the piston. The secondary seal keeps fluid from leaking from the pedal end of the bore.

The piston has a diminished diameter between the ends, much like a sewing-thread spool, so that fluid can flow freely about it. The piston end facing the brake pedal has a conical hole in it to locate the actuating rod coming from the pedal. The other end of the piston (toward the cylinder head) has some small holes drilled in it so that communicating passages exist between both sides of the piston crown. A piston-return spring is fitted between the cylinder head and the piston crown. In the cylinder head there is a two-way inlet-outlet valve assembly and a threaded hole that takes the line fitting. Two ports connect the reservoir with the cylinder. The smaller of the two is just barely uncovered by the primary cup when the brakes are released and serves as a vent to relieve pressure build-up in the cylinder. This is the reason for an atmosphere vent in the reservoir. The large port is located behind the piston crown and allows the fluid to pass into the cylinder around the annular space between the piston ends. When the brake pedal is mashed, the piston moves in, closing off the small port between cylinder and reservoir. The fluid in the rest of the cylinder is then under direct pressure. Mash harder and the pressure causes the poppet valve in the cylinder head to open and pressure is forced into the brake lines. When the pedal is released the return springs between the brake shoes pull the shoes together and force the fluid from the wheel cylinders back up the lines into the master cylinder. The returning fluid closes the inlet valve in the cylinder head and pressure is put on a disc which serves as a seat for the valve and for the piston-return spring, forcing the disc and valve assembly off its seat. The fluid can now flow back into the cylinder. When the pressure on the disc falls below the pressure of the piston-return spring

(which is inside the cylinder), the disc and valve assembly returns to its seat.

During the time that the pedal is being released, brake fluid can't enter the cylinder from the line fast enough because of flow restrictions around the valve. Here's where the small holes drilled in the piston crown come in. Fluid from the reservoir and the area behind the piston crown can flow through these holes upon demand as a sort of pressure equalizer. After the piston is back at rest position, additional fluid coming into the cylinder from the line can pass directly into the reservoir through the relief, which is now un-covered. The piston-return spring keeps the outlet valve disc seated at line pressures below 10 to 15 pounds per square inch. This pressure stays in the lines and wheel cylinders to keep air from getting into the system in the event of small breaks or leaks. The valve as-sembly is normally made of brass and the springs are usually cadmium-plated steel wire.

The cups in both master and wheel cylinders are made of tough, flexible, nonporous synthetic-rubber compounds. and they are relatively impervious to chemical actions. The cupped end of the unit always faces the pressure, and as this pressure increases it merely tends to force the cup tighter to the cylinder-bore walls.

If you've had any experience with brake systems at all, then you've heard it said time and again that the two greatest enemies of the master cylinder (and in effect, the entire system) are water and dirt. And for a good reason. Since the reservoir is vented to the open air, condensation water can form on the walls above the fluid level when tem-perature and humidity conditions fluctuate. The specific gravity of water is greater than that of brake fluid, so it naturally seeps to the bottom of the reservoir and eventually through the ports into the bore. Since the fluid and the water both have an oxygen content, the cast-iron cylinder bore is thus susceptible to corrosion and eventual scoring of the primary cup. As for dirt, this can be avoided by really cleaning the area around the reservoir filler cap before inspection, and being careful when removing and replacing the cap.

If the master-cylinder bore is worn because of either of these conditions, you will usually notice that you have to increase pedal pressure, or you have to pump the pedal, or that the pedal slowly creeps to the floor under prolonged pedal pressure. There's a leak in the cylinder or somewhere in the lines or wheel cylinders. Normally, the master cylinder will show signs of an approaching bad brake condition before the lines or wheel cylinders will.

Brake Lines

In most cases there is a brass fitting screwed into the master cylinder. The brake line fits into this fitting. Normally a two- or three-way fitting, one side may contain the stoplight switch, which deserves mention. The fitting is normally secured to the cylinder by a hollow bolt that lets fluid go to the connecting line(s). A pressure-tight seal is effected between the bolt head, both sides of the fitting, and the master cylinder by concentric rings machined into the fitting and copper gaskets. Make absolutely sure every time this fitting is removed that all areas are extra-clean and new gaskets fitted before the fitting is replaced. The stoplight switch will have two electrical connections on it: one for input current and the other for current to the lights.

The rigid lines of a brake system are usually seamed steel tubing with an inside diameter of $1/8$ to $3/16$ inch. Copper line will crack under certain conditions and will tend to swell more than steel under the high pressures in a hydraulic system. On the other hand, just because a tubing has a copper look to it doesn't mean it is. Some brake-line tubing is coated with copper, so to make sure just check a freshly cut end. The steel color will be unmistakable.

At the fore and aft ends of the brake lines will be found flexible hoses connecting to the wheel cylinders. Two hoses are used at the front and usually just one hose at the rear. As for hose, just be sure to buy a good brand and to install it properly so that it doesn't get chopped off by flailing shocks, steering apparatus, or springs.

Wheel Cylinders

We're finally down to the wheel cylinders. In its most common form the wheel cylinder consists of a plain open-ended bore, a couple of pistons, cups, a compression spring, two openings, and a couple of flexible boots to keep out dirt, dust, and mud. The cylinder itself is made of a close-grained cast iron, like the master cylinder. Mounting bosses are provided to bolt it to the backing plate. The bore is machined to exacting standards and lapped to a high polish. Cups are much the same as in the master cylinder and rest in the same position relative to pressure. The pistons are normally made from aluminum alloy, and the outer ends are made to accept the ends of the brake shoes or the strut that transmits pressure to the shoe. Between the two cups is located a light compression spring that keeps the cups in contact with the pistons when pressure is released.

There are two openings in the cylinder bore to the outside. One goes to the brake-line hose, the other to a threaded bleeder fitting. This bleeder fitting is used to release air trapped in the system. The cylinder's operation is simple: When pressure is applied the two pistons separate, causing the brake shoes to come into contact with the drum. When the pressure is released the tension springs on the shoes pull the pistons toward each other, forcing the fluid back up the lines and into the master cylinder. This, in a nutshell, is the hydraulic system.

TESTING BRAKES

You can get an excellent idea of total brake condition with a simple road test. While you may think you are aware of brake efficiency during everyday driving, chances are you never notice problems that might exist. Find a quiet road or large parking lot for your test. At about 25 mph, apply the brakes hard, but do not lock them up. That is, stop as fast as you can without skidding.

If the brake pedal goes to within 2 inches of the floorboards or less, you have three possible problems: low brake-fluid level, shoes that need adjusting, or shoes that are badly worn. If the pedal feels spongy, you have air in the hydraulic lines (some disc brakes are designed this way, go check with a garage mechanic about your particular car). If the car tends to pull or swerve to one side or the other, you can have several things wrong. These might be incorrect adjustment (one brake tighter than the other), grease or brake fluid on the linings, loose backing plate, reversed secondary and primary shoes, shoes not arced to drum shape, bad pedal adjustment, out-of-round drum(s), or plugged master-cylinder relief valve.

While you're going through these tests, listen for sounds. A grinding or squeaking sound can mean worn linings, dust or dirt trapped in lining depressions, wrong lining material, glazed lining or drum, oil or grease on linings, or warped backing plates. If front-wheel bearings are excessively loose, they will allow the drum to "float" and give a chattering sound. (Some Chrysler products make a chattering sound and have an erratic pedal feel when stopped from higher speeds. This is a design problem and you can't do much about it in the way of repair.) If you hear a rubbing sound, it can be poor adjustment, broken or loose return spring, or binding wheel cylinder or shoe guides.

With the car at rest, push down on the brake pedal and hold it down. If the pedal holds momentarily, then starts to creep down, there is a bad master cylinder or wheel cylinder, or a leak somewhere in the hydraulic lines.

To test a power-assist unit, turn off the engine, put the transmission in neutral, and pump the brake pedal several times. This will bleed away any vacuum reserve. Now push down lightly on the pedal until you feel slight resistance, and hold it there while the engine is started. If the pedal then drops away slightly and seems to require less pressure, the assist system is OK. If the pedal doesn't move and there is no change in the foot pressure, suspect a problem with the assist unit.

REPAIRING DRUMS AND SHOES

Doing your own brake job is really something of a pleasure for any mechanic, professional or amateur. The professional wants to get maximum braking effectiveness by doing an outstanding job, and the amateur is just happy that he can do the job himself and save lots of money. Anyone can do a brake-repair job. But—and this is extremely important—make it a good job. Be sloppy or casual with a brake job and you are inviting an accident.

You might get away with doing a brake job one wheel at a time, but this is not the best way. If there is a problem with one wheel only, such as a leaking wheel cylinder or foreign material on the linings, then just fix one wheel. But any time the brakes show excessive wear of linings or poor drum condition, all four corners should be fixed.

The best way to do a brake job is with the car on four jackstands. Not two, or three, but four, and not jacks. Jackstands are cheap, and they'll keep you from having a bad driveway accident. Elevate the car in a level place just high enough so each wheel clears the ground.

Remove the wheels and then the drums. Begin with the front ones. In most cases, except later-model GM cars, the wheel-bearing housing is part of the brake drum, and when you remove the front drums you must consider wheel bearings, seals, and lubricant. The brake shoes may have to be backed off to allow the drum to be wiggled off. The star wheel, similar to a coarse-toothed gear, is located at the bottom of the shoe assembly and is accessible through a slot in the drum.

If the car has self-adjusting brakes, the adjusting lever must be held out

When the wheels are removed from drum brakes, the hubs are exposed. At the rear the drums will usually be loose, as they are held on by wheel lug nut pressure. At the front, the spindle bolt nut must be removed. Since the hub assembly is already apart, it is wise to go ahead and repack the front wheel bearings at this time. Check for leaking hub seals that will allow grease into the brake area.

Component call out of a typical shoe brake assembly. If automatic adjustment assembly causes accelerated lining wear it can be removed.

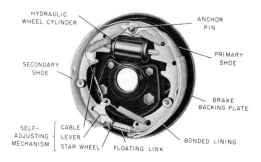

Exposed rear brake assembly shows build-up of grime, which should be removed as part of the rebuild job.

The brake shoes can be removed by detaching the shoe hold-down discs, springs, and pins, and then the return springs from the anchor pin. In shop practice, this latter operation is done with a special tool, but you can do it by grasping the long shank of the spring firmly with vise-grip pliers, stretching the spring sufficiently to remove it from the anchor pin. On rear brakes where the parking brake operates on the rear shoe only, disconnect the parking-brake cable and remove parking-brake strut and lever. Final removal of the front and rear shoes on single-anchor brakes is done by spreading them to clear the wheel-cylinder connecting links, whereupon both shoes will come off as a unit, still held together by the adjustment screw and spring.

Total-contact brakes, used on earlier Chrysler products, have a slightly different hold-down and return-spring arrangement, and a special tool is required to prevent damage to the shoes. Once guide springs, retainers, and return springs are removed, further dismantling is the same as with conventional assemblies.

Clean and inspect the brakes, and also the front-wheel bearings. If air pressure is available, use it to clean drum dust from all parts, being careful not to blow it into the wheel-bearing assembly. A stiff brush is a good substitute for compressed air. If they are very dirty, wash the drum, the backing plate, and the metal part of the shoes in clean solvent and dry them thoroughly. Be careful to keep the solvent away from cylinder boots and brake lining. Check for pits or dark spots on the bearing races; if there is bearing wear you should replace the bearings before reassembly. Check for oil leaks

of the way while the star wheel is turned. This means inserting two tools—a thin screwdriver to hold the lever up, and a brake-adjusting tool—into the slot at the same time.

Mark the drums and shoes so that each complete assembly can be returned to the original wheel position after servicing. Keeping them in paired sets will save a lot of reassembly time. You can scratch them with a sharp instrument or center-punch them with a series of coded dots.

In removing drums, take care to protect front-wheel bearings and seals from dust and dirt. Examine the backing plate to see if it has a wheel-cylinder stop plate. Late-model cars have these stops to prevent wheel cylinders from popping out when shoes are removed, as there is always a slight static hydraulic pressure in a sound brake system. If there is no stop plate, a wheel-cylinder clamp will be required to hold the cylinders in position while the shoes are removed. *Never* depress the brake pedal while drums are removed.

around the rear-wheel bearings and replace the seal if indicated; seepage here
can spoil a good brake job very quickly.

Check all wheel cylinders for piston
leaks by carefully lifting each boot to
note if their interior is wet with brake
fluid. If so, the wheel cylinders must
be overhauled or replaced, as explained
later in this chapter.

Brake Linings

Examine the linings and drums for
wear and grooving, to see if braking
problems might be caused by other than
normal wear. The lining should show
uniform wear both along its contact arc
and across it. Thin spots in the center
of the shoes are normal with oversize
drums, because the shoe radius and
drum radius are not the same. Thinner
edges side to side show that the shoes
have been canted by bent backing plates
and/or anchor pins. Most drums, after
enough normal use, become out of round
and grooved from the abrasive action of

*Drums can distort and have bad wear pat-
terns, which calls for turning on a drum
lathe. Never use drums that have been
turned too much; the local machine shop
will have a gauge to check this measurement for you.*

*Lining wear can be checked to see how
much lining remains. Also check face of
lining to see if it is wearing evenly or if it
is grooved, which indicates the drums are
in need of turning. Always replace the
lining if it is worn down to the rivet heads.*

*Drums usually need turning when new
brake shoes are installed; shoes should also
be shaped to correct radius to get proper
contact points.*

dust and dirt between linings and drum.
Drums can be restored by machining or
grinding on special drum lathes, and it
is safe to remove as much as .030 inch
of material to bring them back to normal

roundness and smoothness. This means that the internal drum diameter will be increased by .060 inch, and the relined shoes must be altered to conform to the new diameter. This is done by use of oversize lining or shimming standard lining, then arc grinding to conform to the new drum diameter.

Modern brake-lining material is molded, then bonded or riveted to the shoes to ensure positive contact and a constant curve and to prevent it from shifting or coming off the shoe. Equipment for relining, drum grinding, and shoe-to-drum matching is not only expensive, but requires training for proper use. It is impractical for the amateur mechanic to own such things as drum grinders, arcing jigs, stocks of lining material and rivets, and bonding ovens.

However, brake lining can be purchased in several ways. Professional brake-servicing companies use rolls of material that must be cut to size, drilled and countersunk for rivets, beveled, and fitted to the shoes. But pre-cut and pre-drilled linings are available to fit specific car models, and replacement shoes, completely lined and ready to install, can be purchased from brake-supply houses and new-car service departments. All forms are available in oversize thickness to compensate for drum grinding, as is shim stock for use under standard lining material, although oversize lining is the usual method. Premium lining materials, such as sintered metallic lining and a wide variety of various degrees of hardness for specific purposes, are available as replacements for standard material. Brake-supply houses which handle name-brand items will have specifications for just about any car made, and following their recommendations will provide the right lining for the indicated purpose.

Clean the entire backing plate assembly, but do not get solvent inside the wheel cylinders.

Apply high temperature grease to points on backing plate where the brake shoes rub. Do not use an excessive amount.

As with riveted linings, bonded materials require special skills and equipment to replace. Old linings must be chiseled or burned off the shoes, which are then carefully sanded in preparation for the liquid cement or special tape adhesive. Cemented shoe assemblies are then clamped in a special jig that applies high, even pressure and heat over the entire contact surface to make a proper bond. It is obvious that the home brake repairman who purchases relined shoes properly arced to his professionally ground drums is getting a better and cheaper job than he could possibly do himself.

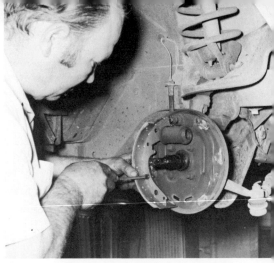

Shoes installation starts with locating pins through backing plate, which are more a convenience for installation than for any special job of later alignment.

Installation and Adjustment

Installing the relined shoes and matching drums must be done with great care and cleanliness. Avoid touching linings or drums with greasy hands, and allow no hydraulic fluid to come in contact with the lining material.

While it is readily accessible, the adjusting-screw assembly should be dismantled, cleaned in solvent, dried, and lubricated. The inboard side of the backing plate should also be cleaned of road grime, which will ease locating the cylinder bleeder valve and anchor-pin adjustment, if there is one.

All brake friction points—except, of course, the shoes and linings—must be properly lubricated. A special grease called Lubriplate is used. It has properties that prevent it from running or vaporizing under the heat the brakes generate, so it may be used without fear of its getting into the drum/lining contact area. However, it should be used sparingly in assembling the adjusting-screw mechanism and at all the mechanical contact points between shoes and backing plate. On rear brakes be

sure to lubricate the parking-brake cable assembly (also see Chapter 15).

If the system has a self-adjusting mechanism, this should be assembled and lubricated before installing shoes. In any case, the star-wheel adjusting nut must be centered over the backing-plate slot (if this type of accessibility is provided) or centered to afford proper adjusting movements (if this is done through an opening in the drum itself). These adjusting assemblies are not interchangeable with the opposite wheels, so be careful to keep the parts for each wheel together.

Place the shoes on the backing plate, engaging them with the anchor pin and the wheel-cylinder connecting links. Be sure the shoes are in proper relative position. Usually the forward shoe has a shorter lining, but not always. The shoes should be marked forward or reverse. If they aren't, and you can't tell by looking at them, ask a professional mechanic who has used that kind of brake lining. Some companies make the

Shoes are attached to cylinder clevii, then springs are attached between each shoe and the anchor pin.

Self-adjusting mechanism should be installed at this time.

forward and reverse linings interchangeable. Others make both linings identical as far as appearance, but the composition is different, and the shoes will not work properly if they are reversed.

Don't feel self-conscious about asking a professional brake man which way the shoes go. It is a problem that has bothered mechanics for years. But be sure the mechanic you ask has had experience with the particular brand of lining or he may not know either. If the counterman where you buy your parts is really sharp, he may be able to help you.

Install the hold-down springs, pins, and washers. On rear wheels, connect the parking-brake cable and install the cable strut. Carefully hook springs onto shoes and over the anchor pin, as well as the adjusting-screw tension spring, making sure that the springs are not bent or over-stretched.

Floating link is installed between bottom ends of shoes, one more spring added, and job is completed.

If the brakes are of the self-adjusting type, take care when assembling the self-adjuster mechanism. These are not interchangeable from one side of the car to the other; if you get them mixed up, the adjuster will retract the shoes rather than advance them. Make sure the parts are not binding on their anchor pin and that both shoe-return springs are installed over the adjuster anchor fitting.

Adjusting screws for self-adjusting brakes are assembled with the thread screwed all the way in and then backed off about one turn. The star wheel is positioned toward the rear or secondary shoe, and the self-adjusting actuating lever is spring-linked to the primary shoe and cable or rod linked to top anchor pin. Before proceeding further, check the operation of the self-adjuster by pulling on the cable or link toward the secondary shoe just enough to lift the lever past a tooth in the adjusting-screw star wheel. The lever should snap into position behind the next tooth and return to its original position when released.

Follow the same Lubriplate procedure when replacing shoes on Chrysler total-contact brakes. Insert the long end of return springs in the shoe web (before placing shoes into position) by sliding them between the support plates and engaging the ends of the wheel-cylinder push rods with the toe end of each shoe. Attach the short end of the return springs to their respective links by prying against them with the proper tool. A long-handled Phillips screwdriver is a good substitute. Install guides and retainers, making sure that the little lip or guide is positioned in hole in support plate.

Bendix-type brakes employ two types of anchor-pin adjustments for shoe

The only difference at the rear wheels is installation of parking brake lever during shoe installation.

centering, making it possible to center without grinding or using gauge bars if the refurbished shoes and drums have been properly arced. Some anchor pins have eccentric threaded ends, and others are mounted through a slotted hole, allowing them to shift when the nut is loosened. In either case, shoe-centering procedures are the same.

Back off adjustment so drums fit easily onto mounting flanges or axles. In the case of front wheels with bearings integral with drum, be sure that the bearing assembly is complete and lubricated, and that the bearing nut is snug enough to prevent any play in the bearing.

Turn the brake-shoe adjusting nut until maximum effort is required to turn the drum with both hands. Mounting the wheel will ease this effort, but

it should take two hands to turn the wheel. Loosen the anchor pin nut not over ¾ turn (with the eccentric-pin type it will be necessary to hold the pin with a square-end tool while loosening the nut). Turn the eccentric pin to shift shoes. With a slotted anchor-pin mount, loosen the nut and rap the backing plate smartly with a hammer to ease shifting of the pin in the slotted hole. Tighten the nut and check brake drag by turning the drum by hand, noticing any difference in drag from the initial setting. If drag is the same, the shoes are properly centered. If drag decreases, it indicates that the anchor pin has shifted. Repeat by again setting the brake-adjuster nut to hard two-handed drag and effecting further shoe shifting by either turning the eccentric or loosening the anchor-pin nut and then tapping the backing plate with a hammer.

Some cars use a nonadjustable anchor. If the lining and drums are standard this works fine, but when you have oversize drums there is a problem in getting the shoes centered. Some replacement shoes have the anchor hole relocated so that they fit properly.

Whether late-model, self-adjusting brakes or older manual models are relined, an initial adjustment is required for proper operation. After the shoe-centering operation on new brakes, or to correct for normal lining wear and to raise effective brake pedal, a minor brake adjustment is necessary to provide proper clearance between lining and drum. For brakes without self-adjusters, this is best done with all four wheels off the ground. Using a suitable tool through the backing plate or drum slot provided, turn the adjusting wheel so there is a slight drag as the wheel is

Some brakes are adjusted with a special flattened tool through the backing plate. Tool lip reaches through to intersect with brake's star-wheel adjustment. Small rubber covers keep out dust and water; they are available from parts shop if misplaced. Cars with self-adjusting brakes often have access holes in the drum, which means that wheels must be removed to adjust brakes manually.

turned. Repeat with each wheel, trying for the same amount of drag. Then, back off an equal number of notches on the adjuster at each wheel (12 to 15 notches are average), making sure that there is no drag. If any is detected, back off an additional 1 or 2 notches on that wheel. Apply brake pedal firmly several times and check for drag again. Repeat as often as necessary until drag is the same before and after shifting anchor pin.

Bleeding Hydraulic Lines

Bleed the hydraulic system and make several slow-speed stops to check equal braking. With self-adjusting brakes, centering procedures are the same and setting shoe-to-drum clearance is not as critical. Just be sure that the shoe-adjusting screw for each wheel is backed off enough to clear shoes from any detectable drag, then achieve final adjustment by braking while car is moving in reverse, which will activate the self-adjuster and bring the shoes to proper clearance.

Following any brake-relining job it is good business to bleed the system, eliminating any air that may have entered. The purpose of bleeding is to drive air out of the master cylinder, lines, and wheel cylinders, through special bleeding valves on each wheel cylinder. These are small fittings, looking very much like Zerk grease nipples, located on the backing plate directly behind the wheel cylinder. Unscrewing them slightly opens a passage into the wheel cylinder, acting like a small faucet with a ball-like end on it. As these bleeder valves are usually covered with road grime, they should be cleaned thoroughly for easy access and operation.

Make sure that the master-cylinder reservoir is filled and that a supply of new, clean hydraulic fluid of the proper specification is available to top this level off as the fluid level drops. Professional brake mechanics pressure-bleed lines, using a large reservoir of pressurized hydraulic fluid that is coupled to the system at the master cylinder and supplies a flow of fluid through all the lines while each wheel-cylinder bleeder valve is opened. However, bleeding can be done without this aid with two persons for the operation—one to operate the foot pedal, the other to bleed each wheel cylinder.

For bleeding by the two-man method, a bleeding tube and a glass jar or soft-drink bottle are required. The tube can be procured at any auto-supply store. It should be long enough to reach from the bleeder ball end to the bottom of the glass jar when the jar is on the ground. Put about an inch of clean hydraulic fluid into the jar. Slip one end of the bleeder tube onto the bleeder valve,

and put the other into the jar so that it is submerged in the fluid. Open the bleeder valve about ¾ turn and at the same time have an assistant slowly press the brake pedal a full stroke. Close the bleeder valve just before the brake pedal hits bottom and allow the pedal to return slowly to full-out position. Repeat until the expelled fluid flows in a solid stream with no air bubbles. Tighten the bleeder valve and remove the hose. Be sure to check the fluid level in the master cylinder and top it up with new clean fluid only.

It is possible for one man to bleed brakes, using the bleeder nose method. Just be sure the end of the hose is below the surface of the fluid in the jar. Open the bleeder fitting, then go to the pedal and stroke it easily once or twice, using about three-quarters of the full stroke. Replenish the fluid in the master cylinder, then go to the wheel and close the bleeder fitting. Repeat at each wheel. If the lines are empty it may be necessary to run as much as a cupful of fluid through each cylinder to get all the air out. This would require several strokes of the pedal for each cylinder.

The best procedure is to follow a wheel-to-wheel sequence, beginning with the one closest to the master cylinder. This applies to caliper-disc units and to later-model cars with dual master cylinders. Begin with the left front, then do the right front, left rear, and right rear. This procedure minimizes the possibility of trapped air entering lines already bled. Under no conditions must the master cylinder be emptied during the bleeding process, as this will pump air into the system. For total-contact brakes on early-model Chrysler front wheels with two wheel cylinders, bleed the lower wheel cylinder first.

Repairing Lines and Cylinders

Hydraulic brake fluid has a distinct, sharp, alcohol-like odor in its fresh fluid state and becomes sticky after prolonged exposure to air. This makes it easy to locate leaks in lines, master cylinder, or wheel cylinders. Check all lines from the master cylinder to each individual wheel, examining any grime-coated wet spots for evidence of hydraulic fluid. Should any lines need replacing, do not attempt to save any of the fluid for reuse. It may be contaminated and cause damage to the system. Note: Hydraulic brake fluid will ruin automotive paint finishes and brake-lining material, so be careful with it.

Use only steel brake-line tubing, properly flared for the fittings. The flexible lines from tubing terminus to wheels are armored for maximum protection and should be replaced only with stock replacement parts.

While it is possible to hone and rebuild wheel cylinders, the job can be just as easily farmed out to a brake shop or machine shop. In fact, replacement cylinders are inexpensive.

With the drums removed, examine each wheel cylinder for leaks by carefully lifting the boots from the cylinder housing. Evidence of hydraulic fluid under the boot indicates a bad wheel cylinder, and the shoes must be removed before you can work on the cylinder.

To remove the wheel cylinder, loosen the line where it connects to the cylinder at the backing plate. Remove the cylinder mounting screws, detach the cylinder from the backing plate, then finish uncoupling the line by rotating the cylinder. Some hydraulic fluid can be saved by placing a well-fitting wooden plug into the end of the flex line. This should not be driven in hard enough to distort the line.

Remove boots, springs, pistons, and cups from the cylinder and place them in alcohol brake-parts cleaning fluid. (All parts of the system activated by hydraulic fluid should be cleaned only with 188 proof clear industrial alcohol or special fluids compounded for this purpose and available at automotive-supply houses.) Clean the cylinder casting inside and out, but do not let it soak in fluid. Examine the bore for scoring and pitting and the cups for swelling. Scored cylinders can be honed to restore the desired mirror finish, but no more than .005 inch may be removed. If more is required, the entire cylinder must be replaced. Replacement kits containing all necessary parts for rebuilding wheel cylinders are readily available from parts houses. Obviously all doubtful parts should be replaced while the cylinder is apart; a minor saving here might result in another major repair later.

If the cups are swollen or mushy it is an indication that the hydraulic fluid has become contaminated with oil,

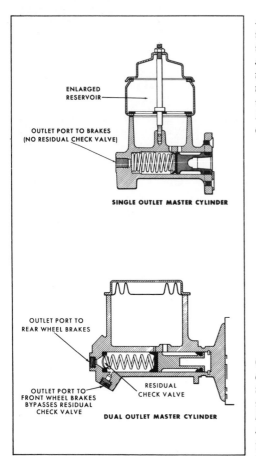

ENLARGED RESERVOIR

OUTLET PORT TO BRAKES (NO RESIDUAL CHECK VALVE)

SINGLE OUTLET MASTER CYLINDER

OUTLET PORT TO REAR WHEEL BRAKES

OUTLET PORT TO FRONT WHEEL BRAKES BYPASSES RESIDUAL CHECK VALVE

RESIDUAL CHECK VALVE

DUAL OUTLET MASTER CYLINDER

After there are many miles on the car the master cylinder may start to fail. Early indications are odor of hydraulic fluid inside car, erratic action of brake pedal, continual loss of hydraulic fluid. Shown are two single chamber master cylinders, one with single outlet, one with dual outlet. Dual outlet is used so separate brake lines can go to front and rear wheels.

Cutaway of a power assist unit behind a dual chamber master cylinder, considered the very latest in safety equipment. As a rule, the home mechanic should leave rebuilding the power assist unit to a professional. Rebuilding the master cyclinder is possible, but replacement with a new unit is not expensive.

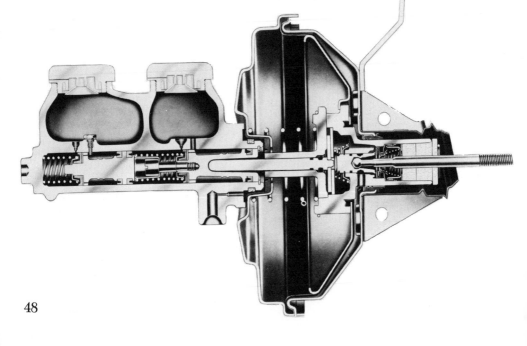

kerosene, or gasoline. Should this condition be evident, the entire system must be flushed, and all wheel and master-cylinder cups (and in severe cases the rubber flex lines) must be replaced.

Reassembly of wheel cylinders must be carried out under clean conditions. They can be contaminated by dirt, oil, water and solvents, or even by dirty or greasy hands. With the finger, coat the inside of the wheel-cylinder wall, as well as the piston and cups, with clean hydraulic fluid. Assemble them carefully in proper sequence for each side, ending with the boots on the ends. Clean the end fitting of the line and screw the cylinder onto the line by rotating the cylinder until snug. Place the cylinder in position on the backing plate. Secure the cylinder to the backing plate with mounting screws and finish tightening the line. Repeat for each wheel.

Master cylinders fail and require rebuilding for the same reasons as wheel cylinders. Normal wear, contaminated fluid, and dust and dirt entering the system will eventually spoil the sealing and pumping action.

Replacement parts for either single or double systems, with oversize pistons and cups, are available should the cylinder require honing, but the maximum that can be removed is .005 inch. Should this honing depth fail to remove scores or pits, the master cylinder will have to be replaced. The honing of master cylinders is best done by a professional repair shop, because special tools are required to remove the burrs around the small ports inside the barrel.

When overhauling master cylinders, always use all the parts in the replacement kit to ensure long rebuilt life. Be careful in reassembly, being very sure to keep any grease or dirt from entering the system. Clean all parts in alcohol or special cleaning compound for hydraulic systems, and lubricate cups and pistons with hydraulic fluid when assembling.

Dual master cylinders, with their tandem piston assemblies, require a little more care when sliding the cups and pistons into the cylinder barrel, because the outlets are usually at the sides, along the cylinder walls. Observe the cups as they are pushed past these holes to see that they do not turn back the edge and destroy their sealing effect. A piece of small-diameter rod, rounded and smooth on the end, can be poked through the outlet hole to ease the cups past the openings. Liberal use of hydraulic fluid as a lubricant will help slide the assemblies through the barrel.

Follow carefully the instructions packed with dual master cylinder kits. Some of the kits have an adjustable piston which must be set for your car. If it isn't set correctly, the brakes won't work.

To fill the hydraulic system after rebuilding wheel and master cylinders, fill the master reservoirs and proceed as with bleeding the system, only open the bleeder valves fully and keep master reservoir filled as the foot pedal is used to pump fresh fluid into the entire system. Then bleed the system as previously described, after bleeding the master cylinder first.

Some masters are equipped with bleeder valves which operate much like the wheel cylinder bleeders. To operate, press the brake pedal slowly, opening the bleeder valve near the bottom of the stroke, then closing it before the pedal is released. Repeat, making sure that the master reservoir is full, until the fluid flows in a steady stream without bubbles. For bleeding without a valve, loosen the fitting to the brake line and force air and fluid out by pressing the brake pedal. Air in the system can be heard as it squirts out through the fitting. Tighten and proceed with bleeding wheel cylinders. On dual masters, loosen both outlet fittings and proceed as described for single cylinders.

When preliminary examination of a wheel or master cylinder indicates swollen or mushy piston cups, the fluid has probably been contaminated by oil, kerosene, or some other foreign liquid that has destroyed the rubber cups. All wheel cylinders and the master should be rebuilt with new parts, but only after the system is flushed. About a quart of 188-proof alcohol or special flushing fluid is required, plus a small amount of extra brake fluid for flushing out the alcohol or cleaner. Follow the same procedure as for bleeding, but open the bleeder valves a full 1½ turns to speed up passage of the old fluid being pushed through by the flushing liquid. After flushing, expel as much fluid from the system as possible by pumping the brake pedal while bleeder valves are open, then proceed with overhauling the wheel and master cylinders. When finished reassembling, bleed the system completely with new hydraulic fluid before the final bleeding to make sure that all flushing fluid has been removed from the system.

REPAIRING POWER ASSISTS

The power-assisted brake systems generally used on passenger cars do not shorten the stopping distance of the automobile. They are designed to assist in applying pedal pressure to the hydraulic system, thereby reducing the pedal force normally required in a non-assisted system. Two basic types are used on passenger cars: the Bendix and Moraine composite units, composed of a vacuum-actuated power unit combined with a hydraulic master cylinder; and the type used by Ford and Chrysler, which uses a vacuum-operated power unit that applies assisting force to the brake pedal linked to the master cylinder. Both systems use engine intake-manifold vacuum to operate them, but will operate with increased pedal pressure should the system fail or if the engine is off.

Power units are composed of three basic elements, all of which must function to achieve assisted braking effort. These are the vacuum chamber, which provides the power as long as manifold vacuum is available; the hydraulic master cylinder, which transmits hydraulic force to the wheel cylinders; and the control valve, which is operated by mechanical linkage to the brake pedal and triggers the vacuum force in proportion to the brake-pedal pressure and travel distance.

Whether of composite or isolated type, power units require much the same replacement of parts as do hydraulic systems in that every phase of their operation depends on good sealing and proper operation of the valves.

Repairs of either the composite Bendix/Moraine or the auxiliary assist units are complicated and require a thorough knowledge of specialized repair procedures. It is best to leave repairs of power assists to an expert, or replace the entire unit with a new or rebuilt one. However, before removing a unit for repair, check all vacuum lines from the engine manifold to the diaphragm housing, as breaks or poor connections will hamper proper vacuum-to-atmospheric-pressure balance and the unit will not operate as it should.

Pedal adjustment is also critical, especially if the proper ¼ to ⅜ inch free play in the pedal action has been reduced and the vacuum valving is not releasing properly. Pedal adjustments are incorporated in the linkage to the power units and on suspended-pedal systems are accessible from inside the car. Before adjusting any pedal clearance, make sure the return spring is operating with sufficient force to return the pedal unassisted to its full-out position. If there is no return spring, be sure the pedal is free on its pivot.

Disc brakes on the front end have become almost standard equipment on most American cars. Early problems were squeaking discs, but this has been cured in most cases. Note how massive the caliper housing is to control deformation when system is working.

REPAIRING DISC BRAKES

Modern caliper disc brakes are highly sophisticated versions of the original single-piston types. Four pistons are used on each caliper, allowing larger pads and more even distribution of pressure to increase both braking force and lining life. With the exception of the main hydraulic supply line, fluid connections to the pistons are by machined internal passages except on early Kelsey-Hayes versions. Self-adjusting, and with visible indication of lining wear, caliper discs are relatively easy to reline but require care and precision to rebuild. Unaffected by water, dust, and dirt—since the close-fitting pucks wipe as they are applied and water cannot be trapped on the spinning disc—they are sensitive to oil or hydraulic fluid just as drum brakes are. Passenger-car disc systems do have a splash shield to divert dust-laden air and water and avoid disc and lining wear caused by abrasives that might filter in between them.

Most larger cars use the vented rotor, which is a heavier disc that can be cooled better.

Relining Discs

The procedure for relining or replacing the pads on Corvette disc brakes is similar to that for all GM discs. The lining material is bonded or riveted to a thin steel backing plate. Bonded shoes

 51

have a groove in the center of the pad to indicate wear. When the groove is completely worn off, linings should be replaced. Riveted material should be replaced when worn to within .020 inch above the rivet heads.

Before proceeding with lining replacement, siphon about two-thirds of the fluid from the master cylinder to prevent its overflowing as the wheel-cylinder pistons are pushed back by the new thicker linings. It is not necessary to remove the caliper assembly to replace linings, nor to bleed the system afterward. A simple guide pin, secured by a cotter key, slides laterally, clearing the holes in the pads themselves and allowing them to be slid out. *Never depress the brake pedal with lining pads removed.*

When inserting new linings, note the directional arrow on the steel backing of each one, which indicates wheel rotation direction and enables you to line up the grain of the material in proper relation to the disc direction. The wheel pistons will have to be pushed back slightly with a thin smooth tool such as a putty knife to accommodate the new linings. Repeat with each wheel, top off the master reservoir to proper level, and test the pedal for firmness. If the pedal is spongy, bleed the line as with regular drum brakes, using the valve on the caliper assembly.

To service the internal-expanding parking brake on Corvettes, it is necessary to remove the caliper and pull the entire disc/drum assembly to expose a conventional internal-expanding two-shoe brake, cable-operated. Shoe replacement is almost the same as for conventional drum brakes, including a final adjustment by star wheel so that there is no drag when the drum/disc assembly is replaced.

Budd caliper discs, used on earlier Chrysler cars, must be removed to replace linings. This can be done without detaching the hydraulic line by removing the mounting bolts to the wheel spindle. A special tool is required; it slides in between the lining pads and piston insulator to hold them in position during removal. Then carefully slide the assembly off the disc, invert it, and remove the shoes one at a time. Replace them with new linings, slide the assembly back on the disc, install the retainer and anti-rattle springs, tighten the mounting bolts, and remove the special retaining clips. Apply medium pedal pressure while finishing the final tightening of caliper mounting bolts.

The Kelsey-Hayes discs, also used on earlier Chrysler and Ford cars, can be relined without removing the caliper assembly. They can be identified by an external hydraulic line that connects opposing piston assemblies. The lining material has a metal backing with tabs at each end and small telltale detents. These detents create a scraping metal-to-metal noise against the disc, indicating that the linings need replacing. To replace them, the splash shield and anti-rattle spring must be removed and the pistons pressed back into the cylinders by prying against the old lining with a thin smooth tool. It is a good idea to check the level of master-cylinder fluid to guard against overflowing during this operation.

With two pairs of pliers, grasp the tabs at each end of the lining pad and withdraw. Slide new pads into position, with the lining material facing the disc and the tabs seated firmly on the caliper. Replace the splash shield and anti-rattle spring, then pump the pedal hard several times to advance the pistons and properly seat the linings. Check the master-cylinder fluid level and bleed the system if the pedal is spongy.

The brake disc itself is machined to very precise dimensions and finish. Disc thickness is critical to proper lining clearance and piston travel, and the finish is critical to proper coefficient of friction between pads and disc. The discs cannot be warped either, since the calipers are solidly mounted to the spindle and must not be twisted by run-out or wobble. Run-out can be checked by removing the lining pads and clamping a dial indicator to the caliper. Tighten the wheel-bearing nut to remove all play from the hub. Pick a smooth spot about an inch from the outer edge of the disc for the indicator ball and turn it slowly. A total run-out of .004 inch is maximum, and the disc must be replaced if it exceeds this. Machining a disc is not recommended.

Disc wear as to thickness also has limits, and this can be checked with a micrometer. Overall wear that reduces the new thickness .035 inch for 1-inch discs, or .010 inch for 1¼-inch Corvette discs, indicates the need for disc replacement. Once a normal wear pattern has developed through use, minor scores in the disc surface have a negligible effect on braking efficiency. As most discs are riveted to the hub assembly, replacement involves removing the entire hub, drilling out rivets, and installing a new disc. They do not have to be re-riveted on GM cars, as the wheel-mounting studs provide the necessary alignment. Be sure to secure with the wheel lug nuts when checking a new disc for run-out.

Rebuilding Calipers

When relining caliper disc brakes, inspect the inner cavity with pads removed. Any indication of hydraulic

Cutaway of opposing piston caliper, using four hydraulic chambers to squeeze large pads against rotor.

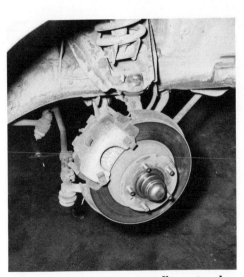

Disc brake servicing is actually easier than drum brakes. Inspect rotor for unusual wear, caliper for cracks.

If caliper must be removed to replace disc pads, the brake line must be disconnected. Plug the end with a fitting to keep system from draining dry.

Removal of dust boots and seals is easier if the pistons are pushed back into their caliper half as far as they will go. Carefully pry off the boot with a thin screwdriver, remove the pistons, seals, and springs, and clean them all in alcohol or special fluid. Clean out bores and all fluid passages and dry them before examining them for scoring or pits. Be careful with any tool you use to remove any part of the piston assembly; avoid puncturing seals and boots, or scratching cylinder walls or piston.

While all rubber parts should be cleaned and examined to determine the specific cause of piston leakage, it is a good idea to replace them all from the standard rebuilding kits available. Pistons and bores should be free of scores and pits. Minor ones can be removed by

fluid means that seals, pistons, or both need replacing. To rebuild caliper piston assemblies, the entire caliper assembly must be removed.

Calipers are made in two halves, with the mating surfaces carefully machined for perfect fit. Before proceeding with any further disassembly, wash the caliper thoroughly in alcohol or the special brake-cleaning fluid prescribed for regular drum-brake wheel-cylinder service. Dry thoroughly and separate caliper halves by removing large cross bolts. Note that the fluid passages where they cross from one side of the caliper to the other are sealed with small O rings. Remove these carefully and keep with other parts so that they are not forgotten on reassembly. Early Kelsey-Hayes calipers do not use internal crossovers and the external tube must be removed before separating caliper halves. Do not bend excessively or reassembly will turn out to be quite difficult.

If the rotor face seems scored, it may need to be turned on a lathe by the machine or brake shop. Remove the entire hub assembly; do not disconnect hub from rotor.

honing, but not more than .020 inch can be removed for cleanup. Beyond that the caliper must be replaced. Bores that show very light scratches or corrosion can be cleaned with crocus cloth, a light abrasive material similar to jeweler's rouge.

With the caliper half clamped in well-padded vise jaws, begin assembly of springs, pistons, seals, and boots. Most of the assembly can be done by hand, using hydraulic fluid liberally to lubricate all parts. GM brakes require a special tool to compress the piston seal and another for installing the boot seal. Use of any other tools for this purpose will result in damage to rubber parts.

Kelsey-Hayes and Budd units, if held securely in a vise, can be hand-assembled with a small smooth screwdriver

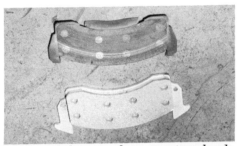

Worn pad here is down to rivet heads, which is beyond where the replacement point is. Rivet heads can wear grooves in the rotors, and replacement of rotors is not inexpensive.

used carefully to work the lip of the boot into the groove provided around the bore diameter. Use no lubricant other than specification brake fluid, as any solvent, grease, or oil with a mineral base will damage the rubber parts and void all the work of the overhaul. Make sure that pistons and seals slide easily into cylinder bores, then place O rings in cavities around fluid crossover passages and fit the caliper halves together. Make sure the mating surfaces are clean and free from nicks before installing cross bolts and hex nuts. To insure proper pressure between caliper halves, a torque wrench is recommended for tightening assembly nuts. About 55 ft.-lbs. for $\frac{7}{16}$-inch bolts, and 155 ft.-lbs. for $\frac{1}{2}$-inch bolts, will mate the caliper halves without damage or distortion. On caliper assemblies with external crossover, check the tube for dirt and fractures before carefully screwing the coupling nuts to fittings.

Replace the caliper assembly, using a putty knife to keep the pistons and boots from hanging up on the edge of disc. Line up the caliper to the spindle mounting holes and secure it with the proper bolts, and shims if any. Check

When disc pads are removed from the caliper, hydraulic cylinder pistons may pop out. If there is any sign of fluid leaking around the cylinder the unit should be rebuilt by a professional. Be careful when installing new pads so the pistons return to the cylinders squarely.

hydraulic-line fitting for cleanliness and thread condition. Some systems use a small copper gasket in the male end of this connection, which should be replaced to ensure a good seal at this critical point. Install lining pads, retaining pins, anti-rattle springs, and splash shield.

UNDERTAKING A BRAKE JOB

Obviously, a brake job is more than a thirty-minute adjustment, but it is something any amateur should be able to handle. Most brake service and repair operations are done with basic tools, but one special inexpensive tool should be in every toolbox. It is called a brake pliers, and it makes easy work of shoe-spring and disc-retainer removal and reassembly. Should the particular job you are confronted with require some other special tool, haul the brake assembly to the local parts store or brake shop, where they can do the repairs at a fraction of the cost they would charge for the entire brake job.

As a guideline, plan to spend an entire day on your first full brake relining/service job. You'll spend most of your time just becoming acquainted with the various pieces, to ensure that you get each brake assembly reinstalled properly. Here's a tip in that direction: Always leave one brake assembled as a guide. Chances are very good that about the only things you'll do with a typical brake rebuild will be new linings, shoe adjustment, and possibly drum turning. Normally, the wheel and master cylinders do not need repairs until the car has around 100,000 miles on it.

3 steering

IT MIGHT SEEM that there is no possible connection between how a vehicle steers and various chassis control features, such as shock absorbers, sway bars, and spring rates (see Chapter 2). However, automotive engineers learned long ago that steering is directly affected by every movement of every wheel. This effect, furthermore, will dictate exactly how well the car steers (which is a function of overall handling), how easy the car is to control, and to some extent how comfortable driving is.

There is an alarming number of accidents reported yearly that are attributed to "loss of control." In the majority of these cases, it simply means the driver no longer could control the steering. In few cases has there been a total failure of the steering system, such as a broken tie rod, but in almost every case the steering is probably much less effective than when the unit was new. A steering system can and does wear to the point

where adjustment is necessary. At the same time, there are tremendous forces working on the steering system, forces that help make marginal parts fail or become sloppy. In many cases, these forces cause the steering parts to loosen on their mountings.

Every automobile owner should know how to perform routine steering-system maintenance at home. The amateur mechanic can take things even further by performing many repairs.

MECHANICAL PRINCIPLES

A steering system is really a very basic assembly. Force exerted on a steering wheel (which might as well be nothing more than a lever or tiller) is transmitted through a shaft to some kind of gear at the lower end of the shaft. This gear mates in some way to another gear and shaft, changing initial shaft-turning direction 90 degrees. At the end of this second, shorter shaft (usually called the sector shaft) will be attached a connecting rod called a pitman arm, usually about 7 inches long. From this pitman arm will extend a rod to one of the wheel spindles. In early cars, and some contemporary trucks, this rod is parallel to the left frame rail and connects to the left front spindle. Such a unit is called drag-link steering. Most cars have a tie-rod connection between the two spindles. This entire unit may be composed of three or four short rods connected together by rod ends (spherical joints). In one popular design, a tie rod goes across the chassis parallel to the front crossmember and connects the pitman arm to an idler arm on the right frame rail. Connecting to this cross link are two shorter tie rods that go to each front spindle. In another design, the idler arm is mounted at midpoint behind the front crossmember, with tie rods linking to

each spindle and a short drag link connecting to the pitman arm. Both of these methods are generally referred to as cross-link steering. A power-steering assist can be adapted to any steering system, even rack-and-pinion, and the basic steering-system design will not be radically changed.

In earlier days, steering was the most simple combination of linkages, often with no gears. The tiller type of steering on ancient vehicles would be a good example. But as cars became heavier, and speeds increased, there was definite need to create a steering system that could make mechanical leverage work in both directions.

Although all the steering commands would seem to originate at the vehicle steering wheel, such is not the case since the car front end is engineered to be somewhat self-aligning, and road conditions will cause deflection in steering situations. This is a Pinto steering unit, which uses a flexible cable shaft between wheel and rack and pinion gearbox.

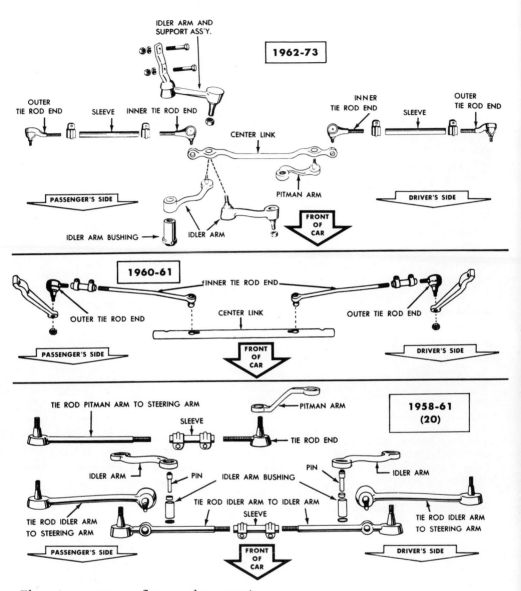

There is a constant effort on the part of engineers to improve steering linkage, as evidenced by the changes in link designs on this medium sized car from 1958 through 1973. At every point where there is movement in the linkage there will be wear, which will accelerate when lubrication is lacking.

It is vital to inspect and repair any part of the steering linkage that is worn. Often overlooked on modern cars is the fabric vibration damper used in the steering shaft above the gearbox. While this is not prone to failure, the rubber/fabric compound can be adversely affected by chemicals.

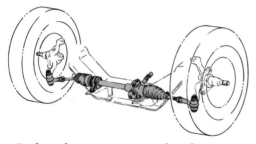

Rack and pinion steering has been very common on foreign made cars for several years; it made its American debut on Ford Pinto as an attractive package for lightweight cars. New Pintos and Mustangs may offer a power assist rack and pinion option.

Steering Ratios

The modern car will usually have a steering gearbox ratio of approximately 22:1, which means 1 pound of force at the steering wheel will be equal to 22 pounds at the spindle steering arm. This gearbox ratio will vary from car to car, with some of the lighter cars having as low as 18:1 and some heavy cars well up toward 30:1. The reason is quite simple. While the car is moving, it does not take a great deal of pressure on the steering wheel to get road-wheel response. Indeed, the entire front-end geometry has been engineered to make steering at speed easy. But while the car is going slow, or stopped, it takes a great deal of force to overcome the friction between tire and pavement (see Chapter 4). Sometime note how much easier it is to turn the front wheels while parked on ice or dirt than while parked on pavement.

This opposition of forces is what wears on a steering system. The constant heavy loading on the steering gearbox may tend to loosen the gearbox mounting bolts. Even the slightest bit of sloppiness at this point will tend to make the steering feel loose. Heavy loads on the tie-rod ends will increase wear, and the sum total of wear in four or more rod ends will also give a loose steering feel. Heavy leverage loads will ultimately take their toll on the gearbox components, also, and the results can be anything from broken gears to galled gear teeth to gearing high spots to a broken gearbox housing. Gearbox loading failures are much more likely if significantly larger

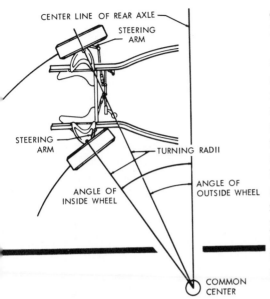

CENTER LINE OF REAR AXLE

STEERING ARM

STEERING ARM

TURNING RADII

ANGLE OF INSIDE WHEEL

ANGLE OF OUTSIDE WHEEL

COMMON CENTER

When the front wheels are turned, the inside wheel must turn in a tighter radius than the outer wheel. All this is taken care of in design of the steering linkage (Ackerman principle).

(wider) tires are used on the front end than the car was originally designed for. The more resistance there is to turning, the greater the gearbox loading.

But the steering-system leverage can also be used to reduce the amount of road-shock feedback into the steering wheel. It would take considerable shock at the wheel to give a 10-pound shock at the steering wheel.

Power-steering ratios are usually in the area of 17:1. They could be faster, perhaps in the realm of the 10:1 sometimes used on racing cars, but this would be far too touchy a system for the average driver. If you think you are capable of handling any type of quick steering, get a ride on a neighborhood kid's go-

cart, which will have a ratio of about 10:1 also.

It is possible to change steering-gear ratios by either adding high-performance steering/pitman arms (these are normally listed as options by most dealers), or by changing the diameter of the steering wheel. The larger a steering wheel, the longer the leverage from wheel rim to center, thus the slower the total ratio. Unless you're really hooked on performance, it is best to stay with the steering ratio originally intended for the car. If you change to a faster ratio (manual design, no power assist), you will find the car correspondingly harder to turn at slow speeds and when parked.

Preload

Construction of a typical steering system is simple enough. The lower end of the steering-wheel shaft has a spiral worm gear pressed on. The gearbox housing has a bearing support for this shaft immediately above and below the worm gear. If this worm gear is moved closer to or farther from the sector shaft, the steering "preload" will be adjusted. A slight amount of play is necessary between worm and sector gears to avoid binding as the gears are cycled. This preload will be by either metal shims between the housing and end plate, or by a threaded bearing adjustment nut at the end of the housing.

Just below or above the worm gear passes the sector shaft, or pitman-arm shaft, or drop shaft; all three terms mean the same thing. This shaft is supported by a bushing or bearings in the gearbox housing. This shaft sometimes also has an adjustment nut, which will move it in relation to the worm gear. The shaft receives movement from the worm gear by a roller or lever connection.

ADJUSTING MANUAL STEERING SYSTEMS

There are five basic types of manual steering units on American cars, not counting those imported under U.S. names. These types are: Gemmer worm and roller (Chrysler to 1961, American Motors to date); Saginaw recirculating ball (GM and Rambler section of American Motors); Ross (Jeep and Studebakers to 1961); Chrysler recirculating ball; and Ford recirculating ball. The change to recirculating ball from the older designs was to get a smoother steering "feel" without heavy spots.

Before you start any steering maintenance, it is wise to make sure the gearbox is aligned. All that heavy loading may have caused the gearbox to shift on its mounting slightly. Make sure the wheels are pointed straight ahead and there is no load on the pitman arm. Loosen the gearbox mounting bolts slightly. The gearbox can then shift back into alignment if it is out, and then you tighten the bolts. Make sure they are tight.

It might be wise at this time to mention a special tool that all home mechanics should have in their toolbox: a rod-end fork. Tie-rod ends have a

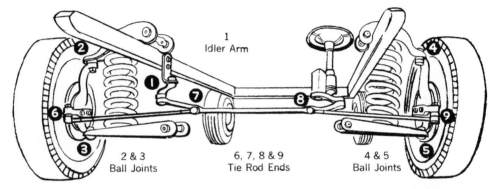

1
Idler Arm

2 & 3
Ball Joints

6, 7, 8 & 9
Tie Rod Ends

4 & 5
Ball Joints

The various points on a front end that the home mechanic should check at least twice a year, and more often as the vehicle piles up mileage. These are: 1) idler arm; 2, 3) ball joints or king pins; 6,7,8,9) tie rod ends; 4,5) ball joints or king pins.

Pitman arm on steering gearbox determines ratio of steering. Special replacement arms are available from most car dealers to speed up the steering ratio. A special gear puller is normally needed to remove the pitman from sector shaft after the large nut has been removed.

A link sleeve that has been distorted like this from a severe front end crash should never be reused. On occasion a home mechanic might use a pry-bar wedged in the sleeve opening to adjust the linkage and cause a similar distortion.

The steering gearbox "load" is adjusted most often by a locking threaded shaft. This shaft increases or decreases the clearance between the worm and sector gears; adjustment must be done carefully to avoid placing too much bind on the gears. When a steering system seems to have too much "slop" in the gearbox, this is the adjustment that takes it out.

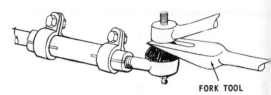

FORK TOOL

When tie rods are to be replaced it is necessary to free rod stud from tapered hole in spindle or idler arm/pitman arm. A tapered fork tool is best for this; do not pound the rod end housing or rod stud with hammer

Front wheel toe-in and toe-out are adjusted by small sleeve links on each side. It is imperative that these links be adjusted so the securing clamps have a good "bite" on the rod or rod end shaft. This is where the linkage is adjusted when the steering wheel is being centered.

tapered stud that mates with a taper in the spindle arms and pitman arm (as well as any intermediate cross shaft). When this stud nut is pulled tight (and always cotter-keyed), the mating tapers may be so tight the rod end is hard to break loose. Often you can give the tapered arm a smart slap with a hammer to free the stud. Don't hammer on the stud threaded end or you may distort the threads. The fork has a wedged face and is inserted between the steering arm and rod end. A hammer blow on the fork end is usually sufficient to free the stud.

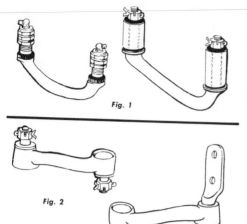

Fig. 1

Fig. 2

Fig. 3

There are three basic idler arm units: fig. 1 is the kind that is rubber bushed; fig. 2 pivots on a stud; fig. 3 pivots on a support arm bolted to the frame. Do not bend these arms in any way, as this would affect the steering linkage alignment.

The idler arm rubber bushings can and do wear out. When this happens there is too much play in the steering system and the only cure is to replace the bushing or the entire idler arm (the latter is usually the case).

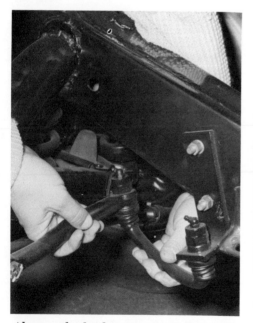

Always check the steering linkage idler arm for excessive play. This will usually occur in a small part of the overall operating arc.

Front end alignment is taken care of in several places; at the two bolts holding the upper arm tiebolt in place is where shims are added or subtracted. This shaft can become worn as vehicle miles pile up and should be replaced to avoid a total shaft failure which can cause a serious accident.

Bushings on the tiebolt are not generally lubricated, so they will wear out after so many miles on the car; the wear will be accelerated if the road conditions are poor. Although you can replace these bushings at home, it is usually done as part of a general front end overhaul and alignment.

Gemmer Worm and Roller

Let's look at the Gemmer worm-and-roller unit first. The worm is integral with the steering shaft, with an hour-glass shape, concave in the middle. It is supported at both ends by tapered roller bearings. The cross shaft has a triple roller (instead of a sector gear), which fits into the worm teeth. An adjustment screw in the cover permits cross-shaft end-play adjustment, which determines play between roller and worm. The pitman arm is fastened with a master spline to the roller shaft by a large nut.

Worm-bearing adjustment: If adjustment is necessary, disconnect the steering linkage from the pitman arm. To eliminate end play in the steering shaft, loosen the four end cover-plate screws, then loosen the cover plate and separate the shims with a knife, being careful not to damage the shims. Remove one shim at a time, retighten the screws, and check for end play by turning the steering wheel full right and left. Repeat this procedure until there is no end play and

no noticeable tightness in the wheel movement to full right and left. Retighten all four screws. Then check the bearing preload with a spring scale on the rim of the steering wheel. If the pull is less than 1½ pounds, remove another shim and repeat the operation. If the pull is more than 1½ pounds, add shims to decrease the preload until it is satisfactory. Be sure all screws are tight when scale-testing.

Cross-shaft adjustment: Loosen the cross-shaft adjusting-screw lock nut (in the cover). With the steering wheel in center position, tighten the adjusting screw slightly. Check amount of end play by grasping the pitman arm. When end play has been removed, use the spring scale again on the steering-wheel rim; if there is more than a 1-pound pull (above the first scale reading), loosen the adjustment screw slightly. Do not overtighten. The steering wheel should turn freely from one extreme to the other without binding or stiffness. Tighten the lock nut on the adjusting screw and recheck with the scale.

Saginaw Recirculating Ball

The low-friction Saginaw recirculating-ball system is widely used in manual steering gears.

Worm-bearing adjustment: Turn the steering wheel slowly from one travel end to the other, being careful not to turn the wheel hard against the ends of travel. Damage to the assembly can result from jamming. Any binding or stiffness may require the disassembly of the entire gearbox. Turn the steering wheel to about one turn from either extreme end of its travel, then loosen the lock nut at the bottom of the gearbox and turn the adjusting nut in until no end play is felt (some models have the

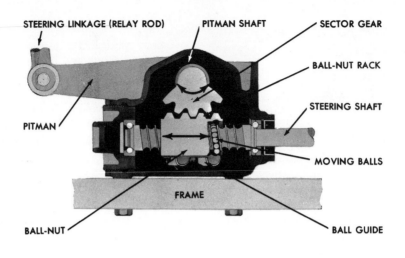

STEERING LINKAGE (RELAY ROD) PITMAN SHAFT SECTOR GEAR

BALL-NUT RACK

STEERING SHAFT

PITMAN

MOVING BALLS

FRAME

BALL-NUT BALL GUIDE

FRONT-END VIEW

adjusting nut at the top of the gearbox). Attach a spring scale to the rim of the steering wheel. A spring pull of ½ pound is desired. Readjust until the spring pull is approximately ½ pound, then lock the adjusting nut and check spring pull.

Cross-shaft adjustment: Turn the steering wheel to one-half the total number of turns. This should be the "high point" between the gear nut and the pitman-shaft gear teeth. Loosen the lock nut, and tighten the pitman-shaft adjusting screw until all end play has been taken up. Rotate the steering wheel back and forth through the high point, and feel for tight spots. Attach a spring scale to the rim of the steering wheel— a pull of about 2 pounds is desired (this includes the preload of the worm-gear assembly). Readjust the pitman-shaft screw as necessary and tighten the adjustment-screw lock nut.

Fill the gearbox with proper lubricant. Recirculating-ball gear assemblies require a special lubricant.

Chrysler Recirculating Ball

Used on Chrysler cars since 1962, the Chrysler recirculating-ball system has the same basic operating principles and general construction, with variations, as the Saginaw recirculating-ball gear.

The front end and the steering linkage should be inspected and all worn or damaged parts replaced and adjusted to specifications before starting steering-gearbox adjustments for worn bearings. Disconnect the steering linkage from the pitman-arm; gear unit is self-aligning.

Worm-bearing adjustment: Loosen the large lock nut on top of the housing. Move the steering wheel gently through its extreme travel to check for stiffness and rough spots. Attach a spring scale to the rim of the steering wheel. Adjust worm-bearing adjustment at top of housing until approximately 1 pound pull is obtained on the spring scale when passing through the high point (tight spot) as the steering wheel is centered. Tighten the lock nut and recheck with the spring scale.

66

Cross-shaft adjustment: Loosen the lock nut on the cross-shaft adjusting screw. Adjust until no more than 2 pounds of pull is obtained from the spring scale on the steering wheel at the high point or the middle of the wheel movement. Rotate the wheel from one extreme to the other, then recheck. Do not overtighten. The maximum of 2 pounds of pull includes both worm and cross-shaft spring pull. Tighten the lock nut and recheck with spring scale.

Ford Recirculating Ball

The basic operating principles and construction of the Ford recirculating-ball steering gear are also the same as the Saginaw gear with some variations.

Check the front-end alignment as usual and adjust and/or replace worn or damaged parts if necessary. Disconnect the steering linkage from the pitman arm.

Worm-bearing adjustment: Loosen the steering-column clamps at the bottom of the instrument panel. Remove cap screws from the top of the gear housing. Move the cover and column up and remove one shim, being careful not to damage other shims. Pull the cover down and retighten the cap screws.

Now turn the steering wheel from one extreme to the other. Turn gently, being very careful not to damage the gear assembly by turning the wheel hard against the extremes of its travel. Check the wheel for any binding or stiffness. Attach a spring scale to the rim of the steering wheel. A 1-pound pull is desired.

Cross-shaft end-play adjustment: The adjusting screw is located on the top of the steering box. Loosen the lock nut and turn the screw to the right to remove end play. Check with the spring scale. Do not overtighten. The total spring pull should not exceed 2¼ pounds. Tighten lock nut and recheck with the spring scale. Readjust if you find it necessary.

STEERING-GEAR DISASSEMBLY

After adjustments of worm, worm sector gear, and cross shaft, if rough spots, binding, or excessive play still exists in the gear assembly, it will be necessary to remove and replace or recondition the gear assembly. This will necessitate the removal of the gearbox assembly and steering column and assembly. Some later models have a flexible steering shaft. If the car is so equipped the joint can be disconnected without disturbing the upper column and wheel. A shop or maintenance manual for the specific car is important for anyone attempting this job.

Parts or complete steering units can be found at a local car junkyard. Occasionally a low-mileage wrecked car can be found, and with a little bartering and work in removing the units, you can obtain a serviceable system. This will save time and money rebuilding your unit.

The steering-gear assembly, column, and wheel can be removed with a minimum of special tools, though the disassembly, reconditioning, and overhaul of the assembly will require additional special equipment. Here are specific directions for the removal of a typical steering assembly. If you must drop it out through the bottom, jack up the front end of the car.

1. Disconnect battery clamps.
2. Disconnect wires at bottom of steering column and tag each wire.

3. Disconnect steering linkage from pitman arm.
4. Remove jacket tube clamps at steering-gear housing (if any).
5. Disengage steering-shaft flange from flexible housing. Some late cars have a flex connection between gear shaft and steering-wheel shaft. This will make it unnecessary to disturb the steering column and wheel.
6. Remove support clamp at instrument panel.
7. Remove horn and signal wires from steering column below instrument panel.
8. Remove horn ring and steering wheel—a wheel puller is needed.
9. Remove dust shield at firewall.
10. Remove floor opening panels (if any exist).
11. If car has manual shift lever on steering column, disconnect gear shift rods at the bottom of the steering column.
12. Disconnect neutral safety switch wire at bottom of column and tag it.
13. Unfasten steering gear from frame (attached with 3 or 4 bolts).
14. If car has automatic transmission, disconnect gear indicator from the dash dial.

To remove the horn switch or steering wheel, disconnect the battery to prevent the horn from sounding. In all cases a wheel puller should be used to remove the steering wheel. Before removing the wheel, make a scribe mark on the end of the steering wheel shaft and on the wheel hub, so the wheel can be reinstalled correctly. Some cars have a blind spline for this purpose.

POWER STEERING UNITS

Many modern cars are equipped with power steering, which includes two basic units: the hydraulic oil pump and the steering unit. The hydraulic pump is engine driven and supplies oil pressure as needed to the steering unit. It is usually belt driven and mounted at the engine front (see Chapter 15).

All power steering pumps are constant displacement type, delivering from 650 to 1300 pounds pressure, depending upon the type and make of the system and the car. Special power steering fluid or Type "A" automatic transmission fluid is used. This fluid is stored in a reservoir attached to the pump with a filter in the reservoir to prevent foreign matter from entering the system. The pressure relief valve located in the pump prevents the fluid pressure from exceeding the predetermined maximum pressure of the system. Flexible hoses carry the fluid to the control valve of the steering unit. The smallest or high-pressure hose carries fluid to the control valve of the steering unit. The larger of the two hoses is the return, or low pressure hose. A flow control valve is combined with the pressure relief valve (located inside of the pump).

When the fluid circulation reaches about 2 gallons per minute, the flow control valve is forced to open a passage between the inlet and outlet sides of the pump and all excess oil is sent back to the intake side of the pump and recirculates. When oil pressure exceeds the fixed pressure limit, the relief valve opens and allows fluid to flow back to the inlet side and recirculate in the pump without raising the pressure in rest of the system.

There are five types of pumps in use: vane, rotor, roller, sleeve, and slipper. Detailed information for the pump concerned can be found in the shop service manual.

Before any major service operations are started the following items should be checked and corrected.

Fluid level: Check level at regular intervals. Wipe the cover before opening to prevent dirt from getting into the system. Maintain fluid level 1 inch below the top. If fluid is very low, check the system for leaks. If only a small amount of fluid is needed, automatic-transmission fluid can be used. When adding larger amounts or changing fluid it is advisable to use special power-steering fluid. Oil should be at operating temperature, wheels in a straight-ahead position, and the engine stopped when checking or adding power-steering fluid.

Belt tension and condition: Belt tension should be maintained between 60 to 90 pounds (for a new belt). If a belt-tension gauge is not available, deflection of approximately 1 inch in the middle of the two belt pulleys (with a medium pressure) is too loose and the tension should be tightened. Using a pry bar can damage the pump or reservoir. Check the belt for evidence of age and wear. Frayed edges, separation of the layers of the fabric, and cracks on the inside of the belt indicate age and brittleness. Good belt dressing will reduce slipping and noise.

Lubrication and inspection of steering linkage and front suspension: The steering gear, linkage and front end should be serviced and lubricated and the alignment checked before any major pump work is attempted. Check tires for correct air pressure. Steering effort can be checked with a spring scale, with engine idling and front wheel on a smooth floor or driveway. Attach the spring scale to the rim of the steering wheel; while turning wheels from one extreme to the other, the pull should not exceed 10 pounds at any point.

Oil-flow and relief-valve operation: These valves can be checked by turning the steering wheel full right or left, with the engine idling. If the valves are working, a slight buzzing noise can be heard. Do not hold the wheel in this extreme position for more than two or three seconds, because if the relief valve is not working the high pressure might damage the system. If no buzzing noise can be heard, a sticking or malfunctioning valve can be suspected. A power-steering additive, found at most auto-parts stores, will clear up many power-steering problems.

Troubleshooting

Because the power-steering gearbox is usually more complicated and sophisticated than the manual design, the amateur mechanic usually leaves rebuilding to the professional. However, it is not difficult to remove and replace the unit, and there are some conditions that you can remedy. If there is a noise around the pump, you can look for a slipping belt, hoses touching the fender splash panels, air in the oil, dirt in the oil, a low oil level, loose pump mounting, pump worn excessively, faulty relief valve, bad flow-control valve, or excessive back pressure, caused by bad hoses of the gearbox. Obviously some of these things you can fix, others must be taken care of by the professional.

If the pump leaks, look for a reservoir that is too full, damage to the inlet or outlet connections, a leaking pump shaft seal, air in the fluid, loose hose connection (cross threaded connections), gasket or O-ring damage. If the system seems to get "heavy" when you turn the steering wheel fast, it may be low fluid level, pump belt slippage, or high internal leakage somewhere in the system. You can normally turn the wheel fast

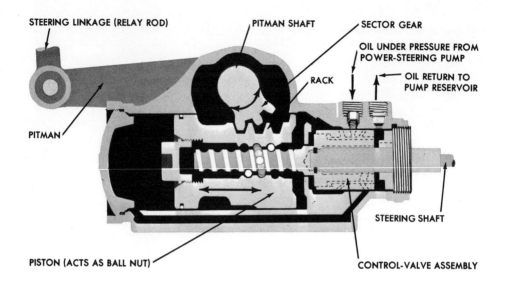

STEERING LINKAGE (RELAY ROD)
PITMAN SHAFT
SECTOR GEAR
OIL UNDER PRESSURE FROM POWER-STEERING PUMP
OIL RETURN TO PUMP RESERVOIR
RACK
PITMAN
PISTON (ACTS AS BALL NUT)
STEERING SHAFT
CONTROL-VALVE ASSEMBLY

enough to "catch" the pump, but it is easy to tell the difference from this kind of loading and when something is wrong.

A hissing sound from the system is not abnormal, and you'll probably notice it most at full turn in either direction. If the steering wheel jerks when you're turning or parking, suspect a loose belt or sticking flow-control valve. If the system just doesn't seem to be giving much help, it can be caused by low oil pressure from the pump, an excessively worn pump, low oil level, or a loose belt.

In most power-steering systems the gearbox is specially built for power assist. However, there is another type, an add-on unit that is really more of an assist. This type of unit consists of a control "head" usually mounted near the pitman arm on a manual gearbox, and a slave cylinder that mounts between the frame and a tie rod. Such systems are no longer in wide use. If you have one that needs repairs, you'd better leave it to the professional.

RACK-AND-PINION STEERING SYSTEMS

Rack-and-pinion steering was found primarily on imported cars until the Ford Pinto was introduced, and the Pinto system is German-built. There isn't much that can go wrong with a rack-and-pinion system. A shaft-mounted worm gear (pinion) moves a cross-mounted rack. This pinion-and-rack assembly is enclosed in a small-diameter tube housing, with the rack extending out either end. A ball joint at either rack end connects to two tie rods, which in turn go directly to the spindle steering arms. Such a straightforward steering design is good for lightweight cars, but it does give considerably more steering-wheel feedback of road shock than the traditional American type of steering.

If anything does go wrong with an r&p unit it is usually lubricant-seal failure, and this is easy to fix. In rare cases either the rack or pinion gear may be damaged and need replacement, which is also easy. If the steering gear has sustained damage from a collision, the entire unit should be removed and given to a professional for thorough checking (alignment).

STEERING AND HANDLING

How well a car handles, or fails to handle, is the combined result of suspension, tires, steering, and other factors. Braking might be considered as a part of handling, but in this case we'll limit the subject to how effectively a vehicle reacts to changes in road surface, changes in center of gravity and center of pressure, and changes in vehicle direction. No single element of the automobile can be singled out as most involved in the cause/effect relationship of handling. Each involved element contributes, and a change at one place will usually result in a different total result. There are exceptions, of course, but not with the typical passenger car.

So let's start with the steering. To get excellent handling, at least up to specifications for a particular make of car, it is necessary for the entire steering system to be adjusted correctly, with no binding spots in either gearbox or linkage. Tie rod ends are not prone to failure, but it's possible for them to get flat spots on the balls after many thousands of miles use. Always replace any component in the steering system with quality parts. After the steering is in excellent working order, and the front end alignment is correct, you can turn attention to other handling areas.

Shock Absorbers

The very first thing you must consider if you suspect your car's handling is shock absorbers (see Chapter 1). While the prime objective of shocks is to work in cooperation with the springs, shocks are also involved in controlling the roll of a car. When a vehicle turns a corner, the height of the car will work like a pendulum, and the shocks help control this roll to a small extent. The best method of getting improved road handling is to go to a slightly "stiffer" shock absorber. The rule of thumb for racing-car builders is to use soft springs

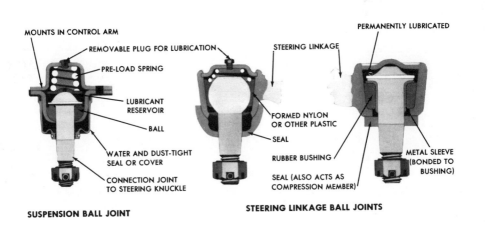

MOUNTS IN CONTROL ARM
REMOVABLE PLUG FOR LUBRICATION
PRE-LOAD SPRING
LUBRICANT RESERVOIR
BALL
WATER AND DUST-TIGHT SEAL OR COVER
CONNECTION JOINT TO STEERING KNUCKLE

SUSPENSION BALL JOINT

STEERING LINKAGE
FORMED NYLON OR OTHER PLASTIC
SEAL
RUBBER BUSHING
SEAL (ALSO ACTS AS COMPRESSION MEMBER)

PERMANENTLY LUBRICATED
METAL SLEEVE (BONDED TO BUSHING)

STEERING LINKAGE BALL JOINTS

TIRE SIDEWALL MOVEMENT

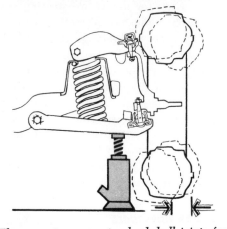

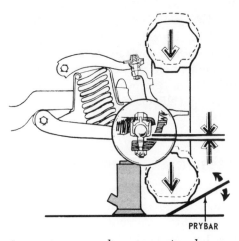

There are two ways to check ball joints for excessive looseness. Some manufacturers recommend the axial movement method, while others recommend the tire sidewall movement. Moog Company personnel (Moog makes a top line of replacement ball joints) recommend the axial movement check as the most accurate. In the tire sidewall check you end up with the multiplied reading at the wheel, which depends on what point on the wheel you take the reading.

In the axial movement check, you are checking only ball joint movement within the joint housing, and is a reading at only one point.

AXIAL MOVEMENT

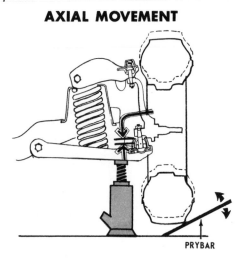

In most cases where excessive looseness develops, the load-carrying ball joint is the culprit and should be checked first. The prime load-carrying ball joint is the lower one in all cases where the coil spring is seated on the lower control arm, and on vehicles with torsion bars. Jack the car under the lower control arm near the ball joint; if axial movements exceed .050-inch, replace the joint.

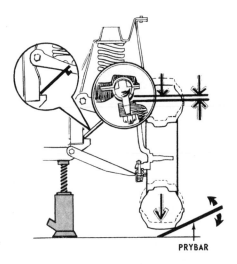

When coil spring is seated on upper control arm, the upper joint is the primary load-carrying joint. Place a support wedge between the upper control arm and the cross-member to lock out the spring pressure. Relocate jack under the chassis frame; axial movements should not exceed .050-inch.

Motor Vehicle Manufacturers Association

(Maximum allowable vertical clearance† for load carrying ball joints)

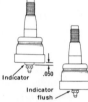

WEAR INDICATOR♦

Indicator

Indicator
flush

In a new joint the
indicator protrudes
from the bottom
plate approximately
.050 inches.

When the indicator
is flush or inside the
bottom plate, the
joint should be
replaced.

Do not jack. Use
frame lift or leave
weight of vehicle
on wheel.

TABLE 1

Clearance specification for those cars
having the coil spring or torsion bar
mounted on the LOWER CONTROL ARM.

Model	Year	Vertical Movement
BUICK	57-60	.150″
	61-70	.100″
LeSabre, Wildcat		
Electra, Centurion	71-72	.020″**
	73-	Wear Indicator♦
Special	61-63	.080″
	64-68	.060″
Special, Skylark,		
GS, Sport Wagon	69-70	.070″
	71-72	.0625″
Century, Regal	1973	.020″**
Apollo	1973	.0625
CADILLAC		
Calais, DeVille		
Fleetwood	57-73	.062″
Eldorado	67-73	.125″
CHEVROLET	55-63*	.093″
	64-70*	.060″
Biscayne, Bel Air,		
Impala, Caprice	71-72	.020″**
	73-	Wear Indicator♦
Chevelle	64-70*	.060″
Deluxe, Malibu,		
Monte Carlo, Laguna,		
El Camino	71-72	.0625″
	73-	.020″**
Corvair	60-63	.093″
	64-70	.060″
Corvette	55-63	Not Applicable
	64-70*	.060″
	71-73	.0625″
Camaro	67-69*	.060″
	70-73	.020″**
Nova (Chevy II)	62-67	See Table II
	68-70*	.060″
	71-73	.0625″
Vega	71-73	.0625″
CHRYSLER	57-64	.050″
	65-73	.070″
COLT-CRICKET	71-73	.020″**
DODGE	57-67	.050″
	68-72	.070″
Dart	60-67	.050″
	68-73	.070″

Model	Year	Vertical Movement
DODGE (Cont'd.)		
Polara, Monaco	1973	.070″
Coronet, Charger	1973	.020″**
EDSEL	58-60*	.200″
FORD	54-72*	.200♭
IMPERIAL	57-66	.050″
	67-73	.020″**
LINCOLN	52-72*	.200″
MERCURY	54-72*	.200″
OLDSMOBILE		
98, Delta 88, Custom		
Cruiser, Etc.	57-70	.125″
	71-72	.020″**
	73-	Wear Indicator♦
F85, Cutlass, Etc.	61-63	.090″
	64-70	.125″
	71-72	.0625″
	73-	.020″**
Toronado	66-73	.125″
Omega	1973	.0625″
PLYMOUTH	57-60	.050″
	68-72	.070″
Valiant, Barracuda	60-67	.050″
	68-73	.070″
Fury	1973	.070″
Satellite	1973	.020″**
PINTO	71-73*	.200″
PONTIAC		
Catalina, Bonneville,		
Grandville, Etc.	58-64	.060″
	65-70	.050″
	71-72	.020″**
	73-	Wear Indicator♦
Tempest	61-63*	.093″
	64- *	.060″
LeMans (Tempest)	65-69	.050″
Grand Prix LeMans,	70-72	.0625″
Grand Am	1973	.020″**
Firebird	71-73	.020″**
Ventura	71-73	.0625″
THUNDERBIRD	55-60*	.200″
	61-66*	See Table II
	67-72*	.200″

TABLE 2

Clearance specifications for
those cars having the coil
springs mounted on
the UPPER CONTROL ARM.

*Horizontal movement in the ball joints for these cars should
not exceed .250″ with the exception of American Motors
1970-72 models which should not exceed .160″ horizontal
movement. On all other vehicles, a horizontal check for ball
joint looseness is not valid.

**Preloaded by rubber or springs, up to .020 vertical move-
ment allowed.

†Applies to original equipment ball joints.

Model	Year	Vertical Movement
American Motors—All Models	70-73*	.080″
Chevy II	62-63*	.093″
	64-67*	.060″
Comet	60-62*	.200″
	63-73*	.200″
Cougar	67-73*	.200″
Fairlane (Torino)	62-72*	.200″
Falcon	60-70*	.200″
International 1000—Travelall	60-73	.095″
Maverick	70-73*	.200″
Meteor	62-63*	.200″
Mustang	65-73*	.200″
Thunderbird	61-66*	.200″
	67-72	See Table I

3 73

Original equipment ball joint housings may be riveted to the control arm. These rivets can be removed with heavy duty chisel; replacement housings will bolt in place.

With level and square, find the exact wheel centerline and make a mark on the cardboard. Now draw a line perpendicular to the first line, passing through the axle centerline point. Where this line intersects the tire, make a mark on the tire with chalk.

You can check front end alignment by making up a graph. Pointer is attached to carpenter square with C-clamp, square is leveled at rear of wheel on axle centerline. Make a mark on the cardboard. Repeat this procedure at front of wheel. Draw a mark on the cardboard between these two points. The pointer in this fashion can also be used to indicate out of round wheels, and by moving it to front of tire tread it will show significantly out of round tires.

A piece of waxed paper between tire and cardboard may make the turning of the wheel easier. Turn the steering wheel to full lock in each direction (don't let the car roll). Mark where chalk mark intersects every ½ to 1 inch of tire travel. Don't let the cardboard move around while tire is moving. Roll the car from the cardboard and connect the points where the tire moved. This will come out as an arc. Now locate the center of this arc by trial and error with a compass. This centerpoint is thus the steering axis inclination, and if it is not the same on both sides (at least very close) and slightly ahead of the centerline, the caster must be adjusted.

(so the wheels are on the pavement as much as possible), but stiff shocks to control rebound. You can get good service from adjustable shocks, moving the setting progressively stiffer as the shocks "wear" during use.

Anti-Sway Bar

It isn't likely that you'll ever do anything with the springs, except replace broken or sagging units. That leaves the anti-sway bar, and here is where you can make a tremendous difference in the way a car handles. The anti-sway bar is simply a solid steel bar running across the chassis. Each end connects by linkage to a suspension member, and the unit becomes something of a secondary torsion bar. Most cars have a minimal-size sway bar, at the front only. You can buy optional heavy-duty front sway bars from the dealer, and often options for the rear end also. Most auto-parts stores know of accessory suppliers of rear-end sway bars. These add-on's really help, especially the rear-end units.

Wheels and Tires

Finally, you have the wheels and tires (see Chapter 4). The way your car rides and handles will be affected in no small part by these companions. If the tire air pressure is set to the normally recommended 24-28 psi, the car may ride well, but tend to be mushy in turns and slow in steering response. Raising the tire pressure to 32 psi will sacrifice a small part of the soft ride, but handling response will be better. If wider wheels are added to the car, the general handling will seem slightly improved, but the tire used should never have a wider tread width than the rim width. Never combine a very wide rear tire with a narrow front tire, such as a 10-inch rear with a 5½-inch front. The extra traction at the rear will cause the front end to "push"—that is, the front end traction is not enough to turn the car on its normal course. Never, never mix radial tires with other designs, as such a combination causes strange things to happen to handling and the car may spin out of control in unusual conditions.

Understeer and Oversteer

Generally speaking, you want the average passenger car to have just a degree of understeer. Understeer means that in a turn you must keep applying steering-wheel pressure to keep the car in the turn. Oversteer means that you must keep diminishing steering-wheel pressure to stay in the turn. Tire air pressure, wheel and tire size combination, tire type, and roll center of the car will all play a part in oversteer/understeer characteristics. The center of gravity you can't do much about, of course, unless you've been carrying a sailboat on your roof, but you can change the other factors to maximize your car's handling.

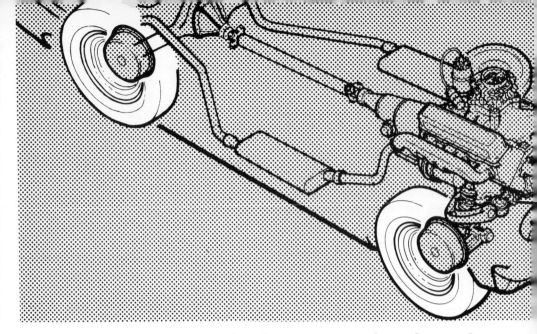

4 tires and wheels

LIKE EVERYTHING ELSE on an automobile, the tires and wheels have been designed for a specific purpose. Any deviation from this purpose will have direct effect on how the vehicle performs and how long the tires can be expected to last. Sometimes the overzealous car owner will tinker with tire size and inflation just enough to ensure poor rubber mileage and performance. Getting the best performance from tires and wheels means the car owner must carefully assess his vehicle, the type of driving he will normally be doing, and the kinds of adverse conditions he may subject the vehicle to. If he is really honest with himself, the owner will then select the correct wheels and tires, with initial purchase enonomy taking a back seat to function. It may be far better to use wheels and tires that will have an initial cost of three or four hundred dollars than to "save money" on tires and wheels that will cost half that.

If you really know how to select tires and how to care for them—and for wheels—you can expect to get maximum performance and mileage from even medium-quality products.

WHEELS

The wheel is ordinarily so troublefree that most modern drivers have come to regard it as foolproof, which it definitely is not. To begin with, practically every automobile wheel not installed by a really conscientious mechanic is fitted incorrectly! Wheels are held on either by lugbolts or lugnuts, and in either case, they have a factory-recommended torque specification. If this specification is not met, and it seldom is, the wheel and drum/hub flange can be damaged.

When installing a wheel, first inspect the lugbolt or stud threads. If they are slightly disfigured, which can be caused by overtightening or cross-threading,

Automobile wheels are not indestructible, particularly those used on the smaller, lightweight cars. These two wheels are part of set of four that were destroyed by hitting a low curbing at high speed, straight on. The tires flexed sufficiently to allow the wheels contact with the curb. Hitting an object at an angle or flat sideways is even more destructive. There is no satisfactory low-cost repair for wheels damaged this badly.

they should be cleaned up with a thread chaser (available at all auto-parts stores). In the case of lugbolts, which are inexpensive, it is wise to replace any bolts that have bad threads. In a pinch you can use a special three-cornered file, called a thread file, to clean up studs. Lug studs are pressed into the hub flange and cannot be replaced at home by the average mechanic. If the very end of a stud should be damaged, no more than ⅜ inch can be cut from the tip for temporary repairs. If lugnuts or lugbolts have been used many times, it is wise to purchase new replacements, since constant torquing will distort the threads.

Inspect the wheel for cracks or signs of abuse. If the wheel has struck a hard object, the rim lip can be damaged. Because of the drop-center construction of most rims, it is very difficult to strike a rim hard enough to make it significantly out of round. However, if you suspect a wheel is not straight, make a quick test. Nail a piece of board upright on a 2x4 wood base. At a place even with the hub center (wheel mounted to the hub and torqued the correct amount), place a nail or wire pointer on the upright. Spin the wheel and touch this pointer to the

Another example of wheel/tire damage from hitting a curb. Here the speed was only about 20 mph, but the tire flexed enough to break the sidewall (white rubber shows in damaged area) on the tire and bend the wheel slightly. After checking the wheel for run-out and roundness it was determined that only the rim lip had been damaged. This was straightened with a hammer, and rough edges were ground smooth. However, the shock forces of the blow were severe enough to break shock absorber mounting on opposite rear wheel area. Front end alignment was also knocked out.

rim edge. As the wheel rotates, it will be apparent if it is either bent or out of round. The out-of-roundness is checked just inside the outer edge, on the lip where the tire bead seats. Most steel wheels will be slightly out of round, but if one wheel shows a significant amount more than the other wheels, it can definitely be the cause of a frustrating wheel-balance problem, and replacement is the only solution. A bent wheel (one that wobbles from side to side) is more common. Any wheel that shows more than about 1/8 inch of wobble, which may seem to be only a tiny amount, can cause balancing problems.

If the lugnuts or lugbolts are not tightened correctly, the wheel can be improperly stressed, which will cause it to run out of alignment. Pulling one or two nuts too tight can also distort the brake drum to the point where the brake "bumps." This is a condition where the distorted drum has effectively set up a series of high and low spots, causing the brakes to grab and release almost as though the drum were out of round.

Never, never mix lugnuts or lugbolts between car makes! Wheels all have different lug face tapers, and while the thread size may be the same, the tapers can definitely vary. If the lug does not match the taper on the wheel center it will often distort the wheel. The lug can also work loose in a few miles.

Any wheel that shows cracks around the lug opening should be replaced. Cracks where the wheel center is riveted or welded to the rim are also signs of weak points. When fitting a new or used wheel to the car, always check the center mating face to make sure it is like the original. If the center looks different, but the wheel bolt pattern fits, install the wheel and make sure the wheel rim or center does not interfere with any

As a wheel gets older, check the area around lug nut/stud holes for cracks. This is especially important if wheel has been installed with overtightened nuts. Always use a torque wrench on lug nuts/bolts; otherwise wheel and brake drum can be warped.

Overtightening the lug nuts/bolts (as with an impact wrench) can bend the wheel center just as badly as a sideways crash. Check the rim-to-center alignment with tape measure and straightedge; if there is a detectable difference in this method of checking the wheel, it should be given to a mechanic for straightening, or it should be replaced.

balance weights on the drum. Never remove a balance weight to make a wheel fit!

"Mag" and Other Custom Wheels

A special word on custom alloy wheels is in order, since they are finding such widespread use. Alloy wheels are usually called "mag" wheels, but this is a misnomer, since magnesium wheels are used primarily on race cars and some transport trucks (where the weight savings in wheels can be turned over to payload). The overwhelming majority of custom alloy wheels are made from aluminum, and while there are several dozen custom wheel manufacturers, the basic wheel castings come from less than a dozen foundries.

To get wheels that fit properly and do not distort the brake drums it is wise to torque each lug nut to manufacturer specifications. This is almost never done, but it makes a great difference in wheel fit and often in how the brakes operate. An out-of-round feeling in the brake system can often be traced to improperly torqued wheel nuts.

When a car is being assembled the lug nuts are all installed at the same time, to a predetermined torque specification.

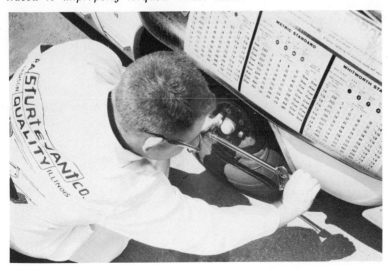

Custom wheels can be either permanent-mold-cast or forged. Forged wheels are by far superior. However, forgings are extremely expensive, and mold wheels have proved excellent even in grueling off-road race use. While an alloy wheel may not be much lighter than the average passenger-car steel wheel, the alloy does pass off generated brake heat faster, and in most cases the alloy wheel is much stronger than steel. It is also machined to a roundness tolerance of approximately .002 inch, which means there are practically no balance problems with an alloy wheel. If you have alloy wheels and experience balance trouble, the tires are surely to blame.

There are some custom wheels made with an alloy center mated to a steel rim. These wheels will not have all the advantages of the full alloy wheel, but they will have the good appearance of "mags," with some slight weight savings.

Custom alloy wheels are more susceptible to fracture than steel, and because of this if there is the slightest crack anywhere in an alloy wheel it should be replaced immediately. Rim damage can be caused by rocks or severe abuse, such as smashing into curbs.

There are custom steel wheels as well. Usually such a wheel is purchased to get a wider rim width, often to be used in conjunction with a wider-tread tire. As a general rule, never use a rim wider than 8 inches for a passenger car. While most production wheels are in the 5½-to-6½-inch category (measured from bead seat to bead seat), the narrow width is a compromise for production economy. If you increase the rim width from 1 to 2 inches, the greater stance support this gives the tire will almost

always improve vehicle handling noticeably. However—and this point is too often neglected—the wider wheel width should straddle the original wheel centerpoint, which has been designed to place a certain load on the front and rear bearings. If you buy a wheel with an extra 2 inches to the outside (positive offset), the added leverage this affords

The type of wheel and tire selected for a particular car will determine much of how the car handles. The wheel offset should not be changed radically (distance from lug nut face on center section to rim lip), but total rim width can be increased and wider tires installed to improve handling. However, using a very wide tire and rim may cause the front tires to "track" or follow a road irregularity. As a rule, increasing tire and rim width about 2 inches over stock sizes is enough.

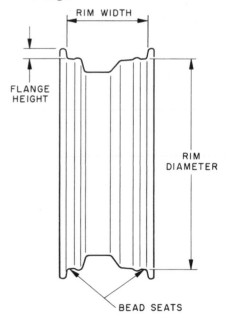

WHEEL RIM MEASUREMENTS

the wheel will often overload the wheel bearings and make them fail prematurely. As a rule, most cars and trucks can handle 1-inch additional positive offset, but more than this is a problem. Discuss this rim-width offset with the dealer before you purchase custom wheels. Remember also that the wider the wheel, the more difficult it is to get correct dynamic wheel/tire balance. A bubble balancer is seldom sufficient for a wheel rim 7 inches or more wide. Spin balancing is usually necessary.

A final word on "custom" wheels: Never buy from a small, unknown manufacturer who cannot show some kind of warranty or guarantee for his product. The larger custom-wheel makers have insured their product, because it definitely does have a direct bearing on your vehicle safety, while some small manufacturers have no such insurance and have no testing results of their product to prove its safety.

A rather common problem nowadays is use of incorrect tire/wheel combinations, such as a tire too wide or too narrow for the wheel rim. In this case the area around rim bead has been broken because the tire was too narrow for a wide rim. If the tire is too wide the tread pattern will crown and display a strange wear pattern in the center, while the sidewalls may flex too much and fail early.

TIRES

Tire troubles are almost universal, and they never seem to be limited to one or the other manufacturer. The number-one tire problem is caused by the car owner. He tries to use a tire that is less expensive, and usually not load-rated for his vehicle. This leads to overloading and early tire failure. Or he seldom, if ever, checks the tire inflation pressure. This leads to over- or underinflation (usually the latter), which increases sidewall loading and heat and causes early tread wear. Poor balance, front-wheel misalignment, and incorrect tire-to-wheel sizing can also be problems. You can spot most of these problems before they cause permanent tire damage (see Chapter 1).

An overinflated tire will show excessive tread wear in the tread center, while an underinflated tire will show excessive wear on the outer edges. Tire pressures can be modified through about 4 psi without adverse problems; usually slightly more pressure can be tolerated than not enough pressure.

Unusual front tire wear can come from one or a number of different mechanical problems, such as worn-out shocks, incorrect front end alignment, worn ball joints, worn tie-rod ends. Scalloping of the tread edges is a good indication of bad shocks or ball joints. This kind of wear will ruin an otherwise fine tire and there is no good way to save the tire.

Tread-wear indicators were introduced by Goodyear in 1967, and appear when the tread pattern is worn down to a depth of 1/16-inch remaining. In many states it is illegal to drive on a tire with the wear "bars" showing.

Problems with front end alignment often cause uneven wear on one side of the tire. Once a tire is worn, as shown, it's usually impossible to save it even if alignment is corrected. At first sign of unusual tire wear take your car to a front end expert.

A peculiar type of tire problem may crop up that has nothing to do with the car, but is rather a result of manufacturing characteristics. One such problem was common recently with the new fiberglass tires. The tread rubber was separating from the casing, a condition that was extremely difficult for the untrained eye to detect. Tires that were nearly impossible to balance at higher freeway speeds would often be found to have this defect. In an advanced stage, these separation spots would appear in the center of the tire as worn sections, or would allow the tread to peel away as shown. The only cure is replacement; usually these tires are covered by warranty.

Another manufacturing defect will show as rubber separation inside the tread groove, caused by incorrect groove depth or curing problems. If allowed to go unchecked, the splits will increase until tread will throw away from casing.

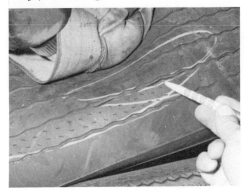

If a tire is wearing on either the inside or outside edge, in a smooth pattern, you have alignment trouble if at the front end, and rear-end-housing trouble if at the back. The most common trouble at the rear is for the inside edges of the tires to wear away. This is caused by a sagging rear-end housing and can be cured by installation of a rear-end support strut, usually available through new-car dealers and frame/front-end shops. This strut should be installed by a professional. Overloading is the usual cause for rear-end sag.

Tires on the front end that wear the inside edges in a smooth pattern may suffer from incorrect alignment in either caster, camber, or toe-out. Smooth wear patterns on the outside of the tread could be caused by camber or toe-in. The only correction is good front-end alignment, but if the tire wear has gone too far, an alignment job will not always save the tire. It will continue to wear irregularly, and should be moved to a rear drum immediately if maximum wear is expected (see Chapter 1).

Tire Rotation

No two manufacturers agree completely as to how tires should be rotated. As the owner you will soon learn that every time the tires are rotated a new balance is necessary. If the wheels are balanced separate from the drums (static or dynamic balance), they will probably swap with minimal balance problems, but if the tires/wheels are balanced in conjunction with a drum, balance can be frustrating.

If the front tires (and sometimes the rear tires) have a series of evenly spaced scallops around the edge, suspect a suspension and/or balance problem. Check for worn wheel bearings, bad shock absorbers (or shocks loose on the mounting bolts), loose tie rods, or bent or loose wheels. "Flat-spotting" of tires can be caused by excessive braking action (locking up the brakes and skidding the tires). Recently, however, the polyester-cord tires have been showing tread-separation flaws that appear as bald or "melted" spots and look like flat-spotting. Often such spotting is accompanied by a balance problem that is almost impossible to find.

BUYING TIRES

Let's assume you're going out for a new set of tires, so you need some guidance in tire selection. First, assume your local tire dealer knows what kind of tires you need. Indeed he does, but only if you're honest in telling him what kind of loads you normally haul, what your driving habits are, and so on. If you habitually corner hard, this will cause early front-tire wear, and maybe he'll have you change front-tire air pressure. Or perhaps he'll suggest a different tire tread pattern that is better for cornering. In all cases, choose a tire strong enough to stand up under the maximum loads you may carry, on bad roads. You can choose a tire that will do a good job under all the conditions you expect, and this will be determined by construction as well as tread pattern, which means you should pay more for the correct tires if necessary. Finally, choose a tire that will have sufficient "footprint" for your style of driving.

A tire footprint is the amount of rubber in actual contact with the road surface under ideal conditions. Thus a wider tire will have more footprint than a narrow tire of the same diameter, and this footprint will vary depending upon tire air pressure and cornering speed.

Tire company worker places "green" tire on machine that will reshape the rubber and various cord combinations into a tire like that on the left. There is still a great deal of physical labor and skill involved in making tires.

Tire manufacturer can check how much tread is actually touching pavement by looking through special grid glass. Darker area is the only part of rubber in contact with surface; this footprint will change as tire bounces and turns.

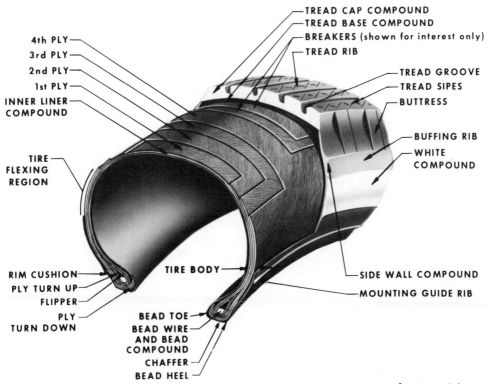

- 4th PLY
- 3rd PLY
- 2nd PLY
- 1st PLY
- INNER LINER COMPOUND
- TREAD CAP COMPOUND
- TREAD BASE COMPOUND
- BREAKERS (shown for interest only)
- TREAD RIB
- TREAD GROOVE
- TREAD SIPES
- BUTTRESS
- BUFFING RIB
- WHITE COMPOUND
- TIRE FLEXING REGION
- RIM CUSHION
- PLY TURN UP
- FLIPPER
- PLY TURN DOWN
- TIRE BODY
- BEAD TOE
- BEAD WIRE AND BEAD COMPOUND
- CHAFFER
- BEAD HEEL
- SIDE WALL COMPOUND
- MOUNTING GUIDE RIB

Composition of a typical tire, giving a breakdown on what each area is called.

You can increase the amount of footprint by using larger diameter tires, wider tires, or lower inflation pressure. All this should be discussed with your tire dealer. In any case, be very careful in mixing tire types.

If you mix bias tires with belted-bias types, don't use two different types on either front or rear. For better handling, mount the bias tires on the front end and the belted-bias on the rear. Do not mix radial tires with any other tire types unless the tire maker specifically says this can be done. There is a significant difference in the way radials and the more traditional tires take a "set" during cornering. For best results, use the same kind of tires all around.

Because there are continuing changes in tire size designations, it is best to check with the local tire dealer as to what tire size numbers mean. But there

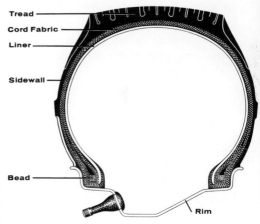

- Tread
- Cord Fabric
- Liner
- Sidewall
- Bead
- Rim

Combination of tire and rim identifications. National Tire and Rim Association sets standards for wheel and tire manufacturing which all manufacturing companies try to observe.

The bias tire is a conventional type which has been around since the early 1920s. In this design, the cords (plies or layers) which make up the body crisscross at an angle (called the bias angle) of about 30 to 40 degrees to the centerline. Cords can be in two, four, or more plies—the number is always even—depending on general tire strength. Such a bias gives good sidewall rigidity and tread strength, but tends to squirm more and run hotter than belted-bias or radial designs.

The belted-bias tire has cords arranged in a crisscross fashion, with two or more layers of fabric "belts" under the tread. Steel-belted tires use steel belts rather than fabric. This design has good sidewall stiffness, but is stiffer in the tread area than the bias design. Thus this type will run cooler and give a bit better mileage. These tires are made of rayon, nylon, or polyester.

The radial tire has a lettered number with an R, such as ER78-14. The cords run at right angles to the centerline (straight from one bead to the other) and may be in from one to three plies. Over this radial section is a belt made from up to four plies, with cords at an angle to the centerline of about 15 degrees. A radial has very flexible sidewalls but an extremely stiff and strong tread area. The tread area usually "wraps over" the edge, giving the tire a rounded tread appearance. The flexible sidewalls make the tire look as though it were underinflated. In some radials the belts are of steel, in others of fiberglass or rayon. Radials run cool, have little squirm, and give excellent wear.

Some car tire cross sections are almost twice as wide as they are high. These are called *low-profile tires,* and are designed to increase footprint. Low-

In 1968 a new federal law was introduced that required all the information about a tire to be embossed in the sidewall rubber. Only the name of the particular tire design is not required; the manufacturer is identified by name or code, and letters DOT show tire is in compliance with Department of Transportation standards. If the tire is a radial, the word "radial" must also appear as an aid to keep from mixing radials with traditional tires.

are some markings on a tire that are there by federal law. This data will include size, maximum inflation pressure, brand name, and manufacturer's code number (often, a premium tire will be sold by a different outlet at a different price, so it will pay to shop and ask pointedly who makes the tire in question), cord composition, number of sidewall and tread plies, tube or tubeless type, an "R" for radial, and DOT to indicate that the tire design meets Department of Transportation regulations.

Tire Types

It might be wise to discuss the different types of tires since so many new tire improvements have been introduced in the past few years.

86

The radial tire has become a great favorite for maximum mileage. This Pirelli design shows low cord angle to reduce tire killing heat. Radials are distinguished in use by a slight "flat" appearance at the sidewalls.

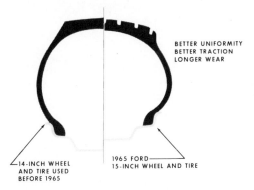

BETTER UNIFORMITY
BETTER TRACTION
LONGER WEAR

14-INCH WHEEL
AND TIRE USED
BEFORE 1965

1965 FORD
15-INCH WHEEL AND TIRE

A good example of changing trend to lower and lower profile tires. By using low profile tire, larger diameter wheel can be used without changing overall diameter of combination, in turn allowing better cooling of brake drum inside wheel.

profile tires may not fit your car, so check with the tire dealer before ordering such a design.

Tire sidewall cords are usually made of nylon, rayon, or polyester. Polyester

has good strength, is not prone to flat-spotting under normal conditions, and is insensitive to water. Nylon is resilient and resistant to heat and water, as well as being strong; it is popular on racing and off-road applications. But nylon tends to flat-spot after getting cold, so that when you first drive on cold nylon tires they are extremely bumpy. These spots smooth out as the tires warm to operating temperatures. New developments may soon eliminate this problem. Rayon is the oldest manmade fiber, with good strength, dimensional stability, and abrasion resistance. But it tends to degenerate if exposed excessively to water.

Belt cords have the special job of keeping the tread flat and in maximum contact with the road surface. Steel wire makes very strong belts and tends to run cool, as well as giving maximum wear for a given thickness of tread. Steel is used mostly in radial-tire designs. Glass fibers have excellent tensile strength and good stability while resisting flex, and thus run cool and wear well. Rayon is competitive to fiberglass for belt-cord use.

FLATS AND BLOWOUTS

When a tire is punctured, the air escapes gradually and the tire can usually be repaired. When a blow-out occurs, the cord gives way and tire repair is unlikely. Blowouts are usually caused by a slow weakening of the cord (overflexing, such as caused by under-inflation or overloading) or by impacts with such things as rocks, potholes, curbs, and so on.

There are various types of blowout- and puncture-resistant tires now being marketed. Some of these special tires have a steel safety belt below the tread,

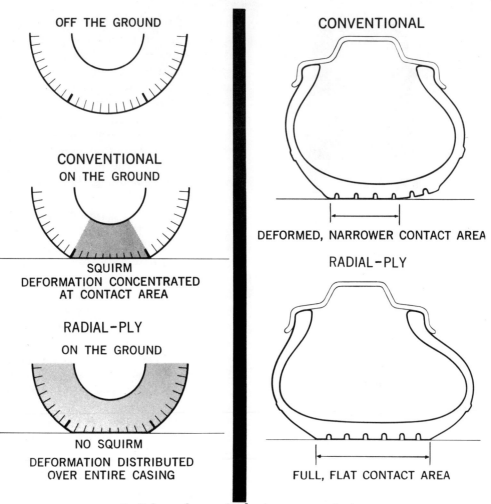

OFF THE GROUND

CONVENTIONAL
ON THE GROUND

SQUIRM
DEFORMATION CONCENTRATED
AT CONTACT AREA

RADIAL-PLY

ON THE GROUND

NO SQUIRM
DEFORMATION DISTRIBUTED
OVER ENTIRE CASING

CONVENTIONAL

DEFORMED, NARROWER CONTACT AREA

RADIAL-PLY

FULL, FLAT CONTACT AREA

*Radials are known for having more contact
area (footprint) than traditional designs.*

others have an inner tire (separated from the tire body by an air space). Still other designs use a sealant to plug the puncture hole. While most of these tires are sold as "premium," they may have problems with balance or high heat buildup.

Incidentally, if you pick up a nail and notice the tire going slowly flat, you can often limp into a station if you don't pull out the nail. Never run a tire flat, as this will surely tear the cords apart and ruin the tire, and often will ruin the wheel rim as well.

If a blowout occurs on the front, the car will swerve and have a steady pull to one side. Here is one situation in which power steering is a definite advantage. A blowout at the rear will cause the car to weave erratically. In neither case should you slam on the brakes. Rather, decelerate with engine compression, and pump the brakes as though you were stopping on ice.

SNOW TIRES

Snow tires are a special subject. Generally, such designs have an open tread pattern with deep grooves. These grooves are designed to displace the snow enough to give traction, something like tractor-tire lugs. The pattern is designed to be self-cleaning, which it may or may not be. Snow tires that will be used on dry pavement as well as snow will have a tread design between the conventional tire and a pure snow tread, because if the grooves are too open, the tire will wear rapidly on dry surfaces. Combination tires are commonly sold on four-wheel-drive vehicles that get a lot of dry-road use.

For some rain use, a snow tread with open channels along the tire circumference will minimize water buildup. If the water has no place to go, it will

In wet weather, a tire has to force water out from beneath it before the rubber can grip the road. In this photo a smooth tire is aquaplaning over the water with no traction.

pack up under the tire and cause "hydroplaning," which is effective loss of tire contact that can cause you to lose control.

Most snow tires designed for use on ice or packed snow have small studs in the tread. These studs dig into ice and packed snow, but they will wear rapidly on dry pavement. They also damage roads, so some states have rules as to numbers of studs allowed per tire, exposed maximum length, and so on. A studded tire will have between 100 and 150 studs; more than this will put too much steel on the surface (dry or wet pavement) and actually decrease traction.

If radials are used on the vehicle front, radial snow tires should be used at the rear.

Snow tires used in mud will not be as self-cleaning as you would like, and mud packed into the deep grooves will unbalance the tires. The only cure is to dig the mud from the tires before doing any moderate-speed or high-speed highway cruising.

CARE OF TIRES

So now you have some new tires, which are not at all cheap, and it behooves you to take good care of them. Start by making sure the wheel is good (as explained previously), with no more than .035-inch radial runout of the wheel. Total runout of wheel and tire should not exceed .050 inch. If it does, you might try rotating the tire on the rim (since the runout may be a compound problem). If the runout is still excessive either the wheel or the tire is at fault. It is not impossible to get a tire that is so out of round that no amount of balancing will get it to run smooth.

Such a tire might be turned true on a tire trimmer, but the only sure solution is a replacement. If you suspect the tire is really out of round, return it to the dealer immediately for an adjustment.

Keep tires cleaned of all petroleum products, which will sometimes cause early deterioration. You can increase the life of exposed rubber by washing the tires with a solvent to remove stubborn substances, followed by clean water mixed with baking soda. If there is a cut in the tire, watch it closely, as rayon cords exposed to water will rot. Smog can cause tire rubber to deteriorate. Cleaning with water and soda will help resist smog checking.

Tire Balancing

You can balance your tires at home with a portable bubble balancer, but this is really a questionable economy, since a really good balance job may not be expensive in a local shop. It may not be necessary, but tires usually require two types of balance: static and dynamic. When a wheel/tire combination has a heavy spot relative to the center-plane of rotation, it is a static imbalance. If you had a flat, round disc out of balance on one side, a small weight at the opposite edge would cure the problem.

But it is possible for a tire/wheel unit to have dynamic imbalance. In this case, the wide wheel may have a heavy spot on the circumference, but this spot is also located on one side of the rim. The imbalance causes a wobble as well as a pure centerplane force disturbance. To illustrate this point more graphically, suppose you had a 50-gallon drum rotating about its centerline. If you placed a 1-pound weight on the circumference of one end, the drum would wobble. If this same weight were placed on the circumference, but halfway between each drum end, you would have static imbalance and there would not be a wobble to accompany the imbalance.

Bubble balancing will not find dynamic imbalance, so if you have low-profile tires and a balance problem, go to a place that will do a good dynamic as well as static balance job. In an emergency, you can get a pretty fair balance job by jacking up the rear end and spinning the wheels with the engine. The speedometer will show the speeds to use, which will be best at 30, 50, and 65 mph. When a vibration shows up at a certain speed, stop the wheel and add a small weight to both inside and outside rim (in line with each other). Move this weight around until the vibration lessens. Slowly, but surely, you can balance a wheel in this manner, but it isn't worth the effort, really. A professional job isn't that expensive.

Tire Repair

Something you definitely can do at home is repair tires and inner tubes, because the cost of a repair steadily increases. Inner tubes are no longer common, but if you must repair one the best repair is with a vulcanizing kit, still available at auto-parts stores. To find a small hole in an inner tube, fill it partially with air (a hand pump still works as well as it did on Grandpa's car) and immerse the tube a section at a time in a tub of water until air bubbles appear. If the tube just springs a leak (without a puncture), chances are it is going to continue to deteriorate, so it should be replaced.

If an inner tube has been punctured, the tire may also have been damaged. If the puncture has been by a large object, such as a spike nail, the tire should have a patch applied over the fracture on the inside wall. If the puncture has been small, such as with a roofing nail, no tire repair is normally required.

When replacing the tube in the tire, install the inside tire bead over the wheel rim. Put a small amount of air in the inner tube, then stuff it inside the tire with the valve stem through the wheel-rim hole. Work the tube around by hand until it feels like it fits the tire correctly. Soapy water will make the tube slide around better, as will talcum powder. A slight amount of air in the tube will keep the tube from getting pinched when the tire outside bead is rolled onto the wheel.

Installing a tube-type or tubeless tire is the same from here on. Step on one side of the tire so that the bead is pulled into the dropped center section of the rim. Then use a tire iron to pry the remainder of the bead onto the rim. Sometimes the iron will not quite get the bead over the wheel rim, so a few blows with a rubber hammer or mallet are necessary. This is where you can pinch the inner tube. Be sure the tube is not caught between tire bead and rim at this point, or between tire iron and rim.

After a tube-type tire is in place, work it around the wheel until the tube stem is straight in the rim hole. Now fill the tube with air to about 20 psi. Let the air out of the tube, and refill to the recommended pressure. This double filling will let the tube "seat" properly.

A modern tubeless tire is harder to repair at home, mainly because the tire bead is stronger than old tube tires, and because of the so-called "safety rim." When a tubeless-tire bead seats on the rim, it is difficult to break loose for repair. Beating the bead with a mallet usually won't do the job. But you can very carefully run over the tire with a car. This pressure will be spread out more and is enough to break the bead away. Once one place breaks away the full bead will follow easily. You may have to break both sides loose in this manner. Remember to run over just the tire, not the wheel too. As a rule, if you have to break down a tubeless tire for repair, the job is too big for the home mechanic (requires a large patch, or whatever). When inflating a tubeless tire, remember that at no time should more than 40 psi be used to seat the beads. More pressure might cause the beads to break, which can seriously injure the mechanic.

Small punctures in tubeless tires can be repaired with special tools by a service station or tire shop, or you can make temporary repairs with special "plugs." These plugs are coated with a cement and literally stuffed through the puncture. The remaining end on the outside is snipped off. This is a temporary repair, however, and should never be considered permanent.

On the subject of puncture sealants that you squirt into the valve stem: They may or may not work, and at best they, too, are temporary. It is not advisable to carry around the small pressurized cans of air and sealant, as they may explode when heated or handled improperly. For tubeless tires, a temporary plug kit and a hand pump remain the most sensible emergency equipment.

If you take the time to maintain the wheels and tires on your car, they will give you thousands of extra miles. But at the same time, you must couple sane driving techniques to regular maintenance. No amount of care will compensate for excessively hard braking or cornering, or high-speed driving on terrible roads. Take care of your tires with the accelerator pedal as well as with the hands.

LOAD RANGE TABLE

LOAD LIMITS (LBS. PER TIRE) FOR TIRES USED ON PASSENGER CARS, STATION WAGONS AND MULTI-PURPOSE PASSENGER VEHICLES*

Tire Size or Designation

Bias		Bias and Belted Bias				Radial	
1965-On	Pre-1965	'78 Series'	'70 Series'	'60 Series'	Metric	'78 Series'	'70 Series'
6.00-13					165 R 13		
		A78-13	A70-13			AR 78-13	AR 70-13
6.50-13		B78-13	B70-13		175 R 13	BR 78-13	BR 70-13
		C78-13	C70-13			CR 78-13	CR 70-13
7.00-13					185 R 13		
			D70-13			DR 78-13	DR 70-13
			E70-13		195 R 13	ER 78-13	ER 70-13
			A70-14		155 R 14		AR 70-14
6.45-14					165 R 14		
	6.00-14						
		B78-14	B70-14			BR 78-14	BR 70-14
6.95-14							
		C78-14	C70-14		175 R 14	CR 78-14	CR 70-14
	6.50-14						
		D78-14	D70-14			DR 78-14	DR 70-14
7.35-14					185 R 14		
	7.00-14						
		E78-14	E70-14			ER 78-14	ER 70-14
7.75-14					195 R 14		
	7.50-14						
		F78-14	F70-14			FR 78-14	FR 70-14
8.25-14					205 R 14		
	8.00-14						
		G78-14	G70-14			GR 78-14	GR 70-14
8.55-14					215 R 14		
	8.50-14						
		H78-14	H70-14			HR 78-14	HR 70-14
8.85-14					225 R 14		
	9.00-14						
		J78-14	J70-14			JR 78-14	JR 70-14
			K70-14				KR 70-14
	9.50-14						
			L70-14				LR 70-14
					165 R 15	BR 78-15	
	6.00-15						
6.85-15			C70-15		175 R 15	CR 78-15	CR 70-15
		C78-15					
	6.50-15						
		D78-15	D70-15			DR 78-15	DR 70-15
7.35-15					185 R 15		
		E78-15	E70-15	E60-15		ER 78-15	ER 70-15
7.75-15					195 R 15		
	6.70-15						
		F78-15	F70-15	F60-15		FR 78-15	FR 70-15
	7.10-15				205 R 15		
		G78-15	G70-15	G60-15		GR 78-15	GR 70-15
8.25-15							
	7.60-15				215 R 15		
		H78-15	H70-15			HR 78-15	HR 70-15
8.55-15							
8.85-15					225 R 15		
	8.00-15						
		J78-15	J70-15			JR 78-15	JR 70-15
9.00-15							
	8.20-15						
			K70-15				KR 70-15
9.15-15					235 R 15		
		L78-15	L70-15			LR 78-15	LR 70-15
		M78-15					
		N78-15					
8.90-15							
6.00-16							
6.50-16							
7.00-15							
7.00-16							

COLD INFLATION PRESSURES—POUNDS PER SQUARE INCH										
20	22	24	26	28	30	32	34	36	38	40
770	820	860	900	930	970	1010	1040	1080	1110	1140
810	860	900	940	980	1020	1060	1090	1130	1160	1200
890	930	980	1030	1070	1110	1150	1190	1230	1270	1300
950	1000	1050	1100	1140	1190	1230	1270	1320	1360	1390
980	1030	1080	1130	1180	1230	1270	1310	1360	1400	1440
1010	1070	1120	1170	1220	1270	1320	1360	1410	1450	1490
1060	1110	1170	1220	1280	1320	1370				
1070	1130	1190	1240	1300	1350	1400	1440	1490	1540	1580
780	820	860	900	940	970	1010				
810	860	900	940	980	1020	1060	1090	1130	1160	1200
860	910	960	1000	1040	1080	1120	1160	1200	1240	1270
840	900	930	980	1020	1060	1100	1130	1170	1210	1240
890	930	980	1030	1070	1110	1150	1190	1230	1270	1300
950	1000	1050	1100	1140	1190	1230	1270	1310	1350	1390
950	1000	1050	1100	1140	1190	1230	1270	1320	1360	1400
930	990	1030	1080	1130	1170	1210	1250	1300	1330	1370
1010	1070	1120	1170	1220	1270	1320	1360	1410	1450	1490
1040	1100	1160	1210	1260	1310	1360	1400	1450	1490	1540
1030	1100	1140	1190	1240	1290	1340	1380	1430	1470	1520
1070	1130	1190	1240	1300	1350	1400	1440	1490	1540	1580
1150	1210	1270	1330	1390	1440	1500	1550	1600	1650	1690
1150	1230	1280	1340	1390	1450	1500	1550	1600	1650	1700
1160	1220	1280	1340	1400	1450	1500	1550	1610	1650	1700
1250	1310	1380	1440	1500	1560	1620	1670	1730	1780	1830
1240	1320	1380	1440	1500	1560	1620	1670	1730	1780	1830
1250	1310	1380	1440	1500	1560	1620	1680	1730	1780	1830
1360	1430	1510	1580	1640	1710	1770	1830	1890	1950	2000
1330	1420	1480	1550	1610	1670	1740	1790	1850	1910	1960
1360	1440	1510	1580	1650	1710	1770	1830	1890	1950	2010
1430	1510	1580	1660	1730	1790	1860	1920	1990	2050	2100
1430	1500	1580	1650	1720	1790	1860	1920	1980	2040	2100
1460	1540	1620	1690	1770	1830	1900	1970	2030	2090	2150
1540	1640	1700	1780	1850	1930	2000	2060	2130	2200	2260
1520	1600	1680	1750	1830	1900	1970	2040	2100	2170	2230
870	910	960	1000	1050	1090	1130				
890	930	980	1030	1070	1110	1150				
890	940	980	1030	1070	1110	1150	1190	1230	1270	1300
950	1000	1050	1100	1140	1190	1230	1270	1320	1360	1390
950	1000	1050	1100	1140	1190	1230	1270	1320	1360	1400
980	1040	1080	1130	1180	1230	1270	1320	1360	1400	1440
1010	1070	1120	1170	1220	1270	1320	1360	1410	1450	1490
1070	1130	1180	1240	1290	1340	1390	1440	1480	1530	1570
1070	1130	1190	1240	1300	1350	1400	1440	1490	1540	1580
1150	1210	1270	1330	1380	1440	1490	1540	1590	1640	1690
1110	1190	1230	1290	1340	1400	1450	1500	1550	1590	1640
1160	1220	1280	1340	1400	1450	1500	1550	1610	1650	1700
1240	1300	1370	1430	1490	1550	1610	1660	1720	1770	1820
1190	1270	1320	1380	1440	1500	1550	1600	1660	1710	1760
1250	1310	1380	1440	1500	1560	1620	1680	1730	1780	1830
1250	1310	1380	1440	1500	1560	1620	1670	1730	1780	1830
1340	1410	1480	1550	1620	1680	1740	1800	1860	1920	1970
1310	1400	1450	1520	1580	1640	1710	1760	1820	1880	1930
1360	1440	1510	1580	1650	1710	1770	1830	1890	1950	2010
1360	1430	1510	1580	1640	1710	1770	1830	1890	1950	2000
1430	1510	1580	1650	1720	1790	1860	1920	1980	2040	2100
1380	1470	1530	1600	1670	1730	1800	1860	1920	1980	2040
1430	1500	1580	1650	1720	1790	1860	1920	1980	2040	2100
1460	1540	1620	1690	1760	1830	1900	1970	2030	2090	2150
1470	1570	1630	1710	1780	1850	1920	1980	2050	2110	2170
1460	1540	1620	1690	1770	1830	1900	1970	2030	2090	2150
1510	1600	1680	1750	1830	1900	1970	2030	2100	2160	2230
1520	1600	1680	1750	1830	1900	1970	2040	2100	2170	2230
1610	1700	1780	1860	1940	2020	2090	2160	2230	2300	2370
1700	1790	1880	1970	2050	2130	2210	2280	2360	2430	2500
1700	1810	1880	1970	2050	2130	2210	2290	2360	2430	2500
1075	1135	1195	1250	1300	1350	1400	1450	1500		
1215	1280	1345	1405	1465	1525	1580	1635	1690		
1310	1380	1450	1515	1580	1640	1700	1760	1820		
1365	1440	1515	1585	1650	1715	1780	1840	1900		

5 the engine

THE AUTOMOBILE ENGINE has changed very little since the first internal combustion engine was adapted to a four-wheeled chassis in the 1800s. Even so, to compare a modern engine with one of those early designs would be like comparing a jet fighter plane to the Wright brothers' invention. Today's car may rely on essentially the same form of engine design as the first car in history, but that simple design has become sophisticated almost beyond recognition. To the home mechanic, the contemporary automobile engine may seem more a maze of mechanical and electronic accessories than a basic form of controlled energy.

Most nonprofessional mechanics (and some of the professionals) are scared away from working on a car engine by the diversity and complexity of the accessory components under the hood. But if all these "luxury" items were removed, few men would be afraid to

attempt even the most difficult engine repair. The secret is to isolate the engine from the accessories, at least in your mind, and proceed from there. But you can't hope to really repair, or even do routine maintenance on an engine unless you understand exactly how it works.

HOW AN ENGINE WORKS

In its simplest definition, the automobile engine is a heat engine. This means that its main product is heat from which an energy potential is extracted and converted into a means of doing mechanical work. So much for the basic theory. Just how the engine goes about accomplishing this process is also quite simple. The engine breaks the complete process down into four distinct steps, or cycles. Starting at top dead center (TDC), the piston moves down in its cylinder, creating a low-pressure area,

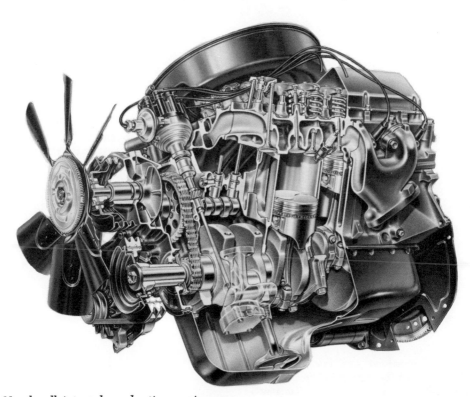

Nearly all internal combustion engines are constructed along the same general principles as the Ford V-8 shown in cutaway. Home mechanic should become familiar with engine construction details of his car, best done through service manuals. If he learns the engine, he can service minor mechanical problems, such as valve troubles or ignition problems and gain thousands of extra miles. The modern engine should be able to get well over 100,000 miles before deep internal rebuilding is necessary.

or partial vacuum, above the piston. At the same time the intake valve is caused to open, allowing air, pushed by normal atmospheric pressure at 14.7 psi, to move into the cylinder. As the incoming air rushes through the carburetor, it is mixed with fuel (see Chapter 7). This is known as the intake stroke, or cycle.

Reaching the lower limit of its travel,

or bottom dead center (BDC), the piston is caused to reverse direction and move back up into the cylinder. About this time the intake valve is closed, sealing the cylinder from the atmosphere. As the piston again approaches TDC the air-fuel mixture, trapped in the cylinder, is compressed between the piston top and the combustion chamber in the cylinder head. This is the compression stroke, or cycle.

As the piston reaches TDC on the compression stroke, and the compression of the air-fuel mixture is at its greatest point, the spark plug ignites the mixture (see Chapter 8). (Actually, ignition takes place just before TDC, to allow for the tiny fraction of a second it takes for the mixture to ignite. As the engine runs faster, the ignition comes earlier in the stroke so the time lapse

Front cutaway of small block Chevrolet V-8 engine, showing relationship of major components. Note how oil pump pickup is at bottom of pan. Large cylinder and short crankshaft throw are apparent here, a part of modern engine design that allows higher sustained rpm. Camshaft is located immediately above crankshaft, works valves through lifters and pushrods. Valve assembly is usually first area to show effects of mileage wear; home mechanic can do a large part of any valve job. Intake system is shown on left side of this cutaway; exhaust routing is on the right side.

Still very much a part of American automobiles is the inline engine design, whether six or four cylinder. This is the basic Chevrolet 6 which has long been considered one of the easiest-to-repair engines ever built. Disassembly of an inline engine for in-chassis repairs is much easier than V-8.

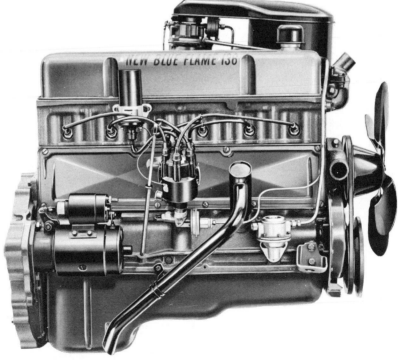

The major components of a Chevrolet V-8 on display. If an engine is disassembled for complete overhaul, it is best to keep the major components together and work on a component system as a whole rather than unbolting everything and mixing the pieces. By doing most of the disassembly/reassembly the home mechanic can save over 50 percent of the cost of an engine rebuild.

can remain the same.) As the mixture burns (it doesn't explode), it rapidly expands, creating pressure which works on the piston top to force it back down in the cylinder on what is known as the power stroke, or cycle.

Then, as the piston again approaches and passes BDC, the exhaust valve is caused to open. The piston has again reversed direction and is moving up the cylinder, forcing the burned gases out through the exhaust system to the atmosphere. This is the exhaust stroke, or cycle.

Strung together, the four strokes, or cycles, make up one complete operating cycle of an engine. The four strokes are spread out over 720° rotation of the crankshaft. Thus, in any engine like this, regardless of the number of cylinders it has, it will take two complete revolutions of the crankshaft to fire all the cylinders. There are also two-stroke engines, in which the intake, compression, power, and exhaust strokes are confined to one crankshaft revolution. Since no two-strokes are produced for use in American cars, we won't concern ourselves with their characteristics. Both two-stroke and four-stroke engines

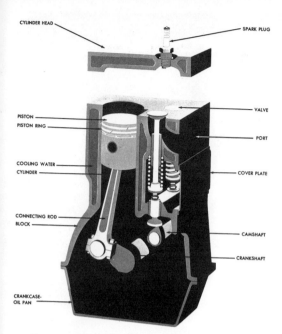

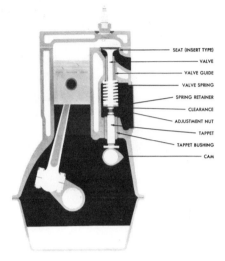

Four-stroke-cycle cylinder and related parts. The essential elements of every four-stroke-cycle gasoline engine cylinder are embodied in this diagram, but the details of the various parts, as well as the number of cylinders comprising an engine, vary from design to design. (Mobil Oil Corp.)

Head construction. In this widely used design, valve ports, valves, and valve-operating mechanism are incorporated in the cylinder block. The cylinder head serves merely to seal the upper end of the cylinder and houses no part of the valve mechanism. Valve movement is effected by rotation of the camshaft, which is driven by the crankshaft at one-half engine speed by gears or silent chain.

operate on the same complete operating cycle of intake-compression-power-exhaust, which is commonly referred to as the "Otto Cycle" in honor of its inventor.

Horsepower and Torque

Referring back to the third stroke, the power stroke, we see how the heat produced by the burning air-fuel mixture is converted into a means of doing mechanical work. As the air-fuel mixture burns, it releases energy in the form of

increasing pressure, which in turn exerts force against the piston, causing it to move down in the cylinder. The force is transferred from the piston through the connecting rod to the crankshaft, causing the crankshaft to move in a circular direction. A flywheel is attached to the end of the crankshaft and it is at this point we can measure the performance of the engine.

There are actually two measures of engine performance: horsepower and torque. Both terms are widely used, but in many cases they are misused. They

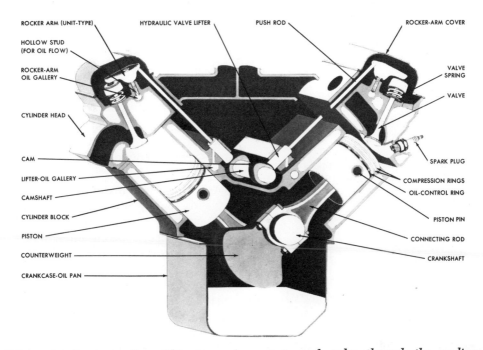

ROCKER ARM (UNIT-TYPE) HYDRAULIC VALVE LIFTER PUSH ROD ROCKER-ARM COVER

HOLLOW STUD (FOR OIL FLOW)

ROCKER-ARM OIL GALLERY

VALVE SPRING

VALVE

CYLINDER HEAD

CAM

SPARK PLUG

LIFTER-OIL GALLERY

COMPRESSION RINGS

OIL-CONTROL RING

CAMSHAFT

CYLINDER BLOCK

PISTON PIN

PISTON

CONNECTING ROD

COUNTERWEIGHT

CRANKSHAFT

CRANKCASE-OIL PAN

Valve-in-head construction. This type of construction is also popular in passenger-car engines. In contrast with L-head construction, valve ports, valves, and valve-operating mechanism, with the exception of the camshaft and tappet, are incorporated in the cylinder head. A push rod, actuated by the tappet, serves to convey cam movement to each valve through the medium of a pivoted lever called a rocker arm. This construction is sensitive to valve-stem deposits, from the oil used to lubricate the rocker arms. Seals or deflectors are provided at the valve tips to minimize lubricant contact with the hot stems.

don't mean the same thing, but they are related to the extent that one cannot exist without the other. Torque is the measure of the amount of work an engine can do, and horsepower is the measure of the amount of work done in a given time. The time factor for horsepower computations is the engine's crankshaft speed expressed in revolutions per minute (rpm).

The exact measurement of engine torque requires the use of a large, expensive piece of equipment known as a dynamometer. The "dyno" has provi-sions for applying a varying load to the engine by means of a "brake"—usually a water brake. The engine's resistance to this load is measured on a large scale and reads directly in foot-pounds (ft./lbs.) of torque. A foot-pound is a force of 1 pound acting on a lever 1 foot long. 33,000 foot-pounds of work done in 1 minute, no matter by what means, equal 1 horsepower. Horsepower determined by this method is referred to as brake horsepower (bhp).

It is a good thing to know the formulas that apply to torque and horsepower and illustrate their relationship. The formula for computing horsepower when torque and rpm are known is:

$$\frac{\text{Torque} \times \text{rpm}}{5252} = \text{Horsepower}$$

The number 5252 is a constant and is actually a simplification of the previously mentioned 33,000 figure; the original formula is:

$$\frac{2\pi \times \text{Torque} \times \text{rpm}}{33,000} = \text{Horsepower},$$

the 2π being another constant representing the circular motion in which the force acts. When horsepower and rpm are known, torque can be determined by transposing the formula:

$$\frac{\text{Horsepower} \times 5252}{\text{rpm}} = \text{Torque}.$$

One interesting fact about torque that many car owners don't realize, is that it is multiplied by the car's transmission and rear-axle gearing, while horsepower isn't. Since it is available torque at the drive wheels that really gets the job done, this measurement becomes the more significant of the two. We can determine how much total torque is available for tractive effort at the drive wheels of any given car, in any gear, and at any speed with the following formula:

$$\frac{T^1 (G^1 \times G^2)}{r} = T^2$$

T^1 equals engine flywheel torque, G^1 is the gear ratio of the transmission, G^2 is the gear ratio of the rear axle, r is the rolling radius of the driving tire in feet, and T^2 is the total torque available where the tire meets the road.

Volumetric Efficiency

Getting back to basic engine operation, let's take a look at the rest of those terms we mentioned earlier in the chapter. Just how much torque and horsepower a given engine will develop depends mainly on how much heat it can produce and effectively use. The heat produced depends on how much air-fuel mixture the engine can breathe into its cylinders, burn, and exhaust during one complete operating cycle. Just how big a breath an engine can take will depend on the cubic-inch displacement of the cylinders, the intake valve area and the length of time the camshaft holds it open, the size and shape of intake ports, and the carburetor venturi, or throttle area (see Chapter 7). In engineering terms the ability of an engine to breathe is called volumetric efficiency. This is the ratio, expressed as a percentage, of the volume of air actually inspired by the engine per intake stroke and the nominal swept volume of one cylinder. (The formula for swept volume, or displacement, is: bore diameter $\times$ bore diameter $\times$ .7854 $\times$ stroke $\times$ number of cylinders.) Volumetric efficiency will naturally be low at part-throttle and will reach a maximum value at full-throttle at some point near the middle of the speed range. This speed will be fairly close to the speed at which maximum, or peak, torque is reached. At higher speeds volumetric efficiency will fall off, mainly because of the fact that less time is available for the cylinder to fill, and the engine is depending on atmospheric pressure to deliver the

100

air. At maximum torque the normally aspirated, high-performance engine will have a volumetric efficiency approaching 90 percent, while at maximum power the figure will drop to around 75 percent.

Other Measures of Efficiency

After the air-fuel mixture gets into the cylinder it has to be compressed, then ignited and burned. This brings us to the term "combustion efficiency," meaning how completely the mixture is burned. The factors influencing this process are the basic air/fuel ratio, the combustion chamber shape and related compression ratio, the ignition timing and spark-plug heat range, and the grade of fuel. Even with everything perfect, combustion efficiency can never reach 100 percent, and there will always be a certain part of the mixture that remains unburned and is lost out through the exhaust. This is due partly to residual exhaust gases that remain in the cylinder from the previous cycle and tend to dilute the fresh mixture, and partly to the impossibility of igniting the mixture at the perfect instant.

Another term, "thermal efficiency," describes the ratio (as a percentage) between the actual energy potential in the air-fuel mixture and the energy that actually gets put to work. In the average engine this is around 35 percent, mainly because of losses to the engine's cooling system.

Another term we should be familiar with is "mechanical efficiency." This describes (again as a percentage) the ratio between indicated horsepower (ihp), which is the theoretical power available at the pistons, and the brake horsepower (bhp) that is actually available at the flywheel. Actual bhp will always be less than ihp because of the

losses from piston and bearing friction, and also because of the power it takes to drive the valve gear, oil pump, distributor, and other engine accessories.

This brings us around to the last term, "efficiency losses," which are the sum total of all the losses. To understand how important they are in the overall operating efficiency of the engine it should be realized that first of all, our heat engine, if all systems were perfect, would have a theoretical maximum efficiency of around only about 60 percent. This is an inherent characteristic of the Otto Cycle engine and we're stuck with it. Losses in the combustion chamber (including the losses to the cooling system) add up to around 24 percent. Pumping losses (caused by the amount of work involved in the intake and exhaust processes) can account for another 5 percent, while mechanical losses (friction, accessories, and others) run about 7 percent. Drive-train efficiency will drain another 2 percent. Add these all up and deduct them from our 60-percent figure and we're left with 22 percent for tractive effort at the rear wheels.

While this information might seem too theoretical for the person only casually interested in keeping his car in premium shape, it is really not difficult to understand, and if you learn how an engine works, you've taken the first step to being a great mechanic.

Engine Stresses

Obviously, since an engine is a method of transferring heat to useable torque/horsepower, metallurgy must play a great deal in engine design and maintenance. Indeed, it is the failure of engine parts that dictates most repairs, rather than the wearing of a specific part. When originally designed, the metal parts that make up an internal combustion engine are intended to work under certain conditions. If these conditions are altered, through abnormal metal wear or by inconsistent operating temperatures, the engine parts will begin to fail.

We've said that the air/fuel ratio inducted into the combustion chamber is ignited by the spark plug. When this happens, the mixture burns rapidly and causes an extremely high pressure and temperature build-up. As mentioned, the pressure pushes downward on the piston to turn the crankshaft. If there is too much clearance between the connecting-rod bearing and the crankshaft journal (see Chapters 9 and 15), this pressure will tend to overcome the lubricating oil and "beat" the bearing clearance larger. A vicious progression is started. At the same time, if coolant surrounding the combustion chamber does not keep the area at the proper temperature—which can happen if the car is running low on coolant, or has an incorrect thermostat, or has faulty timing, causing mixture pre-detonation, etc. (see Chapter 10)—the increasing heat from combustion temperatures will burn valves, burn pistons, dry oil from cylinder walls, distort metal surfaces, and so on. The point to be made is simply that metal in an engine has been chosen and used because it will perform in a certain way under a certain condition. If the necessary condition is altered drastically, the engine will probably fail prematurely.

DIAGNOSING "FUNNY NOISES"

Once you understand, even vaguely, how an internal combustion engine works, it is then much easier to begin perhaps the most important part of automotive engine maintenance—diagnosis of problems. Just as the human body will invariably send out warning signals of an impending system failure, so will the car engine. Learning how to isolate and recognize the mechanical ills of a car engine is a special talent that almost anyone can achieve.

Under normal conditions, the automobile will make a variety of noises, from the click of valve lifters to the whine of an automatic transmission converter to the squeal of disc brakes. Sometimes these noises are peculiar to a particular car, such as the disc-brake noise, and sometimes they would be common to any car, such as the sound radial tires make. Peculiar sounds also come to the ear via different routes; sounds in the rear end will transmit through the sheet metal structure. You can learn how to isolate these noises while driving.

If you have what sounds like a rear-end bearing on the verge of failing, move the transmission lever into neutral while travelling a level road at about 50 mph. Speed up the engine several times, and if the noise remains constant relative to vehicle speed, rather than speeding up and slowing down in harmony with the engine, you've narrowed it down to either front or rear end.

Sometimes a noise that sounds like it is coming from the left rear wheel actually will be coming from the right front wheel and so on. If you have recently changed tires, did the strange noise start at about the same time? If not, and if it seems to have been getting gradually louder, chances are good it is a wheel bearing. Or it might be a third-member bearing in the rear end. The idea is to keep up your search until you're fairly positive you've located where the noise is coming from, and then it is a far more simple job of repair. We can't cover all the little knock-knocks and thumpety-thumps you're likely to encounter with a car, but here are a few typical examples of audio sleuthing.

Fan Belt: A loose fan belt is perhaps the most common of unusual engine noises, especially with cars that include a heavy load of accessory equipment, such as air conditioning. A loose V-belt will make a high-pitched screech when the throttle is suddenly opened, and you'll usually hear it only when the transmission is in neutral. The modern V-belt is very narrow, with a high V-angle and only a minimal contact with the pulley. While most car manufacturers will recommend that the belt have approximately ½-inch play, you'll note that it is necessary to pull the alternator/generator, or idler pulley, really hard to get the belt tight. If the belt still squeals after you have it tight, the contact surfaces may have glazed. Sometimes you can rough them up slightly with 80-grit sandpaper, and often a belt dressing will give them more friction. If nothing seems to stop the screeching, it's time for a new belt. If the belt is frayed on the edges, it may make a barely audible slapping sound. If you have an accessory drive system that uses matched-length V-belts, make sure replacement belts are also matched sets.

Alternator/generator: If you hear a continuous squeal, suspect the alternator/generator bearings, especially if the sound seems to rise and fall with engine rpm. Nearly always noise traced to the alternator or generator will be caused by either dry bearings or a worn shaft, and immediate repair is needed. If you continue to drive with a defective charging unit, chances are very good it will eventually destroy itself. If you're not really sure if the noise is alternator/generator, loosen the drive V-belt. If the noise stops, you've found the problem (see Chapter 8).

Radiator: How many times have you watched a summertime traveler drive along unaware while water steam builds below and behind his car until it finally looks like Old Faithful? Good driving habits include sweeping the dash gauges often, and any sudden rise in engine temperature should be almost immediately recorded. But you might also hear a strange little humming sound coming from under the hood, and not show an overheated condition. The pressure escaping around the radiator cap can make such a sound, but never touch that radiator cap until the engine has cooled and much of the pressure has been released. If the sound persists, but the engine has no other symptoms of overheating, you may have a faulty cap (see Chapter 10).

Water pump: If you hear a kind of deep-throated rattling sound that seems to rise and fall with engine rpm, and seems to be located somewhere toward the front of the engine, it is probably the water pump. When a pump bearing starts to go bad, it will often have a very dull squeak also. If you catch this squeak in time, you can add a water-pump lubricant or radiator conditioner to the water, which will soon lubricate the bearing. A rattle means the shaft or bearing wear has gone too far. Regular anti-freeze is also a lubricant.

Manifold heat valve: A sneaky rattle that is often hard to locate is caused by the exhaust manifold heat-control valve. If the temperature-control spring has broken or been lost, the valve is free to rattle around in the exhaust flow. On sudden engine revving the valve will flutter. It is important to replace this spring, as the valve shaft can eventually bind itself into a closed or nearly closed position if the car is allowed to sit idle for long periods.

Engine/transmission mounts: If the accelerator pedal or gearshift lever seems to move around on hard acceleration or when you drive on bumpy roads, suspect worn or broken engine/transmission mounts. Such a condition is potentially dangerous, as a shift in engine location could bind the throttle open. Engine and transmission mounts are made by bonding rubber directly to metal, and it is difficult to see if a mount has become separated. Use a long pry bar and try to jiggle the engine around on its mounts. A broken mount will quickly show. The sound most normally associated with a broken mount is a dull thud on acceleration, or when going over bumps. Incidentally, accessory mounting brackets can loosen so check them occasionally.

Steering: If a power-steering pump gets too low on fluid, or runs dry, it will become noisy, and there will be a groaning sound as the wheels are turned while parked (see Chapters 3 and 15). When you turn the steering to full right or left lock, you may get a screeching noise, caused by the power-steering piston at maximum limit. Release some pressure on the steering and the sound goes away. This is a normal sound. If you hear any kind of click, or snapping sound from the steering system while turning, suspect either bad ball joints at the spindles or bad tie-rod ends. A snapping sound accompanied by a hard spot in the steering indicates something wrong with the steering gearbox.

Lines, cables, etc.: You can get some really frustrating little sounds from lines and cables in a car. If there is an incessant rattle below the car, kind of like slapping a clothesline pole with a metal bar, it is probably a parking-brake cable slapping against the drive-shaft tubing. A rattle that seems to be of high frequency, but is not the kind of screech normally associated with a loose bumper or sheet metal, can often be traced to a hydraulic brake or fuel line rattling against the frame. If you turn on the heater or air conditioner and get a sound like a playing card being held against spinning bicycle wheel spokes, the heater or A/C fan is hitting something, often just a piece of paper that has somehow gotten into the ducting. If you hear a kind of klunk-klunk that seems to come from beneath the flooring on both acceleration and deceleration, it is probably a bad driveline universal joint.

Engine Noises

It's easy to suspect any noise of coming from the engine. But never overlook the possibility that noise is coming from something much simpler, like a loose object inside the car or in the trunk. It is not impossible to find a soft-drink bottle or can inside doors, even on new cars, and quite often the mechanic will find that a strange noise is little more than a loose spare-tire clamp. Noises that truly come from inside the engine are a bit harder to diagnose.

Bearings: Most drivers suspect every new engine noise to be bad bearings. If the noise comes on suddenly, usually when the engine is under a load (as climbing a hill), and sounds like the ratchet of a machine gun, it is probably the bearings. Immediately stop the engine before extensive crankshaft/connecting rod damage is done. A heavy-sounding knock at higher engine rpm

104

(under load) may indicate main-bearing failure, especially if accompanied by severe vibration. Rod-bearing knock will show up when the engine is decelerating (release the throttle suddenly), and when starting a cold engine. The oil pressure would drop if you have a direct-reading gauge. It is possible to isolate the bad rod bearing. Disconnect one spark-plug lead at a time; if the sound stops, or is lessened, when a spark-plug wire is removed, the rod bearing for that cylinder is the culprit. You can also get a pretty good idea of where the sound is originating (although you can't always tell what is making the sound until you get experience) by using a doctor's stethoscope or even a length of tubing between ear and engine block.

Piston: It is sometimes difficult for the novice audio mechanic to distinguish between bad bearings and a faulty piston. A piston pin with excessive wear will make a very distinctive tapping sound, and the noise will be regular and with two beats. It goes something like, tap-tap (pause), tap-tap (pause), and so on. If you hear the double sound, you can almost bet you have pin problems. If you hear a kind of slapping sound, more of a clack-clack, without the pause, you can suspect a collapsed piston, or a piston with a broken wall. Broken rings will not normally make a noise. You might occasionally get a large piece of carbon on top of the piston. This will make a tapping sound for a short time, but revving the engine will usually force it out through the exhaust. A note of caution: Any time you have the air cleaner off the engine, always set the air cleaner hold-down thumbscrew well away from the carburetor before you remove the air-cleaner top. It is easy to unknowingly drop this screw into the carburetor, and from there it will go

directly to a piston. If you hear a loud tapping sound immediately after having had the air cleaner off the car, and you couldn't find the thumbscrew, now you know where it is. Immediately stop the engine. While you might be extremely lucky and be able to remove the battered screw with a flexible magnet through a spark-plug hole, chances are you'll have to remove a head. The valves on that cylinder are probably hurt anyway.

Flywheel: If your car is equipped with a standard transmission and you find it hard to locate an erratic knocking sound that seems to be a rod bearing (but isn't), you might have a loose flywheel. If the bolts that hold the wheel to the crankshaft flange are loose even the slightest amount, the wheel can make a noise.

Fan: A noise that doesn't come from inside the engine but can be hard to locate is made by the fan blades hitting something. They can just barely be ticking the radiator, fan shroud, or radiator hoses. The sound is something like those made by heater and air-conditioning fans, but louder.

Camshaft: The rest of the sounds you're likely to hear originate usually from the cam assembly and valves. If the camshaft has somehow worked forward slightly, it may hit the front cover plate. This will cause a grinding, scraping sound. A similar sound might possibly come from an excessively worn oil pump, but the sound would be considerably muted.

Timing chain and gears: If you hear a slapping sound from the cam cover plate area (front of engine), it is probably caused by a loose timing chain striking the cover. Worn timing gears will make a whirring sound from the same area.

Hydraulic lifter: Probably one of the most common funny noises to come from the modern car engine is that caused by a dry or worn hydraulic lifter. The hydraulic camshaft lifter is nothing more than a hydraulic cushion between the camshaft lobe and the pushrod. An engine without a hydraulic lifter must have the clearance between pushrod and rocker arm periodically checked and set. The hydraulic lifter automatically keeps this "clearance" available. Hydraulic lifters are fed oil from the pump through galleries in the cylinder block. If one of the lifters should become dry for any reason, it will begin to clatter, the sound being a rapid stacatto click in direct relation to engine rpm. If the sound does not go away, or recurs regularly, that lifter should be replaced.

Pushrod: Not at all unusual is a bent pushrod, especially if the engine has been revved higher than its factory "red line." A bent pushrod will often make the same sound as a collapsed hydraulic lifter.

Rocker arm: A similar tapping noise can come from a rocker arm that is out of adjustment, but this is not common with hydraulic lifters. It is possible, however, to have a rocker arm break, which will cause a tapping sound, accompanied by an engine running erratically and on one less cylinder than usual. A strange squeaking sound from the valve-cover area can indicate a rocker-arm bearing running dry of oil on the rocker shaft.

Distributor: Should there be a noise coming from the vicinity of the distributor, it will have the same frequency as a noise in the camshaft assembly, but it is usually quite subdued. Any kind of clicking sound from this area would indicate a rotor hitting the distributor cap, or something loose or worn inside the distributor.

Spark plug: It is definitely possible to get a sound from the spark plug, even though this mechanical item has no moving parts. Some engines will actually "unscrew" the spark plug unless it is set in place with a torque wrench. Usually such a condition is precluded by the engine running erratically, and often a little whistle is heard on each compression stroke.

Wiring: If the spark plug wiring is "leaking," a spark can jump to nearby metal. These leaks usually happen only with older wiring. They may occur anywhere from the distributor to the plug. The sound will be a snapping that is audible even inside the driving compartment. In some cases it will happen only at higher engine rpm, under load.

Combustion knock: The worst has been left till last. Because of the very heavy degree of engine "de-tuning" automobile manufacturers have been forced into (to meet stringent smog-control measures), it is most common to find that an engine produced after 1971 has a tendency toward combustion-chamber knock. Two things can be taking place: detonation, or pre-ignition. In pre-ignition, the mixture being compressed by the piston on an upward compression stroke is fired prematurely. In years past, an engine might have as much as 30° to 40° ignition lead, meaning that the spark plug actually fired on a high-revving engine that many degrees before the piston reached top dead center. This was necessary in a high-compression engine so the burning mixture would have reached maximum possible combustion just after the piston passed TDC. To get mixture combustion (but not more power) with low compression, engines now have ignition much later, sometimes as much as 4° after TDC at idle. If a particle of carbon happens to be glowing hot enough to ignite the mixture while the piston is still before TDC (but before the spark plug ignites), you have pre-ignition. This is a very definite pinging/knocking sound, sometimes associated with sudden throttle openings. It should be avoided at all costs. Detonation occurs when the compressing mixture suddenly "explodes"—that is, the mixture does not have a controlled flame front as it would under normal firing. Such an explosion makes a knocking sound that can't be ignored, and it will usually knock the top from a piston, or crack the combustion chamber in a cylinder head. Of the two, detonation is far more dangerous (see Chapter 7).

TROUBLESHOOTING

Sounds are perhaps the very best guide a mechanic has to making a correct diagnostic study of an ailing engine. But sounds are only a part of troubleshooting, and troubleshooting is the real test of a mechanic. If you take half a minute, or half a week, to troubleshoot a poorly performing engine, you'll be much money, and labor, ahead. Troubleshooting an engine isn't easy, especially if the problem seems minor and it only has to do with the tune of the engine, not with a serious mechanical failure. A tiny air leak in the intake system can drive the mechanic—amateur or professional—nutty. But the problem can be found.

If an engine will not start, or even turn over on the starter, chances are overwhelming that the problem is in the ignition or fuel system. Of course, on rare occasions the problem can be mechanical, such as a slipped timing chain, but this is unusual. Generally, a troubleshooting procedure is indicated. If the engine doesn't crank—the trouble is usu-

ally just in the starting system, but it could be something more serious, like a hydrostatic lock (water-filled cylinders) or a seized engine. To check for these, you will have to remove all spark plugs and then try to crank the engine. If the engine cranks, this indicates that water is leaking into the cylinders. You will have to remove the cylinder head and inspect the gasket and/or head for cracks, and also check block for cracks. But most problems are simpler. Some common ones are listed below.

Engine will not crank and starter relay does not click: The battery may be dead. The ignition switch, starter relay, or starter neutral switch may be malfunctioning. The starter relay control circuit may be open or contain high resistance.

Check the battery. Perform a battery capacity test. If the battery does not test as having good capacity, make a battery test charge. Replace the battery if tests indicate it is worn out (see Chapter 8).

Check the starter relay, the neutral switch, and the ignition switch. Place the transmission lever in neutral or park position. With a fully charged battery, turn the ignition switch to crank the engine. If the engine will not crank and the relay does not click, connect a jumper lead from the battery to the ignition-switch terminal of the relay, thus bypassing the ignition switch. If the engine still does not crank, and the relay does not click, the relay is defective.

Some cars use a different wiring setup. Instead of going to the relay through the ignition switch, the current goes through the battery cable so that the relay is "hot" at all times. When the driver presses the starter switch (usually separate from the ignition switch), the relay circuit is completed to ground, which operates the relay. In that case, to make the relay operate with a jumper wire, you would connect the wire between the starter-switch terminal on the relay and ground.

To avoid damaging the system during testing, use a test light to determine which terminals are hot or dead. On early Chrysler products the neutral switch can be destroyed by connecting a hot lead to the wrong terminal. On General Motors cars with lights instead of gauges, always put the ignition switch in the "on" position when cranking with the jumper wire. If you don't, the ground circuit in the switch will be damaged.

If the engine now cranks, remove the wire plug connector from the starter neutral switch and connect a jumper wire between the terminals. Operate the ignition switch to crank the engine.

If the engine cranks, the starter neutral switch is defective.

If the engine does not crank, there are three possible defects: The hot wire from the battery terminal of the starter relay to the battery terminal of the ignition switch is loose or broken; the ignition switch is defective; or the wire from the ignition switch to the automatic transmission neutral switch or from the neutral switch to the starter relay is loose or broken. Trouble inside the starter is a possibility, too. But rarely does this result in a dead starting system.

Engine will not crank but starter relay clicks: If the relay clicks when the ignition switch is operated, and the engine will not crank, connect a heavy jumper from the battery to the relay starter terminal. If the engine cranks, replace the relay. If the engine does not crank, observe the spark when connecting and disconnecting the jumper. If there is a heavy spark, check the engine and starter drive as explained below. If the

spark is weak or there is no spark at all, proceed as follows:

Check cables and connections. If the spark at the relay is weak when the jumper is connected, inspect the battery starter cables for corrosion. Check the ground cable to see if it is broken, corroded, or loose. If the cables are corroded, clean them with a file or wire brush and tighten them securely. Replace any broken or frayed cables. If the engine still will not crank, the trouble is in the starter and it must be repaired or replaced.

Check the engine and starter drive if a heavy spark is obtained when the jumper wire is connected. Remove the starter and examine the starter-drive gear for burred or worn teeth. Also examine the teeth on the flywheel ring gear for burrs and wear. Replace the starter gear or the flywheel ring gear if they are worn or damaged.

If the engine cranks with the spark plugs removed, water has probably leaked into the cylinders, causing a hydrostatic lock. The cylinder heads must be removed and the cause of the internal leakage eliminated.

If the engine still will not crank, the engine is seized and can't be turned by the starter. The engine will need to be disassembled for repair.

Starter spins but will not crank engine: The starter drive may be worn out, broken, seized to the shaft, or have a broken armature bypass switch or actuating lever. Repair or replace.

Engine cranks slowly: The battery may be low in charge, the starter may be faulty, the engine may have excessive friction, or there may be excessive resistance in the starter circuit.

Check the battery. If the battery is discharged, recharge it and check the car for possible shorts or a light left on that may cause the battery to discharge. Perform a battery-capacity test. If the battery does not test as having good capacity, make a battery-test charge. Replace the battery if it is defective.

Check the external circuit voltage drop. If the battery was fully charged in the previous test, check the starter-cranking circuit for voltage drop. The drop in voltage will be either "excessive" or "normal."

To correct excessive resistance in the battery-to-starter-relay cable, starter-relay-to-starter cable, or battery-to-ground cable, clean and tighten all connections. If voltage drop is still excessive, replace the cables.

To correct excessive resistance of the starter relay contacts, replace the starter relay.

If voltage drop is normal, make a starter load test. If load current is not to specifications, proceed as follows:

If cranking current is low, repair or replace starter. If cranking current is normal or high, remove the starter from the engine and test the starter current draw at no-load. If the no-load current draw is above or below specifications, repair or replace starter.

If the current draw at no-load is normal, the starter is not at fault; the engine has excessive friction and must be repaired.

Engine cranks normally but will not start: First, check fuel supply. If there is fuel in the tank and the proper starting procedure is followed, the cause of the trouble lies in either the ignition or fuel-delivery system. To determine which system is at fault, perform the following:

Disconnect a spark-plug wire. Check the spark intensity at the end of the wire by holding it $\frac{3}{16}$ inch from the exhaust manifold and cranking the engine. If there is no spark or weak spark

at the spark plugs, the cause of the trouble is in the ignition system.

Next, determine if the cause of the trouble is in the primary or secondary circuit by removing the coil high-tension lead from the top of the distributor and holding it $\frac{3}{16}$ inch from the cylinder head. With the ignition on, crank the engine and check for a spark.

If the spark at the coil high-tension lead is good, the cause of the trouble is probably in the distributor cap, rotor, or spark plug wires.

If there is no spark or a weak spark at the coil high-tension lead, the cause of the trouble is probably in the primary circuit, the coil-to-distributor high-tension lead, or the coil.

If there is a good spark at the spark plugs and they are clean and in good condition, remove the air cleaner and look straight down into the venturi. Work the accelerator arm and see if fuel is being discharged by the accelerator pump. If fuel does not spray out into the venturi, disconnect the fuel line at the carburetor and crank the engine. Fuel should spurt out in a good stream.

If fuel is not reaching the carburetor, check:

The fuel filter—it may be clogged, or it may be an in-line type that has been mounted opposite the direction of fuel flow.

Loose connections.

Fuel line for obstructions.

Fuel-pump flexible line; it may be collapsed.

Fuel pump.

Manual choke. Check choke linkage for binding. Make certain the choke plate fully closes when choke is pulled and fully open when choke is pushed in.

Automatic choke. Check the position of the choke plate. If the engine is hot, the choke plate should be open. If the plate is not open, the engine will load up and will not start. If the engine is cold, the plate should be fully closed. If the plate is not operating as such, check the following:

Choke plate for binding.

Fast idle cam linkage for binding.

Thermostatic spring broken or needs adjustment.

Fuel supply at the carburetor: Work the throttle by hand several times. Each time the throttle is actuated, fuel should spurt from the accelerator pump discharge nozzle. If fuel is discharged by the accelerator pump and the engine still won't start, it is probably flooded or there is water in the fuel system.

Check for restricted fuel tank vent line.

Check fuel inlet system including inlet needle and seat assembly, and the float assembly.

Engine starts but fails to keep running.

Fuel system:

Idle fuel/air mixture needle(s) not properly adjusted.

Engine idle speed set too low.

Float setting too low.

Choke not operating.

Fuel inlet system not operating properly.

Water or dirt in the fuel lines or in the filter.

Fuel pump defective.

Ignition system:

Defective spark plugs.

Leakage in the high tension wiring.

Breaker points not properly adjusted or defective.

Engine runs but misses. First determine if the miss is steady or erratic —and at what speed the miss is worst. Try running the engine at various speeds under load. If it misses steadily at all speeds, isolate the miss by running the engine with the ignition wire removed from one spark plug at a time, until all cylinders have been checked.

If the engine speed changes when a particular cylinder is shorted out, that cylinder was delivering power before being shorted out. If no change in engine operation is evident, that cylinder was missing before being shorted out. If you have found a dead cylinder, check its ignition lead by holding it $3/16$ inch from a ground and cranking the engine. If you don't get a good spark, the trouble is in the secondary circuit of the system. Test the spark-plug wire and check the distributor cap for a crack or corroded terminals. If you do get a good spark, check the spark plug. If the spark plug is not at fault a mechanical component of the engine, such as a valve, is probably to blame. You will have to perform a manifold vacuum or compression test to determine the mechanical problem.

Misses erratically at all speeds: With this symptom, the problem may be in the exhaust system, the electrical system, the fuel system, or the engine itself. It might be:

Exhaust system restricted.

Breaker points defective or not properly adjusted.

Defective condenser, secondary wiring, coil, or spark plugs.

High-tension leakage across coil, rotor, or distributor cap.

110

Defective ignition switch.
Worn distributor shaft.
Carburetor float setting incorrect.
Fuel inlet system not operating properly.
Dirt or water in the fuel lines or carburetor.
Restricted fuel filter.
Engine mechanical problem, which will require a manifold-vacuum or compression test to determine the cause.

Misses at idle only: The problem could be in the ignition system, the fuel system, or the engine itself. Check the following for these possible faults:

Idle fuel mixture needle(s) not properly adjusted.
Restriction in idle fuel system.
Worn distributor shaft.
Worn distributor cam.
Defective coil, rotor, condenser, breaker points, ignition wiring, or spark plugs.
Valve lash (engine with mechanical lifters) or valve clearance (engine with hydraulic lifters) set too tight. Worn camshaft lobe or lobes. Perform a manifold vacuum or compression test to determine which mechanical component of the engine is at fault.

Misses at high speed only: When this condition exists, the problem could be either in the ignition system or the fuel system. Check for the following:

Power valve passage clogged.
Low fuel-pump pressure.
Fuel inlet system not operating properly.
Restricted fuel filter.

Restricted main fuel line.
Positive crankcase ventilation system restricted and not operating properly.
Defective spark plugs.
Parting of graphite in spark plug wire(s). Replace wire(s).

Engine idle is rough: The problem could be either in the fuel system, the ignition system, the exhaust system, or the engine itself. Check the following:

Engine idle speed set too low.
Idle fuel mixture needle(s) not properly adjusted.
Incorrect float setting.
Air leaks at carburetor mount, intake manifold, hoses and/or fittings.
Idle fuel system air bleeds or fuel passages restricted.
Fuel bleeding from accelerator pump nozzle.
Secondary throttle plate not closing on four-barrel carburetor.
Improper stop adjustment on secondary throttle plate (four-barrel).
Incorrect idle speed setting on secondary carburetor.
Improperly adjusted or defective breaker points.
Improperly adjusted or fouled spark plugs.
Ignition timing incorrect.
Inoperative exhaust-control valve.
Engine mounting bolts loose.
Incorrect valve clearance.
Defective crankcase ventilation valve.
Worn camshaft lobes.

Poor acceleration: This is usually an ignition-system or fuel-system problem. Check the following:

Incorrect ignition timing.

Improperly adjusted, fouled, or defective spark plugs.

Improperly adjusted or defective breaker points.

Distributor not advancing.

Accelerator-pump nozzle restricted.

Float setting too low.

Throttle linkage not opening carburetor fully.

Acceleration pump rod not properly adjusted.

Leaky power valve, gasket, or accelerator pump diaphragm.

Distributor vacuum passages in the carburetor restricted or vacuum line broken.

Fuel filter restricted.

Fuel pump defective.

Poor high-speed performance, or engine won't develop full power: Here almost anything can be at fault. Check the following:

Air cleaner restricted.

Clogged fuel filter.

Low float setting.

Undersize secondary jets.

Low fuel-pump pressure.

Distributor vacuum line restricted.

Automatic choke not opening fully.

Secondary throttle plate not opening fully.

Secondary carburetors not working properly.

Incorrect ignition timing.

Defective coil, condenser, or rotor, or crack in distributor cap.

Distributor not advancing properly.

Excessive play in the distributor shaft.

Improperly adjusted or defective breaker points.

Fouled spark plugs or plugs of incorrect heat range.

Restricted exhaust-control valve.

Restricted exhaust pipe(s)

Incorrect valve clearance.

Positive crankcase ventilation system not operating.

Worn camshaft lobe(s).

Loss of compression (perform compression test to determine problem).

Band out of adjustment (automatic transmission).

Slipping clutch (manual transmission).

Excessive Fuel Consumption

Determine as closely as possible your gasoline mileage. The simplest way is to note the number of gallons at fill-up and the mileage on the odometer. Divide the number of gallons used into mileage driven and you can determine miles per gallon. To make a fair test, drive as you normally would. This is the only way to tell if your mileage is good or bad, or if tune-ups have helped improve your mileage.

Gasoline mileage can be affected by a number of seemingly unrelated systems and components. Check the following:

Tires for correct pressure. Perhaps you can run a few more pounds than recommended.

Front end alignment.

Brake adjustment (too much drag).

Wheel bearings.

Inoperative exhaust-control valve.

Restricted exhaust pipe(s).

Distributor breaker points.

Ignition timing.

Spark plugs.

Spark-advance operation.

Crankcase ventilation valve.

Valve clearance.

Engine idle speed.

Idle fuel mixture.

Automatic choke for smooth operation.

Accelerator pump stroke.

Anti-stall dashpot for proper adjustment.
Air filter.
Float setting.
Choke adjustment.
Accelerator linkage for smooth operation.
Thermostat operation and proper heat range for your climate.
Proper band adjustment (automatic transmission) or clutch (standard transmission).

Overheating

This is a common problem. Obviously the cooling system is the usual culprit, but it is not always to blame. Check for the following:

Low on water.
Cooling system leaks.
Water-pump drive belt loose.
Radiator fins obstructed.
Defective thermostat.
Thermostat improperly installed (sensor should face engine).
Cooling system passages restricted or blocked.
Defective water pump.
Defective radiator cap or wrong pressure gauge.
Cylinder heads not properly torqued.
Incorrect valve adjustment.
Low oil level.
Incorrect ignition timing.
Distributor spark advance not working properly.
Restricted exhaust system.
Temperature send unit defective.
Gauge defective.

If you are losing coolant, there may be many reasons—some trivial and some very serious indeed. Check for the following:

Leaking radiator.
Leaking water pump.
Defective radiator cap.
Leaking hoses or connections.
Defective cylinder-head gasket.
Defective gasket from intake manifold to cylinder head.
Leaking freeze-out (core) plug.
Leaking temperature sending unit.
Cylinder head or intake manifold bolts not properly torqued.
Warped cylinder head or block-head gasket surface.
Cracked cylinder head or block-head gasket surface.
Cracked cylinder block or head (s).

If the engine does not reach normal operating temperature, you may think you just have a nice cool-running engine, but you're wrong. As I've said before, engines are made to run at a specific temperature range. Check the following:

Defective thermostat or incorrect heat range.
Temperature send unit and gauge.
Sending unit or gauge defective.

Noisy Valves

A noisy hydraulic valve lifter can be easily located by two methods. First, run the engine at idle speed and place a finger on the edge of the valve-spring retainer. If the lifter is not working properly, a shock will be felt when the valve seats. Second, using a short piece of flexible hose and with the engine running at idle speed, place one end on the valve-spring retainer and the other end to your ear. Listen for a metallic sound and repeat the procedure on each intake and exhaust valve until the noisy lifter has been found.

Common hydraulic lifter problems are dirt, varnish, gum, carbon, and oil

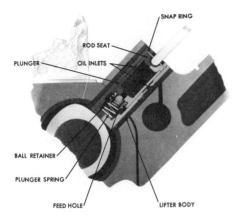

SNAP RING
ROD SEAT
PLUNGER
OIL INLETS
BALL RETAINER
PLUNGER SPRING
FEED HOLE
LIFTER BODY

Hydraulic valve lifter. Engine oil flows under pressure into the upper, or supply, chamber in the lifter body and then past the ball-check valve into the lower, or pressure, chamber. The plunger is forced into continuous contact with the push rod by the spring surrounding the ball retainer. As the camshaft rotates, the cam nose pushes against the lifter body, and thereby increases the pressure in the pressure chamber. This causes the check valve to seat, trapping the oil in the pressure chamber so that it cannot escape. On further rotation of the camshaft, with the resulting rise of the lifter, the confined oil in the pressure chamber functions as a solid member to lift the engine valve from its seat. For the entire period during which the valve is off its seat, the load is carried by this column of oil. As the cam recedes from the "lift" position, the pressure in the pressure chamber is relieved and the hydraulic mechanism returns to its original condition. A slight, predetermined leakage of oil around the plunger provides lubrication and prevents an excessive rise in temperature of the oil within the lifter. This device is also known as the "zero-lash" hydraulic system because the clearance ("lash") between valve tip and plunger is maintained at zero value, either by spring pressure or hydraulically. Some hydraulic lifters may use disc valves instead of ball valves but the lifter functioning is the same. Where the rocker-arm assembly is lubricated by oil supplied through hollow push rods, the valve-lifter push-rod seat has an opening for the required oil flow from the lifter supply chamber.

aeration. When dirt, varnish, gum, or carbon is found in the lifter assembly it can prevent the disc valve from seating, it may become lodged between the plunger and body surface, or it may restrict the oil passages. In any case, the lifter stops working because of failure to pump-up or because internal parts are no longer free to function. To remedy the situation, the lifter must be removed and thoroughly cleaned in solvent. It's also a good idea to change your oil filter more often so the problem doesn't recur.

Air bubbles in the oil can cause lifter noise. Be sure oil is always at the proper level. To check for oil aeration, run the engine and bring it up to normal operating temperature. Stop the engine and remove the oil sending unit. Install a fitting in its place that will permit attachment of a 1/4 to 3/8-inch clear plastic hose that will reach to the oil-filler pipe.

Now start the engine and let it idle. Check the oil flow for bubbles. Increase the engine speed to about 1000 rpm and recheck oil flow. *Caution:* Run the engine only long enough to check flow. If oil aeration is evident, remove the oil pan and inspect the oil pump for wear. Also clean and inspect the oil pickup system. Replace the pump if it is defective.

ENGINE OVERHAUL

There is no reason in the world an amateur mechanic cannot do an actual full engine overhaul, in his home garage and with a minimum of tools. However, to be practical, most home mechanics will pass on any engine mechanical repairs that are deeper than the intake system, timing chain or timing gears, water pump, ignition, starter, or head. This essentially leaves the short block,

Rebuilt (remanufactured) engines may also be purchased in a slightly more complete condition. This one includes the oil pan, oil pump, timing chain cover.

Before any engine rebuild is attempted, it is wise to consider the purchase of a good used engine. Check the serial number of an engine (wrecking yard will show you how) against master list usually kept by wrecking yard or new car dealer. This will verify year of block and sometimes cubic inch displacement. Most wrecking yards have a reasonable guarantee on used engines.

Next up the rebuild ladder is the "long" short block assembly, which includes the reconditioned heads. If present engine heads need rebuilding, such a engine may prove less expensive to install in the long run. Purchase of an engine in this state usually requires trade-in of your old engine as a "core." Removal and replacement of an engine is not nearly as difficult as it might appear, but the amateur should allow a good long weekend for his first attempt.

A good way to install a new engine is to buy a rebuilt short block and add the good pieces from present engine. This is the short-short block, including only block, crank, rods, pistons, camshaft.

a term that means that portion of the cylinder block enclosing the crankshaft, camshaft, connecting rods, and pistons.

You *absolutely* can do much of the work of repairing or rebuilding a short block. However, you'll find that you won't save much money in that area. Where you can save a bundle is in engine removal and replacement in the chassis, and this definitely is something you can do in the driveway.

Pulling the Engine

You can remove the engine with or without the front-end sheet metal in place. In the interest of saving time, especially if you've never removed an engine before, do not remove the front sheet metal. Start by draining and removing the radiator. On some few cars, the upper radiator support (which ties the front fender assemblies together) does not unbolt. To gain much-needed working room, sever this support at either end, near the fender splash panels. It can be welded or pop-riveted back in place.

Disconnect and remove the battery. Store it on a bench. Never set a battery on the dirt or cement, as it will discharge rapidly. Disconnect every electrical wire that connects to the engine, wrapping a tag of masking tape at each terminal end and labeling where it came from (starter, alternator, etc.). Disconnect any small braided grounding wires that might connect the engine to the firewall or the engine to the frame. Disconnect the fuel line at the fuel pump. Be sure to plug the fuel line in some manner, or fuel may flow from the tank. Finally, remove the carburetor. Never remove or reinstall an engine with the carburetor in place, as it is a relatively fragile casting and can easily be damaged by the engine hoist chain.

You can rent a hydraulic engine hoist from practically any equipment rental yard; the going rate is about $8 a day. If you have everything disconnected, you can lift the engine out and return the hoist with only an hour or two use, and the rental yard will often charge for less than a full day.

The hoist will usually come with a short length of chain that is to be connected to the engine. If the transmission is to remain in the car, this small chain will be bolted to a manifold stud at the extreme rear of the manifold, and to another stud on the opposite side (V8 engine) toward the front. When the hoist hook is attached to the pull chain, the engine will tilt up slightly in front. If the transmission is to be pulled along with the engine, the transmission weight will tilt the engine even higher in front, and the chain may need adjustment at the attachment studs. Attach the hoist hook to the chain, and work the hydraulic lift jack until the weight is just barely picked up by the hoist.

From below the car, release the motor-mount bolts. These are where the rubber insulators fit to the frame mounts. If the transmission is going to be removed, the driveshaft is disconnected at the rear end and slid away from the transmission tailshaft. A small hydraulic or screw jack is positioned at the rear of the transmission, with just enough tension to hold the transmission elevated after the transmission crossmember is removed. It is possible to remove the transmission by unbolting it from the crossmember and leaving the member in place, but the job is more difficult. Disconnect all linkage to the transmission, labeling any electrical wiring.

If the transmission is to remain in the car, place the jack at the transmission

116

usually rusty, a few shots of rust penetrant earlier in the work will speed nut removal. Finally, remove the bolts that hold the engine and transmission together. If you have the transmission supported by a jack, and the hoist has taken the engine weight, neither assembly will jump away. Drain the engine oil at this time.

Just in case you may have forgotten, never work beneath a car that is resting on a jack! Always use jackstands!

Now raise the engine with the hoist. It will usually come out with just enough room to clear the grille (that's why you took out the cross brace between the

If you're having your present engine rebuilt, any work on the cylinder block must usually be left to a machine shop. Most auto parts stores have this service available. If there is excessive wear in the cylinders, the block must be rebored and new pistons fitted. The machine shop will tell you how much is excessive. Sometimes an engine will not have enough "taper" to require new pistons, but enough taper to require a straightening bore, which will mean new rings at least.

forward end, with slight tension. There will be a small half-circle cover plate between the engine oil pan and the transmission bellhousing, or the lower half of the bellhousing will be removable. With this out of the way, you can remove several short bolts that hold the starter ring gear to the automatic-transmission torque converter. No such connection must be removed for a manual transmission. At this time, remove the exhaust-head pipes from the exhaust manifolds. Because they are

While your engine cylinder block might not need a crankshaft bore alignment, most remanufactured engines get this treatment as a matter of practice. Some engines are more prone to crank bore "shift" than others; the machine shop will tell you where your engine fits in the picture.

 117

If the engine block is being bored, it is also wise to check the head surface for any warpage. The machinist can do this with a straightedge (so can you) and a feeler gauge. If there is excessive warpage (which can happen if the engine is run extremely hot) a head "checking plate" such as this one shown will not seal air blown into water jackets. Most remanufactured engines must go through this test successfully.

If the engine has experienced a connecting rod or piston failure (breakage), definitely have the crankshaft checked for tiny breaks that are hard to see. This is usually done by Magnafluxing.

If the crankshaft must be reground, which is almost certain on an engine with a great amount of mileage, the machinist will normally take the same amount off both connecting rod and main bearing journals. A common regrind would be called a 10–10, meaning .010-inch off all journals. New bearings must be used, also called 10–10 oversize. Never replace a questionable crankshaft without having it checked by an expert.

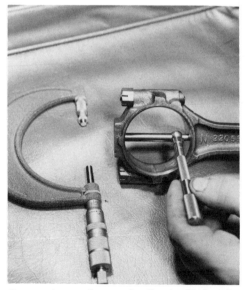

Connecting rods can be "resized" by the machine shop at nominal cost to make sure both big and little end bores are correct and the rod shaft is straight. Use new locking nuts on rod cap bolts.

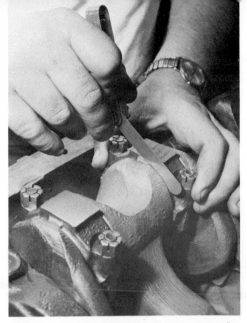

It is imperative that new piston rings be carefully checked in the pistons. Ring sets will have information on how much side clearance (shown being checked with a feeler gauge) and end gap is necessary. To check end gap, squeeze individual ring into cylinder bore and square it with cylinder, then measure gap with feeler gauge. If gap is not enough, ring can bind when it expands with heat. To get additional gap, use whetstone on ring ends. Gaps are staggered when installed on piston.

Rod big end side clearance must be checked. If this clearance is less than recommended by service manual the gap will be even less when the engine gets hot, reducing the flow of oil and leading to quick engine failure.

fenders earlier). Make some kind of wooden engine support from 2 × 4s. If you set the engine aside you can now return the hoist.

You are saving about $12 an hour by removing and replacing the engine yourself, which will account for roughly $150 in an average overhaul. Assuming that you are going to have the short block rebuilt by a local professional (why else pull the engine?) or replace the short block by one from a supply house (even your Sears or Wards store will offer short blocks), you save more money by stripping the engine.

Piston is installed on rod, a special ring squeezer tool used to compress well lubricated rings on piston, then assembly is gently tapped into cylinder bore from above. Be careful to align the rod big end with crankshaft.

 119

Unless camshaft lobes are worn there may be no need to remove cam. However, any rebuild of engine with 50,000 or more miles should include a new timing chain. Old chain stretches and changes timing relationship of valves to pistons.

Remove the head (or, in a V-engine, the heads), the intake and exhaust manifolds, flywheel, starter, distributor, water pump, and perhaps even the timing gear cover. Also remove pushrods and lifters at this time. If you are going to buy a replacement short block, check to see how complete the block is. If it comes with a new oil pump and oil pan, you won't need these items from your engine. If you are delivering your short block to a garage for overhaul, it can now be lifted into a sedan trunk compartment or pickup bed by three or four people.

While the engine block is being rebuilt, you can start on the other items that are likely to need attention.

Head Overhaul

If you do not intend to remove the engine block for any kind of work, but the heads need attention, they can be removed while the engine block remains in the car. No need for a hoist, or any of the previously described work, other than removing wiring and accessories. The carburetor need not be removed to remove the intake manifold, although on some V8 engines the manifold stud nuts or bolts may be difficult to reach with the carburetor in place. Set the intake manifold aside, and unless the distributor has been very recently rebuilt, it should be removed for servicing. To keep nuts, bolts, or similar small parts from falling into the oil pan through block openings, lay rags in the lifter valley (below the intake manifold) and the distributor opening.

Overhaul of automotive engine heads is not a difficult job, but the degree of work done will rest largely with the amount of equipment the mechanic has, and not so much his personal experience. Heads do not "wear out" as do other moving parts of an engine, although one point of wear is the valve guide portion of the head. Heads are subject to tremendous forces associated with combustion: intense heat, high pressure loads, rapid changes in temperature. Since they do little more than just lie there, the head will seldom require more work than servicing the valve mechanism (assuming the car is an overhead valve engine design, as most modern cars are).

Basic head repair is of a distinct mechanical nature, with emphasis given to valve seats, cracks, distortion, and valve guides. A cracked cylinder head may be caused by water freezing (expansion), combustion (pressure), distortion (bolt torque), or running without water (ex-

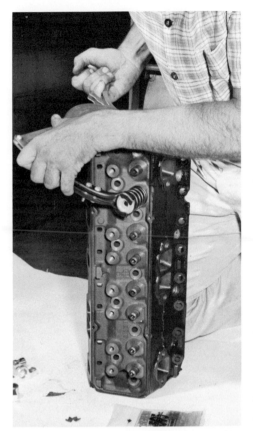

Head work starts with removal of valves with large C-clamp tool that can be rented. Valve spring retainer is held by the clamp, spring is depressed, then keeper locks are removed from valve stem. Valve assembly is then taken apart. Keep all assemblies numbered to indicate which cylinder they came from.

is not too difficult. However, a severe crack in the top of the combustion chamber caused by excessive pressure or mechanical interference will usually mean a new head is needed.

Discounting cracks, and special valve-refacing tools, the amateur can do as good a job as the professional, provided he takes time and works thoroughly. After the rocker-arm assembly has been removed (during initial disassembly), the only moving parts left on the head are valves and springs. To remove the valves, a special compression C-clamp is used, one end holding the valve head and the other pressing down on the valve spring. In this way, the valve spring may be depressed enough to remove the keeper locks. The valve spring and retainer then slide off over the valve stem. This C-clamp tool is usually available at any equipment-rental yard.

As each individual valve and spring assembly is removed, it should be kept together. Mechanics use a yardstick drilled full of holes as a handy valve organizer, with numbers at each hole to denote what engine cylinder the valves come from. If the valves are in reasonably good shape, and the valve guides in the head are not worn excessively, each valve should return to its original location, because all the valve-stem/guide combinations will not have the same amount of wear. Under such a condition, average repair calls only for valve and valve-seat refacing.

With the valve assemblies removed and the spark plugs taken out, there is nothing left in the head that can come out, with the exception of the valve seats and possibly the guides. Both will require attention in a general overhaul of an engine with many thousands of miles on it.

cessive metal heat). Of these, pressure and excessive heat are the common villains. For this reason, head cracks are generally confined to the immediate combustion-chamber / valve-seat area, and are repairs that only a professional can do. As long as the crack is within the valve-seat/throat area (that is, normally well into the port but partially in the combustion chamber), the repair

If the valve seat is the "insert" variety, as in this VW head, it can be removed and a new one installed if the seat is cracked. This job should be left to a machine shop.

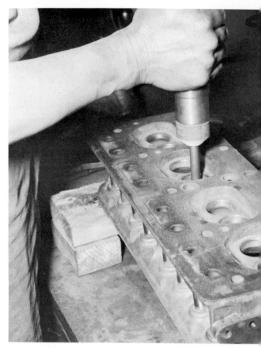

A valve seat grinding tool can be rented, along with the correct stones to renovate valve seats. Touch the seat with repeated light touches; do not make the seat "wider" than service manual calls for. This is not a difficult job.

Before work is started on either of these areas, the head should be thoroughly cleaned. This consists of chipping away all carbon deposits in the combustion chambers and ports, either with a sharp instrument (putty knife, screwdriver) or a rotary wire brush. This is a time-consuming job, but it should not be overlooked. Oil passages should be cleaned with a small wire brush, and blown clear—and this should be done again before reassembling the head.

If valve guides are worn, the valve can hardly be expected to do a good job. Wear is caused by the standard rubbing of metal against metal, a factor aggravated by difficult lubrication requirements (see Chapter 10). The intake-valve stem is constantly being washed by the fuel mixture, and the exhaust-valve stem is subjected to intense heat. Add to this the fact that a guide is just that—it must guide the valve in a straight line while the force moving

Valve seat width and angle may be indicated as slightly different from the: on the valve. This is called an interference angle and is done to insure maximum seal.

the valve is working through an arc. The tip of the valve stem in contact with the rocker arm is being pushed up and down as well as back and forth, and therefore guide wear is likely to occur in a slotted fashion in line with the force exerted by the rocker arm.

Before guides are replaced, the originals should be measured to see how far each protrudes into the intake or exhaust port. These special-shaped bushings can be pressed out, or driven out by hammer if a special punch is available. Stems are made of a number of different metals, depending upon the punishment they must take.

Contemporary engine designs are leaning toward the integral head/guide system, wherein the head metal is also the guide. This has several advantages, one being reduced valve temperature as heat is whisked from the valve stem easier, and another being lower production cost. However, when an integral guide wears, it cannot be replaced. Instead, valve stems are made in oversizes, such as .003, .005, .015, and .030

inch. In this way, the worn integral guide is reamed to the next applicable size, allowing for clearance. This takes special tools, however, and is usually left to the machine shop.

Another type of guide repair, or modification, that has been favored by engine builders is guide knurlizing. Just as knurling the skirt of a piston will effectively increase the diameter of the piston, so will knurling the inside diameter of a guide decrease the internal diameter. The guide may be reamed to a larger true size, then knurlized back to stock clearances. An advantage of this procedure is the creation of hundreds of small oil traps in the guide wall, which will give better stem lubrication. This, too, is a machine-shop operation.

Clearance is a very special problem with guides, and the specified measurement for a particular engine should be adhered to exactly. Excessive clearance around an intake valve is a sure way to encourage high oil consumption. A good insurance against oil sucking into the combustion chamber is the valve-stem seal, a nylon insert that fits around the valve stem on the rocker side of the head. These are reasonably priced and easy to install.

Seat Grinding

No engine overhaul should be attempted without at least refacing the valves and valve seats. It may be nothing more than a touch with the grinding stone, but it is essential to a successful job. While some engines seat the valves directly against the head metal, most designs call for specially hardened valve-seat inserts shrunk into the head.

These inserts must be carefully checked, as they crack, and may be loose in the block head. A loose insert or

Clean the combustion chamber of all carbon deposits with a wire brush in an electric drill.

one that is cracked or burned beyond repair must be replaced. They can be punched out from the back side (through the port), or pried out with a curved bar. They are brittle and the small pieces fly every direction when they break, so place a rag over the pry bar and wear protective goggles.

The insert does not fit a perfect hole in the head. Instead, the machined depression is an interference fit, from .005 to .008 inch smaller than the diameter of the insert. From this it is obvious that the head must be perfectly clean or the little insert won't go in so well. On the other hand, a loose insert will allow carbon to build up around the edge. This tiny bit of insulation is sufficient to keep the exhaust valve from transferring heat to the head rapidly enough (see Chapter 10). A burned exhaust valve will follow.

If the original insert hole in the head is the proper size, a new insert can be set in place as is. Otherwise, the hole must be machined to the next insert oversize. To make insert installation simple, place the insert in a freezer. This will shrink the metal more than enough and it will drop right in place. When the insert warms to room temperature it will be tightly wedged in the block or head. To make sure it stays put, the edge is clinched with a peen in several places.

Valve seats may be reworked in one of two ways, either by reaming or grinding. Cast-iron seats can be reamed, but the hardened inserts must be ground by a tapered stone. With either type of repair, it is absolutely essential that the pilot shaft fit the guide snugly. Too loose a fit allows the reamer or stone to wander, one reason the guides are reconditioned or replaced before the seats are fixed.

It is possible to rent seat grinders, but machine shops and professional mechanics are well equipped for valve work, so this job is a snap for them, and if the head or block is disassembled, the cost is quite low.

Valve-seat grinders usually come in a case, complete with a full range of stones of varying angles. The most common angle is 45°, with some 30° designs still in existence. It is imperative that the stone be dressed before use, to ensure maximum accuracy. Seats should not exceed .002 inch off center; they can be checked by a dial indicator.

A soft touch is required when using a seat grinder. Do not press down. In fact, the weight of the driving motor should be supported by the hands. To do a good job, raise and lower the grinder about twice every second. This will let the stone revolve at high rpm and the cut will be made rapidly. It only takes a few seconds to true up a valve seat.

A coarse stone is used for the initial grinding, then a fine stone to finish the seat. Because any grinding of the seat face will also widen it, a third stone with a different (greater) angle is used to face the inside or outside diameter of the seat and return it to the correct width. This width is quite important and should not be overlooked. Exhaust-valve seats should measure between .090 and .100 inch, while intakes are .070 to .090 inch. The exhaust valve has more heat, and therefore more contact area to transfer heat better.

Final head work includes grinding away any sharp edges inside the combustion chamber. The threads of the spark plug holes are an example of this, and although not absolutely essential, this just makes a good job better. Of course the head must be checked with a feeler gauge and straight edge for warpage.

Valve Grinding

The automobile engine is a bag of compromises, and the engineers have been able to perform seeming miracles over the years in making it as efficient as it now is. Part of the problem stems from getting the right amount of fuel mixture into the combustion chamber at precisely the correct time, then effectively sealing the chamber for subsequent fuel burning expansion. It all boils down to some kind of valve in a four-stroke engine.

Inventors have spent hundreds of thousands of hours trying to develop a better or more efficient valve, with the list including sleeve valves, rotary valves, poppet valves, slide valves—and still the search continues. In the interim, the standard poppet valve as we know it continues to be developed to ever greater degrees as engine performance requirements continue to increase.

Operating conditions for a poppet valve are brutal, to say the least. Unlike the other parts of the engine, a valve is exposed to the intense combustion temperatures with almost no chance to cool off. While the head of a piston is also exposed to these high temperatures, it can pass off heat through the skirt and the rod, as well as the surrounding water-cooled cylinder block. The valve is not so lucky. Instead, it must have a large-diameter head to give maximum breathing capacity for best performance, and a small stem. Heat can be passed along only through the tiny stem and during the very few moments of each revolution when the valve face is in contact with the valve seat (see Chapter 10). Considering that the temperature

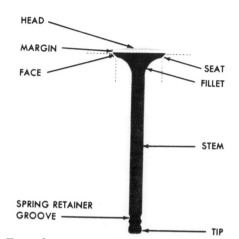

Typical poppet valve. Basic purpose of the valve is to permit gas flow in or out of a cylinder, while providing a gas-tight seal when closed against the valve seat.

inside a combustion chamber may reach 5000° F. for a split second, the task would seem impossible. Furthermore, the poor old exhaust valve must open at the most inopportune time and pass the hot gases out the exhaust port. This is why valve jobs are so common even for an engine that is in otherwise excellent condition, and why keeping the valves adjusted is so vitally important.

Temperatures of a valve head may reach 1000° F. or more under these conditions, and they go even higher in racing engines (racing engines use exotic valve materials). It is easier to understand just how difficult a job the valve has when you consider how short a time the valve is seated. If the engine is turning 3000 rpm (the average cruising speed of most cars), it means that each of the several cylinders will have ignition 1500 times per minute, and that means the valves are off the seat the same number of times. Not very much time for a valve to cool off.

The seating-surface area of the exhaust-valve head may reach 1000°, the center will be 200-400° hotter, and the stem just below the head will be slightly below 1000° F. This is red-hot in any language. If the valve does not seat against the insert exactly right, because of a bent stem or a piece of foreign material, the edge will burn immediately. Once decay starts it spreads rapidly. The intake valve does not have these great temperature problems, because it is seated when the heat is being passed out, and the incoming fuel mixture is at or below atmospheric temperature. This is ironic. Adjacent to each other are two almost identical mechanical items. One is burning up, literally, and a smidgen of an inch away is all the coolant it could possibly want, but can't take advantage of.

Because of the extreme temperatures involved, exhaust valves are normally made of heat-resistant alloy steel. Sometimes the stems are made hollow and filled with mineral salts such as sodium, which is a fast heat conductor. All the exhaust valve's operating problems are further aggravated by operational changes in the engine. The engine may be in perfect condition cold, but when it warms up to running temperatures, some kind of distortion is likely to occur. This in turn may cause localized hot spots near the valve, with attendant heat problems transferred to the valve. The metal may distort enough to slightly misalign the valve between guide and seat, causing an improper heat transfer, and so on. All this just goes to prove that valves are one of the most important areas of engine overhaul, and must be treated with care and precision. Of course, if the deposits on the upper part of the valve stem just below the

head could be minimized, this would in turn cut down on the chances of a valve sticking slightly open—and most of the valve problems would be solved. One way to reduce the effect of such deposits (caused by the combustion particles sticking to the exhaust valve as they flow out) is to have the exhaust valve rotate slightly each time it is lifted. There are two types of rotating-valve designs currently popular, one called the free type, in which the valve rotates at no particular rate, and the other called the Rotocap system, in which the valve rotates an exact number of degrees each time is is opened.

The amateur mechanic may be tempted to take the easy route when it comes time to do the valves. If they look to be in good shape before disassembly, then it would seem reasonable to reuse them with no refacing. This is just asking for trouble. It's like putting on three new tires, and leaving a fourth one bad. A valve job should be part of any engine overhaul.

Valves may be lapped if precision grinding equipment is not available, but this is not the best procedure. To lap a valve, special grinding compound is placed on the seat and the valve rapidly rotated back and forth against the seat. The required tool is a rounded handle with a small suction cup that sticks to the valve head.

There are two kinds of compound available, coarse and fine. The fine is preferred. They come in either oil or water mixtures (use water to remove excess of one, solvent for the other). When lapping a valve, use a very small amount under the valve head, as it can work down around the clean stem and be just as effective at opening up the guide clearance. Inspect the valve face

Valves can be taken to the machine shop for grinding. If a valve has been damaged excessively, it should always be replaced.

Lightly polishing the valve head with emery will discourage carbon build-up.

often, and when a small even gray ring appears around the full circumference of the face, the width of the seat, the job is finished. Of course, there must be no pits or nicks in the mating surfaces.

Lapping is inferior to precision grinding in every respect. A precision-ground valve should never be mated to a lapped seat, and vice versa. As a guide, restrict lapping to a time when precision grinders are not available, or the valves are in nearly perfect condition to start with.

Ordinary passenger car valves have reasonably thick heads, making it possible to reface burned valves. When the grinding equipment refaces the valve, it also trues the head, and usually very little must be taken from the face to remove minor pits and burn traces. If the valve has burned badly, however, it must be replaced. Normally, there will not be more than one or two badly burned valves involved, since the car will run very poorly with just one bad valve.

After the valves have been ground

they must be cleaned of any stem deposits. The heads are also cleaned, and then the valves can be assembled in the head.

Repairing Rocker Arms

Like the valves, rocker arms can wear rapidly. They should be carefully inspected for wear at three points: where the valve tip touches the face, the shaft bushing, and the pushrod stud. The stud ball tip may be worn away, or the adjusting threads may be bad. All these areas may be repaired, but a cracked or bent rocker arm should be replaced.

If the rocker face is pitted, it may be dressed flat. While such a unit could be retained and the valve lash adjusted with a dial indicator, this would not solve a basic wear problem. If the face pitting seems excessive, it is possible the rocker-arm material is faulty.

It is not uncommon for the adjusting-stud threads to break or gall in the rocker, so these should be run through with a screwdriver several times as a

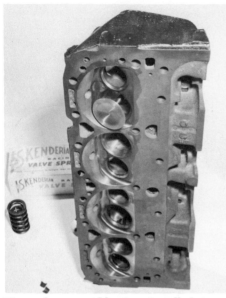

The valve assembly is reinstalled in reverse manner to disassembly. Head surface should be checked for warpage and "surfaced" by the machine shop if it is not perfectly level. This is necessary to ensure correct head gasket seal.

Valve lifters, whether mechanical or hydraulic, tend to wear as fast as any part of engine. Any sign of wear on end that touches camshaft lobe is a good reason for replacement. Carefully inspect rocker arms for fractures and replace as necessary.

check. The slightest bind means some kind of trouble. If the lubrication has been poor, the stud ball end may have become pitted, and in extreme cases will even wear away in the pushrod socket.

Because both valve spring and pushrod are always forcing the rocker upward, all wear of the rocker bushing and the rocker shaft will be on the bottom side. Such wear is readily apparent and common on engines with many miles. To inspect for the wear, force the rocker to the side with a bar. If the shaft is worn, it will show as a ridge of metal riding in the bushing oil groove. Worn shafts should always be replaced. Only in an emergency should the shaft be turned down and reused. The rocker bushing should be pressed out and a new bushing installed, with care taken to realign the oil-delivery holes. The bushing should be honed to fit the shaft, with .002 inch oil clearance being about the average.

When reassembling the rocker and shaft assembly, it is often difficult to get the rockers in the correct place, since exhaust and intake rockers may be of different lengths or shapes, or both. To avoid this, leave one shaft assembled while working on the other. Then you will always know how things are supposed to be put together.

Don't overlook the rocker-shaft supports, as they often break from excessive bolt torque.

Cam-in-block overhead-valve engines use pushrods to connect the camshaft/lifter assembly and the rocker arm. Overhead cam and flathead engine designs do not have the pushrods. A pushrod should be inspected for wear or warpage and discarded if either is found. Wear will be at the ends, either where the rod enters the lifter or at the upper end that contacts the rocker adjustment (some engines do not have an adjustment if the lifters are hydraulic). A slight pit in the lower ball or the upper socket is a sign of trouble, so replacement is suggested.

Lifters come in two versions, solid (mechanical) and hydraulic. The solid lifter is nothing more than a cam lobe follower, but it has been precision-engineered for the purpose.

The hydraulic valve lifter is designed to keep a zero-lash clearance—that is, to reduce engine noise there is no clearance between the cam and ultimate valve stem. If this were the case with solid lifters, the expansion of the metals would cause the valves to remain slightly open. With the hydraulic lifter, any lash in the system is compensated for by hydraulic (oil) action. A hydraulic lifter has three basic parts: the body (housing), plunger, and valve.

Oil from the main oil gallery passes through the lifter check valve, forcing the plunger up from the bottom and into contact with the pushrod, and ultimately the valve stem. This oil is under pressure determined by metering holes in the lifter and the oil galley. Because of the higher pressure, hydraulic lifters require a stronger valve spring to keep the valve seated than do solid lifters.

As the lifter is raised by the camshaft action, there is a further pressure on the trapped oil inside the lifter. This closes the check valve and the lifter then becomes a solid lifter for all practical purposes. A tiny amount of oil is allowed to leak from between the plunger and the housing during this open valve phase so that when the cam rotates to the closed position, the valve will not be kept slightly open. This lost oil is replaced again by oil from the gallery. When an engine with hydraulic lifters is first started, a clattering sound from the lifters indicates that one or more have leaked completely dry and will take a while to pump up again.

It is possible to wear out lifters of this type, although the plunger movement is very small during operation. Dirt, varnish, carbon, and similar foreign materials can get into the lifter and cause the check valve to stick. Keeping the engine oil clean and free from either physical or chemical contamination will protect the lifters.

Replacing Tappets

Economics of engine rebuilding being what they are, novice mechanics often try to get by with the old tappets when a new cam or complete overhaul is really indicated. Good luck. Most modern engines have been designed to include revolving lifters, and this means that lifter-to-camshaft lobe contact points must be absolutely correct. Most cam problems stem from incorrect lifter contact (the contact point should be slightly off center to the "high" side of the lobe).

Camshaft lobes taper from one side to the other, usually between .002 and .004 inch. The face of the lifter is ground slightly rounded, by about .002 inch, and by placing the lifter bores slightly to the higher side of the cam lobes, each revolution of the camshaft will cause the lifter to rotate a few degrees. If either the cam lobe or the lifter face are not ground correctly, or have flattened during use, the valve won't rotate and rapid wear in one spot will ensue.

Repairing Valve Springs

Valve springs are especially susceptible to failure. Even under ideal conditions spring steel will not last forever. Therefore valve springs can be expected to fail from time to time since they operate in unfavorable conditions.

Each and every valve spring should be checked for tension on a special reading scale made for the purpose. The spring must be measured for free (unloaded) height. If this is in the limits prescribed for the particular engine (line them all up together and a comparison check will show minute differences in height), then the spring is compressed a certain distance. At this distance the coils should be exerting a certain amount of pressure. If not, shims may be required between spring and head, or spring and retainer, to get the prescribed pressures.

At the same time, the coils of the spring must not bind against each other, or the spring will break during use. If the springs will not come up to proper pressure with minimum shims, they must be replaced.

Reassembly of the Head

Now everything is ready for reassembly of the head. The valves are replaced in their respective guides one by one. The oil seal is inserted over each stem, followed by the spring and shims if necessary. Using the big C-clamp, the spring is again depressed and the retainer washer and keepers are reinstalled. The head or heads are then ready to be installed on the cylinder block.

The head gasket should be installed as marked, with the indicated top and front portions so placed. Sealing compound or aluminum paint may be used on both gasket surfaces. Always use the gasket prescribed for the engine.

All head bolts should be inspected before reuse. Any slight distortion means the bolt should be replaced. Coat the threads with an anti-seize compound, then torque the bolts to the prescribed

pounds and in the torque pattern established by the engine manufacturer. This pattern usually starts in the middle of the head and works toward either end. It is imperative that the proper torque pattern and pound limits be followed to minimize block and head distortion.

The lifters may be placed in their respective bores before the head is installed (remember, they go back to the same hole they came from), and so may the pushrods. However, the pushrods must be in the rocker-arm pivots before any of the head bolts are tightened.

The valley cover may be replaced now. Since this is separate from the intake manifold on most modern V8s, it should have sealing compound on both sides of the gasket. Also, if small rubber seals are involved around the central hold-down bolt or bolts, new seals

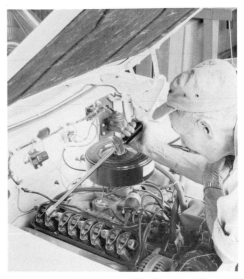

Rocker assembly is usually drawn tight with head bolts; always torque the headbolts to service manual specifications. Torque sequence is normally in a radiating circle from the middle outward. Retorque headbolts after a couple of thousand miles.

After the headbolts are tight, the valves may be adjusted if mechanical lifters are used. Procedure for setting hydraulic valves usually calls for running adjustment down tight, then back up quarter- or half-turn. Specific adjustment recommendations should be consulted and followed, otherwise premature valve failure can result.

should be installed. Nothing is more discouraging than to have an oil leak around these bolt seals after the engine is assembled and back in the car.

When the head was being checked for warpage, one of the surfaces involved was the manifold flat, for both intake and exhaust manifolds. Naturally, this same check must be given the manifolds, and they must be trued up by grinding if necessary.

There is not much that can go wrong with a manifold, but if it is cracked the break must be repaired. This can be done by welding or brazing, the latter being most common, and is acceptable on both intake and exhaust systems. After welding, the manifold should be heated to relieve any stress concentrations, and the mating surfaces machined true.

The manifolds must be cleaned of any carbon build-up, then bolted to the engine with torque specifications observed. A sealing compound may be desirable around the intake gaskets. The

spark plugs are then torqued to the heads, and the exhaust/intake openings taped shut. This will prevent any loose object from falling inside and undoing all the hard work just completed.

Valve covers may be installed at this time. No sealing compound is necessary, since they have thick, soft gaskets. If the engine has an exhaust-emission-control device, it should be serviced and replaced. Keep in mind that the engine was set up to run with such a device, and removal will cause all kinds of tune-up problems. At the same time, this device must be kept in perfect working order at all times, or engine tune will suffer adversely.

Whether or not the water pump must be replaced or repaired is strictly a matter of condition (see Chapters 10 and 15). While the pump is removed, check the impeller shaft for excessive wear. This will usually show up as a trace of coolant leakage out the front of the housing, but not always. Sloppiness of the impeller shaft is an indication of too much clearance. Most pumps have ball bearings, and these bearings are destroyed when a leak develops and the interior rusts.

It is usually easiest to exchange water pumps, since they aren't expensive, but if the pump is to be repaired it must be removed from the housing anyway. Some impeller shafts are a press fit with the pulley, others use a retainer ring. After the pump is disassembled, the worn or bad bearings and impeller shaft are replaced. When reassembling the pump, be sure to observe the clearances advised in the repair kit since everything is being pressed back together permanently.

Under no circumstances should a chance be taken with an old thermostat. Engine operating temperatures are im-

Always install the intake manifold to recommended torque specifications, and recheck after 1000 miles. A tiny air leak at the manifold gasket can make good tuning almost impossible.

All emission control air pumps should be in good operating condition. Check belt tension as regular part of maintenance.

Once valve covers have been drawn tight on an engine they tend to take a "set" and subsequent installations often lead to oil leaks. Use a gasket adhesive to stop the leaks.

Air pumps do fail, and when this happens it is difficult to tune the engine. Most pumps are as cheap to replace as to rebuild.

portant, because an engine can run too cool as well as too hot. If the engine gets too hot it can detonate and eventually pre-ignite, which will mean an immediate loss of power, not to mention damage to internal parts. Excessive engine heat will cause increased oil oxidation and varnish, greater piston-ring and hydraulic-lifter sticking, and obviously increased oil consumption.

Running too cool will cause increased oil dilution, lower gas mileage, oil sludge, coolant rust, and higher ring and bore wear. Every part in an engine has been designed to run at a specific temperature, and should not be required to do otherwise.

The fuel pump completes the engine reassembly, and the unit is ready for replacement in the chassis. If the novice

Clean the breather cap to ensure that it is not plugged and restricting air flow in emission control devices.

Air cleaners play an important role in emission controls. Plugged cleaners tend to choke the carburetor, resulting in a richer-than-normal mixture.

Seals around inlets to air cleaner covers should be cleaned and replaced if badly worn.

mechanic has worked diligently, he will have spent an average of two to four hours removing the engine, two days overhauling it, and four hours replacing it. This is not much time, considering the amount of money he has saved.

After the engine is back in the chassis, the carburetor and ignition may be replaced, along with power accessories, belts, etc. Since all the wiring was tagged

when the engine was first removed, the electrical hookup is simple.

Final Adjustments

Setting valve lash and timing the distributor are where many amateur mechanics fall down. They may have assembled a very good engine, only to have things unravel in either or both of these categories.

To time an engine, rotate the crankshaft until the No. 1 piston is on top dead center (TDC) of the compression stroke. Move the crank back and forth a few degrees either way and watch the No. 1 rocker arms. If they move, the engine is on the exhaust stroke and must be rotated again. With the piston on TDC of the compression stroke, the timing marks on the crankshaft pulley should be aligned with the timing pointer attached to the timing cover.

Before the distributor is installed and before the engine is fired up for the first time, the oil system may be primed by running a long driving shaft down through the distributor (see Chapter 10). Turn this shaft with a drill motor and watch for oil exhausting through the rocker arms.

Now install the distributor (see Chapter 8) with the rotor pointing directly to the No. 1 distributor cap terminal (the secondary, or ignition, wires were taped with the correct spark plug number, remember?). Adjust the distributor by turning it in the direction of rotation until the distributor points just barely begin to open. In this way, a very slight lead is involved and the engine will start. Final distributor adjustment is then made with a timing light.

It is common for amateurs to get the ignition installed to fire on the exhaust stroke, and this leads to all kinds of frustration. If the engine does not start right away, recheck to see if the distributor is not out of phase with the cylinders.

Setting valve lash is not difficult, but is often done carelessly. Hydraulic lifters require no lash adjustment, but some engines call for one turn adjustment from zero lash. This places the lifter plunger in the center of the housing travel. To make this kind of adjustment, loosen the rocker-adjustment stud until the valve clatters, then tighten it to zero lash, or when the valve is quiet. Now tighten the adjustment screw one additional full turn, making the adjustment ¼ turn at a time to allow the lifter to bleed down. Some engines have different-length pushrods for adjustment.

Adjustment of the solid lifter is made with a feeler gauge and requires nothing more special than patience. The lifter must be on the heel of the cam for this adjustment—that is, the valves must be fully closed. Turn the adjusting screw in the rocker until the feeler is a snug but removable fit, and tighten the locknut. Until you are proficient at adjusting mechanical lifters, you should recheck the initial cold settings after the engine has warmed up (the settings are different and are specified in shop manuals).

How an overhauled engine is broken in will determine how well it runs. As soon as it is started, it should be set at an rpm equivalent to 20 to 30 mph, or slightly over 1000 rpm. This allows the oil to circulate through the engine galleries well, and throws oil onto the cylinder walls.

As a rule, don't let the engine idle, and don't operate it with cold water running through the block. So that takes care of the idea of letting the engine break in with a garden hose stuck in the radiator. The engine must reach operating temperature for the rings to seat, and the closer to the boiling point the better, although it shouldn't be allowed to boil.

After the engine has run awhile, drive it around to get everything loosened up. This will be but a few miles. Then retorque the head and manifold bolts and reset the valve adjustment if you have solid lifters. The ignition timing should be rechecked, and the carburetor adjusted for correct idle speed. Adjust the idle mixture screw by turning it in to the lean position. When the engine bucks, or misses, slightly, back the screw out just enough for a smooth idle.

To seat the rings, accelerate the car at full throttle briefly from 30 mph. This will load the rings and cause the slight wear necessary. Hard rings will take slightly longer to seat. Drive the car under 50 mph for the first 250 miles, and at no sustained high speeds for the first 1000 miles. Drain the oil and change the filter at 1000 miles and then observe regular lubrication maintenance.

If I have made an engine overhaul seem not as difficult as you might have thought, that's because it isn't difficult. Most amateur mechanics are reluctant to start engine work because they consider the engine mechanical magic. But don't be afraid to tackle the engine. As long as you do the work in a careful and orderly way, you'll probably amaze yourself at how well it turns out.

PCV valves should be cleaned often, replaced if they do not work smoothly. If the valve plugs up, it can cause excessive crankcase pressure, leading to excessive oil burning, poor engine tune.

ANTI-POLLUTION DEVICES

Pollution controls are the natural enemy of automobile performance, no matter how you measure it: engine horsepower, or miles per gallon, or operating cost per hour. But like them or not, these controls are here to stay, in one form or another. Most experts agree that within the next decade some outstanding advance will be made in pollution-control technology, but meantime the driving public is stuck with a compromise that is better for the environment but murder on the petroleum industry and the individual automobile.

There is not a great deal of work you can do on pollution-control devices, even to make sure they are doing the job efficiently, but there are a few things. The better the home mechanic keeps a car in tune, with all the pollution controls working correctly, the better performance he can expect. Admittedly, this performance is nothing to shout about, but it can get considerably worse if the engine condition is not kept razor-sharp.

The positive-crankcase-ventilation system, better known as the PCV valve, was the first device to be required on all cars. Formerly, combustion-chamber gases escaping by the piston rings would mix with crankcase oil vapors and then vent to atmosphere by a road draft tube. By closing off this draft tube and routing these gases back to the intake system, some harmful pollutants can be corralled.

There are four types of PCV systems. The first has a hose from the crankcase to the intake system, with a valve in between. Manifold vacuum pulls vapors from the crankcase into the manifold, where they are burned. Should there be an intake-system backfire, the safety valve prevents the flame front from leading back into the crankcase, where it might explode the vapors. This isn't a perfect system, and about all the mechanic can do is make sure all the hoses are good, that no hoses are drawing extra air or being flattened by vacuum, and that the valve is operating. The valve can be rinsed in solvent or replaced if it will not work at all. A simple mouth suction test will show if it works.

The second system is similar, but designed to keep the crankcase under slight vacuum at all times (in the first type, the oil filler is free to the atmosphere). Here, the mechanic must see that there are no open air leaks into the crankcase, which would cause the valve to open, in turn leading to a very lean fuel mixture. Such a lean mixture

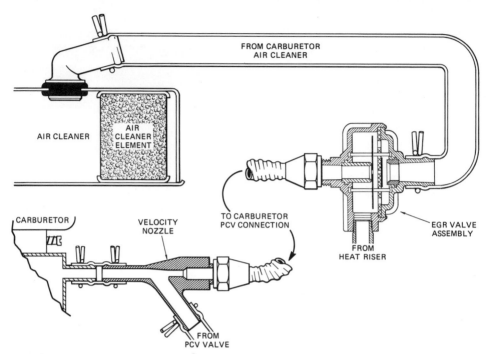

Retrofit EGR NO$_x$ emission control systems are now being required on some older cars in some states. This unit by STP is a typical aftermarket item.

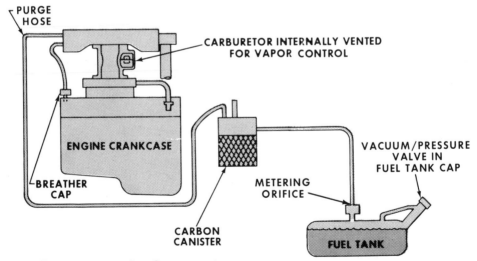

Eventually, car equipped with evaporative emission control systems will perhaps experience problems in the system. Filters must be kept clean, all connections tight.

can quickly damage the engine valves.

The third type is simply a hose from the crankcase to the air cleaner. Since the vapors involved are already gaseous, such a system tends to richen the mixture and the carburetor must be adjusted accordingly.

In the final system, an air hose goes from the air cleaner to the valve cover, and the same system as in the first design gets vapors back to the intake manifold. This way fresh air goes from the air cleaner to the closed crankcase, and then back to the intake system (this is often called the CCV, or closed-crankcase-ventilation system).

The air-injection system is a motor-driven pump that pumps clean air into the exhaust manifold. This air will then give enough oxygen base for the unburned (and still extremely hot) exhaust gases to burn thoroughly in the exhaust system. About the only service this system requires is making sure the pump works freely and that the air-inlet valve on the pump is not plugged.

Unfortunately, this air pump also requires some changes in the carburetor, ignition, cooling system, and even the internal engine parts. All you can do is make sure these related systems are adjusted according to the specifications for your particular car.

Things get more complicated with the ignition-induction system, in which the carburetor is adjusted so the mixture is not too rich at idle. Here, carburetor air flow dictates advance/retard activity in the distributor, and the only thing the mechanic does is make sure the system is not plugged or leaking air. The system is sophisticated and includes some significant changes in engine internal design, so the mechanic won't

The catalytic converter has been added to many exhaust engines in 1975. This unit allows the removal of some of the other restrictive emissions control equipment, but it is controversial and may not stay on automobiles in its present form. Acting very much like a filter, it absorbs harmful exhaust products. Aftermarket catalytic converters will soon be available for older automobiles.

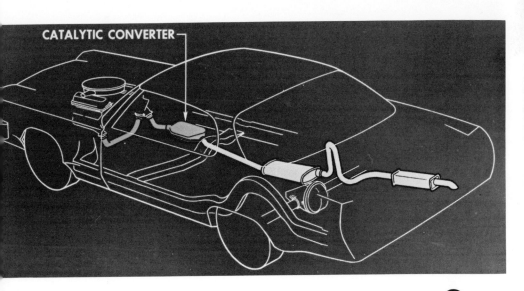

CATALYTIC CONVERTER

be working with these parts much. This is called the exhaust-gas-recirculation-valve system (EGR) in most cases, and the control units are essentially not repairable. If one goes on the blink, it must be replaced. Tests for this system are best left to the professional mechanic.

Fortunately, there are some brighter days ahead. The Vega dual-overhead-camshaft four-cylinder engines designed for 5000 cars during 1974 both give high performance and are able to meet the stringent emission-control guidelines. Here the secret is use of a highly refined combustion chamber of a relatively low 8:1 compression ratio coupled to an electronic injection system. The real secret is the intake system, perfected by Bendix, which meters only the amount of gasoline the engine needs (as demanded by the engine) and no more. Thus the engine will be much more efficient without giving up horsepower or economy.

Obviously emission-control systems with complicated disorders must be repaired by professionals, although the home mechanic can keep an eye on all the plumbing to see that it is in good operating condition.

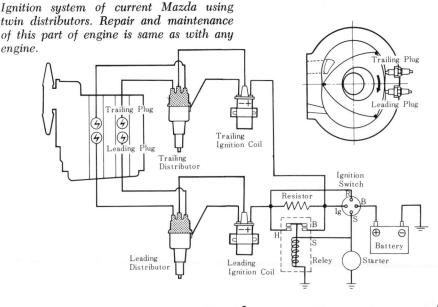

Ignition system of current Mazda using twin distributors. Repair and maintenance of this part of engine is same as with any engine.

6 the rotary engine

AUTOMOTIVE HISTORY is choked with accounts of this or that amazing mechanical invention that supposedly will revolutionize vehicle travel. Unfortunately, these dreams never seem to come completely true. Sometimes an idea doesn't prove workable, and sometimes it never makes it into the production line because it is not economically practical. For a time, it seemed like the rotary engine would be just another of these interesting thoughts destined for an early death. But thanks to the ecological crisis, the persistence of the Germans, and the willingness to gamble of the Japanese, this unique engine of few parts has not been relegated to oblivion.

The rotary engine isn't something that came along in a flash of inspiration during the past decade. The idea dates back more than 300 years to the time that a Mr. Ramelli invented a water pump based on this principle (1588). From then on it was a matter of periodic investigation by various inventors, perhaps more as an intriguing mechanical problem than as a serious search for improvement of the reciprocating engine. In 1859, a Mr. Jones tried a rotary engine based on the Roots supercharger configuration; Cooley tried a similar idea in 1903 (but with a single rotor in a three-lobed housing); an oscillating piston engine was tried sometime during the same period; BMW of Germany did some rotary research in 1934; in 1960 Renault built an experimental rotary; and in 1963 two different designs were offered by Franke and Kraus. It was a German inventor named Felix Wankel who finally got the job done.

Felix Wankel was an engineer with a keen interest in the theory of rotary engines dating back to the 1920s. He felt that failure to create a workable rotary might simply be the fault of engineers not taking into consideration the essential qualities and requirements of a basic

139

internal-combustion engine. Earlier attempts at a rotary had failed because these requirements were not satisfied. No systematic research had been carried on, few experiments continued because no superiority over the conventional engine could be seen, and the necessary industrial technology seemed lacking.

Wankel outlined in his own mind the conditions that a successful rotary engine must meet: None of the moving parts (including the timing system) should make a reciprocating motion; gas sealing within the working chamber must be reliable; replacement of gas must be accurate; the engine must be compact in relation to power output; all component parts must have sufficient strength and wear resistance to withstand the high speed and high pressures of a modern engine; and the engine must be sufficiently cooled and lubricated. On the surface it might seem that other inventors would take this same practical approach to building a rotary, but apparently Wankel was the only one who followed through. From these conditions came the design criteria for the modern Wankel rotary.

The idea of a rotary kept nagging Wankel, and although the occupation forces took over the Wankel laboratory after World War II, his enthusiasm for the project did not die. In 1951 he built a small workshop in his home, and help appeared from a German company known as NSU Motorenwerke AG, a firm that made motorcycles. NSU was interested in the rotary as possible power for a small car they were considering, so the company entered into a joint research and development agreement with Wankel. By 1957 the first engine, called the DKM, had been built, but it was overly complicated by a rotor and housing that both rotated. Further development led to the KKM type in early 1958, which had the stationary housing now common. Although the idea was introduced to the public that same year, it was still a long way from practical use in production cars.

Refinement of the Wankel patents have been carried on in many countries since 1958, the most notable being by Toyo Kogyo in Japan, makers of the Mazda. Their engineers concluded by 1960 that such an engine could certainly be built with existing production technology, and in a span of ten years they perfected the engine for use in the Mazda.

Other companies, including Mercedes-Benz of Germany, were clamoring for a chance to work with the NSU complex as licensees. In America the aircraft-engine manufacturer Curtiss-Wright secured the license, and through C-W many American cars may someday run under rotary power.

Nevertheless, the rotary engine is not the cure-all super-engine that rumor and myth have suggested. The engine is small in all areas: outer dimensions, inner displacements, overall weight—and total power. It does not appear that the engine can be made sufficiently large to compete toe-to-toe with the common large-displacement V8 engines normally used in American cars, so the design will be used only in smaller cars, at least for the near future. Furthermore, advertising has been ambiguous on the point of emissions. The rotary is really rather an inefficient engine. The good emission level of the Mazda results from a highly advanced exhaust reactor which burns the remaining gases before they enter the atmosphere. This reactor is heavy, and without it the engine would have a serious emission problem, as well as much more power.

One of the problems of a rotary design is cooling, a problem aggravated by emission-control requirements. Some of the first Mazda engines had a very unbalanced cooling structure (core casting for water flow); one side of the engine, the combustion side, was very hot while the other side was cool. This caused some interesting problems with construction-material expansion rates. Changes in the design have eliminated most of the heat problems.

The rotary is an extremely smooth engine, almost unbelievably so, but it does require the mechanic to keep all working tolerances within factory specifications. As an example, there is very little room between the side of the rotor and the rotor housing. When more than two rotors are stacked in line to add displacement, these tolerances are also stacked. If there is too much clearance, performance is lost; if there is not enough clearance, heat builds up. While workable rotaries do exist, and will indeed be in some American cars during the 1970s, there is still much design improvement to be done.

HOW THE ROTARY WORKS

Because we are so accustomed to working with the traditional reciprocating engine, it is rather difficult at first to understand exactly how the rotary engine works. Take a good look at the drawings and photographs of the rotary and keep one thing firmly fixed in your mind: that little round gear in the middle of the rotor area does not move! This is important to understand. The larger gear rotates about the stationary central gear in a kind of figure-8 path, and behind the large gear there is a large-diameter sleeve bearing in the rotor housing. This bearing rides directly on a crankshaft journal, so that the figure-8 circular motion (which is somewhat like the up-and-down motion of a traditional engine-piston/connecting-rod assembly) becomes pure circular motion.

But on initial inspection, it doesn't seem possible to rotate a three-cornered object (the rotor) inside a "pinched" circle (the correct term would be epitrochoidal curve). And this is where some very clever engineering begins to show up. From a geometrical viewpoint, the rotary engine is composed of a combination of an epitrochoidal curve and its inner envelope. The pinched-waist oval-shaped curve of the rotor housing inner surface is the epitrochoidal curve, and the curve forming the base of the triangular rotor is the inner envelope of the epitrochoidal curve. With this kind of beginning, the engineer can figure that when the central stationary gear is exactly the perfect size in relationship to the large inner rotor gear, and the rotor shape includes flexible tips that can account for slight changes in clearance, the rotor will clear the housing at critical points. All that remains is to get the various chambers the correct size for compression, combustion, exhaust, and intake.

As the triangular rotor turns inside the housing, the chamber volumes vary. This is because the rotor is not rotating about a fixed center point. When the rotor is in one position during the intake cycle, there is a large volume on one of the rotor sides. (It is important to remember that there are three sides to the rotor, and that each side is a separate "cylinder" which will have all the four internal-combustion cycles during one crankshaft rotation.) As the rotor turns, the volume of incoming charge is squeezed down because the rotor face comes closer to the housing wall. At just

Cutaway display Mazda rotary Wankel engine seems much more complicated than traditional engine at first, until one realizes that must of the housing is consumed with mounting the necessary accessories. The

basic rotary engine has very few moving parts. New Mazda engines are being designed with a single distributor to replace the two shown on this display.

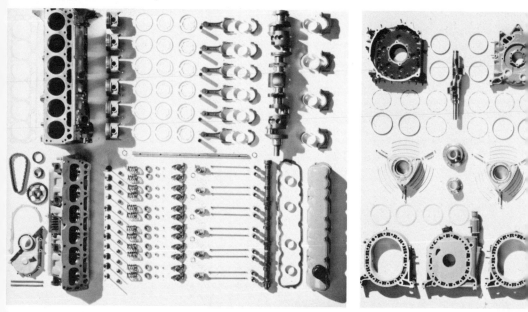

All the parts of a typical six cylinder traditional engine are shown, versus those parts that make up the basic Mazda rotary. The Mazda engine has only 70 basic parts,

of which only 3 are moving. The rotary is scheduled to be introduced in GM cars during the mid-1970s.

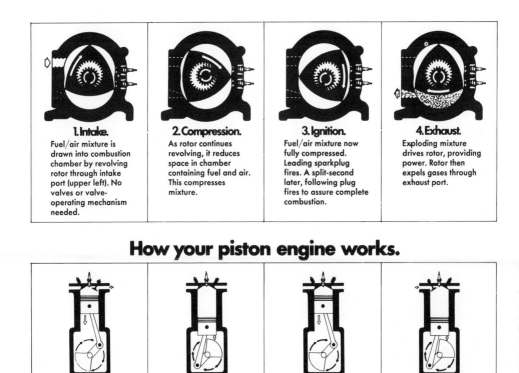

1. Intake.
Fuel/air mixture is drawn into combustion chamber by revolving rotor through intake port (upper left). No valves or valve-operating mechanism needed.

2. Compression.
As rotor continues revolving, it reduces space in chamber containing fuel and air. This compresses mixture.

3. Ignition.
Fuel/air mixture now fully compressed. Leading sparkplug fires. A split-second later, following plug fires to assure complete combustion.

4. Exhaust.
Exploding mixture drives rotor, providing power. Rotor then expels gases through exhaust port.

How your piston engine works.

1. Intake.

2. Compression.

3. Ignition.

4. Exhaust.

The key to the rotary engine operation is a triangular shaped rotor that revolves inside a chamber that looks like an oval which has been pinched at the sides (technically, called an epitrochoid). As each of the rotor's three sides make a complete sweep of the chamber, it performs the same four "strokes" that a piston does in a conventional engine—intake, compression, power, and exhaust. There are no valves; as one rotor tip passes an open intake or exhaust port in the chamber wall, fuel and air enter or burned gases escape.

The gap between the side of the rotor and the chamber wall increases as the rotor continues to turn. When the next tip passes the port, the fuel-air charge trapped between the leading rotor side and the chamber wall is compressed to above one-ninth its original volume. When fully compressed, the rotor side is next to the spark plugs, which fire to ignite the mixture. As the gases expand, the rotor is driven along its path. When the leading rotor tip passes another port, exhaust gases escape.

Through mechanical techniques of gearing and camming, a shaft running through the center of the rotor turns smoothly three times during one complete revolution of the rotor. This shaft transmits power to the transmission the same as a conventional engine.

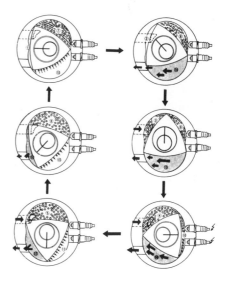

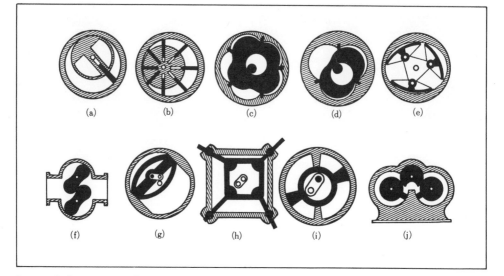

Some of the many and varied types of rotary engines and pumps that have been used since the idea was first tried many decades ago. The twin rotor design in (f) is still in common use in supercharger design on GM diesel engines.

the right time a spark plug fires the mixture. The Mazda uses two spark plugs, one called a leading plug and the other a trailing plug. In this way the maximum amount of mixture can be ignited.

The rotor movement on the stationary central gear causes this initial compression/combustion chamber to continue to decrease in size, but there is another chamber just beginning to open. Again, because of the rotor position on the central gear, force of the combustion spins the rotor into its third "chamber," which is the exhaust. As the rotor tip continues to turn, it decreases the volume in this final chamber and forces all exhaust out through a port opening. There are no intake or exhaust valves in the rotary, and in this respect the engine is very similar to the two-cycle engine.

This similarity to the two-stroke engine is possible because the flexible rotor tips are in constant seal with the housing wall, which also stops any bleed-through

between the three revolving chambers. Because all sides of the rotor are in some phase of the power cycle at the same time, the engine is smooth as silk. The crankshaft makes three revolutions as the rotor makes one, so if the rotor is turning 2000 rpm, the crankshaft is turning 6000 rpm, a kind of built-in overdrive that saves wear on the rotor.

The rest of the rotary, as currently used in most Wankel applications, is like conventional engines. There is an oiling system, a cooling system, an ignition unit, and carburetion. In the case of Mazda, a rather large muffler/reactor (which weighs about 80 pounds) is used, but rumor has it that improved versions of the engine have been built that do not require this type of exhaust-emission control.

REPAIRING A ROTARY

It would seem, then, that normal owner repair and maintenance of the

144

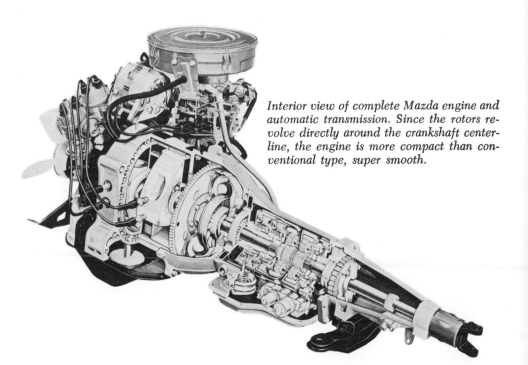

Interior view of complete Mazda engine and automatic transmission. Since the rotors revolve directly around the crankshaft centerline, the engine is more compact than conventional type, super smooth.

Intake system is mounted on the right (passenger) side of the engine; ignition takes place on the left side. Early problems with rotary engines were caused by differences in temperature—left side was very hot all the time and right side was very cold, leading to different rates of metal expansion and consequent sealing problems.

engine would be little different from any current car. Indeed such is the case. Furthermore, because there are so few moving parts in such a basically simple engine design, complete engine teardown and reassembly is considerably less complicated to work on than with the traditional designs.

Before you attempt any work on a rotary, however, it is absolutely imperative that you get a service manual from the new car dealership. This will be vital to all phases of tune-up, but it is especially necessary when doing any internal engine work. The only problems to expect from the inside of a rotary engine will be rotor/gear/crankshaft/housing failure, and this has not proved to be a great problem so far. Overheating may cause housing deformation or rotor-tip (blade) failure. There is no real repair for this problem; repair is a matter of parts replacement.

When a rotary engine fails, chances are a bad seal in either rotor or housing is to blame. Housings are made of alloy; the sealing surfaces must be parallel to each other within very small tolerance, shown being measured here with micrometer.

Each hole that shows here has a long bolt running through it to hold the cylinder block "sandwich" package together, and there is a small O-ring seal necessary at every hole.

Engineering experiments have been carried on in Mazda rotary to find best way to control housing metal expansion, which will in turn control seal failures and chamber shapes. Pin points to methods of letting some areas around chamber "float" and thus be less susceptible to total housing expansion. Water flows through the dark openings between bolt bosses for cooling.

Special seals fit inside and outside diameter of the housing. There have been continued improvements in sealing effectiveness of Mazda engines.

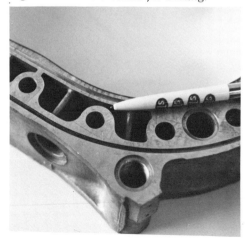

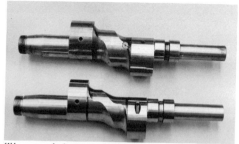

The crankshaft is designed much like a conventional engine camshaft; moving face inside rotor gearing rubs on the lobes and causes the crank to spin. The upper crankshaft is from a later model Mazda engine as compared to earlier, smaller crank. Increase in lobe (journal) size was done to improve load carrying area.

The rotor also uses seals to seal it inside the chamber, including the three tip seals and side housing seals. This latter area is being checked with a mike to discover any major change from required width.

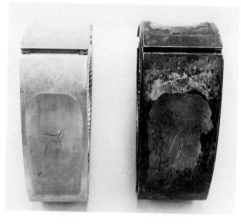

New, clean rotor at left as compared to a rotor just removed from engine. The only way to increase displacement in rotary engine is to increase the volume of the rotors, which can be done by adding a rotor, increasing the rotor diameter, or increasing the rotor width. Note how much wider the used rotor is than the older, small-displacement style.

One of the real problems with rotary engine design has been rotor tip control. Mazda uses three wiper type tips that should be carefully checked for size during any overhaul.

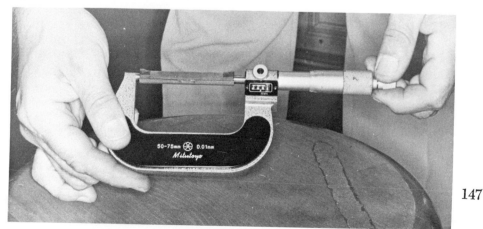

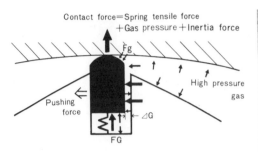

Contact force=Spring tensile force
+Gas pressure+Inertia force

High pressure gas

Pushing force

The rotor tips are so designed that a small spring holds them in constant contact with the chamber wall, and centrifugal force will also assist. But some of the combustion gases are allowed to leak along the tip wall and underneath it, to further ensure a seal.

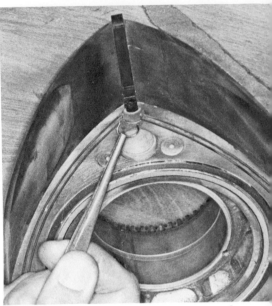

The parts may be small, but they are vital, as shown by this circle clip that serves to locate the end seal and tip.

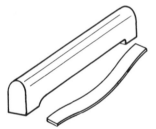

The rotor tip and spring. If there is any doubt as to condition, replace both items.

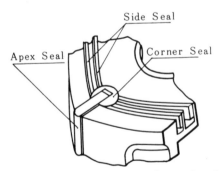

Side Seal

Corner Seal

Apex Seal

Because the secret to a revolving chamber is good sealing, the Mazda rotary has received an unusual amount of engineering effort in this direction.

When the rotary performance is increased for any reason, the tip side and bottom shape is redesigned to allow extra combustion gas to enter for better sealing.

148

To hold all three tips in place while rotor is assembled in housing, a couple of rubber compression bands are wrapped around the unit.

The rotors are marked as to rotation direction only as a matter of convenience. Two inner seals and two outer seals keep combustion gases from entering gear train.

The rotary is assembled in the "build-up" fashion of a racing engine, everything starting at the crank and working outward.

As mentioned earlier, the rotor works in a tremendously restricted area, as far as working clearances are concerned, so sealing the various parts has been a major headache for all engineers. Mazda engines use O-rings to seal the various pieces of the engine "sandwich," and in some of the earlier engines these rings did give trouble. Again, they are a matter of remove-and-replace.

If an engine is disassembled—and this job is definitely not beyond the scope of a home mechanic with some small bit of experience and confidence—reassembly must follow factory directions to the letter. This is especially important when it comes to torquing all bolts and nuts. If the specified torque ratings are not followed, the engine "sandwich" can be distorted, which can cause binding of the rotors and/or defective seal of the O-rings. As a general rule, there will be no need to retighten these tension bolts on a new engine, or even after an engine has been rebuilt. The initial torque should be enough to hold the five housing pieces together. No gaskets are used between the housings.

Because the rotary engine is so different from the traditional engine, I have included an extra number of illustrations to show operation and repair of the basic assembly. Repair and maintenance of the external systems, such as the electrical system, carburetion, and so on, is essentially the same as with conventional engines and is covered elsewhere in this book. Repair and maintenance of the Mazda pollution-control devices are specialized procedures which should not be attempted without a factory service manual.

End plate facing is checked here with a dial indicator, which is the best way to check for warpage.

Face of end plates can wear, and the smallest bit of warpage can make the engine lose performance and fail early.

A feeler gauge and straightedge can also be used to check the end plates for warpage.

Final crankshaft support and seal plate is bolted to housing.

End plates sandwiched between and on either side of rotor housings complete the basic "cylinder block." Dowels are used for alignment; long bolts pass through entire assembly to squeeze it together. Because clearance at all points is critical, it is imperative that all bolts be given exact factory torque.

One of the balance factors to work with entire engine rotating mass is small amount of crankshaft deflection that can be caused by accessory drive chain. This is not normally a problem for an overhaul, however.

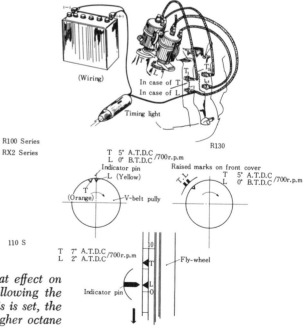

As the initial timing has a great effect on the engine, it should be set following the procedure shown here. Once this is set, the timing need not be reset for higher octane gasoline.

152

Distributors look much like those of any engine using a single set of points, and they are adjusted in traditional manner.

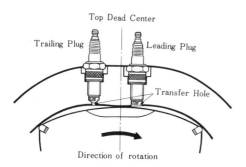

The leading spark plug starts the gas mixture burning; the trailing plug fires to ensure the most complete combustion possible.

Mazda induction system looks like something from an ordinary four cylinder engine, but note difference in two outer and two inner port sizes. By using two intake ports to each rotor chamber, maximum air flow is generated giving better performance.

The Mazda carburetion is much like any car's, but it is essential to follow factory specifications exactly on rebuild to get performance, emission levels correct.

Oiling schematic of the Mazda rotary. Note that a small amount of oil is available at the carburetor, where it enters the fuel-air mixture and thus serves to help lubricate the seals in the chambers.

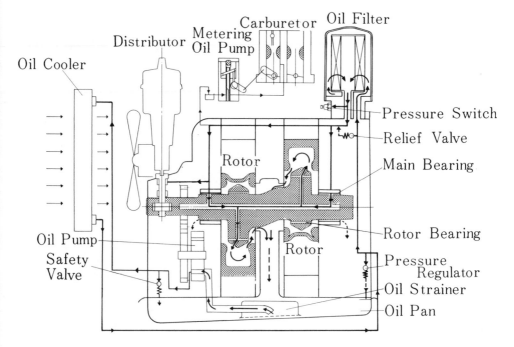

Mazda has developed a three-speed automatic transmission (full cutaway) as well as the standard type transmission shown in drawing.

The exhaust "header" as it might be called is rather bulky and quite heavy, but there are no parts to wear out or chemicals involved.

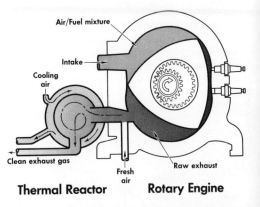

Thermal Reactor   **Rotary Engine**

Essentially, the Mazda reactor works by mixing raw exhaust gases with fresh air, causing a total burn of any remaining combustibles, and the reactor is where toxic hydrocarbons and carbon monoxide pollutants are oxidized to form water vapor and carbon dioxide.

And it all comes out here at the rear of the reactor. Small holes pass air flow, and the result is a twin exhaust pipe system.

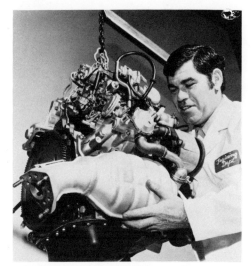

The big secret to Mazda's success in meeting stringent U.S. emission control standards is the thermal reactor exhaust system. A refined version helps the engine meet rough 1975 standards.

155

Because the rotary engine is a form of "two-stroke" engine, it is susceptible to intake port "timing"; thus any change in port shape or location relative to the rotor tip can modify performance highly. Racing Mazda engines have the intake ports enlarged significantly.

The engine is as susceptible to supercharging as any normally aspirated conventional engine. Here a Paxton supercharger has been installed, and the result in terms of usable road horsepower is significant. It is possible that more usable horsepower without emission problems will be available through supercharging than in any other way.

Improved carburetion is used on high performance racing Mazda engines also, including the popular Italian Weber and Japanese Hitachi carburetors.

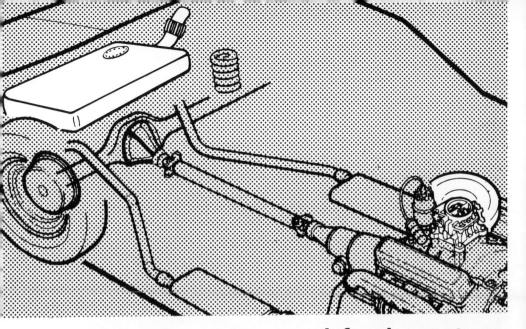

7 carburetor and fuel system

FUEL, in the correct mixture, is essential if any internal-combustion engine is to run properly (see Chapter 5). In the beginning of the automotive era, the engine itself was an extremely simple mechanism, and therefore sophisticated fuel systems were unnecessary. But the modern car places such extreme demands on the fuel system that engineers pour hundreds of thousands of hours into a tiny improvement a driver may never even notice. Any time you work on the fuel system, from gas tank to carburetor, you must consider the entire fuel-delivery system as a whole.

Since the greatest part of almost any automotive repair bill is labor costs, it stands to reason that any work you can do at home on the fuel system will save you hundreds of dollars in the long run. For instance, it isn't uncommon to have foreign material of some kind lodge in the fuel system and starve the engine of gasoline. Many times the amateur

mechanic will automatically assume the problem is in the carburetor, when in reality the carburetor is perhaps the last place to look when gasoline delivery problems are experienced. Perhaps water or dirt has accumulated in the gas tank to such a degree that gas delivery is restricted, sometimes intermittently so that the engine runs erratically for no obvious reason. Perhaps an in-line fuel filter that has become plugged is starving the engine for fuel. The home mechanic can do practically any maintenance, and even some repairs, to the fuel system of any car, antique, classic, or modern.

GAS TANK

The fuel system starts with where you store the gas—the tank. Unfortunately, the gasoline tank is perhaps the most ignored part of any automobile, simply because it isn't a mechanical contraption likely to wear out. Besides, it seems inaccessible. Yet the gas tank has been in for its fair share of engineering improvements over the years. Car builders once put drain plugs in the bottom of tanks, placed there so the owners could unscrew the plugs periodically and drain any foreign matter. In days past, water was not an uncommon partner to gasoline, and this was a quick way of getting it out of the system. Sediment bowls on fuel pumps had the double capacity of cleaning dirt and rust from the gas, as well as water, so by the time a carburetor got the gas, it was nearly water-free. But every few months the shade-tree mechanic would pull the simple carburetor top and soak up water residue from the float bowl. There isn't as much trouble from water in gasoline now, but the fuel system is considerably more complex.

The very new cars are equipped with a fuel-vapor-control system that is designed to keep gasoline vapors from entering the atmosphere, which means that essentially the gasoline operates in a sealed system. Cars of five or ten years ago had a vented-to-atmosphere system. Originally, the manufacturer used a vented gas-tank cap, which would allow atmospheric pressure to equalize pressure in the tank but exclude most foreign material. The problem with this type of cap was sealing when the car was parked on a grade. Gasoline would slosh out through the cap vent. If this vent became plugged, as it was prone to do, the car would finally quit running, because the fuel pump could not operate without atmospheric pressure in the tank. Someone would invariably open the gas tank to see if there really was fuel in there, and as if by magic the car would start and run for a way, until too great a vacuum built up again in the tank.

Until recently, cars have been equipped with a vent in the tank filler pipe, located just below the cap fitting. Here a piece of tubing or rubber hose is looped higher than the tank, so there is no spillage on hills, and nonvented cap can be used for a perfect seal. Other manufacturers used a cap that would let air enter the tank, but not escape. This was called an antisurge cap, and when the sun heats gasoline, the extra pressure is trapped in the tank and serves to push the gas along to the fuel pump, helping prevent vapor lock.

In most gas tanks, the fuel-delivery tube exits at the top side of the tank. The open end of this tube does not touch the tank bottom, where it might pick up debris, and in some cases the tube end has a small brass-wire screen. Keep this screen in mind, for on occasion it is the culprit in a clogged system. If you get this far in the search for a plugged line, you'll note that the pickup tube is secured by a twist-on cap, which is not hard to remove. Do not pry on the tubing, as it is rather fragile. If you should damage the tank or tubing, ordinary rosin-core solder should be used for repairs.

Rust is a common ailment in many gas tanks, usually as the result of water. While water in gas is no longer common, it is possible to pick up a good load of it from a gas station that does not keep the large underground storage tanks clean. Such dirty storage tanks can also be a source of dirt and rust scale. However, if the foreign matter has gotten into the tank, you'll want to get it out.

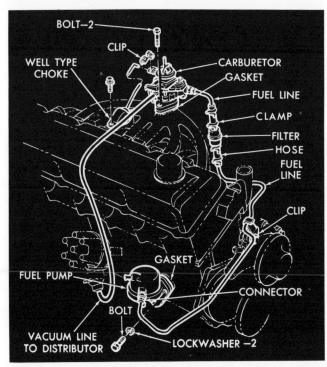

Fuel system at the engine (a Chrysler slant six).

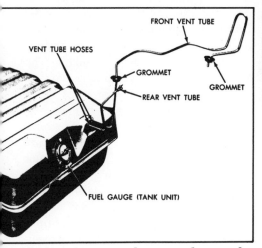

Fuel tanks on modern cars have rather sophisticated vent tubes and overflow return lines; care must be exercised not to damage these lines when tank is being removed from chassis for repair or cleaning.

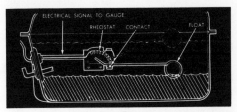

Fuel tank sending unit for the gas gauge may be mounted anywhere on the tank, and can usually be removed for repair or replacement if necessary.

Fuel tank filler necks attach to the tank by various methods; two attachments are shown here. As a rule, the neck must be separated from the main tank if the tank is being removed from the car. It is important that the neck be secured during reassembly so there will be no leakage of gas.

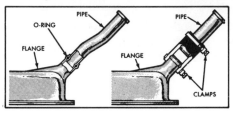

Taking Out the Tank

Most modern gasoline tanks are held to the body or frame by two metal straps. Before these straps are loosened, drain the tank by siphoning or by loosening the fuel line near the fuel pump. Don't reuse this gasoline. The filler neck may have some kind of flexible connection to the tank, which should be loosened, and the new vapor-control lines should be disconnected, as well as the gas-gauge wire. Loosen the tank straps and drop the tank.

It is possible to clean the tank at home by filling it with about two gallons of cleaning solvent and several large ball bearings or hard pebbles. Slosh the solvent around in the tank, and the bearings or pebbles will knock whatever rust scale is built up loose and it can be flushed. Better by far, however, is letting the local radiator shop boil the tank in a caustic solution overnight. This is very inexpensive, and really gets the job done.

Should there be a hole in the tank that needs repair, proceed with caution. If the tank has been boiled, it can be welded on. But if the tank has not been boiled, you should never weld or solder on it unless the tank has been almost completely filled with water. There are alternatives, but this is the best for an amateur. Incidentally, it is wise to carry a small bar of soap in the glove compartment for emergency repairs to the fuel system. Should you be out in the boondocks and knock a hole in the tank, quickly park the car so the gasoline doesn't come through the hole. This saves whatever gas remains, and allows you to patch the tank with soap. That's right, ordinary hand soap. Soak the soap bar in water until you have a soft paste. Rub this on the tank split,

where it will harden. You can make it back to civilization for more formal repairs. At one time, hardware stores sold a type of glue for repairing gas-tank breaks, and you can still occasionally find this in country hardware stores. It will last indefinitely.

One last word on water in the tank. Water will plug up the fiberglass filter used on the pickup tube in some late-model cars. If you think there is water in the tank, but aren't sure, you can buy a gas additive at the parts store which will soak up the water and move it through the carburetor. Ordinary wood alcohol does the same job.

FUEL LINE

About the only problem the main fuel line will give is from clogging caused by dirt or rust. However, it is possible for the line routing to be a problem. If the line passes too close to the exhaust pipe, for instance, the gas may overheat before reaching the fuel pump. If the line rubs against the frame or a sharp metal edge, it can chafe a pinhole. This kind of problem would usually show up only on a car at least four years old.

Gas lines may be steel tubing, neoprene hose, or flexible line. Flex line has not been used much in recent years, but if you still have one always assume it is bad. The flex line can look perfectly good, yet it can have a small hole that allows air into the system. This in turn robs the pump of a full fuel supply, resulting in fuel starvation at the carburetor. The effect, if you check the fuel delivery, is not unlike that caused by a bad pump.

It is possible for steel fuel line to crack, particularly in the flanged area where the end fittings are used. Should you have a stubborn problem of air getting into the system, check these flanged ends and use rosin-core solder as a repair. Solder can also be used to repair a split elsewhere in steel line.

Fuel-line fittings are seldom a problem, although the single wire clamps common to most all new cars will perhaps lose their tension once removed. Should this happen, you can replace them with a screw-type clamp. A note on fittings and tools: It is wise always to use a wrench of the correct size when working on a fitting, rather than a pair of pliers or an adjustable wrench. Fittings are usually of brass and can be chewed up unless the wrench fits perfectly. Vise-grip wrenches can distort the fitting as well as chew it up and should never be used.

FUEL FILTER

Fuel filters can be a source of sore trials to the amateur and professional mechanic alike. A filter may appear all right, and it may test acceptably, and yet it may not be working at all. When an in-line fuel filter finally clogs, it is almost impossible to pass gas through the unit, even enough for the engine to idle. The most obvious test is to blow through the filter; if it seems to restrict the air flow, it is probably clogged.

Filters may be built into the fuel pump, they may be in the fuel line between pump and carburetor, they may be attached to the carburetor, and most carburetors have a final fuel screen as a part of the needle valve/seat arrangement. Obviously, such a fuel filter is important. Some filters have an element that can be cleaned, made of ceramic or metal screening, while others use paper or fiberglass elements that can be

replaced. When cleaning a filter, make sure the solvent can run through it freely, and blow through the screen element to make sure it is not clogged internally. If there is any doubt at all about the filter condition, replace it. The cost is small. It is wise to replace the bronze filter element at the needle valve/seat point any time the carburetor is worked on, or any time the fuel system is cleaned. This particular element never seems to blow as clean as it should, and even a small bit of restriction at this point is too much.

Some in-line filters are made for air-conditioned cars and have a bleed hole that bleeds fuel back to the gas tank. This is done to help control vapor lock. When the fuel in a pump or line between pump and carburetor is heated, it can vaporize. This vapor will pass into the carburetor all right, but then it escapes through the carburetor bowl vent, and thus the carburetor is starved for gasoline. By letting this vapor escape back to tank before it reaches the carburetor, vapor lock is alleviated slightly. In the case of air-conditioned cars, where heat is likely to be a bit higher, this little bit is helpful.

FUEL PUMP

There are only two kinds of fuel pumps to consider, electric and mechanical. The mechanical pump is perhaps the most common on American-built cars, and the electric pump is common on many imported cars and on American-built trucks. Originally, the mechanical pump could be disassembled for repair—usually a problem arising from a fractured diaphragm. The mechanical pump is driven by an eccentric on the engine camshaft. Sometimes the pump lever rides directly on this cam lobe, as with many in-line engines, or there may be an actuating rod between lobe and lever, as with V8 engines. As the pump lever moves up and down, it works a diaphragm. This diaphragm sucks gasoline from the gas tank and pushes it up the short fuel line to the carburetor. If there is a fracture in the diaphragm, the pump loses efficiency.

Mechanical Pumps

Older mechanical fuel pumps could be disassembled and repaired. There was a row of small screws around the pump circumference, and the diaphragm was sandwiched between upper and lower portions of the pump body. A repair kit consisted of a new diaphragm, and perhaps a valve or two and related springs. New cars do not use repairable mechanical pumps; the body halves are crimped together. When a pump goes bad, you buy a replacement. But they're not expensive.

To check a fuel pump, either electric or mechanical, start first by checking what kind of fuel "head" you have at the carburetor inlet. Remove the fuel line. To get a really accurate reading of the fuel delivery, you need some kind of pressure gauge that reads in increments of pounds. Fuel pressure at this point should be anywhere between 1½ and 6 psi at idle, the variance depending upon the displacement of the engine and cfm (cubic feet per minute) flow of the carburetor. The larger and more powerful the engine, the larger will be the carburetor cfm requirements, and consequently the higher the pressure needed from the fuel pump. You'll need to find out what the particular pump pressure for your engine should be.

If you have a pressure gauge, which is available from any parts store and is inexpensive, hold it securely against the fuel line and have someone spin the engine (on the starter, with coil wire removed to prevent the engine from starting) several times. If you are getting a good pressure head, fuel problems will be either the carburetor or a plugged vent on the gas tank. Some older pumps would hold the line pressure, but the bleed-off characteristics of newer pumps negate any pressure retention. This lack of pressure in the fuel line when the engine isn't running is a benefit, as the carburetor float and needle valve need not work against the pressure, and the pressure cannot overcome the needle valve and flood the static engine.

If you don't have a pressure gauge, hold your finger tightly over the fuel line (have some kind of can handy to catch the gas) and spin the engine. If you can't possibly hold back the pressure, chances are good the pump is OK. Check fuel flow into the gas catch-can at this time also. You might have good pressure, but have a restriction in the fuel line that limits fuel flow—a flattened line, a collapsing hose, etc. If you do find an indication of poor pump pressure or fuel-flow restriction, suspect the in-line fuel filter first. Clean or replace the filter, and pump pressure should return to normal.

If you must remove a mechanical pump, first remove the inlet and exit fuel lines. Two bolts hold the pump to the engine block. These are invariably in cramped quarters, so you'll probably need a ratchet and socket, and you may need to remove the pump from below the car. As the pump comes loose you'll notice it seems to bind on something slightly. This is the lever pressure against the cam lobe (there is a small compression spring on the lever). Never reuse the old fuel pump gasket unless abso-

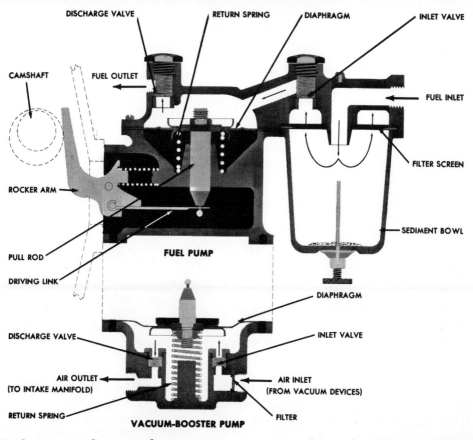

DISCHARGE VALVE   RETURN SPRING   DIAPHRAGM   INLET VALVE

CAMSHAFT   FUEL OUTLET

FUEL INLET

ROCKER ARM

FILTER SCREEN

SEDIMENT BOWL

PULL ROD

FUEL PUMP

DRIVING LINK

DIAPHRAGM

DISCHARGE VALVE

INLET VALVE

AIR OUTLET
(TO INTAKE MANIFOLD)

AIR INLET
(FROM VACUUM DEVICES)

RETURN SPRING

FILTER

VACUUM-BOOSTER PUMP

Fuel pump and vacuum-booster pump. The pumps are separated here for clarity, but in actual practice are combined into one unit, with a single rocker arm actuating the pull rod of each. (Mobil Oil Corp.)

lutely necessary, and in that case always coat the gasket liberally with some form of gasket cement. The lever chamber of a mechanical fuel pump is usually open directly to the engine crankcase. Pressure inside the crankcase can blow oil past a poor gasket.

When you replace the fuel pump, you'll have to overcome the lever-spring pressure as you align the bolt holes. Also make sure any actuating rod between camshaft and pump lever is in position. On some V8 engines, this rod will slip downward when the pump is removed. It can be slid upward again with a screwdriver and the lever slipped below. Should you have trouble getting the rod back in place, most V8s have an access plug in the engine block in line with the rod. Torque the pump bolts, as there is continual pressure on the case and a slightly loose bolt will work itself free.

Electric Pumps

An electric fuel pump works differently from the mechanical pump in that it pushes the fuel rather than pulls it to the carburetor. It is in operation whenever the ignition switch is on, which means it has a constant fuel-pressure head whether the engine is running or not.

Because the electric pump pushes fuel, it is located as near the gas tank as possible, and as low as possible in relation to the tank contents. The internal components of the electric pump are similar to those of the mechanical pump, with a diaphragm or cylinder plunger to move the gas along. About the only home repairs that can be accomplished with this type of pump, other than replacement, is cleaning and gapping of the points. Electric points are used to operate the pump, and will sometimes corrode and close. If you don't hear the fuel pump clicking when the ignition is turned on, chances are the points are at fault.

CARBURETOR

Carburetors usually do not cause the engine to fail suddenly. Instead, the carburetor problem will be almost unnoticeable; the engine performance will drop off ever so gradually, acceleration will suffer, mileage will decrease slowly, and so on. Generally you can expect to get between 30,000 and 50,000 miles between carburetor overhauls on the modern car. Even then, it is usually not a matter of carburetor parts wearing out (the wear points would be throttle shafts, accelerator pumps, etc.), but more of foreign material in the carburetor air/fuel-mixing galleries. To help eliminate wear from the few points that do exist, use a white high-temperature grease at all metal-to-metal contact points. This will also eliminate binding in the throttle operation (see Chapter 15).

From the standpoint of wear, the accelerating pump is the most troublesome. This is a kind of plunger that throws a charge of raw fuel into the carburetor throat when the throttle butterflies are opened. The fuel keeps the engine from running lean at this point in transition between idle and high-speed jetting. If the accelerater pump is worn, you'll notice a definite flat spot in engine acceleration when you step down on the throttle. Of course, this isn't the only thing that can cause such a flat spot, but it is the most common.

Carburetor Blockage

If you have trouble with the carburetor the chances are good that it is caused either by foreign matter reaching the carburetor through the air or through the fuel, or by a reaction between the air and the fuel.

Anyone can be a shadetree mechanic when it comes to overhauling and adjusting a carburetor, no matter how complicated the unit may seem. No special tools are normally required, and the job can be done in a matter of minutes. It is best to secure a carburetor overhaul kit before taking the carburetor apart; also have a gallon of carburetor cleaner handy to soak the parts during internal cleaning phase.

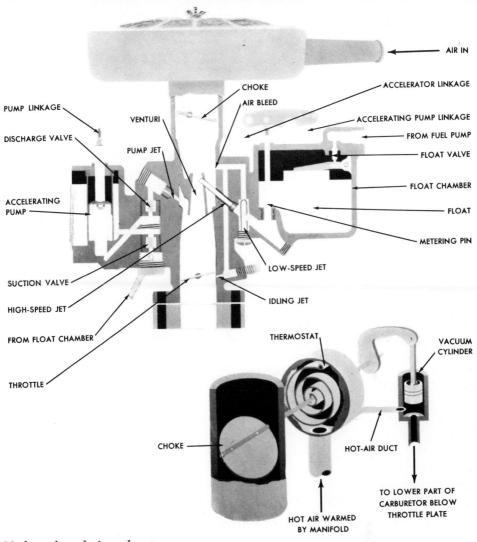

Modern downdraft carburetor.

The dirt or foreign matter may be rust particles that sluff off the sides of the gas tank or dust in the air that is inside the tank. When the dirt is carried up to the carburetor by the fuel, it means trouble. Airborne dirt gets lodged in the air bleeds and passages, upsetting the balance between air and fuel.

Even if you had a perfectly clean atmosphere for the engine to operate in, with hygienically clean gasoline and a scrubbed fuel system, you would still have a dirty carburetor in time because of the way gasoline evaporates. Unfortunately, not all the substances that make up gasoline will readily pass into the air. The heavier fractions of gasoline turn to a kind of gooey mess which eventually hardens into a material that is about the same as a good brand of varnish.

Dirt is the primary enemy of the carburetor. A good tune-up consists

mostly of disassembly, cleaning, and reassembly, without making any adjustments at all. This is true even when replacing parts, such as accelerating pumps
and needle seats. The old and the new
parts go back into the same positions,
so that all you have to do is make careful checks of specifications.

How Carburetors Work

Trying to correct malfunctions can
take a lot of time if you don't know what
you're doing. You could spend days taking a carburetor apart, putting it back
together, running the car, and then going back through the same procedure
all over again, simply because when you
get the carburetor apart you don't know
what to look for.

Other malfunctions cannot be seen,
but once you know how a carburetor
works all you have to do is stop, look,
and listen, because that carburetor is

*Carburetor sizes are determined by CFM,
which means cubic feet per minute of air
flow; thus a large displacement engine will
need more CFM for a specific maximum
rpm than will a small displacement engine.
It is common practice to get economy by
restricting size of carburetion placed on an
engine, but this in turn restricts the performance. Current generation of carburetors
are far superior to older designs in ability
to carefully meter fuel/air mixture to
cylinders.*

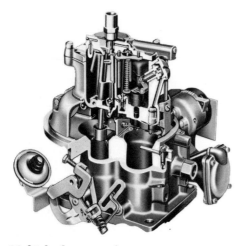

*Multiple-throat carburetion is now very
common on most larger displacement engines, but it was fairly new when this four-
barrel unit was first introduced on 1956
Ford products.*

*The famous Holley three-barrel carburetor,
which uses the large opening as a secondary
when the engine load calls for vastly increased airflow. It is possible to adjust and
tune an engine so that it runs most of the
time on the smaller primaries, which is great
for fuel economy, but the large secondary(s)
can be available in a situation when power
is necessary.*

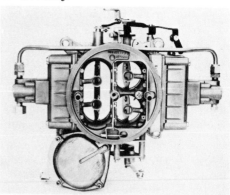

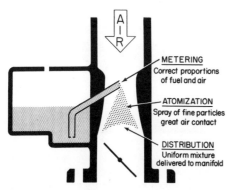

METERING
Correct proportions
of fuel and air

ATOMIZATION
Spray of fine particles
great air contact

DISTRIBUTION
Uniform mixture
delivered to manifold

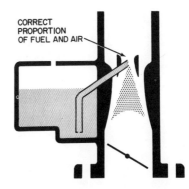

CORRECT
PROPORTION
OF FUEL AND AIR

Purpose of a carburetor is to meter, atomize, and distribute fuel throughout the air entering an engine. These functions are carried out automatically by the carburetor over a wide range of engine rpm, and by controlling the amount of air/fuel mixture which flows on to the engine, the carburetor lets the driver control engine rpm.

Good combustion requires a correct air/fuel ration, or mixture. Too much fuel causes a "rich" condition, too much air causes a "lean" condition. The metering system must maintain the correct ration for all engine load conditions.

trying to tell you something if you have the knowledge to understand it.

Fuel enters the carburetor through the inlet seat and fills the float bowl. The fuel rises in the bowl, lifting the float, which pushes the needle into the seat and regulates the flow of gasoline.

The object is to keep the fuel in the bowl at just the right level. Too much, and the engine will run rich. Too little, and the engine will run lean, maybe even coughing back through the carburetor. Sometimes the coughing-back results in a flame shooting from the air horn.

To adjust the fuel level you bend an arm on the float or bend a little tab that is attached to the arm and pushes on the needle. The "float level" specification is a measurement from some part of the carburetor casting to the float, when the float is resting on a closed needle. If the float is attached to the bowl cover, the measurement is taken between the float and cover, with the cover inverted so that the weight of the float closes the needle.

If the float is attached to the bowl itself, then the measurement is taken from the top of the float to the top edge of the bowl, with the float and needle in the closed position. To get the needle and float into the closed position on this type of float system, you might push the float and needle closed with your finger.

That was okay in the old days when we had steel needles, but now there are Teflon-tipped needles, neoprene-tipped needles, and Teflon or neoprene inlet seats. These needles and seats will last a long time with only the pressure of the float against them, but the pressure of your finger pushing on the needle may be too much and you will end up with a groove in the neoprene. The soft material will slowly come back to shape, eliminating the groove, so that a few hours later the float level has changed from where you set it. If the neoprene or Teflon does not come back to shape, the groove may cause flooding because it provides a place for particles of dirt to lodge.

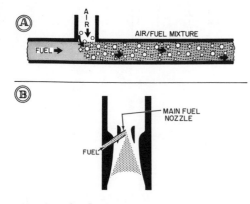

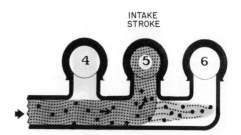

Liquid fuel is broken down into small particles so they will readily vaporize and mix with air. This is accomplished by (A) bleeding air into the fuel in internal carburetor passages and (B) at the main fuel nozzle where high velocity air tears the fuel into a fine spray.

For good combustion, the air and fuel must be thoroughly and uniformly mixed and delivered in the same quantities to each cylinder. A perfect distribution is difficult to achieve, since the liquid particles will try to puddle in the manifold, or continue in a straight line at corners. This is shown here where cylinder 5 on the intake stroke is not getting all the fuel it should. Engineers design manifolds to compensate for these problems.

To get the float and needle into the closed position on a carburetor with the float attached to the bowl, invert the carburetor and take the measurement. With the carburetor on the car the easiest way to do it is to pour some gasoline into the bowl until the float rises to its maximum height, then take the measurement. There is usually a tolerance on float adjustments, and a good mechanic will adjust to one end or the other of the tolerance because he knows a particular carburetor will run best with that setting.

It's important that you don't confuse fuel level and float level. Float level is a measurement from the float to some part of the carburetor bowl or the cover. Fuel level is an actual wet measurement of how far the fuel is from the top of the bowl. If the float needle and seat are attached to the bowl, then the actual fuel level can be measured with a scale. If the float needle and seat are attached to the bowl cover, then the fuel level

cannot be measured in most cases unless the carburetor manufacturer has provided sight holes in the end of the bowl. The fuel-level specification, if given, is really nothing more than a double check to be sure you have set the float level correctly and accurately.

When the engine uses fuel and the float drops, it is possible on some carburetors for the needle to fall out of the seat. If this happens the carburetor receives more gas than it needs. The engine would be flooded, not only on the inside but probably on the outside. To keep that from happening there is a little tab on the back side of the float that limits the drop. The float-drop measurement is taken with the bowl cover off the carburetor and held in the normal position, measuring from the underside of the bowl cover to some part of the float.

If the float is attached to the bowl itself, there usually is no float-drop measurement. The float in that case may be

168

designed so that at maximum drop it rests on the bottom of the bowl.

If by some chance the little tab that limits float drop has become bent, then the float may not drop enough. In this case the needle will not pull away from the seat far enough and we might have fuel starvation at wide-open throttle.

Dirt, as mentioned, is a big enemy of the float system. If it weren't for dirt there probably wouldn't be any need for all the fancy filters that we have on cars nowadays. That needle and seat are so sensitive to dirt that the smallest particle can cause flooding. This is the reason for Teflon and neoprene seats and needles. The theory is that Teflon and neoprene have enough give so that they will conform to the shape of the speck of dirt and seat around it. Sometimes they do, sometimes they don't.

If a particle of foreign matter should cause the needle valve to leak, then enough fuel can be pumped into the engine to kill it, and make restarting almost impossible until the excess fuel evaporates. If you ever see a carburetor that is all beat up around the needle and seat area, it's a good bet that the driver was standing there beating on the carburetor trying to jar a piece of dirt out of the seat so the flooding would stop.

The base of every carburetor is really nothing more than an air valve with throttle plates hung on a shaft controlled by your foot. Wide-open throttle means just that. When you step on the gas you are opening the throttle valve so that the maximum amount of air can enter the engine. But in order for the engine to run, this air has to have gasoline mixed with it in the right proportion. This is done by running a tube from the float bowl to the middle of the air stream where it goes through the car-

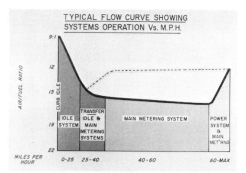

This typical flow curve shows the approximate speeds at which the various carburetor systems may operate. These are only approximate speeds, but if your carburetor is acting up in a certain speed range this indicates which system is acting up.

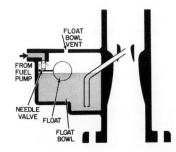

Fuel in the float bowl must be maintained at a specified level for correct metering under all driving conditions. The float opens and introduces additional fuel as the fuel level drops, and shuts off the flow at the needle valve. A carburetor that constantly overflows will have a sticking needle valve.

buretor. The end of the tube, called the main nozzle, is positioned so that it is in the center of the venturi, a narrow section of the air passage in the carburetor. Because this section is narrow, it causes reduced pressure at the end of the tube, and this reduced pressure (or suction) draws fuel from the float bowl, where it mixes with the air, then goes past the throttle valve and on to the combustion chamber. The tube begins in a well at the bottom of the

 169

float bowl called the main well. Fuel enters the main well through a calibrated hole called the main jet, which is located at the bottom of the float bowl so that during all types of engine operation it will always be submerged and able to draw fuel.

The main metering system has had many refinements since the first simple carburetor was made. There may be air bleeds or little baffles in the main nozzle, and there may be vacuum or mechanically operated metering rods in the main jet. The object of all of the refinements is to be sure that the engine receives more fuel when it needs it and less fuel when it doesn't.

Metering rods are designed so that they stay in the main jet when the engine is running at low power. But when the engine is running at maximum power the rods will lift out of the jet so that the engine gets the fuel that it needs. At any point between closed throttle and maximum power, the rods will be partially in or partially out of the jet, according to how much fuel the engine needs at the time.

The main metering system controls the economy range of a carburetor. It consists of a main jet and a main nozzle with air bleeds open to air flow at the head of the venturi area. As the throttle is opened, air velocity through the venturi increases, which decreases the pressure at the main nozzle. Air pressure through the bleeds into the main well pushes extra gas into the nozzle.

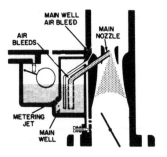

Mechanically operated rods are lifted by a lever hooked to the throttle. Vacuum-operated rods are pushed out of the jet by a spring and pulled down into the jet by engine vacuum acting on a piston hooked to the top of the rod. A passageway from the intake manifold runs up through the carburetor so the engine vacuum can act on the piston.

Without engine vacuum the carburetor wouldn't work. This vacuum exists below the throttle valve when the engine is running, and at idle on a good engine is about 18-21 inches. As the throttle is opened, engine vacuum drops off until there is zero vacuum at wide-open throttle.

It's rare to have a main metering system plug up completely unless it is done deliberately for a test of mechanics, such as at the Plymouth Trouble-Shooting Contest. If the main nozzle is plugged but the main jet still open, the carburetor will idle perfectly, but gasp and die completely the second the throttle is opened.

We have to have an idle system because at idle the throttle valves are almost completely closed and there is not enough flow of air through the venturi to draw fuel out of the main nozzle.

At idle the engine is drawing air around the throttle plate, which is just barely open, but this air has no fuel in it. The fuel is coming through the idle port hole in the throttle body below the throttle plate. An idle-mixture needle screws into the outside of the throttle body and is used to regulate the amount of fuel flowing through the port and into the engine.

Fuel enters the idle system through a tube mounted in the carburetor, usually between the float bowl and the carburetor throat. The end of the tube is a calibrated hole, called the idle jet.

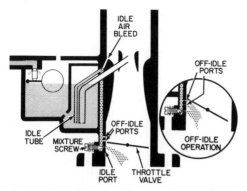

IDLE
AIR
BLEED

OFF-IDLE
PORTS

OFF-IDLE
PORTS

IDLE
TUBE

MIXTURE
SCREW

OFF-IDLE
OPERATION

IDLE
PORT

THROTTLE
VALVE

At engine idle, air flow is low and not enough to meter the fuel properly from the main discharge nozzle. The idle system is provided to pass a regulated amount of fuel to the back side of the throttle butterfly. Just as the butterfly moves off idle, the engine needs extra fuel but the air flow is still not high enough, so extra ports (off-idle) are exposed.

Fuel comes up through this tube, makes a U-turn, picks up some air through air bleed holes, then goes through a long passage to exit underneath the throttle plate. Some idle tubes can be changed merely by unscrewing them, but others are part of the metering cluster and the whole cluster must be changed.

As the throttle is opened, the high vacuum beneath the throttle plates starts to fall off and fuel flow lessens through the idle port. To keep the engine from faltering at this crucial moment, another hole, called the idle transfer, is uncovered which feeds more fuel to keep the engine going. By this time enough air is coming through the venturi so that the main metering system will start to take over. However, in most carburetors the idle system will continue to feed even up to as high as 70 mph.

It's important to keep clear in your mind that the engine idles on air from two sources and fuel from one. Air goes into the engine around the partially opened throttle plate, and a fuel and

air mixture enters through the idle port, controlled by an idle-mixture screw. The screw is spring-loaded, and you control the idle mixture by setting the screw.

Engine idle speed is something else. You control that with a spring-loaded screw on the throttle shaft. When you take your foot off the gas, the throttle will close to the setting you have made with the idle-speed screw. If you have made the wrong setting and the throttle closes too much, the engine will die.

If you open the throttle suddenly on an engine, the air reacts instantly and rushes past the throttle blades, but the fuel coming out the main nozzle takes a little while before it catches up. During this period the engine will run lean and stumble. The problem is solved by using an accelerating pump. It's nothing more than a piston hooked to the throttle linkage and operating in a cylinder so that every time you step on the gas a squirt of fuel goes into the carburetor. The pump only squirts when the throttle is moved. At all other times it does not feed any gas.

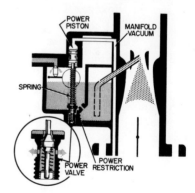

POWER
PISTON

MANIFOLD
VACUUM

SPRING

POWER
VALVE

POWER
RESTRICTION

Maximum engine power requires use of all available air for combustion; to get this a slightly richer mixture is needed, which the power system supplies. A spring loaded power piston in the Rochester carburetor receives a command through a manifold vacuum gallery and opens a power valve.

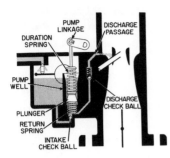

When the throttle is opened rapidly, air flow and manifold vacuum change almost instantly. Because of the difference in weight between air and fuel, any sudden change in throttle opening results in an immediate increase in air intake but not so in fuel weight. A mechanically operated pump forces extra fuel into the airstream when the carburetor must operate in this situation.

The pump system includes an inlet check valve and an outlet check valve so that it can suck fuel into its cylinder from the bowl on the upstroke and then squirt this fuel into the carburetor throat on the downstroke.

Some pumps are not directly operated by the throttle linkage but allowed to operate by the linkage. They have a duration spring that actually pushes the pump down. This is done so that the length of time that the pump is operating is always the same, no matter how fast the driver opens the throttle.

The well known "flat spot" on acceleration is usually caused by something wrong in the accelerating pump. Most of the time it is a pump piston that doesn't fit well in its cylinder, either because the piston is worn out or because it is made of leather and the lip of the leather curled up when the piston was installed. Or it could be maladjusted linkage, so that the pump stroke is too long or too short.

The jet that controls the amount of

squirt on an accelerating pump is usually built into the pump nozzle, mounted above the venturi.

Main metering jets with or without metering rods work fine above idle at almost any cruising speed, but when the engine is really called upon to put out, with the throttle wide open, the main jet just doesn't let enough fuel in. In order to admit more fuel there is another passage into the main well and up into the main nozzle. This passage is closed at all times except when the throttle is opened enough to allow engine vacuum to fall below about ten inches. At that point a spring opens the power valve and additional fuel is allowed to enter the main well and go through the main nozzle and into the venturi.

Power valves can be vacuum-controlled or mechanically controlled. Some Stromberg carburetors have the power valve at the bottom of the accelerating pump cylinder so that when the throttle is open wide and the accelerating pump bottoms, it tips a little plunger that opens the power valve. Other power valves operate off engine vacuum opposed by a spring, and they can be either a piston operating in a cylinder or a diaphragm.

The unfortunate thing about a power valve is that you may not know it is bad until it is too late. If a power valve should fail in the closed position, the engine would not get the fuel it needs at wide-open throttle, and it might even run lean enough to burn a hole in a piston, depending on how long you ran the engine wide open.

Luckily, vacuum-operated power valves are held closed by engine vacuum, and opened by a spring. So if they fail, they usually fail open, allowing a lot of fuel to go into the engine at all speeds above idle, and in some designs even allowing fuel to dribble out onto the top of the engine, which is a handy warning if the driver pays attention to the smell of gasoline.

Chokes

If an engine could be heated up to operating temperature before you started it, you would never need a choke (see Chapter 10). This is one reason why people who live in California with its warm climate can in many cases take the choke off their carburetors and never have any trouble. But if they had to live in the Midwest or in the East through one winter, they would find out just what a choke is for.

A cold engine is just that—so cold that the fuel condenses out of the mixture onto the intake manifold passageways and the walls of the combustion chamber.

The choke system provides a richer mixture for cold engine starting and operation, because fuel vapor has a tendency to condense on cold engine parts, thereby decreasing the amount of mixture available in the cylinder. When the engine is cold, a thermostatic coil holds the choke valve closed. This reduces the air supply and raises the vacuum applied at the fuel outlets, so that more fuel is pulled into the manifold. As the engine warms up, the coil relaxes and opens the choke butterfly.

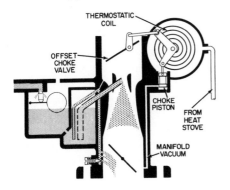

Fuel alone will not burn. It has to be mixed with air. The only way we can get a mixture in a cold engine is to feed more fuel into the engine than we need to make up for the fuel that condenses. The choke is an air valve placed above the main nozzle, so that it can shut off all the air going to the engine. This allows the full force of engine suction to operate on the main nozzle and on the idle ports so the engine gets the excess fuel that it needs.

The problem with chokes is not in making them work but in getting them to shut off at the right time. Automatic chokes are closed by a thermostatic spring and opened by this same spring when heat from the exhaust manifold allows it to relax. However, the spring control alone is not enough. To get a more positive control there is a vacuum piston that opposes the strength of the spring, and the choke valve itself is offset so that the air entering the carburetor tends to push it open. When it all works right we have what is called an automatic choke, instead of the old-fashioned manual choke that the driver had to remember to open himself. When it doesn't work you have a big problem, and the engine will lope and blow black smoke out of the tailpipe.

Sticking chokes have been so much of a problem that now some carburetor manufacturers are coating choke shafts with Teflon. It seems to work, although the adjustment of a choke will probably continue to be a touchy affair.

Nobody should ever open the throttle wide when an engine is cold, but some drivers will. Other drivers will absentmindedly pump the throttle when trying to start the engine, thus flooding it. Both of these mistakes are compensated for by the choke unloader. It's a little

 173

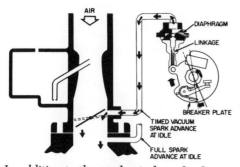

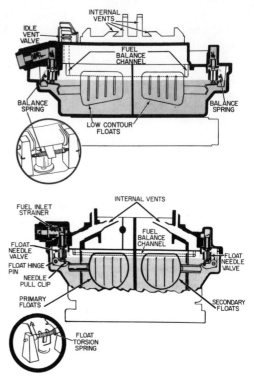

In addition to the mechanical spark advance incorporated within the distributor, vacuum advance is available to advance spark when the engine is under load (throttle suddenly opened). As the throttle varies position from idle to full open, vacuum in the line to the advance mechanism on the distributor will increase or decrease, moving the breaker point plate in direct relationship to vacuum load. Always remove this vacuum line when setting ignition timing in order to get a true reading.

thing that opens the choke enough to clean out the engine when the throttle is pushed to wide-open position.

While the choke is operating the engine can't use the extremely rich mixture unless it is run at a faster-than-normal idle. To accomplish this we have a fast-idle cam and linkage that works in conjunction with the choke to raise the idle speed whenever the choke is operating.

Barrels

All of the systems described so far apply to a carburetor in its simplest form, but we haven't said anything about the number of barrels or throats on the carburetor.

Most engines from one cylinder up to six cylinders have a carburetor with only one throat. In that case there is only one of each carburetor system. Some six-cylinder and some V8 engines come

When there are more than one carburetor bore and venturi, as in most modern automobiles, all the systems previously described are duplicated. For the Rochester 4G and 4GC four-barrel carburetors, these are the types of float system involved.

with a two-throat carburetor. In that case the main metering system and the idle system are duplicated for the second throat.

The float system does not have to be duplicated because the bowl has enough fuel capacity to serve two main jets with ease. The same reasoning applies in the accelerating-pump system. One pump is used, but it has two nozzles, one for each throat.

The power system also stays basically the same as in a one-barrel carb, except that it feeds two main metering

174

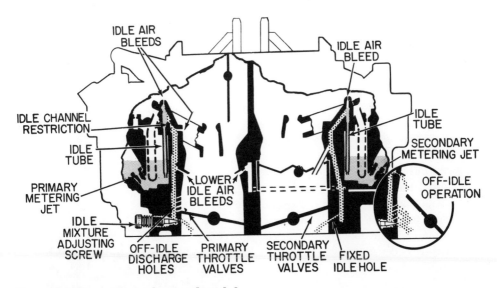

Idle System Labels:
- IDLE AIR BLEEDS
- IDLE AIR BLEED
- IDLE CHANNEL RESTRICTION
- IDLE TUBE
- PRIMARY METERING JET
- IDLE MIXTURE ADJUSTING SCREW
- LOWER IDLE AIR BLEEDS
- OFF-IDLE DISCHARGE HOLES
- PRIMARY THROTTLE VALVES
- SECONDARY THROTTLE VALVES
- FIXED IDLE HOLE
- IDLE TUBE
- SECONDARY METERING JET
- OFF-IDLE OPERATION

Trace the idle system in this four-barrel design and note how it works the same as a basic single-throat carburetor does. When the carburetor is being rebuilt, instructions that come with the rebuilding kit give all measurements needed and identify where the various parts go. Still, it is advisable to be thoroughly familiar with all the parts and where they came from as carb is disassembled.

systems instead of one. In the choke department there isn't much change either; they just make the choke valve big enough to cover both carburetor throats.

When we go beyond two barrels, however, there are some real differences. In a four-barrel carburetor the two barrels that the engine runs on normally are called the primaries. The extra two barrels only operate at high engine speed, when they are most needed.

As mentioned before, the carburetor is really nothing more than an air valve. At idle the air valve or throttle is closed because the engine doesn't need much air. As the engine goes faster it needs more air, or we might say that if the

engine gets more air it will go faster.

At low speeds around town only a small throttle opening is needed to make the engine do its job. When you get out on the highway you open the throttle and go faster, up to the wide-open throttle. But the engine won't go as fast as it is capable of running because it isn't getting enough air.

To solve this problem the four-barrel carburetor was invented. The engine runs around town at low speeds on the primary barrels, but when you get out on the highway and really want to go,

As the carburetor design becomes more complex for better air/fuel mixing, slight design changes are incorporated, such as the idle air by-pass system shown.

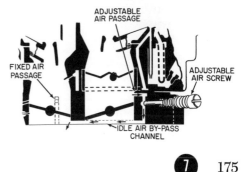

Adjustable Air By-Pass System Labels:
- ADJUSTABLE AIR PASSAGE
- FIXED AIR PASSAGE
- ADJUSTABLE AIR SCREW
- IDLE AIR BY-PASS CHANNEL

all you have to do is step on the gas and the secondary barrels open up.

Admittedly, the job could have been done with a larger carburetor, eliminating all the complicated vacuum and mechanical controls that operate secondaries, but then you have to educate the driver. An engine needs just the right amount of air to do its job. With a large carburetor the driver has to have an educated foot, and open the throttle just the right amount so that the engine doesn't get too much air. A four-barrel with primaries and secondaries is the only answer, because it gives the driver more positive control of his car.

There is no general rule about what systems feed the secondary barrels. Of course there is a main metering system, but there may be a power system or even an idle system. It all depends on what problems faced the designer and how he went about solving them.

Secondaries can be either vacuum-controlled or mechanically controlled, with maybe a velocity valve to boot. Mechanically controlled secondaries start to open when the primaries reach

about three-quarter throttle. The secondaries open at a faster rate, so that all four barrels reach wide open at the same time.

It is possible, on mechanically controlled secondaries, for the driver to

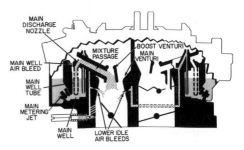

The main metering system is located on the primary side of a four-barrel carburetor and flows fuel between the idle and power ranges.

open the throttle wide at a low speed when the engine doesn't need all that air. To correct this mistake, there is usually an air valve or velocity valve in the secondary barrels above the throttle valve. This air valve does not open until there is a sufficient rush of air past it to raise a weight or compress a spring. Of course the only time we have sufficient airflow is when the engine is going fast, which is the only time we need the secondaries anyway.

Vacuum-controlled secondaries do not have this problem. They are controlled by either manifold vacuum or venturi vacuum, so they open only when the engine needs the extra air, regardless of what the driver does.

An idle compensator is used on some standard and some air conditioned cars to help when the engine might get into an extreme "hot idle" condition. This valve cannot be repaired; replace if necessary.

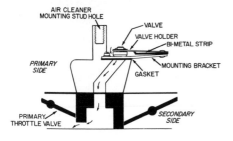

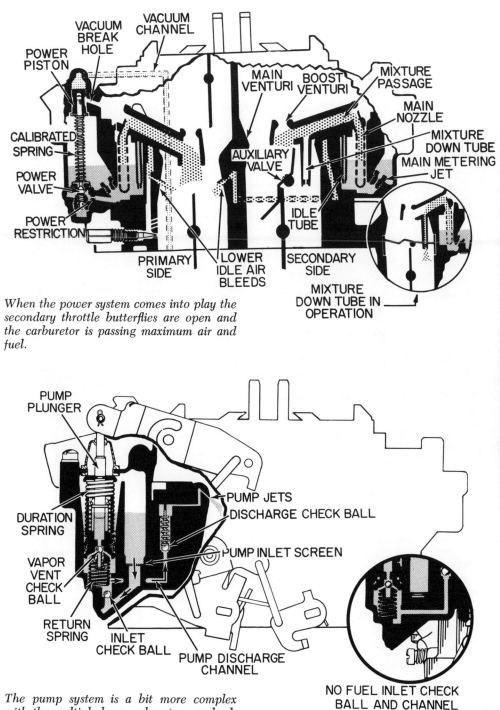

POWER PISTON
VACUUM BREAK HOLE
VACUUM CHANNEL
MAIN VENTURI
BOOST VENTURI
MIXTURE PASSAGE
MAIN NOZZLE
MIXTURE DOWN TUBE
MAIN METERING JET
CALIBRATED SPRING
AUXILIARY VALVE
POWER VALVE
POWER RESTRICTION
IDLE TUBE
PRIMARY SIDE
LOWER IDLE AIR BLEEDS
SECONDARY SIDE
MIXTURE DOWN TUBE IN OPERATION

When the power system comes into play the secondary throttle butterflies are open and the carburetor is passing maximum air and fuel.

PUMP PLUNGER
PUMP JETS
DISCHARGE CHECK BALL
DURATION SPRING
PUMP INLET SCREEN
VAPOR VENT CHECK BALL
RETURN SPRING
INLET CHECK BALL
PUMP DISCHARGE CHANNEL
NO FUEL INLET CHECK BALL AND CHANNEL

The pump system is a bit more complex with the multiple bore carburetors, and adjustment is slightly more difficult.

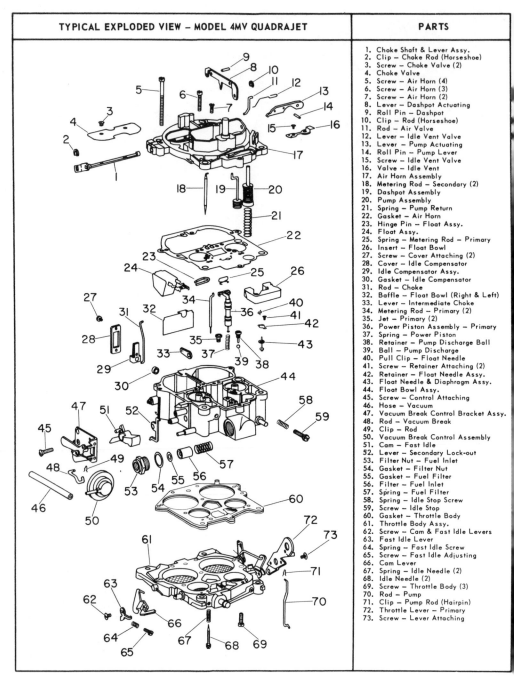

TYPICAL EXPLODED VIEW – MODEL 4MV QUADRAJET	PARTS

PARTS

1. Choke Shaft & Lever Assy.
2. Clip – Choke Rod (Horseshoe)
3. Screw – Choke Valve (2)
4. Choke Valve
5. Screw – Air Horn (4)
6. Screw – Air Horn (3)
7. Screw – Air Horn (2)
8. Lever – Dashpot Actuating
9. Roll Pin – Dashpot
10. Clip – Rod (Horseshoe)
11. Rod – Air Valve
12. Lever – Idle Vent Valve
13. Lever – Pump Actuating
14. Roll Pin – Pump Lever
15. Screw – Idle Vent Valve
16. Valve – Idle Vent
17. Air Horn Assembly
18. Metering Rod – Secondary (2)
19. Dashpot Assembly
20. Pump Assembly
21. Spring – Pump Return
22. Gasket – Air Horn
23. Hinge Pin – Float Assy.
24. Float Assy.
25. Spring – Metering Rod – Primary
26. Insert – Float Bowl
27. Screw – Cover Attaching (2)
28. Cover – Idle Compensator
29. Idle Compensator Assy.
30. Gasket – Idle Compensator
31. Rod – Choke
32. Baffle – Float Bowl (Right & Left)
33. Lever – Intermediate Choke
34. Metering Rod – Primary (2)
35. Jet – Primary (2)
36. Power Piston Assembly – Primary
37. Spring – Power Piston
38. Retainer – Pump Discharge Ball
39. Ball – Pump Discharge
40. Pull Clip – Float Needle
41. Screw – Retainer Attaching (2)
42. Retainer – Float Needle Assy.
43. Float Needle & Diaphragm Assy.
44. Float Bowl Assy.
45. Screw – Control Attaching
46. Hose – Vacuum
47. Vacuum Break Control Bracket Assy.
48. Rod – Vacuum Break
49. Clip – Rod
50. Vacuum Break Control Assembly
51. Cam – Fast Idle
52. Lever – Secondary Lock-out
53. Filter Nut – Fuel Inlet
54. Gasket – Filter Nut
55. Gasket – Fuel Filter
56. Filter – Fuel Inlet
57. Spring – Fuel Filter
58. Spring – Idle Stop Screw
59. Screw – Idle Stop
60. Gasket – Throttle Body
61. Throttle Body Assy.
62. Screw – Cam & Fast Idle Levers
63. Fast Idle Lever
64. Spring – Fast Idle Screw
65. Screw – Fast Idle Adjusting
66. Cam Lever
67. Spring – Idle Needle (2)
68. Idle Needle (2)
69. Screw – Throttle Body (3)
70. Rod – Pump
71. Clip – Pump Rod (Hairpin)
72. Throttle Lever – Primary
73. Screw – Lever Attaching

An exploded view of a Rochester Quadrajet showing the many tiny pieces that make up the assembly. When taking a carburetor apart for cleaning, it is not necessary to tear it down this far; just remove the main assemblies so that cleaning solvent and air can be used to open up all air and fuel passages. Do not put nonmetallic parts in carburetor cleaner as the cleaner will sometimes attack the materials.

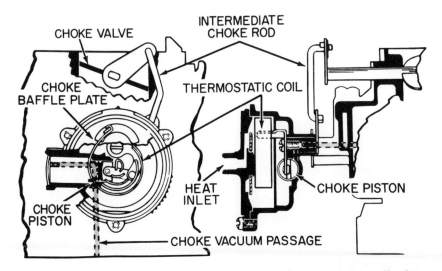

CHOKE VALVE

INTERMEDIATE CHOKE ROD

CHOKE BAFFLE PLATE

THERMOSTATIC COIL

CHOKE PISTON

CHOKE PISTON

HEAT INLET

CHOKE VACUUM PASSAGE

Automatic choke systems will also vary with the more sophisticated carburetors, with Rochester using a hot air type, hot water type, and a manual choke. Usually it is necessary to set the choke about where you think it should be, then check it after the engine has entirely cooled (first thing in the morning is best) and readjust.

Other Carburetor Features

If you do a lot of driving around town, you need a heated intake manifold to improve the low-end response. At low speed the fuel mixture is moving slowly through the intake passages and droplets of fuel have a tendency to fall out of the airstream. A heated manifold helps to keep the fuel vaporized. Heat comes from the exhaust gases, which are usually channeled in some way so that they go up under the base of the carburetor to heat the intake passages. However, we do not want the fuel in the carburetor bowl to become heated, just the intake passages themselves. So you may find carburetors that are installed on manifolds with a large insulating block separating them.

If you step on the throttle hard to go across an intersection, and all of a sudden you decide to stop, the engine may die when you take your foot off the throttle, unless it has an anti-stall dashpot, also known as a slow-closing-throttle dashpot. The engine dies because you have already started a big load of fuel on the way to the cylinders but when you take your foot off the throttle, you shut off the air supply. The large load of fuel then floods the cylinders and kills the engine. An anti-stall dashpot stops this by holding the throttle open for a few seconds and allowing it to come down to idle slowly, which gives enough time for the engine to burn off the rich mixture.

Idle Mixture

One of the tests for finding out if a carburetor is operating correctly is to make an attempt to adjust the idle-mixture needles. (V8s have two needles, six-cylinder engines only one.) If possible, mixture needles should always be adjusted with the fingers. If it is necessary to use a screwdriver because you can't get the needles with your fingers, be very careful that you do not screw them in so far that you force them into the idle port hole. If you do this you may put a ridge on the needle or even break off the end of it.

Idle mixture is adjusted by screwing the needles in for a leaner mixture and out for a richer mixture. The usual setting at which almost any engine will idle is about 1½ to 2 turns unscrewed from the completely closed position. To adjust idle mixture the engine must be at operating temperature. The choke must be off and the fast-idle cam must not be holding the throttle open.

Many other things must be checked before you actually set the idle. In some cars the headlights must be on so that the alternator puts a load on the engine. Some cars are adjusted in drive, some in neutral. Get the correct specifications for the car you are working on and be sure that you follow them to the letter. When the engine conditions are the way they should be, then it's OK to go ahead with the actual idle-speed and mixture adjustment.

Screw one idle needle in slowly. You will reach a point where the mixture becomes so lean that the engine starts to falter. This is called the lean roll point or sometimes the lean fall-off point.

Unscrew the needle and you will reach a point where the mixture becomes so rich that the engine starts to roll; this is called the rich fall-off point. The usual setting for an idle needle is midway between these two points. Again this may vary in different engines, so be sure that you have correct specifications for the engine you are working on. Adjust one needle at a time and go back and forth between the two needles (on a V8) until you are sure that the engine is as smooth and as steady as you can make it.

Air-Fuel Ratio

Air-fuel ratio is a fancy term you won't hear much. What you will hear is talk about a carburetor running rich or running lean. Running rich means that the engine is getting too much fuel; running lean means just the opposite. Sometimes running rich produces an obvious symptom such as black smoke coming out the tailpipe, but most of the time if the mixture is off it will show up either as poor gas mileage or a lack of power.

If you want power it takes gasoline to produce it, so you can usually assume that the engine is running too lean if it doesn't seem to have much push. If the gas mileage is much poorer than it should be then you can be pretty sure that the mixture is too rich.

Carburetor men usually measure the air-fuel ratio with an exhaust-gas analyzer. The analyzer takes a sample of the gas from the tailpipe, and a meter gives the ratio of air to fuel by weight. The normal range is from about 11 to 1 up to 15 to 1. Outside of that range there is either too much fuel or too much air to make a combustible mixture. Some carburetor men don't bother with an exhaust-gas analyzer, but those who do have found that the small amount of

180

time it takes to hook the analyzer up will save them a lot of trouble in the long run because it gives them an immediate check on how well the carburetor is running, both before and after they have worked on it.

It is not necessary for you to go out and buy an exhaust-gas analyzer. A good one is expensive, and a bad one is worse than none at all. And there are some bad ones on the market. The point is that when working on a carburetor you are mainly concerned with mixture control. Power, performance, and smoothness are all dependent upon having the right amount of gasoline in the air to match the needs of the engine.

Carburetor Overhaul

Of course the greatest enemy of mixture control is dirt. If the idle-mixture needles will not adjust or you keep having problems with rough idle and stalling, just look at the outside of the carburetor. If it's all encrusted with fuel residue and dirt, you can be pretty sure it's almost as dirty on the inside. So you have to get it clean, and you start by removing it and taking it apart.

Removing a carburetor is more or less an obvious procedure. It is held on at the base by studs and nuts. Remove the nuts, the throttle linkage, the hot air tube to the choke housing if there is one, and any wires to such things as the transmission kick-down switches or air-conditioning idle speed-up switches.

Exploded views of carburetors usually show the parts as if they had been disassembled by a bomb. Never under any circumstances take a carburetor apart this far for cleaning. A good rule to follow is that anything with a gasket should be removed so that the gasket can be renewed. Also any jet that is screwed

in should be removed so that the cleaning fluid can get up into the passages behind the jet. Choke vacuum pistons should be removed if they are of the type that is built into the carburetor.

The throttle shafts or choke shafts should never be removed for ordinary

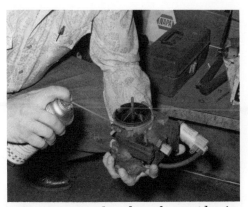

Although sprays that clean the outside of a carburetor make it look good, such a facial does little good for the working parts of the carburetor.

The only way to thoroughly clean a carburetor is to remove it from the vehicle, disassemble it completely, and then do the cleaning by hand. Special carburetor cleaning solvent is available through parts stores; do not get it on your hands for any period of time as it is very caustic. In the absence of a good cleaning solution, use solvent or gasoline.

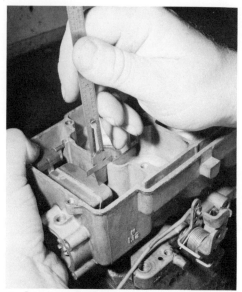

Carburetor rebuild kits will give exact specifications for critical adjustments, such as float level. Follow these rules explicitly. Kits usually include gauges for measurements.

A typical carburetor repair kit. Often a kit will include some gaskets and parts that seem superfluous to the carburetor you are working on. They probably are, since it is less expensive for the manufacturer to make all kits alike, so use only the parts you need. However, make sure you have the correct gaskets in the right place. Do not replace the original jets without consulting a manual for your particular engine.

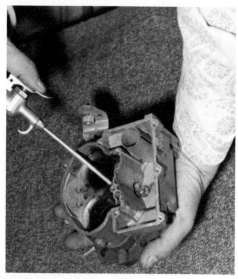

After cleaning the carburetor housing (all pieces of rubber and gasket material should be removed before using carburetor cleaning compound), blow all the orifices clear with compressed air. This is a step which should not be overlooked.

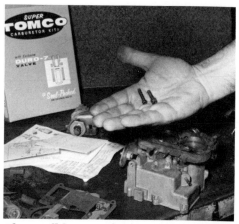

There will be a number of small screws that look similar, so it is wise to separate the basic unit fasteners during disassembly, and remember where they go for reassembly. The screws that hold the base plate to the carb body are usually of a larger diameter than the screws that hold the top plate in place.

cleaning. If you do you'll just be making a lot of extra work and you won't be accomplishing anything, because the cleaning solution easily finds its way alongside the throttle and choke shafts If power valves are the screw-in type, they can be removed. If they are pressed or staked in, they should be left alone.

After the carburetor is disassembled, the large parts should be put in a basket and the small parts in a closed screened container which will allow cleaning solution to enter but keep the parts from being lost. A good holder for small parts is a tea ball, ordinarily used for making tea, available at any store with a housewares counter.

The basket for the large parts comes with either a 3-gallon or a 5-gallon bucket of commercial carburetor cleaner. However, if you are only doing one or two carburetors a year, you can buy the carburetor cleaner in pint cans and pour it into coffee cans to do the cleaning. Use a coat hanger to fish the parts out. The cleaner is a very powerful chemical —you should never put your fingers in it, and be very careful not to splash it in your eyes.

Some cleaners will clean a carburetor in twenty minutes. Others don't do a very good job. You will have to find out by experimenting with what is available in your area. Any cleaner will ruin rubber or neoprene parts, so if there are any parts like this in your carburetor be absolutely certain they are removed before the carburetor is dunked.

After the carburetor has remained in the cleaning solution long enough, the whole basket should be removed and allowed to drain. Then all the parts can be submerged in cleaning solvent or kerosene. If the carburetor cleaner did its job properly, the solvent is only to wash out the cleaner, but in some cases you may have to use a brush with the solvent in order to loosen and remove some of the more stubborn deposits.

Swish the carburetor around in the solvent so that all of the cleaner is washed out. Then remove the carburetor piece by piece and blow all the passages with compressed air. If you don't have an air compressor, then blow the passages out with a tire pump. You must blow the carburetor with something to be sure to remove any remaining pieces of dirt.

After the carburetor is clean it's simply a matter of reassembling it with new gaskets and new parts where necessary and checking the various adjustments on the carburetor. You should never put a carburetor back together with the old gaskets except in an emergency.

The next step up from a gasket set is a zip kit or pep kit. This includes gaskets plus a few of the parts that wear out, such as needle and seat and accelerating pump. If the carburetor is really in bad shape, then you will need an overhaul kit, which includes just about every part on the carburetor that could wear out except the shafts. If even an overhaul kit won't restore the carb, then your only recourse is to buy the parts that you need. However, it is usually cheaper to buy a new carburetor than it is to go that far.

While assembling the carburetor you will set the float level, but that is ordinarily the only internal adjustment. After the carburetor is assembled there are all kinds of external adjustments that make it operate correctly.

When you buy a repair kit for your carburetor there will usually be a sheet included that will show all the adjust-

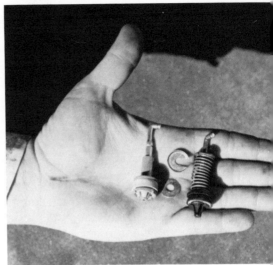

After the base plate is installed, the idle screws are positioned. These should be run all the way in until they gently bottom (do not overtighten them!) then backed out 1½ turns on older cars, 2½ turns on late cars with an abundance of emission control equipment. Sometimes there will be a plastic cover on these screws on later cars, which has been installed originally to control owner adjustment of the idle mixture.

All repair kits will include accelerator pumps. Use them, and make sure they fit into the pump bore correctly. Fill the carburetor body with gasoline before inserting accelerator pump and following top plate.

If the car does not idle very well, it might be wise to check how the throttle butterflies fit the base plate. Hold the unit up to light and if there is more than the tiniest crack visable between butterfly plate and throat bore, loosen the butterfly shaft and adjust the butterflies for a snug fit.

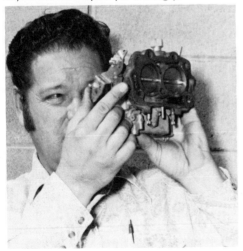

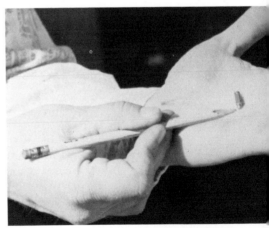

A new needle valve and seat will be included in the kit and should be a part of any carburetor overhaul. The tiny tip of the needle does wear, and it can cause some problems of flooding or needle valve sticking.

It is necessary to clean the intake manifold gasket area very carefully, allowing none of the old gasket to drop inside the manifold. The new base gasket can often go on in two ways, but only one will be correct. Check how the original gasket is on before it is removed.

To get really excellent performance from the carburetor overhaul it is necessary to adjust all the lever linkages as outlined in the instructions which will be a part of the overhaul kit. This particular lever shown adjusts the accelerator pump action.

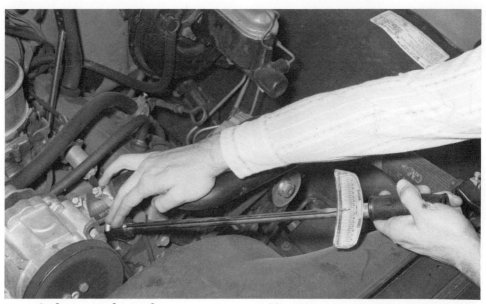

As a final part of the intake system tuneup, check all intake manifold bolts with a torque wrench. A slight leak at this point will give a lean mixture which is difficult to trace down. If there is suspicion of a gasket problem after torquing the bolts, squirt fine oil around the port area—if this oil is pulled into the engine the gasket must be replaced and/or the manifold is warped.

CAM FOLLOWER ON
HIGH STEP OF FAST
IDLE CAM

PRIMARY THROTTLE
VALVE CLOSED

AFTER SCREW MAKES
CONTACT ON LEVER,
TURN SCREW IN 3 TURNS
TO ADJUST.

Typical instructions with rebuild kits; but to get thoroughly into carburetor adjustments for top tune it may be necessary to refer to service manual.

Carburetor bowl area is clean appearing while the throat is dark, but tiny jet orifices in bowl area clog readily and cause poor engine operation.

ments and specifications. If not, there are books available that will give you this information. The factory shop manual put out by the manufacturer of your car has all this data.

Changing Jets

If you get the carburetor back on your car and it still doesn't run right, you may have to change the jets. This is usually not necessary. In fact, in some cases it will increase exhaust emissions to such an extent that it is illegal. But changing jets is a procedure that you must know in order to make a carburetor work correctly.

After the fuel enters the idle jet it picks up air as it moves through the idle passage in the carburetor. When it reaches the idle port below the throttle plate, it is in reality a mixture of fuel and air, and it is the proportions of this mixture that you control with the idle-mixture screw. However, the idle-mixture screw does not control the fuel that comes from the idle transfer port. That fuel mixture is controlled by the size of the idle jet and the idle air bleeds.

If the idle jets are screwed in it's a simple matter to change them. However, if they are pressed into a metering cluster, the only way to change idle-jet size is by drilling or buying a different cluster, if one is available—and it usually isn't.

Main jets are usually screwed in and are easily changed. However, main jets for the secondary side of a four-barrel carburetor may be just orifices which are not removable. When removing main jets be sure to use a screwdriver that fits the slot in the jet. If you don't, it's very easy for the screwdriver to slip partway out of the jet and chew up the soft brass. On a carburetor that uses metering rods the usual procedure is to change the rods. But it really doesn't matter whether you change the rods or the jets, so long as you end up with the right mixture.

If you want a richer mixture at wide-open throttle but want to retain the mixture you already have at cruising speed, then the power jet is the one to change. A lot of ingenuity has been used in the design and placement of power jets and sometimes you have to use almost an equal amount of ingenuity to find them. Some cannot be changed because they are nothing but a restriction in a passageway. Others can be changed or drilled in order to richen or lean the wide-open throttle mixture. In most carburetor tuning on stock automobiles, the power jet is seldom changed. The main reason for this is that the only way you can check the mixture to find out what you have is to put the engine on a dynamometer, and dynamometers aren't common items.

The accelerating-pump jet may also be a restriction in a passageway that is impossible to change or even drill. Sometimes the restriction is in a removable pump nozzle that is screwed into the carburetor throat. If so, the nozzle sometimes has a number stamped on it which indicates the size of the accelerating-pump restriction.

Drilling or changing of accelerating-pump jets is usually done to eliminate a flat spot on acceleration that cannot be cured by lengthening the stroke of the pump. It is possible to have 100 identical carburetors, 99 of which will run well, but on the 100th the accelerating pump might be just a trifle lean, causing a flat spot when you step on the gas. In that case a larger pump jet or pump restriction does wonders to cure the problem. This procedure should only be attempted by a carburetor expert, because ordinarily you can set the pump linkage for a longer stroke to overcome any flat spot.

Adjusting Fuel Level

It's easy to think of the fuel level as the measurement of how high the gasoline is in the float bowl, but this is not the part that's important. The critical point is the main nozzle and whether the gasoline is right at the tip of it ready to spill into the venturi or way down inside where the venturi suction will have to build up considerably before any gas will come out.

Fuel level can be so high with a maladjusted float that gasoline actually drips out of the nozzle when the engine is shut off, or it can be so low that venturi suction cannot pull the gasoline out of the nozzle and the engine will gasp and wheeze instead of cruising along.

A high fuel level can cause dying on turns or dying on sudden stops, and a low fuel level can cause poor response when the main metering system attempts to

Most home mechanics fail to set the float level properly, which leads to a carburetor rebuild that seems to be little better than before the rebuild.

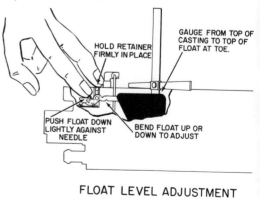

FLOAT LEVEL ADJUSTMENT

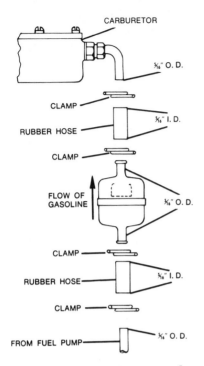

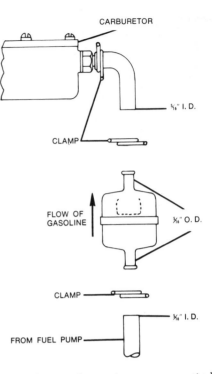

If the engine does not have an in-line fuel filter, one should definitely be installed. The slightest amount of foreign particles entering the carburetor can plug up passages or jets and cause the engine to run erratically. Shown are methods of installing filter in steel or Neoprene lines. Flow of gasoline will be marked on filter.

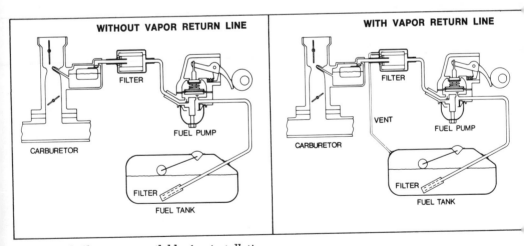

Special filters are available for installation on cars with the new sealed fuel delivery system. They must be used.

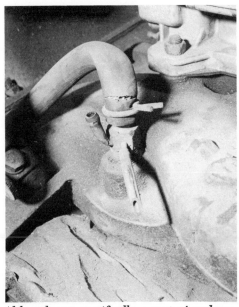

Although not specifically a part of carbure-tion, it is wise to check all intake manifold bolts for correct torque (no air leaks around the gasket to lean the mixture) and all hoses that connect to the carburetor or intake manifold. If the hose has even a tiny crack, the end should be trimmed and remounted, or a new hose fitted.

shape these crankcase vapors are mostly unburned gasoline or just air. On an engine in bad shape there is a lot of oil smoke mixed in with them.

The only thing you can do with smog valves is to make sure that the hoses connecting them do not have any leaks and that the valve itself is clean. If the valve is an orifice type, a visual inspec-tion is good enough. If the valve is a plunger type, you should both visually inspect it and shake the valve to be sure that the plunger is free inside.

Smog valves can be cleaned in car-buretor cleaner, although many car makers recommend replacement instead of cleaning. Since the smog valve al-lows unburned gasoline or air to enter the engine, if you pinch the hose or put your finger over the end of the valve, the engine will actually slow down, because you are taking some of the air and gas away from the idle mixture. If the engine does not slow down then you can be pretty sure that the valve is plugged or restricted.

take over from the idle system. With experience you will be able to recog-nize high fuel level or low fuel level because of the way the engine acts.

Suppose you have a car that runs very well at high speed but extremely rich at idle so that the engine rolls. You ad-just the idle-mixture screws but it doesn't help, so the logical thing to suspect is the fuel level. There are many problems that are obvious if you just give them a little thought and analysis.

Smog Valve

The so-called smog valve can cause mixture problems too, because it allows crankcase vapors to enter the engine (see Chapter 5). On an engine in good

Air Cleaner

Nothing will make an engine run rich quicker than a clogged or restricted air cleaner. If the element in your cleaner is made of foam or steel mesh, it should be cleaned in solvent or kerosene, shak-en or squeezed dry, and lightly re-oiled (see Chapter 15). Foam-type elements must be handled with care because they are fragile and frequently split at the seam where they are glued. If you have this trouble, instead of repairing them or getting another foam element, there are paper elements available that will take the place of the foam.

If you have a paper element you can gently tap it or blow it clean. The best way to fix it is to put on a new one. The

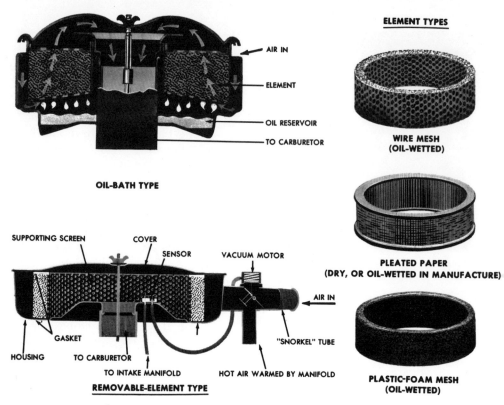

ELEMENT TYPES

AIR IN

ELEMENT

OIL RESERVOIR

TO CARBURETOR

OIL-BATH TYPE

**WIRE MESH
(OIL-WETTED)**

SUPPORTING SCREEN   COVER

SENSOR   VACUUM MOTOR

AIR IN

GASKET

HOUSING   TO CARBURETOR

TO INTAKE MANIFOLD   HOT AIR WARMED BY MANIFOLD

"SNORKEL" TUBE

REMOVABLE-ELEMENT TYPE

**PLEATED PAPER
(DRY, OR OIL-WETTED IN MANUFACTURE)**

**PLASTIC-FOAM MESH
(OIL-WETTED)**

Passenger car air-cleaner types.

best test ever devised for a paper element is to hold it over a bare light bulb. A new element will look bright and clean, and a dirty one will be obviously plugged up.

When cleaning air cleaners of any kind, the housing should be cleaned with solvent, but do not submerge it in a solvent tank. There are inner chambers that can become full of solvent and it's impossible to pour it out. Also be very careful not to cut your fingers when you are wiping out the inside of an air cleaner. The cleaner is made of sheet metal and there are sharp edges that can really cut.

Carburetor Repair Tips

Since a good carburetor overhaul and adjustment is a prime part of any engine tune-up, it is a place where the home mechanic can save considerable money for labor costs. You can expect to do a casual carburetor overhaul in less than four hours, even if you've never seen the insides of a carburetor before. You will need only basic tools (a full complement of screwdriver blade sizes is helpful), and the cost of repair kits is low.

A word on repair kits. There will usually be a small tab on the carburetor somewhere identifying the model. You'll need this information when buying replacement parts. You'll quickly learn that it is not uncommon to get the incorrect kit. To avoid a return trip to the parts store, haul your just-removed carburetor along to the store (before you disassemble it!) and be sure you get what you need. Don't be alarmed if you seem to end up with extra parts in the kit. Many kits are built to work with a variety of carburetor models; just use the parts you need.

As a rule, the final adjustment will be only for idle and accelerator pump stroke, but you may want to make a final choke adjustment. This can best be determined the next morning after the overhaul, when the engine is cold, and most automatic chokes can be adjusted at the choke housing. Make sure that any linkage parts that rub together are greased, to ensure smooth throttle operation, and install any throttle-linkage return springs that were originally hooked up.

As a final check, make sure the throttle linkage will not go "over-center" at wide open throttle. Have someone press the accelerator pedal to the floor. If the throttle linkage causes the carburetor lever to pass over-center—that is, beyond the pivot point of the carburetor lever—the carburetor can be locked at full throttle. Adjust the linkage to correct this.

And that's all there is to carburetor overhaul. You can do it yourself, without an expensive garage bill, and you'll be pleased with the results.

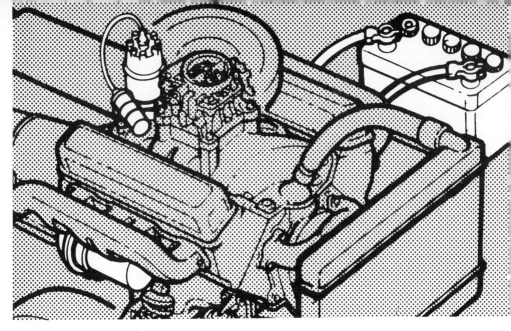

8 electrical system

You MIGHT not need electric devices to make a movable vehicle, but without them you'd have a pretty crude form of transportation. Automotive electrics—and by this we mean everything on a car that operates with electricity in some way—are vital to the modern passenger car. Unfortunately, the increasing sophistication of the automobile has tended to complicate electrical systems, and all this tends to confuse the mechanic. Even professional mechanics often are frustrated by problems in the electrical circuits.

For a quick course in automotive electricity, just remember that electrical current is much like water. The smaller the diameter of a garden hose, the harder it is for a given amount of water to flow. Flow can be increased by turning on the faucet more, or increasing the pressure. The electrical equivalent of pressure is termed voltage, and the electrical equivalent of a smaller hose—or any-

thing that increases resistance to flow—is termed ohms. The measurement of current flow through a wire is in amps, or amperes. Watts are the product of amperes times volts.

WIRING AND FUSES

Right now would be a good time to discuss total wiring. If too many devices are powered by a single wire of a certain size, some of the devices may be starving for enough current. The wire must be large enough to carry all the current to supply all the items in a particular circuit. For example, if a car has a 3-amp radio, a 2-amp windshield-wiper motor, and 7-amp lighting, it will take at least a 12-amp wire to carry common current to these items. Otherwise the wire will be overloaded, get hot, and possibly burn the insulation and short out. Wire larger than neces-

sary may be used, but never smaller. As a guide here are some wire sizes and amp loads you can expect to find on your car:

Amperes	Wire size
35	8-9
25	10-11
20	12-13
15	14-15
7	16-17
5	18-19
3	20-22

There isn't much you're likely to be doing to vehicle wiring other than routine maintenance, but this seemingly insignificant chore can save you countless hours of headaches later.

On really old cars, wiring is likely to become brittle—not the metal strands, but rather the insulation. Such rotten insulation will easily fall from the wiring, and shorts are inevitable. Unless the car is over thirty years old, however, this problem isn't likely. More common now is for insulation to be burned away, as by exhaust-pipe heat, or rubbed away from abrasion. Cuts in insulation are usually not a problem unless a sharp section of chassis or body metal grounds out through the cut, or the wiring is cut enough to reduce the load capacity of the wire.

Always inspect wiring very carefully at least once a year, with special attention to wiring inside the engine compartment and below the floorboards. Wherever you find a frayed insulation, use electrical tape, and find what caused the fraying. If a wire has been slightly cut, peel back the insulation and run solder for about ¼ inch, then tape the wire. Quite often clods of mud will dry on exposed wiring under the flooring. Some-

times these can be very large clods, and heavy. Always break them away.

Wiring ends need special attention. Unless the attachment is tight and clean, some of the current may be lost. If the wire end fitting is slightly broken, replace it with a new one. These fittings are not inexpensive, though. If the wiring into an old fitting seems to be pulling from the fitting or breaking away, run solder into the fitting where the wire connects. Any section of wire that has burned the insulation away because of a ground should have the full section replaced by new wire. This can be spliced into the original wire about 8 inches from where the burned insulation stops.

When you're having trouble with a horn that won't blow, or a light that doesn't work, or a starter that won't spin, never overlook the possibility of a bad section of wiring, a grounded wire, or a wire not making a good end connection. This is perhaps the number-one problem in automotive electrical "failures." Never take any connection or wire for granted; always check. Because wiring plays such an important role in all phases of troubleshooting, it is wise to keep (in the car) a test light—inexpensive, at your local auto-parts store—a short length of replacement wire of at least size 12, and a "jumper" wire. This last item is best made from a flexible length of 8-gauge wire with an alligator clip at either end. It can be used for testing and can even serve as a replacement wire in an emergency.

Integral in any wiring circuit will be fuses and circuit breakers, items with no other function than safety. Some of the electrical components in a vehicle will be combined into a common fuse or circuit breaker. Such a combination might be backup light, cigarette lighter, and dash lights on a common fuse or breaker. Should some component in this system draw an abnormal amount of current, the overload will cause the fuse or circuit breaker to disconnect the circuit. Sometimes, however, the electrical problem might be in a wire not fused, such as the hot wire from battery to ignition switch, or a grounded wire will burn up before the fuse blows.

A fuse is a glass or ceramic insulator with metal contacts at each end joined by a fine wire or thin metal strip. This wire or metal strip is designed to carry just so much current, and when more current is induced, the wire or strip will melt, disconnecting the circuit.

Many new cars come equipped with "automatic" circuit breakers; if a momentary load should cause an overload and break the current circuit, the circuit breaker will reset when the load drops. This is especially useful in the case of windshield wipers and headlights. A circuit breaker is not likely to fail, but should replacement be necessary, always use one with exactly the same rating. Incidentally, some cars have the headlight circuit breaker integral with the headlight switch. If the overload continues to exist, the circuit breaker will not reset, and you must find the cause, which will invariably be a ground somewhere in that particular system.

If you replace a blown fuse only to have it blow again almost immediately, look for the problem. Never wrap tinfoil around a fuse for reuse, or stick a metal object in place of the fuse. There is a problem somewhere, and unless you find it, the whole car can go up in smoke. Literally. If the replacement fuse does not blow immediately, but continues to blow occasionally, suspect a wire that is only occasionally being grounded.

Neutral Safety Switch

If the neutral safety switch on an automatic transmission goes bad it can keep the car from running (see Chapter 11). One kind of neutral safety switch is screwed directly into the transmission, and the other mounts with two or three screws somewhere on the transmission selector linkage. It is commonly inside the console on cars with floor-mounted gear selectors, and somewhere on the steering column of others. In some cases the trouble is burned or grease-coated contacts, but if there is an obvious break, or signs of wear, a new switch should be installed.

LIGHTS

Vehicle lighting is one place where the home mechanic should absolutely become a master. It is not a difficult system, but it is subject to various periodic and continuing problems, so the car owner should know now to troubleshoot and repair it. Start by learning about the headlamps.

Headlights

Dual headlight installations use two different types of sealed-beam units. The high-beam lamps have two terminals on the back, and the lens is marked with a number 1. The other units operate on both high and low beam, and like the sealed-beam lamps found on cars with single headlights, they have three terminals on the back. The lens is marked with a number 2. On cars with the dual lights arranged side by side, the outermost lamps are the three-terminal high/low combination. On cars that have one

194

light mounted above the other, the high/low unit is on top.

Remove the decorative trim surrounding the headlight. On most cars with dual lights there are three or four screws. Cars with single lights usually have only one screw. Once the trim is off, there will be several screws visible around the circumference of the headlight. Three of these are removed to change the sealed-beam unit. The other two are for aiming the lights. These aiming screws are larger than the retaining screws.

Once the retaining ring surrounding the light is off, the sealed-beam unit can be pulled out and the plug withdrawn from its terminals. Putting in the new lamp is a reversal of the removal process.

You can do your own headlight aiming with ease. Find a place where your car will sit level, such as a paved driveway or parking lot. The car should be positioned 25 feet from a garage wall. The wall should have one horizontal line and three vertical lines drawn upon it. The horizontal line can be laid out with the help of a carpenter's level and should be at the same height as the center of the headlights. The center vertical line should be at the car's exact centerline. You can sight through the rear window to do this.

Two other vertical lines are then drawn, the same distance apart as the centers of the headlights. These should be located equidistant from the centerline, which will place them directly in front of the lights.

The adjustment of Type 2 units (with the number 2 molded into the lens) is made with the headlights on low beam. This will assure adequate illumination with the lights dimmed, and the built-in

angle between the high and low beams will take care of the brights. If the car has dual headlights, the high-beam-only Type 1 lights are adjusted separately.

Switch the lights on low beam. Cover the right headlight and adjust the left vertically until the top edge of its high-intensity zone is exactly on the horizontal line. The vertical adjustment screw is at the top of the sealed-beam unit on most cars. When adjusting the aiming screws, move them first counterclockwise until the lights are definitely out of adjustment, and then bring them in gradually clockwise. Otherwise the spring may not expand properly and will later allow the lamps to change their aim.

After positioning the left light vertically, use the same procedure to move the beam horizontally until the left edge of the high-intensity zone is 3 inches (2 inches in some states) to the right of the vertical line in front of that headlight. The light's horizontal adjusting screw is located to one side of the sealed-beam mounting. Then move the covering from the right headlight to the left, and make the same adjustments to the right light. Dual headlight installations must have their number 1 lamps aimed also.

Aiming Type 1 lights is like aiming Type 2 lights, but the beam is positioned differently on the wall. Cover the three lights not being adjusted and adjust the exposed high beam until the center of intensity is 2 inches lower than the intersection of the horizontal line and the vertical line in front of that light. (This measurement depends on your state's motor vehicle requirements.)

If you have a car with single headlights that is equipped with the old 5000 series sealed-beam unit (without the number 2 on the lens), they should be adjusted while on high beam only, according to the instructions given above for aiming Type 1 units (single-filament high-beam).

Other Lights

Tail lights, instrument-panel bulbs, and other small lights are quick and easy to change. The average car has about twenty small lamps, of various sizes. When a small bulb goes out you should check to see that the lamp itself is really to blame. Quite often, parking-light and turn-signal units will suffer from weather, water, and mud until the wires or sockets finally succumb to corrosion and rot. If the bulb turns out to be OK, insert the probes of a test light into the socket (with the switch controlling the light turned on) and see if current is actually reaching the lamp.

If it is, the trouble is probably nothing more than a coating on the socket or bulb contacts. Scraping the terminal contacts on both the bulb and socket should do the trick. Poor ground contact could also be a factor, so don't forget to polish up the lug pins on the lamp base, and also the slots in the socket that they fit into. If no current is reaching the socket, a broken or shorted wire or possibly a faulty switch is the cause. However, most switches operate more than one bulb, or at least something else besides the bulb. If the other components in the circuit are working, the trouble is not likely to be in the switch.

Every bulb has a number printed on its base. When buying a replacement get a bulb with the identical number. Often the parts store will have a chart or booklet listing the bulbs used for particular applications in various makes and models of cars. Tell them what kind of car you drive and which lamp has burned out, and they'll fix you up.

The lights on the outside are easy to work on, but some of those behind the dashboard are hard to reach. These small instrument-panel lamps are usually retained in sockets that can be taken out the back of the instrument panel by turning them about a quarter-turn counterclockwise and pulling them out. The sockets on a few cars press into holes in the back of the panel. Once the socket is out it can be pulled from under the dash and the old bulb replaced by a new one.

Tail lights, backup lights, parking lights, and turn signals are generally serviced by removing the lens and trim ring. Most cars have from one to four screws holding the ring in place, and once these are taken out, the ring, lens, and gasket will come off. On some late-model cars it is possible to replace the bulbs in the tail, stop, and backup lights from inside the trunk. These lights have sockets that can be pulled out.

Many of the bulbs used in rear lighting are combination types that have two filaments and serve as both tail light and turn signal, or as a stoplight and tail light. For this reason it is imperative that the same type of bulb be used.

Light Switches

If the bulbs are all good, but the stop lights or backup lights still won't work, or dimming the headlights for an oncoming car sometimes makes them go out, you've got switch troubles. The cure is to put in a new switch.

In the case of light, heater, and windshield-wiper switches that are mounted through the dash, it's necessary to take off the control knob before the faulty unit can be removed. In most cases a small set screw must be taken from the knob before it will come off the shaft. Some controls may have knobs that are threaded onto the shaft and can be unscrewed, and others have spring retainers that are freed by inserting a small wire into a hole in the bottom of the knob. The knob and shaft on some GM cars is taken out as a unit by pulling the control to the ON position and depressing an under-dash button on the switch body.

Some switches may be fixed by simply tightening, adjusting, or lubricating the switch or linkage. Stoplight switches operated mechanically off the brake pedal can cause two kinds of trouble. Those on older cars with brake pedals that pass through the floorboards are located under the car and are exposed to dirt and corrosion. These switches have a lever which contacts the brake pedal. The lever is spring-loaded, so that it will swing in an arc as the brakes are applied and the pedal arm moves away from it. The switch lever is connected internally to a pair of contacts which trigger the stoplights. If the switch lever shaft becomes rusted or coated with dirt, it will no longer follow the movement of the brake-pedal arm. Usually, a few drops of rust-dissolving oil will free the frozen shaft. In bad cases, the switch can be removed and washed in solvent. After the solvent bath, work the lever a few times and it should start to move freely. It it does not, the spring is probably broken and must be replaced.

The stoplight switch used on late-model cars with "hanging" brake pedals is usually mounted under the dashboard on the brake-pedal stop. Trouble caused by these switches is likely to result from vibration. Should the retaining nut loosen, it may allow the switch to move away from the pedal and the stoplights will remain permanently on. The switch must be remounted tightly so that electrical contact is made when the brake pedal is depressed $\frac{3}{8}$ to $\frac{5}{8}$ inch from the fully released, or off, position.

The backup-light switches on most transmissions seldom cause trouble, since most are mounted on the steering column inside the car. Some cars with floor shifts have the backup-light switch mounted on the side of the transmission. These switches and their connections take quite a beating, and may cause trouble. The small rod connecting the switch to the reverse-gear bellcrank may also become loose or rusty.

If the headlights don't work and you suspect the dimmer switch, check the circuit with a jumper wire. By connecting the center wire leading to the switch to one of the other two wires, you should be able to make the lights operate either bright or dim. If the jumper wire gets results, the trouble is probably in the switch. Make sure that the real trouble is not just poor contact between the wires and the switch terminal connections. Most dimmer switches can be removed by folding back the upper corner of the front floor mat and removing the wire and mounting screws from the switch assembly.

GAUGES

With the exception of the speedometer, and in a few cases the water-temperature and oil-pressure gauges, modern dashboard instruments are electrically operated. It has become common to limit standard instrument clusters to a speedometer and a fuel gauge with only indicator lights to warn of low oil pressure, engine overheating, and inadequate battery charging.

Many of the less elaborate instrument layouts can be serviced without taking the panel out of the car. However, most of the cars that have "extra" instruments installed as "options" must have the panel removed before you can get at the gauges.

Since many instrument panels are now made of plastic, there may also be one or more ground straps to provide ground polarity to the instruments. When replacing the panel be very sure to reinstall these properly to ensure a good ground.

Fuel Gauge

Modern fuel gauges are simple devices capable of measuring the amount of voltage transmitted from a sending unit located in the fuel tank. There is also a voltage-limiting relay in the circuit to prevent inaccurate readings caused by voltage changes. On some cars the voltage limiter is part of the fuel gauge itself, but it may also be a separate behind-the-dash unit. In most cars equipped with electric oil-pressure and water-temperature gauges, these units are connected to the same voltage limiter as the fuel gauge.

A fuel gauge that shows a full tank whenever the ignition is switched on is probably not stuck, as it may seem to be. More likely there is an electrical cause for this malfunction. The most common is an improperly grounded gauge or instrument cluster. If the cluster is not grounded, all other electrical gauges will also be against the peg at the high end. The ammeter, however, will not be affected.

A faulty voltage limiter can also cause the gauge(s) to read high or low, either at one peg or the other, or at any odd place in between. If the needles occasionally make sudden surges to higher-than-normal readings, this is also the result of a faulty voltage limiter.

A quick check of the instrument voltage limiter can be made by connecting one lead of a test light to the temperature-sending unit on the engine and the other lead to ground. Leave the instrument wire attached to the sending unit also and have the ignition switch turned on. A flashing lamp indicates that the limiter is working.

Another possible cause of a full reading is a short in the wire from the tank. If the wire proves to be OK, the gauge well grounded, and the voltage limiter operating properly, any trouble that exists must be either in the gauge mechanism itself or in the tank sending unit.

The place to check is the grounding of the sending unit. Clean a small area on the fuel tank and another at the top of the sender. Attach a jumper wire to a good ground on the car body and touch the other end to the clean spot on the fuel tank. If the gauge reads normally, the trouble is a poorly grounded tank. If the gauge still does not read accurately, touch the jumper to the clean spot on the sending unit. A normal reading here indicates poor ground contact between the tank and the sending unit. Should the reading still be off, the trouble is either in the gauge or in the sending-unit mechanism.

Other Gauges

If your car is equipped with electrically operated temperature and oil-pressure gauges, the tests used on the fuel gauge should work on these as well. An operating ammeter will always show a discharge when the headlights are switched on and the engine is not running. Since ammeter failures are rare, it is always advisable to check the wiring before replacing the instrument.

When the ignition is switched to the on position the oil, temperature, and generator lights should come on. If one fails to do so, the bulb and connection should be checked to locate the trouble. If the generator light stays on after the engine is started, the charging system and the indicator-light circuit should be checked.

A temperature indicator that continues to report a cold engine even after the car has been driven for several miles, or indicates a hot engine immediately after starting, probably has either a defective sending unit or a shorted wire between the sending unit and the indicator light.

Faulty sending units that fail to switch on the indicator light when the ignition is turned on can be spotted by grounding the wire from their terminal. If the lamp lights, clean the sending unit. If it still does not function, replace it.

BATTERY

So far, all the electrics discussed have had to do primarily with accessories. Now we'll get into those electrical components that must be operating correctly for the engine to work, namely the starter, generator/alternator, and ignition. But first, an important commercial for your car's battery (see Chapter 15).

The poor battery is expected to work perfectly, under all conditions, with no maintenance, indefinitely. It never will, of course, and lack of service by the car owner is the number-one reason batteries fail early. They aren't cheap, so a few moments once or twice a month will be time well spent.

It isn't necessary to go into how a battery is made, or what makes it work. You can have the local gas-station operator check the battery condition for you, and unless the test shows a bad cell or two, you can expect to get continued service from your battery provided it and the charging circuit are in good

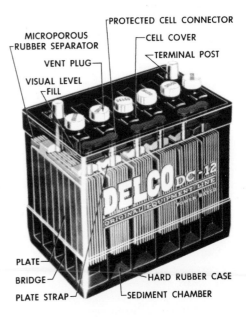

The storage battery is the heart of the automotive electrical system, but it is not the unit that all the electrical components work from. The battery is a storage unit only, a kind of reservoir of electrical energy that will meter into the system as needed. It has the prime function of operating the starting motor. The electrical generating system is responsible for supplying electricity after the engine is running.

A good way to help a battery fail is to let the case become coated with grease and dirt, which will draw a tiny bit of current. Keep the case clean, the terminals and leads free of corrosion. Do not let a battery shake around freely in the mount, as this can damage internal plates and break the housing.

While economy batteries may suit the finances best at the moment, a premium battery will be least expensive in the long run. If the car is equipped with many accessories, such as air conditioning, a premium battery is almost essential.

repair. If the battery goes bad, spend a few extra bucks and get a really good replacement. Trying to scrimp a dollar will always prove a bad bargain in this case. And don't expect a home "trickle" charger to save a dying battery, either. A trickle charger is good if you live in a cold climate and don't run your car long enough on trips for the battery to recharge.

With proper care, a good battery can have a lifespan of four or five years. Most threats to the battery come from an improperly adjusted voltage regulator. Sulfating, which is a result of a constant undercharge, can usually be traced to the regulator. On the other hand, a battery does not "store" electricity, so it can be overcharged too. This will lead to high temperatures in the electrolyte, extreme oxidation of the positive plates, and finally, disintegration of the plates.

At the same time, do not overfill a battery, as this will dilute the electrolyte.

If you let the water level get too low, the acid concentration is too high, and the battery can also fail early. Generally, the water level should be about ¼ inch above the plates. You'll hear all kinds of opinions about the type of water a battery should use; to be on the safe side use distilled water only, since mineral or chemical impurities can harm the battery.

When dirt and acid salts accumulate on the battery case (outside), a conductive layer is formed. (See Chapter 15.) In an extreme case this will become a path for constant discharge. These salts usually show up as a "growth" around the battery posts. Mix up baking soda with water (a thick paste) and apply anywhere you find white salts forming. Let this boil for ten minutes or so and flush with clean water. Repeat until the posts and wiring ends are perfectly clean. Use ordinary dish detergent with water to wash the battery case. Make sure none of this solution gets inside the battery, or it will weaken the electrolyte. Remove the wire terminals and clean both terminal and post with sandpaper. Really inspect the wire where it enters the terminal, as salts can build heavily here, and often unseen, they eventually destroy the wire. After the terminals are replaced on the posts, coat everything with a heavy salve of petroleum jelly. Always use a regular puller when removing battery terminals; never just loosen a bolt and knock the terminals loose or pry them loose. This will break the post away from the internal plates. While you're cleaning the battery, which should usually be done three or four times a year, also check that both positive and negative leads are properly connected at the other end. Finally, make sure the battery hold-down system is tight. Now you can move on to the charging circuit.

GENERATOR

Although the majority of American automobiles now include an alternator in the charging system, there are still enough generators around to make at least a cursory investigation of this unit useful.

The frame of most generators is cast iron. The end pieces, on the other hand, are generally of some material such as aluminum alloy. The pole shoes are of mild steel and may retain a considerable degree of residual magnetism even when not energized by battery current. The pole shoes are held in the frame by large screws like those in starter motors.

The coils surrounding the poles are connected so that current passes first through one coil and then the other. One end of the wire forming the field coils is attached to the "field" terminal, on the outside of the generator housing. This terminal is insulated from the frame by a fiber insert and washer. The wire from the field terminal attaches to the field

terminal on the voltage-regulator unit, which completes the circuit for battery current needed to energize the electromagnetic poles of the generator.

The armature in most generators is relatively long in proportion to its diameter. This reduces the effect of inertia on the armature windings at high rpm.

Each coil of the armature windings is connected at either end to two opposing segments on the commutator. The segments are insulated from one another as well as from the armature shaft by strips of mica, or a synthetic substitute. Commutators are usually made of brass because of its conducive ability and resistance to corrosion. The armature windings are soldered in place on the commutator segments, but the position of the commutator is almost 90° off from the position of the related windings on the armature core.

The brushes in an automobile generator are of a different design and material from those in electric starter motors. Starter brushes are made from a metallic copper-based material, but those in the generator are of carbon.

Cutaway of a generator. Electrical systems on most new cars do not use a generator. Failures are usually in end plate bushings/ bearings, brushes, commutators. Brushes and commutators can be repaired at home with just a few tools.

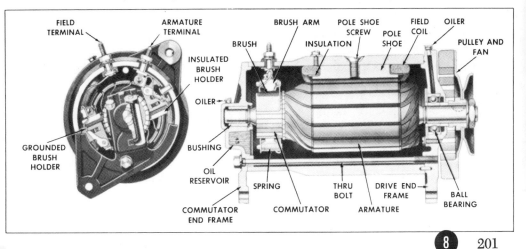

One of the brushes is connected to a terminal which sends the current produced in the armature to the battery via the voltage regulator. The other brush is grounded directly to the frame of the generator. Polarity of the ground brush is the same as that of the grounded side of the battery. The charging system's circuit is therefore completed through the frame of the automobile.

The armature runs in bushings or bearings set into the end plates of the generator. In the past, these had to be oiled every thousand miles or so to prevent excessive friction and possible failure. Later generators are often equipped with ball or roller bearings—at least at the drive end—which are prepacked with a permanent lubricant. While the commutation end of the armature shaft still requires periodic oiling on many generators, some manufacturers have provided it with a metal cap filled with permanent lubricant. Ruined generator bearings and broken drive pulleys are often the result of · excessive fan-belt tension. Incorrect tension is always a prime suspect in cases where bearings fail in spite of proper lubrication.

Generator problems are easily detected if your car is equipped with a dashboard-mounted ammeter. However, trouble normally associated with the generator will usually be caught on indicator lights too. Overcharging, low charging, or fluctuating charge are most likely the result of a malfunctioning voltage regulator. Intermittent charging or no charging are the troubles that most often originate in the generator itself.

Low charging and no charging are the common forms of charging-system trouble. If the ammeter begins to register a constant and steady discharge, or if the generator light comes on and stays on, the generator may be delivering no charge at all. If the cooling-system temperature is rising, the cause of the no-charge condition is probably nothing more than a broken or loose belt.

An ammeter needle that dips suddenly into the discharge zone and then returns an instant later to a reading well up in the charge range is indicating that charging is taking place only part of the time. A winking light can mean the same problem. Check the condition of the battery and its connections. A hydrometer test that shows all the battery cells to be uniformly discharged means definite charging system trouble. If one or more cells are the only ones discharged, or if the electrolyte level is extremely low, battery failure may be the cause of the abnormal ammeter readings. A loose battery connection that is making poor or intermittent contact can cause the generator light to flicker or the ammeter needle to dip.

The next step is to determine if the defect lies in the generator or in the voltage-regulator unit. This can be done by eliminating the regulator from the circuit. On most General Motors and Chrysler cars ("A" circuit systems) you can do this by removing the field wire from the regulator, then grounding the field terminal at the generator. If you don't remove the field wire you will burn up the regulator if it is the double-point kind. Ford uses a different wiring setup ("B" circuit system), so you have to jumper a wire from the armature terminal to the field terminal, either at the generator or at the regulator, and it's not necessary to remove the field wire.

You can perform this test in emergencies with the blade of a screwdriver. The engine must be running, of course, and great care should be taken to keep hands and tools out of the moving fan blades. If eliminating the regulator increases the ammeter reading to a high level, the trouble is in the voltage regulator. But if it does not increase the output, the generator is a fault.

When making this test be sure that everything in the car is turned off except the ignition. Run the engine just fast enough to see if the generator is going to put out, then turn the engine off.

In generators that won't charge, the trouble is worn-out generator brushes. If you have a generator with a removable inspection band at one end, it can be snapped off for checking the brushes. Try pressing down on the brushes with the tip of a screwdriver to place them in firmer contact with the revolving commutator. If doing this causes the ammeter to show a charge, worn-out brushes or a dirty commutator are the problem. Should inspection reveal that the brushes have worn to less than half their original width, they are in definite need of replacement.

In some cases, the brushes may be sticking in the holders. This is particularly true if the generator has become dirty and oil-soaked. Sticking brushes usually call for nothing more than a good cleaning, but if the commutator has become burned or glazed, the unit should probably have the brushes and commutator renovated. Whenever brushes are replaced, the commutator should always be turned in a lathe to make sure that it is concentric with the shaft and that the segments have a smooth, level surface for the brushes to ride against. The mica between the commutator bars should be undercut so it won't interfere with the brushes.

The presence of individual burned commutator segments means open circuits in the armature. This and other troubles involving the wiring of the generator are probably best left to a shop.

ALTERNATOR

The alternator is an especially useful new development. It charges the battery in a different way from the generator. It is also smaller in size, is less likely to fail becauase of high rpm, and uses a less

Alternator works slightly different from generator; it is more difficult to repair because of how the unit is assembled. As a rule, it is best left to a professional to disassemble and repair.

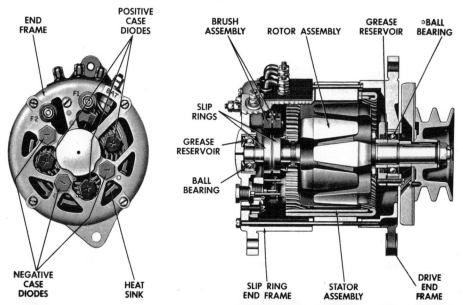

END FRAME

POSITIVE CASE DIODES

BRUSH ASSEMBLY

ROTOR ASSEMBLY

GREASE RESERVOIR

BALL BEARING

SLIP RINGS

GREASE RESERVOIR

BALL BEARING

NEGATIVE CASE DIODES

HEAT SINK

SLIP RING END FRAME

STATOR ASSEMBLY

DRIVE END FRAME

Ford alternator shows compact size. Internal diodes can be damaged if you are careless around car with arc welder or battery charger. Most common failure on units with high mileage is bearing plate cracking.

complicated regulator. The alternator isn't a recent invention—it has been around on motorcycles for some time—but it has become practical for mass production only recently, mainly because of the solid-state electronics which introduced the transistor. The modern alternator uses quite a few positive/negative diodes to rectify its alternating current into direct current.

For converting mechanical power into electrical power, the alternator has certain distinct advantages over the generator both in efficiency and durability. The same principles of magnetism employed in magnetos and generators are also used in alternators; however, there are noticeable differences in actual construction.

In the generator, the magnetic field remains stationary while the armature coils are rotated. This is the most prac-

tical way of designing a direct-current unit which must be made compact, since many coils are needed to produce a steady supply of direct current. In an alternator, the aim is not only to tap the maximum voltage of one particular polarity, but to use the entire output, regardless of the fluctuating voltage. In order to obtain a sufficiently high average voltage, a greater number of cycles must be generated.

An alternating-current cycle is the length of time that it takes for the current output to rise from zero voltage to maximum positive voltage, return to zero voltage, proceed to maximum negative voltage, and again fall to zero. The automotive alternator usually has about fourteen magnetic field poles and produces seven AC cycles for each rotation of the shaft. It is true that a DC generator could be built that would duplicate this feat, but the unit would need to be large and complicated. The important difference between the automotive DC generator and its AC successor is that in the alternator it is field magnets that rotate while the current-producing windings stand still.

To avoid confusion, different terms are commonly used to describe the parts of the alternator than for describing their counterparts in the DC generator. The rotating part of an automobile generator is called the armature. The rotating part of an alternator is called the rotor. The rotor contains the magnetic field coil in an alternator. The stationary windings of the alternator, which correspond to the armature windings in a generator, are called the stator. Since the rotor forms the magnetic field in an alternator, it only needs to be supplied with a steady source of direct current from the battery. It has a segmented commutator such as that found in generators, but only two smooth brass slip rings. The slip rings have brushes riding against them, one supplying the field coil with current of positive polarity and the other providing a negative ground connection.

Although alternator voltage output is proportional to rpm and field strength, its current output (amperage) is much more stable. In addition, since it produces near-maximum current at low speeds, the voltage-regulating function has a more uniform requirement throughout the engine speed range. Some of the first alternator systems employed a regulator not very different from those used with DC generator systems, but in the course of the past several years various developments in both alternator design and regulator construction have served to simplify and miniaturize the regulator to the point that some cars no longer even have a separate regulator but only a small transistorized regulating device incorporated into the alternator itself.

Some car makers are going back to mechanical regulators because the transistorized units can't stand booster-battery starts. When a booster battery is removed after starting a car that has a dead battery, the voltage shoots up so high that it kills the transistor in the regulator. This can be avoided by turning on all the accessories and lights in the car before disconnecting the booster battery.

Never continue to drive a car that has evident charging-system trouble. Should the problem be a loose connection that opens the charging circuit, unregulated current of the wrong polarity may be allowed to enter the battery or the alternator diodes. Never short across or ground any of the terminals on the regulator or alternator on alternator-equipped cars, even though such practices are part of the troubleshooting routine used with generator systems.

Brushes last a lot longer on an alternator than on a generator, but they do wear out. The quickest way to check for this trouble is to pull the field connection off, since it is usually in the form of a plug connector. The "F" terminal uncovered by pulling the plug is the one leading to the insulated brush. Using an ohmmeter with selector set on the x 10 position, or a 110-volt bulb with two test probes, it's possible to check the circuit through the brushes and field windings for continuity, with the engine off. Touch the test probes to the field terminal and ground, and the ohmmeter should register little measurable resistance (or the test lamp should light up). If considerable resistance (or a reading of infinity) is indicated, or if the bulb fails to light at all, there is probably poor contact between the brushes and the slip rings. Actual resistance of the field winding can be as high as 12 ohms, depending on design. You are not interested in the resistance value as in finding a bad connection or broken wire, which would be indicated by a very high reading on the ohmmeter.

On some of the alternators used by Chrysler it is possible to remove the brush holders individually. Sometimes, by wiggling these brush holders with the engine running the unit can be made to charge temporarily. This is a sure indication that the brushes need attention. On most other alternators the housing will have to be taken apart to get at the brushes should the initial ohmmeter check indicate possible poor contact. Once this is done it will be possible to duplicate the test at the slip rings. If the windings are intact, the trouble has to be worn-out or sticking brushes.

If the brushes are making good contact

and the rotor winding are also OK, the diodes should be tested. This is not a hard job once the housing is apart, but the diode leads must be unsoldered. The diodes can be tested either with a 3-volt battery-powered test light, or an ohmmeter or "VOM" containing a 1.5-volt battery. Higher voltage should never be used since it will ruin the diodes. The test lead probes are touched to the wire and the case of each disconnected diode, and then reversed to check current flow in the opposite direction. A good diode will light the lamp or produce a low resistance reading in one direction but not in the other. If both readings are about equally high or low, or if the light will (or will not) light in either direction, the diode is bad. Individual diodes can be replaced, using one of the inexpensive diode-fitting tools available or by replacing the entire heat sink in which the diodes are mounted.

An even faster on-the-car check can be carried out by disconnecting the battery ground cable and taking ohmmeter readings in both directions across the output and ground terminals of the unit. Test results will be similar to tests of individual diodes but will not pinpoint which diodes are faulty. Garages have a diode tester—a small unit that will test the diodes after the alternator is taken apart, but without disconnecting the individual diode leads.

CURRENT REGULATOR
VOLTAGE REGULATOR
CUTOUT RELAY
BATTERY TERMINAL
GENERATOR TERMINAL
FIELD TERMINAL

Regulator for generator has removable cover so points can be adjusted to regulate amount of electricity passed to battery. If unit is improperly adjusted the battery can be ruined as well as the generator. A meter is needed to check the output during adjustment.

Alternator regulators, slightly different from generator regulators, are often sealed. When this unit goes bad, a replacement is about the only repair possible.

VOLTAGE REGULATOR

If you must go further into the alternator to find a problem, leave the work to a garage, since taking the rest of the unit apart is a job for special press tools. The regulator is not quite so complicated and you can do several repairs and checks at home on this vital partner to the charging system.

Certain troubles that indicate regulator malfunctions can often be spotted by the behavior of the ammeter. One of the most common symptoms is an ammeter needle that moves up and down the scale from a high charge rate to a low discharge in direct proportion to engine speed. This condition is harmful to the battery and should be corrected

206

immediately. Since the cause is usually either a burned-out resistance in the regulator or a faulty relay winding, the only practical cure is to install a new regulator. The only regulator troubles to correct by repair and/or adjustment are those involving incorrect charge rates or a no-charge condition. If this is the case, the regulator should be calibrated exactly to the car maker's specifications, and if adjustment proves impossible, the unit should be scrapped in favor of a new one.

A no-charge problem, if caused by the regulator, is limited to two possibilities. First, the contacts controlling current to the alternator or generator field may not be making contact. Second, the regulator may contain fuse wires which are designed to melt under abnormally high charging, for the protection of the alternator or generator. The regulator should be inspected visually to see if it has fuse wires, and if so to determine whether they have been separated. The cause of the burned-out fuse wire probably lies in the regulator itself, so it must be thoroughly tested according to the car maker's instructions before renewing the fuse wires and returning the regulator to service. For the protection of the alternator, these wires must be replaced with fusible wire of the proper material.

A low charging system output, usually accompanied by a low battery, probably results from improper calibration of the regulator. The charge rate should therefore be readjusted to bring it within the manufacturer's specifications. A low, unsteady charging rate is usually caused by a high resistance somewhere in the charging system or its connections, including battery posts and terminals. In some instances this may result from the formation of oxidation deposits on the regulator contacts. The relays can normally be cleaned and the contacts lightly burnished with a riffler file without upsetting the standard adjustment.

An excessive charge rate is the most dangerous condition that can develop in the electrical system. In some cases the regulator may be set too high. This could be the result of recalibrating the unit without first bringing it to the proper operating temperature. It can also stem from nonfunctioning relays, or regulator contacts which have stuck or welded together. Both of these conditions call for replacement of the regulator unit. Another common cause of excessive charge rates is a poorly grounded regulator. Some cars do not have a separate ground connection for the regulator, which must then depend on having its base in good electrical contact with the car body. Try connecting a jumper wire between the regulator base and a clean spot on the body or chassis. If the charge rate becomes normal, it is only necessary to correct the ground.

When installing a new regulator on a generator-equipped car it is of the utmost importance that the generator be polarized before starting the engine. If this is not done, the generator—or regulator—will be burned out in the first few minutes of operation. This is especially important on cars having only indicator lights. An ammeter will show no charge when the engine is started without first polarizing the system; the light may not. Should you accidentally reverse the system's polarity and start the engine, remove the battery ground cable before shutting off the motor to save the generator from possible damage from unregulated battery current flowing "backward" into the windings.

To polarize the generator, momentarily touch a jumper wire between the generator terminal and the battery terminal of the regulator. The jumper should only be connected for a fraction of a second. If you leave it on any longer, you will burn up the points in the voltage regulator on some double-contact regulators.

Alternator systems are never polarized. They do not depend on residual magnetism in the field. Never under any circumstances should you make any attempt to polarize an alternator.

STARTER

Looking very much like a generator, but doing an entirely different job, is the starter motor. The starter may give you no trouble throughout the life of one car, but it can be a continuing source of frustration on another. Actually, starter motors are remarkably durable considering that they usually operate under the most adverse conditions. Fortunately, you can tell that a starter motor is going to fail eventually when it begins to act up. Don't expect a miracle to happen, with the trouble suddenly going away into thin air. Fix the starter and it won't leave you stranded. Remember that push-starting a car with an automatic transmission is much harder than push-starting one with a standard transmission.

Starter-motor design has steadily improved through the past several decades, and the switch to a full 12-volt electrical system has made it possible for starter motors to be relatively small even for large-displacement engines.

Most car makers have their own unique starter designs, so no overall description will fit. But a detailed description of each type of starter is unnecessary here; this information can come from a shop manual. Let's get directly into diagnosing starter troubles and making some home repairs.

Never jump to the conclusion that just because the starter doesn't spin at the flip of a key it has failed. There is a very good chance the trouble is elsewhere.

A weak battery will make any starting-system test unreliable. If you are sure the battery is in good condition, switch on the headlights and try the starter. There are three possible malfunctions: the lights will go out and the starter will not operate; the starter will make sounds, but the lights will dim considerably and any actual cranking will be very slow; the headlights will remain bright but there will be no cranking.

If the lights go out when the starter is switched on, look for poor connections between the battery and the starter motor. Corroded battery terminals are

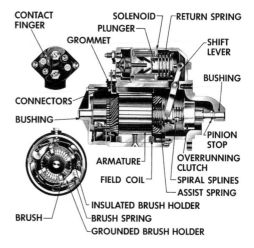

Starter motors are similar to generators; repairs are usually called for at brushes, bushings, solenoids. If starter action becomes erratic in electrical department, the solenoid needs repair or replacement. If it seems to spin okay but not engage, the clutch is usually to blame.

the primary suspect, but don't overlook the ground strap were it is fastened to the engine block or car body. Some cars have the battery grounded to the body of the car and a separate ground strap between the body and the engine. This may be located under the car in the area of the transmission or starter mounting.

If the lights dim noticeably when you operate the starter, and cranking action is sluggish or won't turn the engine at all, there is something throwing an unusually heavy load on the starter and imposing a high discharge rate on the battery. Probably the most frequent cause of such trouble is having too heavy an oil in the crankcase, usually a problem associated with cold weather. It could also be excessive spark advance. If the initial advance has been set too high or if the advance mechanism of the distributor is not working freely and correctly, the cylinders may be firing

Check the automatic advance mechanism by sucking on end of tube to make sure there is no leak in the diaphragm.

About the only thing that ever goes wrong with a horn is burning of the contact points. Housings are usually riveted together; replacement with new unit may be cheaper than repair.

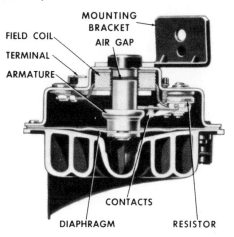

FIELD COIL

TERMINAL

ARMATURE

MOUNTING BRACKET

AIR GAP

CONTACTS

DIAPHRAGM   RESISTOR

before the piston reaches the top of its stroke. The engine tries to run backward, fighting the action of the starter.

If the lights stay bright, but there is no response from the starter, there is an open circuit in the starting system. This could be in the starter motor itself (possibly worn-out brushes), in its wiring, in the starter relay, or in the ignition switch and its wiring. You can make a small jumper cable to test the control circuit, using a 14-gauge wire and two alligator clips, or do it with a screwdriver. Make contact between the main (large) terminal on the starter relay or solenoid and the small terminal that receives the wire from the ignition-switch starter control. If the starter runs, the trouble is in the dash switch or wiring.

On cars with automatic transmission, there is a neutral safety switch that allows the ignition key to actuate the starter relay only when the transmission selector is in the park or neutral position (see Chapter 11). This may also be the site of trouble. Locate the switch and bypass it with the jumper wire (making sure that the transmission is in neutral). If the ignition key will now operate the starter, the trouble is in the neutral safety switch. Chrysler Corp. automatics have a neutral safety switch that grounds the starting circuit whenever the transmission is in neutral. These switches have only one terminal and can be bypassed by grounding the wire.

If these tests of the control circuit fail to provoke action from the starter, you can try connecting a heavy booster cable jumper directly from the battery hot side to the terminal on the starter motor. If this causes the starter to operate, the trouble is in the solenoid or starter relay. If the starter does not run when the booster cable is connected, the trouble is in the starter motor itself.

If the relay or solenoid makes a clicking sound when the key is turned and the starter does not run, but does run with the booster in place, it is not

The majority of starter motor failures can be traced to a faulty solenoid. Check the solenoid plunger to make sure it is free in the cylinder.

If starter makes a rapid clicking sound without engaging, it can usually be a problem of incorrect contact between the copper bolt head shown and contact disc on plunger control. Replacement kits are available.

Check all wiring carefully, as a disconnected wire at any terminal means the starter will fail to work.

necessarily an indication that the relay or solenoid is OK. In many cases the internal contacts are burned, making it impossible for the solenoid to switch on the heavy starter current. Sometimes a solenoid can be repaired, but usually it must be replaced.

The starter motor is usually neatly hidden by the engineers. Because it is mounted low alongside the engine block, it almost always must be removed from below the car. This calls for jackstands. Disconnect the battery before removing the starter, and remember that starter motors are rather heavy when you're working from an awkward position.

The starter will probably be coated with oil and dirt, and it will probably be difficult to reach the electrical wiring. Remove the bolts which hold the starter to the engine. If there is a support strap between the front of the starter and the engine (usually at an oil-pan bolt), make sure this is reinstalled. It is there to keep the starter weight from binding the drive mechanism at the flywheel. After the motor is loose from the engine, the wiring can be removed. Remember, or tag, the wires so they'll go back to the right terminal.

If you're sure the problem is the solenoid, it is probably easiest to install a new unit. If you're not sure what the problem is, haul the entire starter assembly down to the auto-parts store and have them check it out. They'll give you the pieces needed if the problem is minor. If the motor itself must be repaired, leave it to the shop. You're still way ahead on labor costs.

Sometimes the starting system seems to have troubles, but the starter motor is okay. If the motor tries to work, but the engine won't turn over, maybe you have water in one or two cylinders (caused by a broken cylinder wall,

leaking head gasket, etc.). Pull the spark plugs and the engine should turn over. Obviously you'll have to repair the engine. If the engine still won't turn over, maybe all the oil has drained from the bearings (caused by using oil that has been thinned or broken down by excessive heat). The engine will usually crank, but with effort. If the cooling system is clogging up, it can let the engine run too hot and a piston can seize.

If you get antifreeze into the oiling system, it will usually cause the bearings and pistons to seize. If you think this might be the case, drain the antifreeze and fill up with water. If starting improves, you've found the problem. If the antifreeze has really got things gummed up, get some Butyl Cellosolve from the parts store and put it in the oil. Follow the instructions explicitly.

If the starter seems to spin all right, but the engine won't turn over, the starter drive is at fault. If the motor spins and there is an accompanying gear-clashing sound, stop immediately. There is a chance the starter drive gear is not meshing correctly with the flywheel ring gear. If ring-gear teeth are damaged, it means the gear must be removed and replaced, a time-consuming and difficult job best left to a shop. Some GM starters have shims between the starter base and the engine. These are used to adjust clearance between the starter drive and the flywheel ring gear. If your unit has these shims, be sure and get them back in place.

IGNITION SYSTEM

Discounting minor accessory electric devices, such as heater and air conditioner, the only remaining electrical components are involved with the igni-

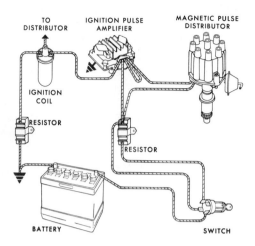

Schematic of new transistorized ignition circuit that is becoming popular. Main advantages of this system are long life and absence of breaker points.

Transistorized ignition system. Shown are basic component and circuit diagrams for two systems. (Mobil Oil Corp.)

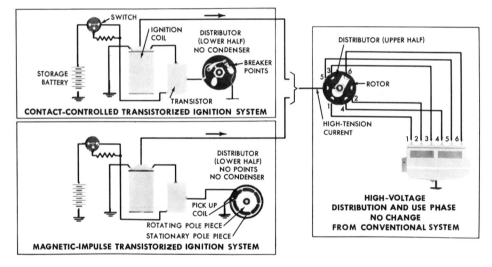

tion. These will include the distributor, the coil, the spark-plug wiring, and the spark plugs.

Distributor

The distributor is really quite simple, although it might seem a maze of mechanical tricks. The distributor has the job of getting spark to the correct spark plug at a precise moment of crankshaft rotation. In itself, this requirement would not be difficult to meet, but at the same time, the spark plug must fire

at different moments of crankshaft rotation depending on engine rpm. That is, the plug may fire at piston TDC (top dead center) when the engine is idling, but it must fire before TDC when rpm increases (to adjust for fuel-charge inertia, flame-front travel, etc.).

The typical distributor is driven off the camshaft at the same speed (one-half the crankshaft speed), and may or may not also be connected to the oil-pump drive gears (see Chapter 5). Like the carburetor, the distributor and its

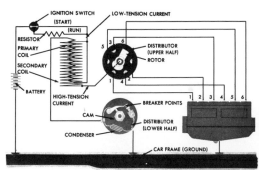

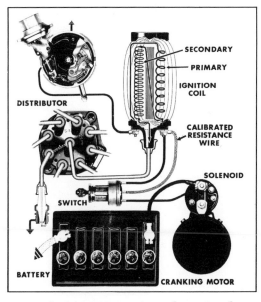

Standard ignition system schematic, showing coil windings which increase electrical output to distributor.

Chevrolet V-8 distributor as disassembled for inspection and repair. Much of the difficulty encountered in home tune-up can be traced to sloppy work on the distributor.

Conventional ignition system. The ignition system supplies current for igniting the fuel in each engine cylinder at the proper time in the cycle. The storage battery supplies the primary current which must be greatly "stepped" up in voltage in order to furnish the proper spark at the spark plug gap. This is accomplished in the coil, an assembly of windings on an iron core. The primary winding carries battery current, the secondary winding the high-tension current induced by the continuous making and breaking of the primary circuit by a rotary switch (cam) driven by the camshaft at one-half engine speed. The switch customarily occupies the lower part of a so-called "distributor," the upper part of which is occupied by another engine-driven rotary switch that "distributes" the high-tension current to the spark plugs in the proper engine firing order. The various circuits are generally "grounded" through the chassis. The condenser is employed to absorb certain unavoidable electrical effects that, if allowed to continue unchecked, would greatly interfere with proper operation of the primary circuit and the breaker points.

Modern circuits employ the resistor shown in the primary wiring. On starting, when a good, "hot" spark is needed for prompt firing, full battery current passes to the primary coil through the START path. After the engine starts, the switch connections are changed so that battery current passes through the RUN path, which includes a resistance that cuts down the current reaching the primary coil. The reduced current, while adequate for satisfactory post-starting operation, helps prolong point life because of its lower intensity.

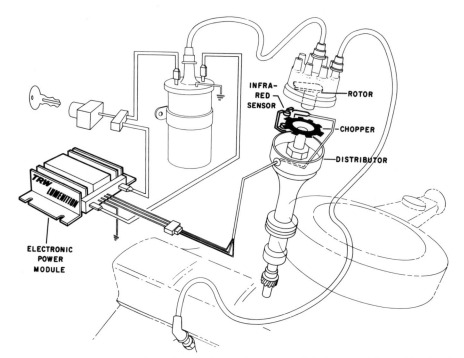

Recent advancements in the electronics field have led to introduction of many new types of ignition systems. One of the most recent is the TRW Lumenition, shown here in schematic form. There are only three parts to this system, other than the traditional distributor and coil. These are the chopper and infrared light unit, which replace the breaker points and condenser, and the power module. The power module switches the coil primary current and thus controls spark energy. The slotted chopper disc fits over the distributor shaft and interrupts the light beam of the sensor.

attendant parts are involved in every action of the engine. Therefore, the distributor is also a place to start looking when the engine acts up.

In most instances, you can detect improper distributor operation by the way the car behaves. Slow cranking when the engine is warm, backfiring, noticeable loss in performance, ragged idling, or "breaking up" at high speeds are some of the usual symptoms. If the compression is good, carburetor properly adjusted, and ignition system in otherwise perfect shape, the distributor and its advance mechanism deserve a close inspection. In fact, just by checking, cleaning, and lubricating the distributor each time it is removed to install new points you can usually prevent most trouble before it ever has a chance to affect engine operation (see Chapter 15).

The device that adjusts the distributor to operate properly relative to engine speed can be either a vacuum advance mechanism or a centrifugal advance mechanism. You can check the condition of the diaphragm and vacuum advance mechanism without removing the distributor from the car. The vacuum line runs from the distributor to the carburetor. Disconnect it from the distributor and take the cap off the distributor. Move the breaker plate by hand

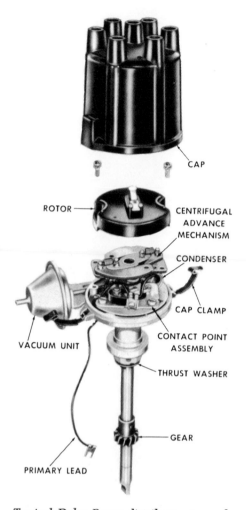

CAP

ROTOR

CENTRIFUGAL
ADVANCE
MECHANISM

CONDENSER

CAP CLAMP

CONTACT POINT
ASSEMBLY

VACUUM UNIT

THRUST WASHER

GEAR

PRIMARY LEAD

Typical Delco-Remy distributor as used on many GM cars. Distributor must be in excellent working order for engine to function properly; on older units always suspect shaft bushing wear.

not hold the plate in "advanced" position, the diaphragm is leaking and the vacuum chamber unit will have to be replaced. If the plate does not snap back to the retard position when the vacuum port is uncovered, the advance parts are binding or the spring is broken. Distributor vacuum chambers are serviced as a complete unit only, so if you find a diaphragm that leaks you'll have to buy a whole new vacuum unit. If the advance plate is binding or sticking, it can usually be put back in serviceable condition by cleaning and lubricating it according to the manufacturer's recommendations.

Centrifugal advance mechanisms can have their efficiency impaired by three things. The most common is plain old dirt and lack of lubrication (see Chapter 15). After a year's service the average centrifugal advance should be removed, cleaned, checked for wear, and properly lubricated. This is absolutely necessary if precise action is to be obtained. The weights and linkage of the centrifugal advance must be completely clean and lightly lubricated with engine oil. Most distributors have a felt wick in the center of the distributor cam which is to be regularly given a few drops of

until the full advanced position is attained, being careful not to bend the points. Place your finger over the vacuum port and release the breaker plate. It should move only very slightly and then stop. After a few seconds, remove your finger from the vacuum port. The advance mechanism should snap smartly to the full-retarded position. If placing your finger over the vacuum port will

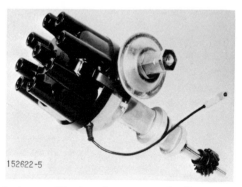

It is possible for the primary load wire to have a hard-to-detect short where it enters the distributor housing.

oil to keep the centrifugal advance properly lubricated. The weights should be checked to see that they are free from rust or burrs which would hinder smooth movement.

The second cause of trouble is wear in the distributor shaft, bearings, thrust washers or cam. This can seriously disrupt the timing and functioning of the centrifugal advance. If the distributor shaft can be moved noticeably from side to side, the shaft or bearings are worn. Shaft end play should be no more than .012 to .015 inch. Most distributors have replaceable bushings in the distributor housing, but some do not. If replaceable, the bushings or bearings can be removed with a bushing driver or arbor press. Excessive end play can usually be corrected by installing new thrust washers on the shaft. Then the repair is made by driving out the pin holding the drive gear and removing it from the shaft. The shaft can then be withdrawn and checked for straightness by rolling it on a flat surface. If all is well, the washers can be slipped on and the shaft then reinstalled. If the distributor cam shows any visible wear at all, you can bet it is seriously affecting the engine timing. In most cases this is a very inexpensive part which can be installed in a few minutes. Proper cam lubrication will usually prevent such trouble. A badly lubed cam can also affect the operation of both the centrifugal and vacuum advances by slowing the motion of the cam and breaker plate. To function perfectly, a distributor must be kept as friction-free as possible.

One third thing which can spoil the accuracy of centrifugal advance units is incorrect point spring tension. Like a poorly lubricated cam, this may also affect the operation of the vacuum ad-

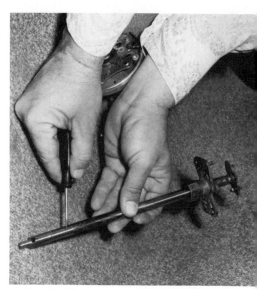

If the distributor is in poor condition, inspect the shaft at lower end for excessive wear. Any indication of wear should be further checked with a micrometer (entire shaft size should be uniform) and shaft should be replaced if wear is severe. Also check the shaft bushings in the housing.

Although the cam lobe does not usually wear, it can if the lubrication is missing. Install a new cam if it shows any signs of wear. The tiniest bit of wear in distributor parts will cause erratic engine operation.

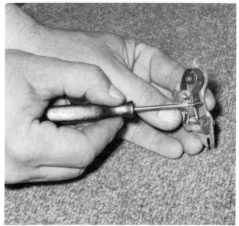

Pin holding drive gear to lower end of shaft should be checked and replaced if it shows any signs of wear or fatigue. On occasion the pin will shear if there is a bind on the shaft or in the oil pump.

Always use quality replacement distributor points, and check to see how much wear is on old point cam rubbing block. This block wears away slowly when lubed well, wears rapidly when there is insufficient lubrication on the cam lobes. It is imperative to use correct cam lube, as ordinary greases will melt and get on contact points.

vance system to some degree. The point spring tension should be adjusted, if possible, but in many cases excessive or inadequate point spring tension is the result of installing the wrong points in the car. Incorrect springs installed in the centrifugal advance can also ruin its precision. When any distributor parts are replaced, make certain they are the correct ones for your particular engine, since the same distributor with different advance rates is probably used in many different makes and models.

The breaker points are the key electrical part of the distributor. The length of time the points stay closed has a very important relationship to coil saturation. That is, the longer they feed battery current into the coil's primary windings, the stronger the magnetic field becomes. As a result, greater spark voltages are produced. However, there is a limit to how long the points can remain closed effectively, because of the design of the

distributor cam. The time the points remain together is called cam angle or dwell. Both terms refer to the number of degrees of distributor rotation that points remain closed. The initial gap to which the points are adjusted determines dwell. And although there is a specific tolerance for these settings, efficiency is lost beyond a certain point. Points that are set too wide open gradually. This can cause excessive arcing and burning of the contacts, and shortens the coil saturation time as well. If set too close, dwell time is increased, but "point bounce" can often occur at higher speeds, and the idle becomes rough and starting is more difficult.

Removing and Installing a Distributor

The distributor should be replaced if you have any doubt as to condition.

Traces of carbon between terminals, a crack in the cap, indications of water residue: all these are reasons for replacement. Sometimes a frustrating miss at all speeds can be traced directly to a distributor cap that looks perfect. They are inexpensive, so replace when in doubt.

A lot of the troubles experienced with ignition points can be avoided by proper installation and maintenance. Undoubtedly the thing that keeps many tinkerers from taking out the distributor for point installation is the fear that they won't be able to reinstall the thing correctly once the job's done. Yes, sometimes it does take a little coaxing to get the oil-pump drive to engage and the gears to mesh properly, but you'll find that with proper techniques you can do the job. After you've done it once or twice you could probably repeat it blindfolded.

In addition to checking the rotor for carbo traces (small lines that appear to run ha hazard across the part, and serve as a rou for errant electrical charge) and physic cracks, file the rotor tip clean to get be charge transfer.

Some distributors have a rotor that is much smaller than the Chevy unit shown, and fits a slot in the upper end of the drive-shaft. Delco-Remy distributors use a large circular rotor as shown; underside has small square and round pegs so it can be attached to drive plate only one way.

First, always aim the rotor in the sam direction before pulling the distributo Probably the best way is to simply tur the engine until the rotor is pointe directly at the front of the car. You als have to remember the position of th distributor body, so that lines and wire will hook up easily when you put back.

After you've mentally marked the roto and body positions, you can remove th distributor hold-down clamp and pu the distributor out. As the distributo is withdrawn one of two things wi happen: either the rotor will not mov at all, or it may rotate slightly as th helical gears disengage. If the distribu tor is the type that is driven by th oil-pump gear, the rotor will not turn Also, you will see no gear on the en of the distributor shaft after it is ou of the car. If it does turn, remembe (or mark) the rotor's final position i

Inspect the rotor for cracks or carbon traces and replace if it is damaged.

Counterweights must be cleaned well before reassembly. If the unit has run dry of lubrication there is sometimes wear at the point shown, which will cause the advance mechanism to operate in an erratic manner. Replace these weights if they show the slightest sign of wear.

The counterweights must also get a special distributor lubricant.

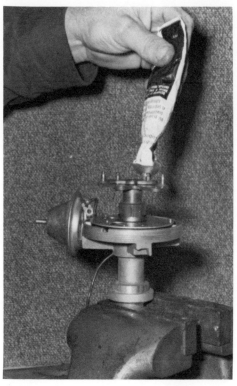

relation to its original location. When reinstalling the distributor, all you'll have to do is place the rotor in the final position, insert the unit into the engine, and the gears should engage and turn the rotor back to its initial place. On a few engines, like the Chevy sixes, the oil-pump drive may not align with the tang on the distributor shaft end. If this happens, don't panic. Just reach down into the distributor hole with a long screwdriver and turn the oil-pump drive until it is in the right position.

If the engine is accidentally rotated while the distributor is out, all you have to do is pull one spark plug and hold your thumb over the plug hole while you turn the engine over (see Chapter 5). Stop when the piston is at top dead center on the compression stroke, as evidenced by the compressed air pushing your thumb away from the hole. (On the exhaust stroke, the exhaust valve would be open and you would feel no pressure.) Practice it several times until you are sure that the piston is on top dead center of the compression stroke. If you can see the piston through the hole, or feel it with a broom straw, so much the better.

Once you have the piston on TDC in one cylinder, you must find out what wire goes to that cylinder. It will be easy if the wires and cap are still in position on the engine. Once you have found the right wire, all you have to do is insert the distributor so that the rotor points directly to that wire segment in the cap, and position the distributor so the points are just ready to open.

If you keep the rotor opposite the correct wire segment, and are sure the points are just about to open, then you can insert the distributor in any position relative to the engine block. It makes no difference to the timing of the engine. However, only the original stock position will allow you to put the cap on the distributor without twisting the plug wires into a pretzel. Also, any vacuum lines or wires will hook up easier if you put the distributor body back in the original position.

Snug down the distributor hold-down bolt, connect all the wires and the cap,

Distributor point plate should have all wiring leads securely fastened. Check to make sure none of the leads is bare, especially the lead passing through the housing body. It is possible to set the points at home with a feeler gauge; a better job of setting dwell is possible on a machine shop distributor machine.

and the engine should fire up. If it won you probably made one of two commo mistakes. First, you may have though the points were positioned about t open, when they were actually about t close. Double-check the rotation of th cam. Second, you may have had th piston on the exhaust stroke instead c the compression stroke.

Distributor Points

For maximum efficiency and min: mum deterioration, the contact poin must meet accurately—both horizontall and vertically as well as at 0° of angl If the mismatching is severe, you shoul probably return the points to the deale and demand a better-made set. In mo: cases, however, a little judicious benc ing of the stationary contact mount wi correct minor alignment problems. Avoi any major bending because you ma damage the points beyond repair. Th points supplied on many foreign car: including some VWs, have a fiber washe that is installed on the breaker-poir pivot post between the stationary an movable point assemblies. This washe must be filed to correct vertical aligr ment errors, since the construction c the movable point arm is such that benc ing it is impossible.

There is one exception to this discu: sion of point alignment, and that's th new pivotless points used by Ford. A cording to a Ford service bulletin, yo can expect a slight irregularity in thei wear pattern, which is "normal."

After the points are checked for align ment, and any discrepancies correctec they can be installed in the distributo and adjusted to specs. This calls for set of flat feeler gauges or an electroni dwell meter. Although most servic manuals give specifications in degree of dwell or cam angle, this is only fc

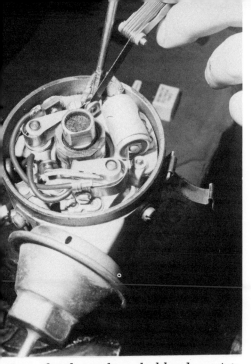

Some distributors have dual breaker points, others have single points. Make sure all wires are firmly attached and not shorting out on housing. Adjust points with feeler gauge to a perfect setting, rotate the shaft by hand several times, recheck the setting.

lubricated. Vaseline and other greases with a low melting point should not be used, since they are rapidly broken down by engine heat and thrown off the moving parts. Never use brake-shoe grease. It dries hard, and then grinds the rubbing block down to a nub quicker than sandpaper. Wheel-bearing grease, chassis lube, and rear-end grease should also be avoided. There might have been some excuse for using the wrong grease years ago when distributor-cam grease was hard to find, but it can be purchased in almost any large auto-parts store now. Some distributors, such as the Delco-Remy, have an oil-saturated wick that distributes lubrication to the cam. This should be re-oiled with light engine oil periodically and when new points are installed. At 20,000 miles or sooner, the wick should be replaced. A new wick is included as part of some replacement sets. For points without a lubricating wick, a light smear of rubbing-block

convenience in modern service garages where electronic testing equipment can be a real timesaver. When properly used, a feeler gauge can be just as accurate. But don't ever attempt to use a feeler gauge on used points. The slightest pitting of the points will result in an inaccurate measurement.

When new points are installed, some mechanics like to adjust the gap .002 to .003 inch wider than specified to compensate for early initial rubbing-block wear, but it's probably better practice simply to recheck the gap after 100 miles or so—particularly if you want top performance from the new set of points right away.

Rubbing-block wear can be a real problem unless the cam is properly

Replacement points should be installed anytime the rub block is worn significantly or the point faces are pitted. It is imperative correct ignition lubricant be used, and that sparingly on rub block only.

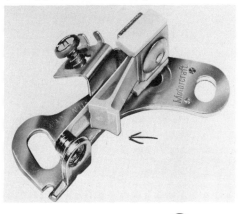

grease works very well for limiting friction and wear. Here's one place where it's mighty handy to have a distributor out of the car, since by rotating the shaft by hand you can "work in" the lubricant to ensure that it is spread evenly on the cam and thoroughly fills the pores of the rubbing block. Nothing can do quite so much damage and cause so much trouble as oil on the point contacts, so go easy.

The practice of smoothing used points with a point file is of dubious value. While badly pitted points can be quickly made reusable by filing them, the surfaces are left rougher than they should be, which reduces effective contact area and speeds further pitting. Another thing to remember is that the tungsten contacts must not be filed so much that they will burn through into the softer metal underneath. The tungsten facing on the contacts of many stock point sets is so thin that even one filing will sometimes seriously weaken it. Filing should only be the first step in reconditioning points. After filing, they should be honed mirror-smooth with either a fine stone or crocus cloth. Points dressed by this method will have the appearance and efficiency of a brand-new set. However, one must be very careful to hone the surfaces flat, absolutely not to a bulging, rounded contour which would severely reduce the effective contact area and result in local burning. After filing (only if absolutely necessary), honing, and polishing, the points may require slight realignment.

Remember that points which show signs of severe burning and discoloration, or have developed deep pits, indicate an imbalance in the ignition system, which must be corrected or the trouble will soon recur. This can usually be done by checking and replacing the condenser, as explained below. Contact point burning may also result from an abnormally high primary voltage or the presence of oil or other foreign matter on their surfaces. Oil or crankcase vapors working up around the distributor shaft are a frequent cause of point burning. This trouble is easy to detect because the oil produces a smudgy line on the distributor's breaker plate directly under the contacts. Over-oiled parts, clogged engine breather pipes, or plugged pollution-control valves are the usual cause of this. Anything other than a lightly frosted appearance of the contacts should be considered abnormal.

Condenser

The condenser is a rugged and reliable part of the ignition system. There is usually no reason to replace it unless actual testing proves it to be weak. Nor is there usually a need to replace the condenser with each change of points, although this is routinely done by most mechanics. It takes less time to put in a new condenser than it does to test the old one. In these days when mechanic's time is so costly, condenser

Always install a new condenser whenever points are installed. A bad condenser can cause poor spark at the plugs.

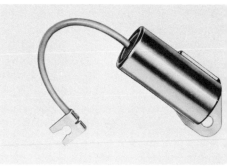

testing is almost a lost art, and installing a new one is insurance against subsequent untimely failure.

If an engine misfires at high speed, or if the breaker points become burned and pitted after only a short time in service, the condenser is often suspected of being at fault. However, simply changing the consenser, may be money down the drain. The missing could be caused by spark plugs or high-tension cables that have an excessive voltage requirement, while oil on the points is responsible for the burning and pitting of the contacts. In many cases, apparent condenser trouble is not due to a bad condenser, but to a poor ground contact. A very large percentage of condenser trouble can be eliminated by making sure that all external connections are clean and tight. This applies particularly to the condenser mounting strap, which must be in good electrical contact with the distributor. When a new condenser is installed, or the old one replaced after testing, the mounting strap and the part of the distributor it attaches to should be brightened with emery paper to ensure a perfect ground for the case.

Most contact-point pitting results from an imbalanced ignition system which causes transfer of tungsten from one contact point to the other. The result is a "mountain" on one contact and a "valley" in the other. The direction in which the material transfer takes place can be used as a basis for analysis and correction of the pitting. For example, if the material transfers from the negative contact to the positive (the movable point on negative-ground cars), the condenser capacity needs to be increased within the specifications given by the car maker, or the condenser has become

weak and must be replaced. If the material transfer takes place in the opposite direction—from positive to negative—the condenser capacity is too great, and the condenser must be replaced by one with a lower rating.

There is a ballast resistor in the primary circuit of some cars which is designed to help stabilize the load placed on the condenser and to further minimize point burning due to excessive voltage. It is simply a compensating resistance in the primary circuit that heats up during low-speed operation when the primary current flow is high, thereby reducing the current flow and prolonging ignition-contact life. At higher speeds the primary current flow is low, since the points are closed for a shorter length of time, and the ballast

Always suspect the resistor in ignition circuit if there is trouble that can't seem to be traced.

FIG. 1

OPEN

FIG. 2

SHORTED

NOTE: If just one side opens up, the resistance will be doubled.

resistance cools off and allows more current to flow—very desirable for good high-speed operation. During starting, the ballast resistor is bypassed, allowing full battery voltage to reach the ignition's primary circuit.

Coil

The ignition coil seldom gives trouble, but sometime it does. Unfortunately, the coil can start to weaken and you may spend days or weeks trying to find the trouble elsewhere. The coil's job is to build enough charge to fire the plugs under the high compression forces inside the combustion chamber. Sometimes a higher-performance coil may be fitted to an engine, but unless a high-performance distributor is also used, there is not much point in it.

Most coil troubles are the result of defects in the secondary windings. Either the insulation that separates the windings from one another has broken down, resulting in a reduction of the spark voltage, or the insulation between windings and ground has broken down, allowing the spark current to escape

The coil may look good externally but be failing inside. A weak spark can often be traced to a bad coil. When in doubt, install a coil you know is good.

internally. Coils subjected to a great deal of vibration are particularly vulnerable, since the windings in shaking against one another can wear away their thin lacquer insulation quickly. Broken windings and internal connections are nearly always the cause of complete and sudden coil failures, but such trouble is actually quite rare. The most common coil defects result from a gradual deterioration of internal insulation, and complete failure is usually preceded by many signs of an impending breakdown.

One of the most common tip-offs that the coil needs a check is hard or unreliable starting. Another symptom is a chronic high-speed miss and cutting out during acceleration. If the car's battery is up to par, the distributor tuned, and the plugs in good shape, yet the trouble still persists, your suspicions should definitely be focused on the coil. You can perform preliminary coil checks without special equipment, and if these indicate that a coil defect does indeed exist, you can replace the coil and that's that. But if your home tests are not conclusive, you can't assume the coil is blameless; you need more elaborate test procedures.

The first test is to remove the high-tension cable that passes between the coil and distributor from the distributor cap. Hold the end of the cable about $\frac{3}{16}$ inch from some grounded part of the engine and operate the starter with the ignition turned on. A bright-blue spark should jump the gap. A weak yellowish or red spark indicates insufficient spark voltage. This last condition definitely points to a weak coil—provided the points, condenser, and battery are all in good shape. To back up your test, take the coil to a garage for a thorough test. Be careful about rejecting any coil unless you have a new coil of the same make and specifications to check against it. A coil tester may tell you that a coil is weak, but maybe all of that type of coil will show weak on that tester. If the coil tests weak when compared with a new coil of that same specification, replace the coil.

If your preliminary test using the high-tension cable produces no spark at all, you should attempt to pinpoint the trouble before replacing the coil with a new one. All you need is a 6- or 12-volt bulb, depending on your car's electrical system, and two test leads attached to it. Start by taking off the distributor cap and either turning the engine until the points are open or separating the points with a small piece of cardboard. Turn on the ignition switch. One testlight lead can now be connected to ground somewhere on the engine and the other lead touched to first one of the coil's primary terminals and then the other. If the lamp lights when touched to the terminal that leads to the distributor, it indicates that the coil is getting current and that the primary windings are OK. If the lamp lights when touched to the other primary terminal, but not when attached to the one leading to the distributor, the primary windings are faulty and the coil is no good. If the light does not go on when connected to either primary connection, the trouble is somewhere else, possibly in the ignition switch. More than one new coil has been installed, only to have the ignition switch or starter relay turn out to be the culprit.

If your tests show that the coil is getting current at both primary terminals, try shorting across the open distributor points with the tip of a screwdriver. If a spark jumps from the high-tension wire to a grounded point on the engine as the screwdriver is removed, the trouble is probably oil, dirt, or water on the points or simply burned points. Should this last test also fail to produce a spark at the high-tension wire, disconnect the primary wire that passes between the coil and the distributor and attach a test wire to the coil in its place. Ground the other end of the wire against the engine block and then pull it away. If the spark jumps from the high-tension cable when the test wire is removed from the ground, the coil is OK, and the trouble is in the points (which are probably grounded) or condenser (which may be shorted). If a spark does not jump during this test, the secondary windings of the coil are probably faulty and the coil should be replaced if a machine test corroborates your own test results.

There is one other thing that could be causing the trouble, and that's poor contact between the engine and the ground pole of the battery. Whenever there is a "mysterious" electrical problem in your car that seems impossible, the battery-and-engine connection is one of the first things to check.

In some cases a coil will test out perfectly. Yet the car remains hard to start and misses at higher speeds, suggesting that there is inadequate spark voltage. If the engine has recently been tuned up, repaired, or newly installed in the car, you have a hint as to what the real problem is. Nine times out of ten the trouble is reversed coil polarity. The cause of this is that the two primary wires leading to the coil have been reversed by mistake. When this happens the spark voltage has positive polarity. It should always be negative, regardless of the way the battery is installed in the vehicle. If it isn't the sparking current has a lower "pressure" in relation to the spark-plug ground electrode that it must jump to. The end result is a weak spark, even though every part of the ignition system is in perfect condition. Another indication of reversed coil polarity is "dishing" of the spark plugs' side electrodes.

Stock coils are most susceptible to damage from high temperatures and vibration. For this reason weak coils are more likely to fail completely on a long summer trip. Cars that have coils mounted in especially hot locations which are subject to a great deal of vibration often show a remarkable tendency toward coil failure. If it's possible to do it without making the high-tension cable to the distributor too long (over about 12 inches), relocate the coil to a cooler, steadier spot. When replacing a defective coil it is very important to make sure that the new one is the correct voltage (6 or 12 volt) for the car. Also, it must be of the correct polarity. Pre-1956 Fords with 6-volt systems and many imports have the positive pole of the battery grounded to the chassis rather than the negative pole. Coils from these cars should not be installed on cars with more common negative ground. If you happen to have a car with positive ground, remember that the coil primary terminal marked positive (+) must be connected to the distributor, while on cars with negative ground it's the other way around. If the original coil is being discarded because of a burned tower, carbon tracking, or any evidence of arcing at the tower, the nipple or boot on the coil end of the high-tension lead should always be replaced. Any arcing at the tower will carbonize the nipple so that placing it on a new coil will invariably cause another coil failure.

Spark Plugs and Wires

There isn't a great deal to say about spark-plug wires. Either they are good, or they are bad. And it doesn't matter whether you are using special resistance cables, high-performance (and high-priced) racing cables, or wires that are twenty years old.

Generally speaking, you will have to change all secondary (plug) wiring about every 50,000 miles. Sure, you can get more miles from the cable, but that's pushing it. And if you drive the car under harsh conditions, or if the wiring is subjected to lots of gas and oil solutions, you may have to change sooner. The best bet you can make is always to keep relatively new wires on the car.

But even with new wires, you can have a problem. You might have damaged a wire during installation, causing an internal break. This will show up as

Spark plug wires can be a frustrating source of electrical problems. Always clean the wires of oil and grease, and replace them if they show signs of cracking. Sometimes a high-speed miss can be traced directly to a single poor plug wire. It is usually best to replace plug wires every 30,000 miles or so.

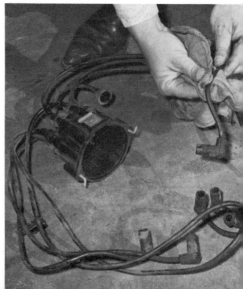

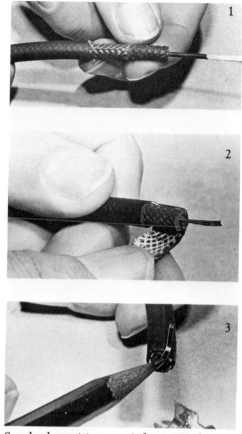

an erratic or missing fire to one spark plug, usually only as a hard-to-find miss at higher speeds. Make sure you install new nipples where the wiring enters the distributor cap, and make sure the plug terminals are not close enough to an engine part (such as an exhaust manifold) to allow arcing from terminal to block at high engine speeds.

The spark plugs need direct and periodic attention if you're going to get top performance from a car, or any performance, for that matter. Unfortunately the modern car usually has so many accessories piled inside the engine compartment that getting at plugs can be a major chore. Generally speaking, if there seems to be little room up top (especially with air conditioning), you can do the job from below the car. It is more tedious, but perhaps necessary.

There is no hard-and-fast rule as to when spark plugs should be changed, although you'll hear claims of everything from 5,000 to 50,000 miles. Change the plugs when the tips indicate a change is necessary. This may be due to

Spark plug wiring can fail, too. If the wiring is old and coated with oil, it should probably be replaced. A good check is to watch a running engine at night and move the cable near metal to detect leaks. Internal failures can cause engine missing at higher rpm and under loads. Figure 1 shows early type of resistor cable used to combat radio interference. Figure 2 shows current type of resistor wire. Figure 3 shows how plug or distributor end staple should be inserted into cable core securely and then bent over exposed end to make sure of good contact.

Check distributor cap for physical damage, look for carbon traces along the inside between contacts. Excessive moisture buildup inside the cap will also cause a corrosion that means cap should be replaced.

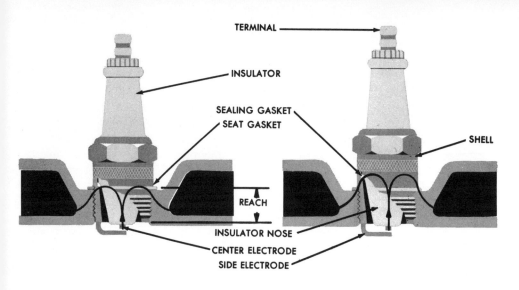

TERMINAL

INSULATOR

SEALING GASKET
SEAT GASKET

SHELL

REACH

INSULATOR NOSE
CENTER ELECTRODE
SIDE ELECTRODE

COLD PLUG

Spark-plug operation; temperature range. High-tension current from the distributor enters at the center electrode and leaves by the side electrode, producing the igniting spark in jumping the gap between the two. The use of an effective, thick insulator is necessary to avoid wasteful leakage of current and short circuiting, the high-tension voltage often being in the magnitude of 18,000 to 20,000 volts. Grounding, or completion of the circuit, occurs between the metal shell and the cylinder head.

HOT PLUG

The path of heat flow outward is up through the center electrode, through the insulator and thence through the interior gas-sealing gasket to the plug shell and the cylinder head. Differences in the length of this path for spark plugs of otherwise similar dimensions and construction result in variations in plug operating temperatures. As shown, a long path means a hot plug; a short path, a cold (relatively cooler) plug.

mileage, it may be due to a weather difference, it may be due to your use of a different grade of gas, or lots of things. Just learn to read the plugs and you can't go wrong. But if you must have a mileage figure to go by, new plugs every 10,000 to 12,000 is usually about right.

Most auto-parts stores have a free chart that shows exactly what spark plugs in all kinds of poor and good condition look like. Keep this chart around, as a handy reference. Generally speaking, a normal plug will have a light tan or gray insulator. There will be few deposits. If your plugs look like this, replacements of the same type should be used. If the plug looks different in

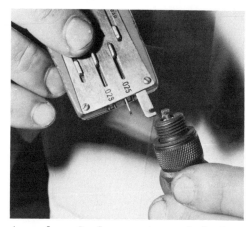

A good spark plug gapping and checking tool is as near as the local auto parts store, and it should be used. Always check the gap on new plugs before installation.

any way, haul it to the parts store and they'll tell you what is wrong and what type you should use for your car.

(following photos courtesy Champion Spark Plug Company)

This is what a normally burning spark plug should look like. The tips will have a brown to grayish tan deposit and slight electrode wear. This indicates correct plug heat range and mixed periods of high/low speed car operation. Regap before reinstalling.

This plug shows reversed polarity in direction of spark travel. It should always be negative, or the current should arc from the center to the ground electrode. Reversing the flow places greater demand on the system. Symptoms of reversed polarity are: hard starting, missing during acceleration or at higher speeds, short spark plug life. The cure is simply to switch the primary leads at the coil. On most systems, the negative lead should go to the distributor.

Improper use of pliers bends electrode and frequently pushes center electrode into the insulator assembly.

Mechanical damage shows in bent electrodes and broken insulator caused by foreign object in the combustion chamber. Can be caused by plug with too long a reach as well.

If one or two plugs of a set have fractured insulators, severe detonation may be suspected. Indiscriminate bending of the center electrode during gapping can also cause the insulator to crack.

A worn-out plug will have eroded electrodes and a pitted insulator, indicating too many miles of service. The only cure is replacement.

Fuel scavenger deposits may be white or yellow and while they may appear bad they are normal with certain branded fuels. Accumulation on the ground electrode and shell areas may be unusually heavy, but the material is easily flaked off. Such plugs can be considered normal and can be cleaned and reused.

Wet, oily deposits may be caused by oil leaking past worn piston rings. A porous vacuum booster pump diaphragm or excessive valve stem guide clearances can also cause oil fouling. Usually these plugs can be cleaned and reinstalled. Hotter type plugs may overcome a chronic fouling condition, but that would indicate an engine overhaul is needed.

Carbon fouled plugs show dry, fluffy black deposits which may result from over-rich carburetion, over-choking, a sticking manifold heat valve, or clogged air cleaner. Faulty breaker points, weak coil or condenser, worn ignition cables can all reduce spark voltage and cause plug misfiring leading to similar deposits.

Splash fouling can occur with relatively new plugs and sometimes right after tune-up. Accumulated combustion chamber deposits are melted and thrown against the plugs. They can be cleaned and reused.

If one or two plugs have melted electrodes, preignition was probably the cause. Check for intake manifold air leaks, possible crossfire, or worn distributor parts which might alter timing.

Burned or blistered insulator nose and badly eroded electrodes are indications of plug overheating, caused by wrong spark timing or low octane fuel causing detonation. Lean air/fuel mixtures, clogged cooling system, or sticking valves may also cause the condition.

TUNE-UP TIPS

Because it is a machine, the automobile works best when each and every part is in excellent working order, and when each group of parts is doing its job at top efficiency. Unfortunately, we too often let the vehicle slip out of top tune, and from there it is constantly downhill. To avoid letting an automobile be out of tune for any length of time, it is wise to plan a yearly maintenance schedule that calls for at least two tune-ups per year, with tune-up checks every three months. If the car gets a great amount of use, say two or three thousand miles per month, then tune-up checks should come every two months, with regular tune-up maintenance scheduled perhaps three times yearly.

Every mile your car runs at anything less than peak effeciency is costing you money, a cost that will far outweigh the expense of a home tune-up on schedule. While most drivers know the value of keeping their car in premium tune, it has been the upward spiral of the professional tune-up that has tended to discourage a regular tuning schedule. Because a professional tune-up may cost as much as $100 or more, many motorists have decided to get the car tuned only in an emergency—usually when it won't run anymore!

Other drivers have opted to shop around for the "bargain tune-up," usually advertised as a certain low fee, plus parts. This, too, proves to be a false economy, since this type of corner gas station tune-up will most often prove to be nothing more than the installation of poor quality ignition points, spark plugs, and perhaps a carburetor adjustment. A good engine tune-up is more than tinkering with linkage and looking at the spark plug gap. Any home mechanic will probably start his automotive career with the basic tune-up, and since it is something that will show immediate results with a minimum amount of labor and expertise, the driveway tune-up should rate priority over raking leaves and working in the garden.

You will need only a minimum amount and variety of basic hand tools for the tune-up, but if you can spare an extra few dollars for a couple of pieces of specialty equipment, such as a compression gauge and timing light, you can

Electronic tune-up instruments are an invaluable aid to the home mechanic, and they are not costly when purchased as individual units. Electronic timing light is especially useful if you have not yet attained a high enough degree of experience to set ignition timing by "feel."

232

expect excellent results every time. Fortunately, these special tools are not expensive, and you will need only the simple home-shop versions. They are available from all auto parts stores and general parts outlets such as Sears and Montgomery Ward; since you will not be using them on the demanding schedule of a professional mechanic, you can get the bottom-of-the-line equipment. Because most of this equipment is sold in a "modular" way, the designers have come up with test equipment sets. As you become better and better with your tune-up gear, you can add more sophisticated testers, all designed to work together as a package. In addition, this electronic test equipment comes with simple instructions that you can refer to for occasional use. When you become totally familiar with such test equipment, you will find it an invaluable diagnostic aid when you are troubleshooting a mechanical or electrical problem.

An engine tune-up is usually thought to be limited to the ignition and carbu-

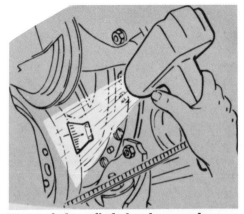

Timing light will flash when number one spark plug fires. The light will show up timing marks at the crankshaft pulley.

retion systems, but this is not the case. There is also the matter of mechanical tune-up, which are covered in Chapters 5, 7, 8, 9, 10, and 15. Essentially, the mechanical tune-up merely means that the mechanic checks the engine's internal parts to make sure they are working correctly. Of course, it could go far beyond this, but as a general rule the home mechanic will be concerned primarily with the cylinder compression

To advance or retard the timing, distributor hold-down bolt is loosened slightly and distributor rotated by hand, then bolt is retightened. Some distributors will also have a timing reference at the base.

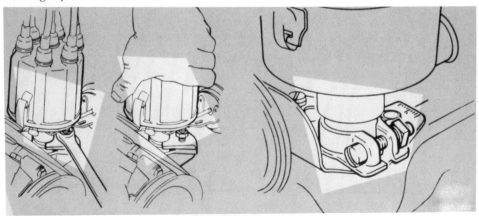

test. This test will tell if there is something wrong with the piston rings or valves, two areas that are directly related to engine tune and final engine performance.

If you suspect an engine may have poor valves, a blown head gasket, or something wrong with the rings or pistons, use the compression (pressure) gauge. This is an inexpensive tool that will register pressure to 200 psi or more on a large dial. It will have different size rubber ends, so there will be one just right for any size plug hole you may find. To use the gauge, remove all spark plugs and test each cylinder in turn. If you have an auxiliary starter button (also available at the parts store), you can spin the engine on the starter while holding the compression gauge in place. Otherwise, you'll need a friend to engage the starter and hold the throttle wide open.

Hold the compression gauge rubber end securely in the spark plug hole while the piston in that cylinder has a chance to revolve through the compression stroke several times (see Chapter 5 for a detailed explanation of the engine's four strokes). Record this reading, along with the cylinder, for later reference. Some home mechanics find it useful to check cylinder pressure on a brand new engine, and keep this for reference through the year. It is a good indication of how the internal parts of an engine are reacting to wear.

If all cylinders show a pressure within a few pounds of each other (from 10 to 15 pounds variance is acceptable), it is safe to assume pistons, rings, valves, and head gasket are in good working order. If there is a mechanical failure problem, this will normally show up at only one or two cylinders. If all the

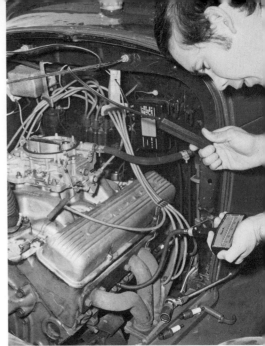

Compression gauges come in a variety of styling designs; all measure the pressure inside the combustion chamber. This will tell if there is internal mechanical problem that must be repaired.

cylinders show an abnormally low pressure reading, it would tend to indicate the engine needs a complete rebuild.

If one cylinder shows a low pressure reading, squirt some oil into the cylinder through the open spark plug hole. Be liberal, as this oil will seal around the piston rings long enough for you to get another pressure reading. If the cylinder pressure increases after this oil treatment, the rings on that cylinder are not seating and you must tear into the engine. If the pressure is still low, you are losing pressure through a bad valve (usually the exhaust valve; see Chapter 5), a hole in the piston, or a blown head gasket. Your local gas station attendant will probably have a tester that will tell if compression gases are leaking past the head gasket and into the coolant. If the head gasket tests well, then suspect a bad valve or piston. Either way, you must disassemble the head from the cylinder block to find out.

Another type of pressure tester you will find handy for the tune-up is for the fuel system. This gauge is most commonly included as part of a vacuum gauge; the vacuum side of the dial reads from zero to about 27 (meaning 27 inches of mercury), and the pressure side reads to 10 psi. Obviously, this gauge cannot be susbtituted for the correct instrument when reading compression chamber pressures!

The pressure side of this guage is used to test fuel pump pressure (3½ to 6½ psi on most modern cars). Remove the fuel line anywhere between carburetor and fuel pump and hold the gauge inlet securely against the fuel line or pump. If the fuel pump does not show pressure very near specifications (these specs are available from the auto parts store), it will be necessary to replace the fuel pump before getting into the tune-up. Full instructions on use of both these pressure gauges come with the instruments.

Once considered more a gimmick than a helpful instrument, the vacuum gauge has suddenly come into its own as a driving aid. Some new cars are now equipped with vacuum gauges, and the driver who learns to use the gauge can register much improved gasoline mileage. For the purpose of engine tune-up, and detecting possible trouble, the external vacuum gauge should be used. Some of these test gauges are really complete, with simple instructions that can be followed to determine a very wide variety of engine operating problems.

The vacuum gauge indicates the difference in atmospheric and engine pres-

A vacuum and low-count pressure combination gauge is used to test engine vacuum and fuel pump pressure.

Electronic tune-up instruments for the home mechanic are becoming more and more sophisticated. Now there is even an exhaust gas analyzer available from Sears.

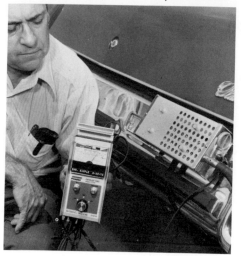

For the home mechanic who would rather have all the instruments combined in one case, the advanced equipment is ideal.

sures; the higher the reading, the greater the difference. Since the difference is based on atmospheric pressure, it is necessary to make altitude scale corrections. These corrections are included in the instructions.

The test gauge will usually include a length of rubber hose. The end of this hose will connect to a fitting as near the intake manifold as possible. If the vehicle has a vacuum booster for the fuel pump, plug off this line, as it disrupts the vacuum and you will have difficulty getting a true reading. Make sure there is no vacuum leak in the gauge connection. Most of the tests will be made with the engine running at idle speed. Other tests can be made at varying engine speeds; these tests are thoroughly covered in the instrument instructions. In this instance, we are interested primarily in whether or not there is an intake manifold leak, which will make subsequent tune-up difficult.

If a vacuum gauge is not available,

squirt some very light machine oil around the intake manifold flanges where they connect to the cylinder head. If the oil is sucked into the engine, or bubbles, the gasket is not sealing. You can generally get a seal by tightening the manifold bolts to the correct torque.

If the carburetor or distributor is to be repaired or rebuilt, this can be done as explained in Chapter 7. If the engine has been tuned within the last six or eight months, it is usually not necessary to remove either carburetor or distributor. Instead, they are checked and adjusted as necessary. Don't overlook the coil condition during this type of tune-up, or the spark plug wiring. If the plug wires are dirty, they should be cleaned; if the wires are more than two years old, they may need replacement with a quality wire. Check the wire ends to make sure they are in direct contact with fittings. Do not wrap these wires together, as it is possible for them to "leak."

Troubleshooting problems in the electrical or fuel systems and performing a tune-up in them are not the same thing, although a good tune-up may alleviate the problem(s). We've covered the various troubleshooting steps in Chapter 7, as well as the mechanical repair and adjustment of carburetors and distributors. For the tune-up, we are concerned only that both electrical and fuel systems are working up to factory specifications.

By testing the fuel pump "head"— that is, the pressure the fuel pump is putting out—the mechanic makes sure there are no restrictions in the fuel delivery system. By checking the fuel filters, it is possible to tell whether or not there is a high probability of foreign material inside the carburetor. Since the carburetor was recently rebuilt and the

Perhaps the ultimate piece of electronic equipment for the home tune-up would combine a full complement of regular tune-up gauges in addition to an exhaust analyzer.

If the carburetor must be cleaned and rebuilt as part of the tune-up, follow the instructions with the rebuild kit.

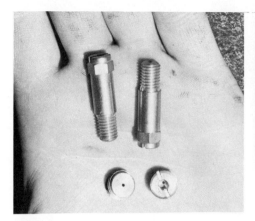

The only time jets and valves in a carburetor should be changed is when the carburetion is being modified to increase power or to get better gas mileage. Normally, the jets and valves are only cleaned.

fuel system checks well, the mechanic will concentrate on the "little things" that make such a big difference in how an engine operates.

These little things include throttle linkage adjustment, fuel line and fitting condition, carburetor-to-manifold fit, heat control valve, automatic choke, and carburetor air cleaner.

Check the throttle linkage carefully. The throttle pedal should "bottom out" on the floorboard or a special stop at the instant the carburetor butterfly is wide open. Worn linkage should be replaced, and check for linkage "overcenter." It is possible for linkage to pass overcenter, thus hanging the trottle in a wide-open (or nearly so) position. This is very dangerous and must be avoided. Throttle linkage return springs should be connected, and be strong enough to snap the throttle closed. If any of the linkage seems to be binding, it might be the result of metal touching metal, or the build-up of dried lubricant. Bend the linkage slightly to clear metal inter-

Float setting in a carburetor is critical to engine performance; this should be checked very carefully each time carburetor is rebuilt.

ference, and clean away old lubricant before adding new grease or silicone treatment.

As a rule, there will be no trouble with the fuel line(s), but you should always check. If any hose has developed a crack, especially around a fitting, replace the hose with a quality neoprene. If the single-wire Corbin-type clamp loses compression, the fuel can seep out around the hose-fitting connection. The remedy is to install a new clamp. On occasion, the home mechanic will find a fuel line that is not well supported, which allows the line to vibrate excessively when the engine is running. Make sure the line cannot vibrate (this can,

and does, aerate the fuel), and see that the line does not rub against some metal part. An abrasion rupture can result from constant rubbing.

If the carburetor is not tight on its mounting, excess air will enter the fuel/air mixture. Use the thin oil again, squirted around the carburetor-to-manifold gasket. If the oil is sucked into the manifold, or if bubbles appear, you have a leak. If the leak cannot be eliminated by tightening the carburetor flange bolts or nuts, remove the carburetor and install a new gasket. Make sure the old gasket material is cleaned thoroughly from carburetor base and manifold. It is possible to "flop" some gaskets; hold the gasket in position and it will be apparent which way it should fit. If the carburetor still will not seal, suspect a warped mounting face on the carburetor flange.

External adjustments on carburetor are usually restricted to the idle mixture screw(s), which will usually be in the carburetor base near the intake manifold, and the engine rpm screw (shown here), which will be part of the throttle linkage assembly. Single and two-barrel carburetors will look something like this unit.

The four-barrel carburetor will appear more complex, but it really isn't. Idle mixture screws are under the carburetor; set them with the engine running at idle rpm.

A dirty air cleaner should always be replaced or cleaned. The paper element cleaners must normally be discarded when they get too dirty; they can be cleared temporarily by blowing air through the unit from the inside toward the outside.

Somewhere in the exhaust manifold(s) you will find the exhaust heat control valve. This is a device very much like a chimney flap, and it serves the same purpose: to retain heat. When the engine is cold, the fuel/air mixture will not atomize well. By closing a flap in the exhaust manifold, much of the exhaust heat can be retained (and circulated through the intake manifold), warming the engine faster.

This valve will gradually open as the engine warms; the opening is caused by a spring. Inspect this valve to make sure it is free and without restriction. If the valve is binding it is probably caused by carbon or rust build-up in the manifold. Tap the butterfly shaft lightly with a hammer while moving the valve counterweight by hand. This will normally free the valve. Lubricate with a mixture of graphite and alcohol; the graphite will not form more carbon whereas ordinary grease will.

The automatic choke will have been serviced when the carburetor was cleaned and rebuilt, but it should be checked for full operation in cold and warm conditions. If this choke is closed even the slightest, it will serve to richen the fuel mixture, or disrupt the carburetor air flow. Adjust the choke if necessary (see Chapter 7).

The carburetor air cleaner can be a tyrant to an engine. If it is clean, it serves to keep out foreign material. If it is dirty, it serves much the same as a choke, and it may begin to pass some of the entrapped foreign material to the engine. Whether the filter is oil bath, paper element, or polyurethane insert, clean it during the regular lubrication schedule (see Chapter 15), and more often under dusty driving conditions. Also make sure it is sealing securely around the cover.

The emission control equipment can usually be at least partially serviced at home, and this normally becomes a part of the tune-up procedure. A good rule for the home mechanic is to service the PCV valve, and inspect the remaining equipment. If something seems amiss, call on the help of an expert. The problem with working on most of the emission control equipment is checking the parts for correct working condition; much of this is now in the realm of electronics, so it is best to leave adjustments to a professional.

It is possible for the carburetion system to be out of adjustment by a rather large percentage and still get excellent engine performance. Such is not the case with the electrical system. It is possible for a slight maladjustment to occur in the ignition after only a few hundred or few thousand miles; in turn this may cause any number of maladies, such as rough idling, stalling, poor acceleration, hard starting, bad gas mileage, and so on. Many of the problems caused by the ignition system are often erroneously credited to the fuel system. Earlier in this chapter, you have learned how the engine electrical system works; you should become very familiar with a typical form of troubleshooting, and always keep the ignition system tuned as perfectly as possible.

Not so strange is the fact that the ignition system starts with the storage battery. Before you do anything to the rest of the system, it is necessary to perform a number of battery "tune-up" operations. Assuming the battery is in good condition, something that you can have checked periodically by the gas station attendant is the battery fluid level. There will be a visable water level mark for each cell; do not overfill. Clean the individual cell caps, and make sure the

It is essential to check and clean the battery as part of every tune-up. Pay particular attention to condition of the cables and cable ends.

vent holes are clear. After replacing the caps, remove both positive (+) and negative (−) battery cables. Loosen the clamp, which may be either the clip type or the bolt and nut type, and pull it from the battery post with a regular battery clamp puller. This tool is available at any auto parts store, is very inexpensive, and should be used any time the battery cable is removed. Never hammer on the post or clamp, and never try to twist a frozen cable free with pliers. This may break the battery post from the cell plates, which will ruin the battery.

Once the battery cables are free, clean the cable ends thoroughly. There is a neat tool for this purpose, which includes a male brush to fit the tapered cable end hole, and a female end to clean the battery post. If such a tool is not handy, a round file for the cable end and a flat file for the battery post will work fine. So will coarse sandpaper, but be sure to clean paper and sand residue from the soft lead cable ends and

battery posts. Check the battery ground strap where it connects to the engine or chassis; the connection should be tight. Check the other lead where it attaches to the starter solenoid, as it must also be tight. Also check this "hot" cable for damage to the insulation, particularly where it might come in close proximity to a metal surface. Plastic tape should only be a temporary repair; replace the cable soon.

Wipe the battery surface clean. Do not pour water over the surface, as it may run in the cap vent holes and cause cell overfilling. If there is any corrosion on the battery, remove it with a solution of damp baking soda, directing the cleansing solution away from the caps. After cleaning, inspect the case for cracks. The battery hold-down clamps should be snug. Now move along to the spark plugs.

Strictly from a comfort standpoint, always change the spark plugs when the engine is cool. Some modern V-8 engines are so loaded with accessories it is practically impossible to change the spark plugs from topside. In this case, the plugs may be reached through the panels in

Remove the spark plugs carefully to avoid damaging porcelain; note condition of tips. Auto parts stores have available plug guide charts to show which combustion chamber conditions will be indicated by the spark plug tip.

There are many different types of spark plug gap checking and adjusting tools available. The ground electrode (piece that is connected to metal base of plug) is gently bent to get correct gap.

the fender splash apron, or from below the engine. In any case, the plug will be near the exhaust manifold, and it is easy to get a painful burn from a hot manifold.

In the way of special plug tools, you'll want a regular spark plug socket and ratchet; the socket has an insert to hold the plug in place, while the ratchet will have a jointed handle so it can be operated in difficult spaces. A plug feeler gauge will be necessary; this is a feeler gauge with round wire and a slotted section for bending the plug ground electrode.

The suggested mileage interval for new spark plugs may vary according to the type of driving you do, but as a rule you can expect between 5,000 and 10,000 miles on a set of plugs. You can squeeze more than this from the plugs, but to do so requires constant attention to the plug (10,000 to 12,000 miles would be a maximum for premium performance). Check with your local auto parts dealer as to the spark plug brand that seems to work best in your particular car

(this definitely may be different from the factory type), and also for the heat range needed.

After the old plug is loosened a thread or two, blow or wipe any dirt from the area so it will not be inadvertently knocked into the cylinder. "Read" the condition of the individual cylinders by looking at the spark plug firing tip. If you do not have the maximum mileage on the plugs, and the electrodes seem to be in good shape, you can probably clean the plug and reuse it.

Wash the plug in solvent, and rub the porcelain stem dry with a rag (or blow dry with air). Handle a spark plug with care, since it is easy to ruin one by dropping it and breaking the insulator. Clean the metal shell and threads with a steel brush, but do not use this brush on the insulator. With some of the new gasolines it is possible to get a rather large buildup of residue on the insulator (the part that runs from the tip up inside the metal shell). If you are very careful, you may scrape this away with a thin-bladed knife. It is best, however, to have the plug ends cleaned on a sandblasting machine made specifically

Another type of plug gapping tool has an adjustable head. When the handles are squeezed the plug is automatically gapped to a predetermined setting.

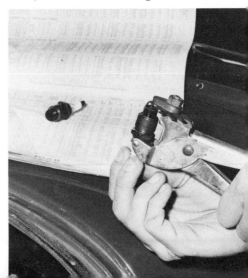

for this purpose. Your gas station may have one, the auto parts store probably does.

File the electrodes flat; there is usually a small electrode file on the spark plug feeler gauge. If not, buy the special file. It is necessary to file the electrodes to remove a high resistance area that forms at the point where the plug fires. Use the round spark plug feeler gauge, because this will compensate for a cavity that forms naturally in the ground electrode. If you use a flat feeler gauge it will "bridge" this gap and give a false reading. Set the spark plug to the specifications for your particular car; to get this gap correct, bend the ground eletrode ever so slightly. It only takes a bit of pressure. If the spark plug gap is off by only a couple of thousandths of an inch, it will be enough to give poor performance.

Make sure the new plug (or the adjusted old one) has a gasket. Although you can use the old gasket again, it is advisable to get new gaskets at the parts store. Start the plug by hand, and tighten it only finger-tight. If possible, always set the spark plugs with a torque wrench (the best reason for the new gasket), and be careful not to tilt the spark plug socket and fracture the porcelain.

A quick test to see if all the spark plugs are working correctly is either to ground across from the plug's external tip to the head (use a screwdriver with an insulated handle!), or remove the plug wire. If the engine slows noticeably you know the plug is working. But you don't know how well the plug is doing its job.

You can replace the entire secondary spark plug wiring at this time if you wish. Clean the surface of the coil, and check for signs of erosion around the large plug-type wire receptacle in the

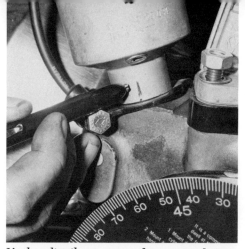

If the distributor must be removed from the engine, mark both distributor base and engine block so the unit can be replaced in exactly the same location. This will insure timing is at least in original position.

Also mark relationship of rotor and distributor case when removing distributor.

Clean the timing mark areas. This VW engine has a mark on the generator support tower that aligns with a slight mark on the crankshaft pulley. If the timing marks are not cleaned, it is difficult to adjust the final ignition timing.

coil. Check that both positive (+) and negative (−) leads to the coil are tight. If you are not quite sure about the coil condition, take it to the garage or parts store where it can be tested.

It is necessary to clean the secondary wiring, coil, and distributor cap because an accumulation of grease, oil, dirt, or moisture will contribute to reduce insulation. A similar reduction in insulation can be caused by cold, heat, and chafing.

There is also a special corona effect. This effects the secondary wiring because it can cause rubber or plastic covering to deteriorate. The corona is caused by a surge of high-tension current through the wiring, which builds an electrical field around each wire, liberating oxygen into the air where it forms ozone. This "glow" is visible in the dark.

Remove the distributor cap and inspect it very carefully for cracks or carbon traces. It is easier to clean and inspect the cap with the wiring removed; mark each cap plug and each wire so it can be mated correctly on reassembly. Wipe the distributor cap clean with a cloth dampened in alcohol; if you find a patch of carbon anywhere on the cap, or a crack, it would be wise to install a new cap. While you are cleaning the cap, use a wire brush (such as that used to clean guns) to clean the plug wire sockets. It is possible to get corrosion inside these sockets (usually from

For normal tune-up the distributor need not be removed; only the cap is lifted off. Caps may be held down by either a pair of side clips, or by a spring-loaded clip that is turned by a screwdriver. Note that all caps have a locating notch in the base, which must align with the distributor before the cap will fit snugly.

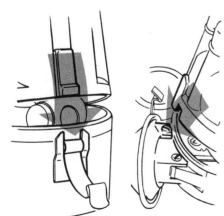

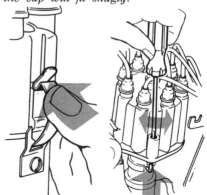

water), and if this corrosion is bad enough the cap should be replaced. Also look for cracks and carbon traces inside the sockets; replace the cap if you find either problem.

Clean the rotor, and check for cracks or carbon traces. There should be a maximum of .010 of an inch clearance between the rotor tip and the distributor cap segments (the stubs that connect directly to the plug wire sockets). If the cap and rotor are reasonably new, chances are this gap will be close to .005 of an inch. You can check the gap by putting heavy grease on the segments and rotating the distributor with cap and rotor in place. Measure the thickness of the grease at a segment and you have the clearance. If the clearance is no problem, clean the segments and the rotor tip with sandpaper, then clean cap and rotor.

To do a thorough job on the distributor, it is necessary to remove it from the engine, but in this case you will probably only be adding points and condenser. It may not be necessary to add points, and replacement is neces-

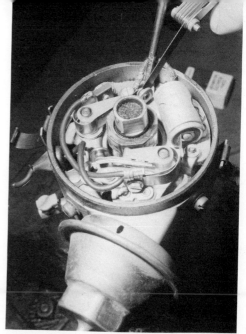

After replacement points have been installed, the gap must be set with a feeler gauge. Some point sets are built so the gap is already adjusted. When working inside the distributor be very careful not to ground any wire leads or break any wires.

sary only if the old ones are badly pitted or worn.

The wear areas will be the cam rubbing block and the point contact surfaces. If only the contact surfaces show signs of early pitting, they may be dressed with a file. But always dress the points when they are perfectly aligned: that would be in both up/down and fore/aft planes. Bend the ground point bracket (the one that doesn't move) for alignment, never the breaker arm (the one that moves). File the points lightly, then clean away the filing residue. Anytime you have the cap off a distributor it is a good practice to add a touch of cam lubricant. This will help retard rubbing block wear, but use only a dab to keep an excess from being thrown on the points. A touch of lubricant should

Replacement points and condenser are available as a set. Full installation instructions will accompany the points.

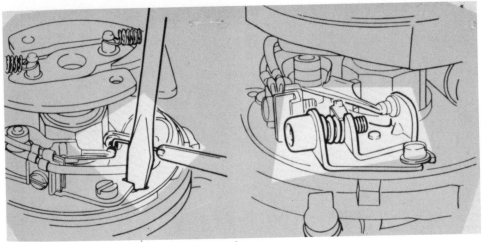

To set points, loosen hold-down screw and move point base. Point rubbing block must be at apex of distributor cam, which gives maximum opening. Some distributors on GM cars will have adjustment screw which is accessible through a window in distributor cap.

also be added to the pivot shaft (where the points pivot), and to any rubbing surface of advance weights.

If new points are to be installed, use small wrenches and work carefully. The new points will include complete installation instructions, but they may not caution to look for a frayed insulation where the small coil wire exits the distributor body. This wire can also be broken.

The new point installation instructions will indicate which screw(s) must be loosened or removed to install the points to the breaker plate, and they will give the amount of gap to set the points at. There will be a wide variation in gap setting methods, so follow the included instructions only. If no instructions are available, note that on most distributors there will be one screw that, when loosened, will allow the point set to move. Rotate the engine until the

point rubbing block is directly on the apex of the cam lobe. Adjust the point set until the contact points are at the correct gap, then tighten the screw. On some GM products, this adjustment can be made from the outside, through a "window" in the distributor cap. This point gap should be checked several times, after the engine has been rotated,

Ignition cam angle, or dwell, is the time points are closed, measured in degrees of cam rotation. Point opening, therefore, has a definite bearing on cam angle. Cam angle can be checked with one of the inexpensive electronic tune-up instruments available through auto parts stores.

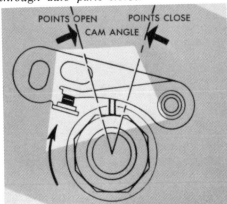

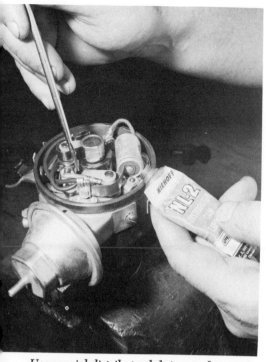

Use special distributor lubricant where point rubbing block touches cam, and at point pivot stub. Do not use an excessive amount of lube, as it can be thrown off and get on the point contact faces.

Clean the segments of the distributor cap (the little stubs that are positioned around the perimeter) and the center contact. If the cap is cracked or has carbon traces, replace it.

The rotor tip can be cleaned with a piece of sandpaper or emery cloth. If the rotor is cracked or has carbon traces, it must be replaced.

to make sure it is precise. As with the spark plug gap, a slight variation here from the manufacturer's specifications can have a great effect on how the engine performs.

After the points are installed and the distributor cap and wiring have been replaced, run the engine for several minutes to get it up to operating temperature. Now you can check the ignition timing, and this is where you will need an inexpensive timing light.

The timing light will include comprehensive instructions on use, but the light attachment is simple. The red clip lead is attached to the battery terminal of the starter solenoid, the black lead

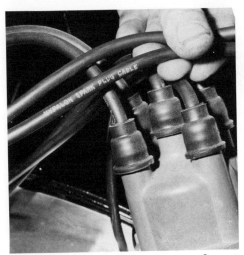

Spark plug wires do deteriorate and must be replaced periodically. Internal condition can be checked for continuity. Always use rubber nipples at coil and distributor to keep water out.

A bad or damaged coil can cause hard-to-find problems in the ignition system. Always check it as part of the tune-up, cleaning the surface and high-tension lead cup.

connects to a ground, and the blue lead fits in an adaptor at the number one spark plug. The spark plug is not disconnected from the distributor for this test. When electric current flows through the number one spark plug wire, it causes the timing light to flash.

Timing marks may be on the vibration damper at the front of the engine (the crankshaft pulley) or on the flywheel. In this case, there is a hole in the block so the timing mark can be seen. Most engines have the timing marked off in degrees on the front pulley. When the engine is running at idle speed, the timing light is aimed at the timing marks, and you can easily read whether the distributor must be advanced or retarded (rotated) to align the mark on the pulley with a pointer attached to the engine.

If the timing is not right, or you want to change it, loosen a hold-down bolt at the base of the distributor and rotate the distributor body until the timing is where you want it to be. In this way you can advance or retard the timing through a number of degrees, and this will have a direct effect on how the engine will run.

Another way to get the ignition timing "about right" is to run the engine at idle speed, and rotate the distributor in the advance direction (against rotation) until the engine just starts to run rough. Engine rpm will speed up slightly. Retard the distributor until the engine just starts to run smooth. This is a good way to set timing if you do not have a light handy.

It may be necessary to change the ignition timing from the factory specifications. In this case, it is wise to consult a professional mechanic for advice, especially if the vehicle is equipped with a significant amount of emission control equipment.

With practice, it is possible for the amateur mechanic to do a typical tune-up (not requiring distributor or carburetor overhaul) in about an hour. By shopping diligently and getting quality parts at bargain prices, you can expect to do such a tune-up for less than $20; sometimes for less than $10. This is far less than what the professional shops are charging, and since you will be doing the tune-ups when they are necessary, engine life and performance will be maximum over much of the vehicle's lifespan.

9 oil system

IT CAN RIGHTLY be said that oil is the lifeblood of an automobile engine. In fact, without lubrication the average car would cease to function in practically every part of its structure. Unfortunately, lubrication is also something too many automobile owners overlook. While they don't have to do the actual work involved in lubrication, these owners should at least make sure a qualified person does take care of the car at the specified intervals.

The contemporary automobile is far advanced over its predecessors of twenty or thirty years past in the technology of metals and lubrication. Where once it was commonplace to change engine oil every 1000 or 2000 miles, and grease the chassis at least every 2000 miles, the modern car usually can go 6000 miles or 4 months between oil changes, and chassis lubrication is similarly infrequent. But lubricants aren't forever!

Lubricants are found in all the major mechanical components of a car, including the rear end, transmission, engine, and front suspension. In structures where a reservoir is not feasible—such as the front suspension—grease is used rather than thinner oils. Lubrication of rear ends and standard transmissions is basic; oil within the housing is thrown on the moving parts by the parts themselves. In the case of automatic transmissions, the hydraulic fluid used to make the transmission function is also the lubricant. However, in the more demanding components such as the engine, special systems of lubrication routing are necessary.

COMPOSITION OF OIL

To fully understand the oiling system of an automobile engine, it is first necessary to understand something about oil itself. In an engine, oil is called on to reduce the friction between moving parts. This will prevent the destructive overheating caused by excessive friction, conserve power, and reduce wear of contacting metal surfaces (see Chapters 5, 11, 12 and 15). Oil acts as a seal between the piston ring and cylinder to prevent combustion leaking down into the crankcase. It washes away abrasive metals worn from friction surfaces. By flowing continually over heated surfaces, it keeps operating temperatures down. It must do all these things even if the weather is desert-hot or arctic-cold.

Under ideal conditions, oil will form a thin film between two surfaces so that these surfaces never touch and no metal wear can ever occur. Unfortunately, this ideal condition seldom exists. When ambient temperature is low, oil viscosity is such that the oil does not flow well during engine warmup. When the temperature is hot, or high, the oil may thin too much and the lubricating film is easily broken. To be of maximum effectiveness, the oil must flow well at cold temperatures but maintain body at high temperatures. During this time, it must also keep an unbroken film between the metal parts.

To help oil perform these functions, various additives have been incorporated in their chemistry during the past three decades. Principal additives are oxidation inhibitors, detergent dispersants, anti-foam agents, rust inhibitors, viscosity-index improvers, and pour-point depressants.

Oxidation and corrosion inhibitors are necessary in the modern engine because of higher operating temperatures and different construction metals. When oil begins to deteriorate, it forms products that will eat up engine bearings. These products also cause varnish, lacquer, and sludges on the inside of the engine. Detergent dispersants were originally created to get rid of the problem of sticking rings. When combustion products reached the ring grooves, they would build up and cause excessive ring-groove plugging. The dispersant additive breaks these products up into tiny particles, which are held in suspension and not allowed to congregate in any single place.

Viscosity-index improvers are necessary to make oil flow better when cold and retain its viscosity characteristics when hot. If air bubbles get into the oil, all kinds of internal lubrication problems occur, starting with rapid metal wear. To reduce foaming, anti-foam agents are used. These agents do not eliminate foaming, but rather encourage rapid movement of air bubbles to the surface of the oil level. Rust inhibitors are added to the oil to counteract the action of corrosive chemicals when the engine is run only briefly and is not at operating temperature long enough to evaporate fuel and water contaminants that are present in the oil.

Sludge in oil is caused by instability of poor grades of oil under high-temperature operating conditions, gums from unburned fuel, and combustion products mixing with the oil through blow-by. Additives can take care of most of this, but the big problem is that of oil contamination caused by blow-by. In an engine in new or good condition, blow-by occurs during cooler-than-normal operation. If the car is driven on short trips only, chances for this kind of sludge formation are greatest, and will cause all kinds of oil-system plugging. The oil-pump pickup screen will become plugged, sludge will form on the inside surface of the block, and in general the effectiveness of the oiling system will be reduced considerably.

Oil Grades and Weights

Oil is classified as either ML (motor car, light service), MM (medium service), or MS (severe service). The MS oil is the only one that should be used in modern engines, or any engine for that matter. Since oil is made in several "weights" and "thicknesses," it will be called SAE 10 weight, or SAE 20 weight, and so on. Generally speaking, the lower the SAE number the "thinner" the oil, or the greater its tendency to flow at low temperatures. The number has nothing at all to do with the quality of oil. Modern oils with additives may be listed as SAE 10-30, etc. This means the oil has multiple viscosity, and will flow well at low temperatures but retain viscosity at higher temperatures (see Chapter 15).

As a guide, use the lightest-weight oil possible with the engine, with 20 weight being average. A newly rebuilt engine with close-fitting parts can take this type of oil well. However, as the engine wears normally, the oil might be increased to 30 weight to compensate for the greater clearances. It must be remembered, however, that the "heavier" the oil, the thicker it will be at cold temperatures. If the engine has been rebuilt with greater than stock clearances, such as is common with high-performance engines, a heavier oil is recommended, at least 30 weight and often as great as 50 weight. In such a situation, always select a specially formulated heavy-duty or racing oil.

OIL CIRCULATION

Automobile engines use either a wet-sump or a dry-sump oil reservoir (see Chapter 5). In the first, the oil is maintained at proper quantity by a sump in the oil pan. In other words, all the oil is carried within the confines of the oil pan, isolated from the revolving crankshaft by a baffled sump. In the dry-sump system, which is something of a misnomer, the main oil supply is kept in a tank outside the engine. The engine oil pump draws the oil from the tank, then another pump scavenges it from the flat pan back to the tank. This type of system is commonly used on aircraft, motorcycles, and racing engines. It is more positive and allows extra cooling because of greater oil capacity, but is also more expensive.

While the transmission and rear-end gears splash the oil around and thus lubricate themselves, the engine needs a more sophisticated approach. Every moving part inside an engine must be oiled, from the crankshaft bearings to the valves. Splash is not now the answer, although it was common to the low-performance engines of years past. It would not work today.

There are three basic types of oiling systems in engines: splash, modified splash, and full pressure. In the first, the crankshaft splashes oil around inside the engine and gravity causes it to drain back to the pan. The modified-splash design has little troughs across the oil pan. When the connecting rod revolves at the bottom of the stroke, oil is scooped up by dippers on the rod cap. In an improvement of this, additional oil nozzle pipes shoot a stream of oil into the approaching dipper. Neither the splash nor modified-splash system is ideal. Most modern engines use full-pressure lubrication. An oil pump packs the oil into a main delivery galley and thence to the points of the engine that need lubrication.

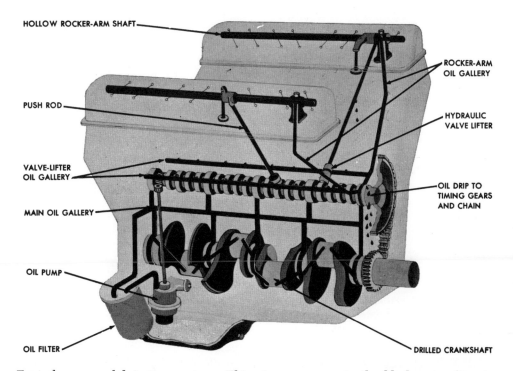

HOLLOW ROCKER-ARM SHAFT

ROCKER-ARM OIL GALLERY

PUSH ROD

HYDRAULIC VALVE LIFTER

VALVE-LIFTER OIL GALLERY

MAIN OIL GALLERY

OIL DRIP TO TIMING GEARS AND CHAIN

OIL PUMP

OIL FILTER

DRILLED CRANKSHAFT

Typical pressure-lubrication system. This schematic diagram is typical of virtually all car-engine lubrication systems today. Oil from the crankcase is delivered under pressure through an oil filter to the main oil header and thence through drilled passages in the cylinder block to the main and camshaft bearings. Drilled passages in the crankshaft conduct oil from the main bearings to the connecting rod bearings. Since this is an overhead-valve engine, the rocker-arm assemblies are supplied with oil from passages in the block connecting, in this case, with the camshaft end-bearing supply. This source also furnishes oil to the hydraulic-valve-lifter oil lines. Oil sprayed and splashed from the connecting rod bearings lubricates the cylinder walls. The timing gears are lubricated by oil issuing from the camshaft end bearing. A common variation of this system is to route the rocker-arm oil supply through hollow push rods receiving oil by way of the hydraulic valve lifters. (Mobil Oil Corp.)

Oil pumps are engine-driven. They draw oil through a screen on the pickup tube immersed in the pan sump. Depending upon the individual pump design, the oil is under a specific pressure and goes first to the oil filter (usually), then to the main oil gallery (gallery or header). From the main gallery (which is usually drilled in the cylinder block), the oil goes through secondary galleries to the crankshaft main bearings, camshaft bearings, timing drive mechanism, rocker arms, and lifters.

All this initial oiling route is usually within the confines of the cylinder block and, in the case of overhead valves, the heads. These passages can get plugged, and that is the reason for emphasis on cleaning during overhaul.

The oil pump is detachable from the cylinder block, and may be located in a number of different places. In some designs, such as Chevrolet's, the pump is actually immersed in oil near the sump; in others, the pump may be outside the block with an internal pickup leading to the sump.

Because different parts of the engine need different amounts of oil, some kind of limitation must be placed in the delivery system. This is normally taken care of by the size of secondary delivery passages between the part and the main gallery, but often a further control is included in the bearing and/or bearing clearance. For instance, in some engines the various main bearings may require different amounts of oil, usually discovered during trial-and-error engineering by the factory. Restrictions in the passages take care of these requirements effectively.

At each crankshaft main bearing, the oil enters the bearing through a hole. Sometimes either the bearing surface or the crankshaft journal is grooved, either partially or the full circumference, to aid oil flow. Part of the oil delivered to the bearing will flow across the surface and out the sides to drop back into the oil pan. More of it will flow into a hole in the crankshaft journal that connects to the rod journals.

At the connecting-rod bearing, the oil will flow across the bearing surface and out the sides to fall into the pan. In some engine designs, the connecting rods are drilled from the big end to the piston-pin bore. If this is the case, the oil then continues up the rod and flows across the pin bushing before falling back to the pan.

Clearance of any and all bearings thus has a direct effect on total oil pressure within the full-pressure system. If all the connecting rods have .0025-inch clearance, but one of the main bearings is worn and has excessive clearance, oil pressure will force more than normal oil through this bearing. Therefore, other bearings will tend to run at reduced oil flow.

While direct cylinder oiling has been tried by continuing the oil from the piston pin to a hole in the piston, the most common type of bore oiling is direct splash. When the crankshaft is rotating in the crankcase, it churns up considerable oil spray, which gets on everything in sight, including the cylinder walls. At the same time, as the rod journal goes through the top portion of rotation, oil being squeezed from the bearing surface is thrown on the walls.

At the front of the engine, some kind of oiling for the timing gears and/or chain is necessary. This may be either a direct or remote delivery, but the common system is from the front camshaft bearing. This oil is then thrown on the gears and chain, and drains back into the block through a hole at the bottom of the chamber.

Oil to the valve system in overhead-valve engines may be via internal or external passages, with the internal passages most common. An oil passage in the block mates with one in the head. The head passage passes the oil directly to a rocker-shaft support and then out the shaft to the individual rocker arms. This supply is usually of low volume, but increases as engine rpm increases. As the oil squeezes out the sides of rocker and support bearings, it splashes onto the valve stem and thus lubricates the valve guides. Getting the correct amount of oil to the rocker system is a definite problem on some older overhead-valve engines, such as the Ford design. In these cases, an extra outside lube line may be installed (kits are available through most parts-supply houses).

Because wear of all the working surfaces is normal, thus increasing bearing clearances and lowering final-point oil pressures, most engines are equipped with pumps of large capacity. To control the oil pressure, then, a special bypass valve is installed, normally in the pump housing. When a predetermined oil pressure is reached, this spring-loaded valve is opened and the excess oil is bled back to the pan. As bearing wear increases, requiring slightly more oil pressure at the pump to compensate for a loss of pressure at the bearing, the relief valve is used less. It is possible to shim the pressure-relief spring, carefully following engine manufacturer instructions, but under no condition should the spring be stretched in an attempt to increase the effective oil pressure.

Although the crankcase ventilation system is not exactly a function of the oiling system, it is inextricably connected with lubrication. The pumping action of the pistons creates a pressure in the combustion chamber. It also creates a pressure in the crankcase, and this pressure must be released. If not, oil contamination will occur because of lack of crankcase venting. For this reason, it is vital to keep the ventilation tubes and breather caps absolutely clean in older engines. Newer engines equipped with positive crankcase ventilation system (smog devices) should also be serviced regularly.

OIL PUMPS

Oil pumps are generally of the rotor or gear type. Location of the oil pump may vary in different engine designs, but the average system has the pump driven by the camshaft, or at half the engine rpm. This is accomplished by placing the actual pump somewhere in the pan cavity (or low on the outside of

Exploded view of Chrysler type rotor oil pump. Although the O-ring seals will occasionally fail, most common type of wear is between the rotor lobes and between rotor lobes and end plate (base). (Illustration courtesy Chrysler Corporation)

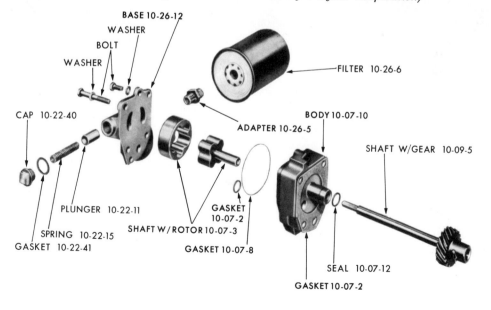

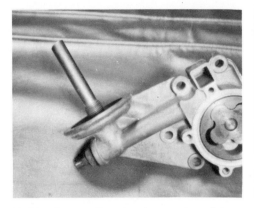

If the oil pump housing is an external type with filter attachment, check area where filter seals, as well as oil feed tube. If the tube is partially plugged the filter flow is hampered.

End plate of Chrysler V-8 oil pump shows scoring. The plate can be buffed flat and smooth with emery paper, or it can be trued by machine shop, but the cost is so low that a replacement part is recommended. Check end of rotors for excessive wear, and replace if wear seems significant. Also check housing around circular outer rotor for scoring. On gear type pump, end plate and gears will have same wear problems.

Pressure relief valve inside oil pump body determines how high pump will raise pressure through block oil galleries. Special stronger springs to raise pressure are available through any dealer. On some cars, the shaft that drives oil pump off camshaft/distributor gear will tend to fail. Special, improved metal drives are also available.

The Chevrolet small block V-8 engine oil pump is typical of most American cars. Although a new replacement is not expensive, it is possible to repair a slightly worn pump housing and replace the gears at a fraction of new replacement pump cost. Condition of the pump will also indicate problem areas that may be occuring inside the engine, such as plugged oil filter, worn bearings, even combustion chamber problems. If there is any foreign matter in the pump, show it to a qualified mechanic for identification. The pump base plate will tend to wear; it can be replaced, but if wear is minimal a flat machine file can be used to resurface the plate face.

Small scores in the pump housing walls can be smoothed with emery paper; be sure the housing is cleaned of any residue grit before reassembly. Large scores in the wall usually mean the pump housing should be replaced. Check idler gear shaft for excessive wear, which will show as uneven discoloration.

If something becomes lodged in the pump drive gear, it will often shear a pin (shown being pointed out). Always check to see if gear is loose on the shaft and if shear pin is fully engaged.

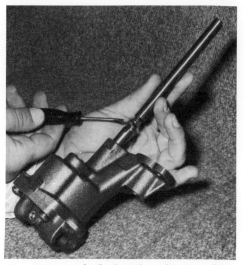

If there is foreign matter in the oiling system it will usually show up as excessive wear between the oil pump gear teeth. Carefully check the teeth on each gear, or the rotors of Chrysler type pump, and replace if there are signs of wear. Also check the drive gear shaft for unusual discoloration which would indicate unusual wear. If there is any question as to pump status, have a mechanic look at it to decide if total replacement is necessary.

Too often overlooked is the oil pump drive shaft, which may or may not be a separate unit from the main drive gear. Some cars which use nylon timing gears experience trouble with small particles of nylon breaking away and becoming lodged in this shaft area, which in turn will often break either the pump shaft or the distributor shaft (the distributor shaft drives off the top of the oil pump drive).

Oil pumps have a pressure release valve built in to control the amount of oil pressure sent to the engine components before excess pressure is bled off. As engine bearings wear, oil pressure will normally drop slightly. Most dealerships have a special relief valve kit (spring, spring and spacer, etc.) that can be installed to bring pressure back to normal. It is advisable to consult local mechanic familiar with your type of engine before modifying oil pressure.

Make sure oil pickup screen is clean and fits into the pump body tightly. If it is loose, air can enter system when oil level is low. Some pumps use an O-ring seal at this point.

the cylinder block), and providing the drive through an extension of the distributor driveshaft. The driving gear which meshes with the camshaft may be on either the oil pump or the distributor.

Two types of pumps are in normal passenger-car use: the rotor type common to Chrysler products, and the gear type on Fords. Both obviously do the job, and the only real difference is in the operating clearances. Since they are literally bathed in oil most of the time, mechanical wear is less likely than with other engine parts; still, the shaft and end plate must be carefully checked and repaired or replaced if needed.

Wear is most common to the end plate, and if this exceeds .001 inch (wear or warp), the plate must be replaced or machined smooth. Anything under .001 inch wear can be dressed out with emery cloth on a flat backing.

To check the clearances of a gear-type pump, place a straightedge across the housing and gears, then slide a feeler gauge between both surfaces. If the distance is greater than .003 inch, either the gears or housing must be replaced (whichever is worn). The gears should clear the pump body by a maximum of .005 inch. Such tight tolerances are imperative if the pump is to operate correctly.

The rotor pump looks very different from the gear type, having a four-lobed cam working inside a five-cavity secondary rotor, but the end-plate clearance must also be .003 inch or less. When one of the primary rotor lobes is pushed into a secondary rotor cavity as far as it will go, the clearance of the lobe exactly opposite must not exceed .010-inch, as measured between the primary lobe and a high spot on the secondary rotor. The outer or secondary rotor is perfectly round, but since it also rotates, clearance between it and the stationary housing should be a maximum of .012 inch.

There are no special assembly instructions for oil pumps other than those contained in repair kits, which may include special clearance gaskets for the end plate (necessary for proper end float of the gears/rotors). However, there should be between .003 and .009 inch end play between the drive gear or shaft retainer and the stationary housing neck.

Use a gasket between the pump and the cylinder block; do not use any kind of sealing compound. The pump may be primed with oil before it is attached to the engine. It is absolutely vital that the oil-pump pickup tube and screen be perfectly clean before reassembly. If the tube or screen rotates in any way, it must be free to do so without binding, and there should be no air leaks in the pickup tubing. Incidentally, the size of a pickup tube is engineered for a particular engine, so if a tube is replaced the inside diameter should be the same.

OIL PAN AND FILTER

Oil pans as supplied on any engine are designed to do a specific job (see Chapter 15). The only reason for using a different, or modified, pan would be to increase the capacity or include additional baffles. Added capacity will be helpful if the engine tends to run hot (remember oil is a coolant), and baffles will keep the oil from sloshing away from the pickup screen on hard acceleration, deceleration, or violent turns. Such modified pans are common to race cars of every type, but not necessary on ordinary passenger cars.

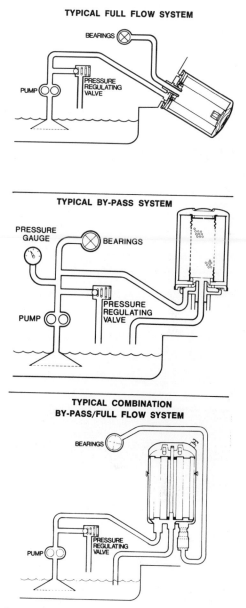

The three types of oil filter flow systems common to American cars, including full flow, by-pass, and combination. Generally, the system included on the car is fine, but in rare cases of oiling difficulty it is often possible to get system modification kit from the dealer for home installation. (Illustration courtesy Fram Corporation)

A few examples of internal seals are shown below

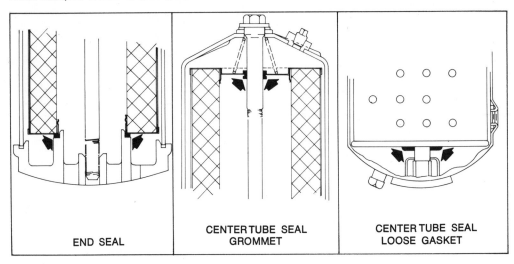

END SEAL

CENTER TUBE SEAL
GROMMET

CENTER TUBE SEAL
LOOSE GASKET

A few examples of external seals are shown below

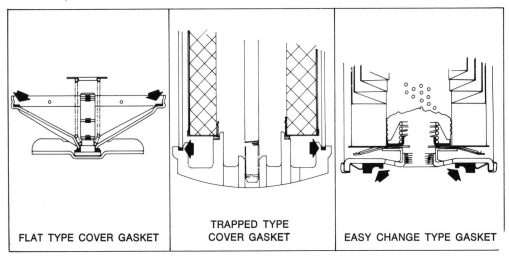

FLAT TYPE COVER GASKET

TRAPPED TYPE
COVER GASKET

EASY CHANGE TYPE GASKET

Both internal and external seals are used for oil filters, and the only problem a mechanic will have is making sure the filter seals completely when a new filter is installed. If an old seal is left in place under the new seal, leaking is common. Always replace filters with recommended units or listed substitutes; never run a filter longer than the recommended mileage limits. (Fram illustration)

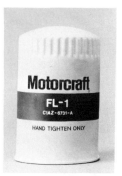

Typical of the screw-on filters now finding great favor with car manufacturers. This kind of self-contained filter is easier to change at home, but you'll need a "compression strap" filter tool for the job. Never use large pliers as they will damage the outer housing.

Unless the pan has been damaged by rocks, it will bolt back to the block with no trouble. Gaskets must be included along each rail and at each end, usually attached with a good sealing compound. Do not overtorque the pan bolts, as the light sheet metal will distort easily and then will not seal well.

Oil filters may be of full-flow or partial-flow design, and the included elements may be of cloth, paper, felt, or combinations thereof (see Chapter 15). In all cases, their prime job is to remove solid contaminants that find their way into the oil.

The full-flow filter passes all of the engine oil through the filter before it reaches the various bearing surfaces, while the partial-flow filter cleans only a portion of the circulating oil at any particular period. The advantages of the full-flow system are apparent; it makes it less likely that anything harmful should reach the bearings. However, the full-flow filter does not filter constantly. Whenever the oil is cold or the filter is plugged with dirt, a bypass valve opens so that the engine can continue to get oil.

Some full-flow elements have a valve built into the element itself to prevent drainback into the pan. If the filter emptied every time the engine was shut off for a few hours, every start would be without lubrication. Because of this extra valve that works with the bypass valve in the engine, it is important that the correct filter element be used. Just because the element fits onto the mounting pad doesn't mean it will work correctly. The wrong element can ruin an otherwise good engine.

If you keep a new car only a few months, then it is doubtful if changing the filter or the oil will give you any benefit, other than keeping your warranty in effect. But if you keep your car, new or used, for several years, then filter elements and oil are cheap. Use the best of each and change them often, and your engine will run longer and with less trouble.

Most popular engines that use the cannister-type oil filter can be converted to the easier-to-use spin-on oil filter. A special adapter is available at most auto parts stores and new car dealerships for this conversion. In the case of this large block Chevrolet engine, the adapter is a small aluminum disc and a sealing gasket.

 261

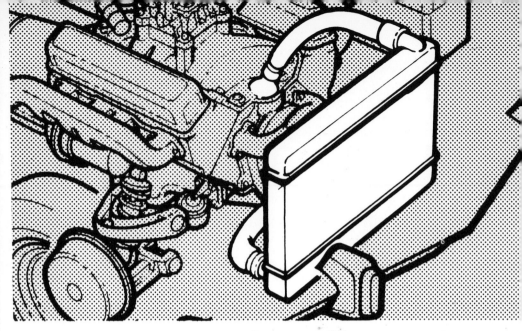

10 cooling system

PRACTICALLY EVERY PART of an automobile has been designed to operate efficiently within a specified temperature range, a range that has been proved from practical experience to be that which an average car driven by an average human being will run within. Unfortunately, too often the average human being assumes the average car is indestructible. Nowhere is the error of this assumption more apparent than in the automotive cooling system.

The most common cause of automotive "breakdown" is simple tire trouble (see Chapter 4), but the second most common malady is overheating. It is practically impossible to avoid tire trouble, since so often it is caused by situations the driver cannot control. However, practically every case of overheating can be avoided by the driver who really takes care of his vehicle.

The radiator is part and parcel of almost every American automobile, but not enough car owners realize that the vehicle cooling system consists of more than a water-filled radiator. Oil is primarily a coolant (see Chapter 9). While it also is a lubricant between two moving metal parts, its basic job is to keep the metal parts below a temperature where they might want to "weld" together. As a coolant, then, oil can also carry off heat from metal surfaces and transfer this heat to ambient air at some other place. In the engine, oil in the oil pan passes off great quantities of heat. In the automatic transmission, oil can be routed through its own small radiator to pass off excess heat. Even power-steering systems often have tiny oil radiators. Most cars have systems that use oil so well designed that no owner-added cooling units are necessary. But let's take a look at what an owner can do if he wishes.

Nothing will kill an automatic transmission faster than excessive heat, and nothing will build heat faster in an automatic than overwork (see Chapter 15). Such an extra load is common when a car is loaded to capacity and driven across the Mojave Desert in 110-degree summer heat. If a trailer is added, even a tiny trailer, transmission heat skyrockets. Most American cars cool transmission fluid by passing it through a cooling tube located inside the water radiator. This is economical manufacturing, but not at all the best way to go. Most serious outdoorsmen, and people who tow trailers a great deal, have found that aftermarket add-on transmission coolers are practically a necessity. Here, the transmission fluid flows through a small, highly efficient radiator of its own. This radiator is most commonly mounted somewhere in the grill opening where it can get a direct blast of cooling air. Actually, such a cooler is so effective that it can be mounted almost anywhere on the car that air flow is present. With this one simple inexpensive little radiator, a conscientious car owner can do more for his cooling system than all the additives and highly advertised products available.

But let's get into the problems of cooling more deeply. While the oil inside an engine controls much of the friction heat build-up, it is water that controls the worst area of all—the combustion chamber. Extremely high temperatures are reached in a combustion chamber. For this reason, a water jacket is cast around the top of a cylinder and in the head above the combustion chamber. Some of the heat captured by circulating oil will be transferred to water, but the greatest majority of water heat comes from the chamber and must be cooled rapidly.

Water enters the engine at the water-pump housing and circulates into the lower block area before it passes to the combustion-chamber area. From the combustion chambers it goes directly to the water pump again, then to the top of a radiation device (the radiator). The extremely hot water trickles (relatively speaking) through the radiator to a bottom tank, losing much of its heat to passing air, and is then ready again to pass through the engine block. Simple enough.

RADIATOR

The majority of radiators are made of brass, although some are of aluminum. Both vertical and cross-flow designs are in use, the vertical flow having a top and bottom tank, while the cross-flow has similar tanks at either side. In both, the water enters one tank, then drains down to the other through rows of brass or aluminum tubes. A typical small American car will have a radiator "core" about $1\frac{1}{2}$ by $2\frac{1}{2}$ feet in size, with two rows of tubes, one behind the other but staggered to the direction of airflow. These tubes are soldered into individual holes in each tank "plate," and spaced throughout the core by fins. These fins are but a single length of brass strip woven back and forth the length of one or two tube rows. The purpose of the fin system is to give strength to the tubes, to help increase the amount of area available to pass heat to passing air, and to some extent, to protect the tubes from external damage.

Interestingly enough, there seem to be no hard-and-fast engineering rules to determine exactly what size, shape, and capacity a radiator need be to cool a specific engine. Most radiators are chosen on the basis of past experience with similar-sized engines in similar-

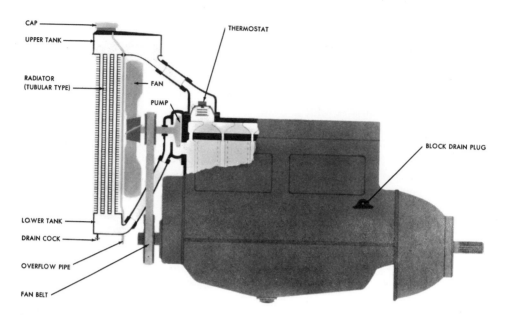

Forced-circulation-cooling system. Relatively cold water, or water-antifreeze mixture, from the bottom of the radiator is picked up by an engine-driven pump and circulated through the engine jacket spaces. The warm coolant is in turn cooled in passing through the radiator, by atmospheric air forced and pulled between the radiator elements by car motion and the action of the fan. The thermostat maintains proper coolant temperature. (Mobil Oil Corp.)

Solder to hold upper and lower tanks in place is run in trough. The slightest pin hole here will allow pressure to escape.

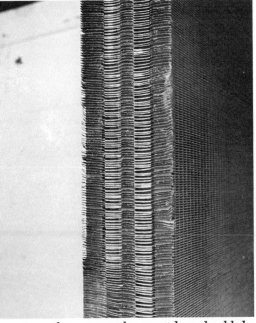

Pins that surround core tubes should be straight to allow maximum air flow. Flush bugs from front of core occasionally, straighten fins.

sized chassis. Thus manufacturers install a radiator that will just barely do the job, because the larger the radiator is, in any way, the more it will cost. If a car is ordered factory-fit with air conditioning, a larger radiator will automatically be installed, along with a fan with more blades. Sometimes if a car is ordered with a heavy-duty trailer-towing option, a larger radiator will be installed. But even these larger radiators are often not sufficient for the job. That's where that little automatic-transmission cooler comes in. If you have a radiator that it is hard pressed to cool the engine water, its burden can be lightened if the transmission cooler tube is removed from the bottom tank. This has the effect of lowering the temperature of the water that enters the block, essentially the same thing a larger radiator would do.

Solder is best quality, nonacid type.

The more tubes in a radiator, the better it will cool. This is a five-row design, which is about maximum thickness for automobiles, and would be used in a heavy-duty condition. Some economy cars have only two rows, most cars have three-row design. These tubes will plug with rust if the system is not taken care of.

Now back to radiator design. It is not the capacity of a radiator that determines how well it will cool, but the area of metal (brass or aluminum) that is exposed to passing air. That small two-row radiator can be increased to three, four, five, and even six rows. Certainly, the water capacity will increase, but most important is the greater area exposed to air. Seldom does a production radiator exceed four rows, or a total thickness of about 4 inches, while it is not uncommon to find five-row and six-row custom radiators.

Most modern radiators are pressurized, from 7 to 20 psi, and for good reason. The higher the pressure, the higher the water temperature can be before boiling, and this is vital now that engine temperatures of 215 degrees are not uncommon (part of the fight on smog). Such a pressurized system will show a failure much faster than an unpressurized system, and it will have its own peculiar problems. A quick way to build too much pressure is to sit in traffic on a hot day with the air conditioner going full blast. The common failure here is for pressure to blow a radiator hose. Usually the hose doesn't rupture, it just pops away from a radiator or engine fitting.

The type of fan will also have much to do with how the engine cools at lower speeds and at idle. Essentially, the more blades the better will be cooling until ram air takes effect. If your car is equipped with an automatic fan, the kind that automatically clutches into operation when engine temperature reaches a certain point, always keep a wary eye on the assembly. Such fans have a tendency to go bad, so if the car overheats, look here first.

The fan shroud is where many home mechanics think they are doing good

Upper hose outlet will be on opposite side of lower outlet, which keeps water in radiator long enough to cool.

when they are actually doing bad. Never remove a fan shroud! In one way or another, the engineers have found that this particular engine with this particular fan needs a shroud in order to get cooling at low engine speeds. Without the shroud, air normally required to pass through the radiator (being pulled by the fan) sweeps in around the back of the radiator, so little cooling effect gets to the radiator.

It is possible to have a radiator/water-pump combination that is too effective. In this case, the water pump moves such a volume of water, and the radiator lets it drain down so fast, that the water does not have time to pass heat off to the air. This is rarely the case in a Detroit vehicle, but it can happen, and the only solution is to place a restrictor in the upper hose to reduce the water flow.

COOLING-SYSTEM LEAKS

There are two kinds of leaks in a cooling system—the kind you see and the kind you don't. If the radiator has a break somewhere, if a hose leaks, if the water pump leaks, or if the cylinder block is cracked on the outside, you'll see the leak. But if the cylinder block is cracked on the inside, or a head gasket is blown, you'll never see the leak.

Anytime you find a leaking system, the first temptation is to rush for a can of guaranteed "stop-leak." While such a temporary fix might be okay, you've got a big problem somewhere that needs a definite remedy. If you have a blown head gasket, the engine is going to run poorly as well.

If you find that radiator water is continually down, and there seems to be foam in the remaining water, suspect a block gasket. The best way to check is to have a gas station run a system dye check. Obviously the only cure is a new head gasket.

You can tell if the water pump is the culprit because almost always the leak will seem to be coming from below and behind the pump pulley. The spring-type clamps used to attach radiator hoses are probably best replaced by the older screw-type clamp, especially if you have a high-pressure system. Definitely replace any hose that looks bad. A smart driver always carries a spare "universal" hose. Incidentally, an emergency repair of a burst hose is very easy. Unlock the pressure radiator cap so there is no pressure, then wrap any kind of cloth tightly around the hose and tie it in place. A necktie or sock works fine. At least it will hold water until you can find a replacement.

Leaks in the radiator are a different story. A radiator will leak from only three sources: a fracture caused by impact, a fracture caused by vibration, or corrosion. Most radiator leaks are caused by corrosion, a kind of cancer that works from the inside out and is extremely difficult to catch early. Corrosion is a chemical problem, and once it starts it is very hard to control.

Glycol-base antifreezes have additives that will combat corrosion, and the better brands of menthol-base antifreeze have corrosion inhibitors, but these are only good for a time. Because additives break down it is advisable to change antifreeze once every year. It is also advisable to use antifreeze year-round, because then the corrosion inhibitors will always be at work, and because most antifreezes also include a lubricant good for the water-pump bushing. If an aluminum radiator is fitted to your car, antifreeze is imperative.

A radiator that has inside corrosion

The only way to do a major radiator repair is to take it to the radiator shop, where it will be immersed in water, filled with air, and leaks spotted. Small leaks at accessible seams can be soldered at home.

should always be removed and flushed by a professional. This way you can assess how far the cancer has gone. Just pouring in an anticorrosion inhibitor at such a late date will usually prove fruitless.

THE BLOCK

Rust in the radiator water comes from the cast-iron block, and it is serious. Rust will accumulate in the engine water passages, and periodically some rust will break loose. These rust flakes are usually quite large, at least large enough to plug up a radiator tube. After a while, continued rust accumulation inside the radiator tubes will so reduce water flow in the radiator that it becomes quite ineffective. To test for plugged tubes, run your hand over the front of a radiator that is at operating temperature. If you find a cool area, it is plugged. This rust can also build up around a thermostat, and even in cylinder-block passages or radiator hoses. Back-flushing the block and "rodding" the radiator are the only cures for a serious case of rust.

Along the cylinder-block side, and sometimes in the head, will be located "freeze," or core, plugs. These plugs are supposed to pop out if the water in a block should freeze solid, thus saving a cracked block. Unfortunately, they seldom do pop out, and they almost always eventually start leaking. If the engine has much mileage, the cores can corrode until they start leaking. Sometimes, they just don't fit well and leak for no other reason. You could stop such a leak with a water additive, but it is better to replace the plug. The old plug is pried out and a new one tapped in place. No special skills are required.

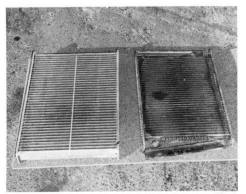

Most often, an older radiator that is filled with rust must be "rodded" (each tube cleaned individually), and small pin-holes somewhere in the core flow soldered. When a new radiator core is installed the original top and bottom tanks are removed and soldered to the new core.

While it is recommended that a professional backflush the radiator should it prove severely plugged, the home mechanic can do periodic maintenance by removing both hoses from the radiator, along with the radiator cap, and inserting a garden hose in the lower outlet. Plug the hose into the outlet with a rag, then turn water on full-blast. This will flush small amounts of accumulated rust from the tube top inlets.

FLUSHING THE SYSTEM

After overheating, whether caused by a leak or clogging, you can assume the cooling system requires a complete chemical purging. Radiator shops and some service stations use "pressure" or "reverse" flushing. These techniques are very effective, but they require special equipment and trained personnel. Fortunately, there is a reasonably thorough method of flushing that may be accomplished at home with no special skills or tools.

1. Set heater temperature control to high. If your car is equipped with a vacuum-operated heater valve (you'll have to check with your dealer—this type of valve is found on late-model cars with factory-installed air conditioning), run engine at idle during all the flushing procedures keeping a close watch on the engine-temperature gauge. The reason the engine must be running is that coolant must be kept circulating through the heater for a fully effective flush, and a vacuum valve will stay open only with the engine running.

2. Open radiator drain cock and let radiator drain. Do not open engine drain cocks.

3. Remove radiator cap and install deflection elbow in the filler neck. This prevents excessive splash into the engine compartment. (Gates #CH-118 hose or equivalent fits the filler neck of most car radiators.)

4. Remove hose from the heater-supply nipple at the engine block. Point this hose downward for auxiliary drain.

5. Connect water to the heater-supply nipple at the engine block. This does not have to be a positive connection. An ordinary garden hose will do. Just be

10 269

sure that most of the water enters the engine.

6. Turn on the water, making sure it is cold. Flush for three to five minutes without the engine running (but see step 1). During the last minute of flushing, squeeze the outlet or upper radiator hose to remove any trapped liquid.

7. Turn off water supply and close the radiator petcock. Reconnect heater-supply hose and remove deflection elbow from radiator. Be sure system is full of water.

The further steps for chemical cleaning require the utmost caution when working in the engine compartment, since the spinning fan blades and various belts can inflict serious injury.

8. Add one can of a cooling-system degreaser (Eskimo RCDL-11 or equivalent). Replace radiator cap and run engine at fast idle for approximately 30 minutes. Then repeat steps 1 through 7 above. The system must be degreased before the rust, scale, and lime cleaner (below) can be effective.

9. Add one can of heavy-duty (not multi-duty) cooling-system cleaner (Eskimo CSL-32 or equivalent) and run engine at fast idle for approximately 45 minutes. Add neutralizer according to instructions on can. Then repeat the flushing operation, steps 1 through 7 above.

10. With the total system partially drained and completely flushed, you are now ready to install new antifreeze. After the flushing procedure described above, again drain the radiator, and check all fittings for tightness. The system will accept approximately a 40 percent fill of glycol, which will protect to about −12° F. The reason, of course, is that the block still contains water. If you need more antifreeze

protection, you can make space for it by draining an equivalent amount of water from the engine block. Fills beyond 68 percent (−75°) do not offer additional protection.

If you're just filling with water for the summer, avoid so called "hard" water with a high mineral content (buy bottled water if necessary), and don't forget to add a good brand of inhibitor (Prestone Anti-Rust or equivalent). No additional inhibitors are needed with an antifreeze fill of 25 percent or more. Avoid water of high mineral content for the make-up water.

REMOVING A RADIATOR

A damaged or thoroughly clogged radiator requires removal from the car and either rebuilding or mechanical cleaning with tools and skills not possessed by even the average professional mechanic. However, you can still save considerable money by bringing the radiator, rather than the car, to these shops.

The radiator may be removed from a car for servicing, and must be removed if rebuilding is required. The latter cannot be accomplished with the radiator installed because soldered components must be separated and then immersed in various chemical baths before they can be resoldered. The first step is to drain the system and separate the hoses from the radiator. On cars equipped with automatic transmissions, lines that lead to the transmission intercooler must be disconnected. The intercooler is usually an integral part of the radiator and is always located at the bottom.

Fan shrouds are attached to the structure surrounding the radiator. These

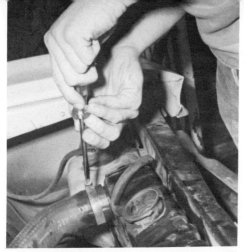

Sometimes the radiator hose clamps will become slightly loosened by engine vibrations and engine coolant will seep from around the outlet. Keep the clamps tight. When installing hose, use small amount of soapy water to make it slip over outlet easily.

If the upper or lower hoses have deteriorated badly and lost their body strength, they will be easy to squeeze flat. Some hoses will have wire spring insert to keep them from collapsing during use (particularly lower hose).

Always keep the fins of any cooling device open. Air conditioner coils are more tightly finned than coolant radiator and should be cleaned carefully with a wire brush, then blown clear with compressed air. Use a knife blade or screwdriver blade to straighten any bent-over fins.

Clean interior passages of dirt and bugs with rifle brush or piece of rag on end of coat hanger.

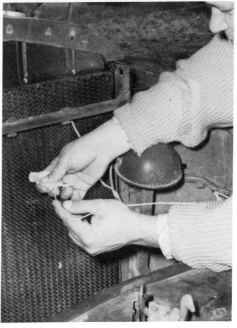

can be either removed or pushed back over the engine out of the way. The radiator itself is attached at each of its four corners by bolts. The detaching points will always be at the car and not at the radiator, where the brackets are soldered. Check the clearance between the radiator and the fan before loosening the radiator attachment bolts. If you have any doubt about working room, it's wise to remove the fan to prevent costly radiator damage, especially on cars equipped with a rear-opening (front-hinged) hood, which might restrict your leverage.

Lift the radiator out carefully. Any inadvertent contact between it and the car structure will damage the fragile cooling fins. Remember, too, that these fins are very sharp; it's wise to wear heavy gloves when handling a radiator. Store or transport the unit vertically if possible to avoid any further hazard to the fins. Installation is accomplished by reversing these procedures.

RADIATOR TROUBLESHOOTING

Just knowing how to correct a cooling-system problem usually isn't enough. Perhaps more important is learning how to diagnose trouble, to recognize trouble ahead, and perhaps to make repairs before something bad happens. Here are some things to watch for.

Always suspect a thermostat if the car is giving heating troubles. Most thermostats will last about two years, and they tend to fail gradually, so overheating can be coming on slowly without your notice. Thermostats are marked with their operating temperature, with the usual range from 170° to 205° F. Always use the thermostat suggested for your particular engine, and go to a slightly cooler one only as a possible overheating remedy. Never, never run without a thermostat on a modern engine. If the engine is allowed to run too cool, accelerated metal wear can result because the metal parts have not been allowed

Thermostat on left controls temperature of water as it leaves engine en route to the radiator. At the first sign of overheating (or even an engine running too cold) suspect this thermostat.

Pressure radiator caps are available in wide range of pressures; use only that rating the radiator was originally designed for.

discomfort. An obvious reason for this is to prevent burns from the scalding coolant vapors. A less obvious reason is to prevent loss of valuable coolant.

If you have any doubt as to condition of the thermostat, remove and check it. Place in boiling water; when water reaches opening temperature, thermostat's valve should open. If it doesn't open, replace thermostat.

to expand to proper operating clearances.

On cars without air conditioning a single belt usually drives both the water pump and the alternator or generator. If this belt has broken or is slipping badly, not only will the temperature gauge start to climb but the ammeter or warning light for the electric system will indicate a discharge. A broken belt to the water pump means stopping immediately until a replacement can be installed. Don't even try to reach a service station, since there is absolutely no circulation and the temperature will rise to the danger point rapidly.

If you're overheating, stop and turn off the engine. Open the hood. Do not touch the radiator cap until you can handle it with your bare hands without

Extra fan blades are necessary if the car is equipped with air conditioning, which increases flow of air across radiator at low vehicle speeds. Thermostatically controlled fans are available, but often give trouble after car has lots of mileage.

Electric accessory fans, available when there is very little room to add larger fan blades, may be mounted ahead of radiator to push the air. Most foreign car auto parts houses have these.

Fan blades must be in alignment for balance purposes; check blade tips for cracks that can lead to ultimate fracture and failure.

This fan is too far from the radiator to pull through a good air flow without installation of a shroud. The solution is to either install a shroud or use a spacer to move fan to within 1½ inch of core.

Once it's safe to remove the cap, it's also safe to add cold water to the system. Pour in small amounts at a time, with the engine running, to prevent the thermal shock of the cold water from distorting or cracking the hot engine.

Check the pressure cap. This could have been only partially tightened by a careless attendant at the last gas stop. Also check the spring-loaded vacuum relief valve in the cap for freedom of motion.

Next check the belt that drives the pump (see Chapter 15). A broken belt will be noticeable by its absence, although it's best to search the entire engine compartment to see if it's caught where it could cause trouble later. A slipping belt can be easily detected by pulling on it. If it's as tight as it should be, you'll have a tough time trying to rotate the fan by hand. If the belt is loose, loosen the support bolts and pry the offending accessory out on its slotted support bar until the belt is taut and tighten the holding nut.

For this reason it is a good idea to carry a medium-size adjustable wrench and a pry bar in the car at all times. A jack handle can be used as a pry bar.

A burst hose will be obvious. It will continue to leak until the coolant reaches a level lower than the break. Where factory-type spring clamps have been reused, it is not uncommon for a hose to work loose from its mounting. Here the leak will be evident. Less easy to detect is the pinhole type of break, too small to see but big enough to spew out a lot of coolant when the system is pressurized. If you suspect this from the presence of otherwise unexplainable coolant residue in the engine compartment, run the engine until it reaches operating temperature, and the leak will undoubtedly show itself. Electrician's

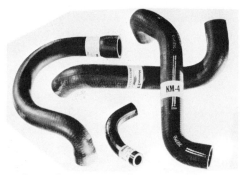

Radiator hoses can fail at any time, even the molded types. As a car gets advanced mileage, it is good insurance to carry spare hoses and clamps. At least carry roll of plastic tape for repair; afterward, the radiator cap should not be installed tightly.

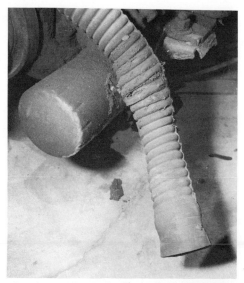

This lower hose finally failed because it was never checked.

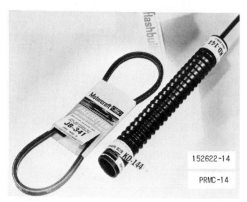

Another way to carry spare hose is to use flexible hose that has correct ends. Extra fan belt is also a good idea.

All heater hoses in the system must be carefully checked for pinhole leaks and tiny cracks. Replace any hose that is cracked.

tape will contain a leak like this long enough for you to get to a service station and purchase a new hose.

Another common cause of overheating is a collapsed inlet (bottom) hose. Most of these contain a spiral-wire reinforcement, the inside of which, over a period of time, can rust and disintegrate. If this hose is not supported, it will collapse when the pump is working hard, blocking the coolant passage. Squeeze this hose at midpoint, and if you can't feel the resistance of the reinforcing

Accessory transmission and engine oil coolers are available, will help considerably to reduce cooling load carried by the radiator. They should definitely be installed on any car that does heavy-duty work, such as towing trailer.

wire, chances are that you've found your trouble. Double-check, if you wish, by racing the engine and observing the hose. If it tends to contract under the suction from the pump, it must be replaced. An alternate to the factory type of reinforced hose is the corrugated, flexible kind of replacement hose now being sold in most service stations. This contains an integral reinforcement, and will bend easily to fit.

Should you spring a radiator leak way out in the desert, chances are good that

Front of Chrysler engine shows relationship of water pump housing and pump (numbers 24 and 21). Replacement of water pump can be done by the home mechanic; old unit is usually required as core trade-in.

(Illustration exploded view courtesy Chrysler Corp.)

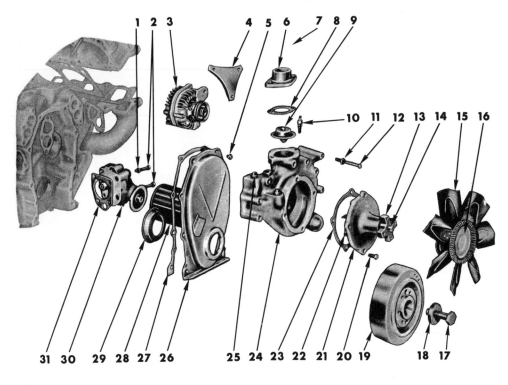

only one tube is affected. A quick repair can be made with chewing gum or a small patch of rag stuffed into the fins at the leak. You can usually pack the area enough to run without pressure (loosen the radiator cap). Should you be caught this way and need water, remember that coffee thermos.

Never leave on an extended trip with a marginal cooling system, since a breakdown in this system will put your car out of operation immediately. If the water pump has been acting up, fix it. If the fan belts need replacement, do it, and adjust them to the ¼ or ½ inch of free play recommended. You can do most of this routine work at home and it won't take time from your golf game.

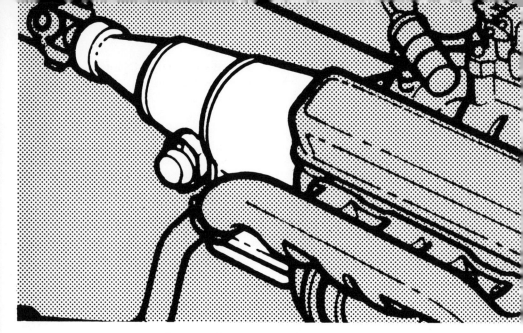

11 clutch and transmission

IT WOULD BE QUITE IMPOSSIBLE for the internal combustion engine to pass available horsepower directly to a drive wheel. Since the engine has a relatively narrow rpm range, and the driving wheels must function within a much larger range, these must be some method of changing the ratio of engine rpm and wheel rpm. This job is done by gears.

If a vehicle is driven by a belt between an engine pulley and a rear-end pulley, this belt can be slipped enough until the vehicle speed is high enough to match engine rpm. Such a drive system was used with vehicles of the late nineteenth century, particularly motorcycles. But belt pulleys must have cumbersome diameters, so a gear-drive rear end was invented, and various types of transmissions and clutches were tried until the "stacked" gearbox common to most contemporary cars came into general use during the 1920s. Interestingly,

the modern manual transmission is not much different from those of fifty years ago, and even the automatic transmission isn't really new.

With either manual or automatic transmission, there must be some method of disconnecting the engine from the drive train. In the automatic transmission this is accomplished with a fluid coupling, and in the manual transmission with a friction clutch. No transmission/clutch assembly is so sophisticated that the home mechanic can't repair it, but the automatic transmission requires so many specialized tools that gear disassembly in the automatics is best left to a garage. Nevertheless, if you want to spend $50 for tools, you can fix the automatic at home as well as any professional. Let's get into the clutch first, then we'll look at the manual transmission, and finally we'll take up the automatic.

CLUTCH

The need for some method of disengaging the engine from the transmission was one of the earliest problems automobile manufacturers faced, and a variety of de-clutching methods were tried. The cone clutch came into great favor immediately after 1900, but this unit had a tendency to grab, and there was very little slippage possible. Because the engine must turn a certain rpm to be effective, some amount of slipping is necessary, especially when moving a vehicle from a stop, and the cone design

The clutch system is used to connect and disconnect a manual transmission. Various important pieces include throwout arm pivot (3, 4), throwout bearing arm (5), pressure plate (10), clutch disc (9), and flywheel (8).

didn't do this too well. Engineers finally settled on the disc type that all modern cars use.

How a Clutch Works

Most modern clutches are the single-plate, dry-disc type. In these units a clutch disc with a facing of material with great heat resistance and a high coefficient of friction is mounted behind the engine flywheel and secured to the transmission input shaft by means of splines. There is no positive attachment of the clutch disc to the engine flywheel. A pressure-plate assembly is interposed between the clutch disc and transmission. This pressure plate is secured to the engine flywheel and turns with it. There is no positive attachment between

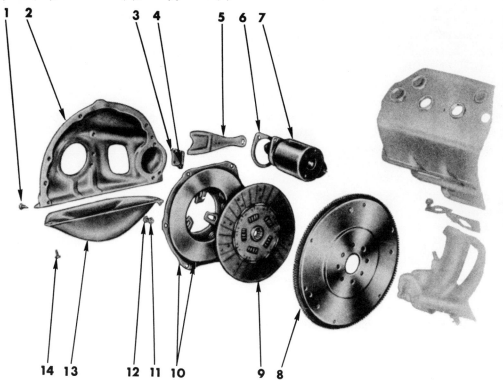

Flywheel usually has ring gear pressed to circumferance to mesh with starting motor gears. Flywheel bolts to crankshaft flange must be torqued to specifications, surface of flywheel must be smooth and straight. There is a tremendous amount of heat generated by clutch disc slipping against flywheel and pressure plate face, but slipping is necessary for smooth starts. The idea is to have minimum amount of slippage, however, and none when pressure plate is fully disengaged.

Another design of pressure plate uses three short arms to release the pressure plate disc.

Diaphragm type pressure plate uses many small arms that touch the throwout bearing at the center. As bearing presses toward face of plate, arms overcome internal spring pressures and pull plate away from free floating clutch disc.

Ford used the Long Borg & Beck type pressure plate for years; counterweights designed as part of the release arms help centrifugal force overcome heavy pressure needed to release clutch disc at high engine rpm. Most auto parts stores have a trade-in arrangement on pressure plates. If the flywheel or pressure plate faces are scored from excessive heat (which comes from excessive clutch slippage, in turn caused by broken pressure plate springs or improperly adjusted clutch linkage) the parts should be refaced or replaced.

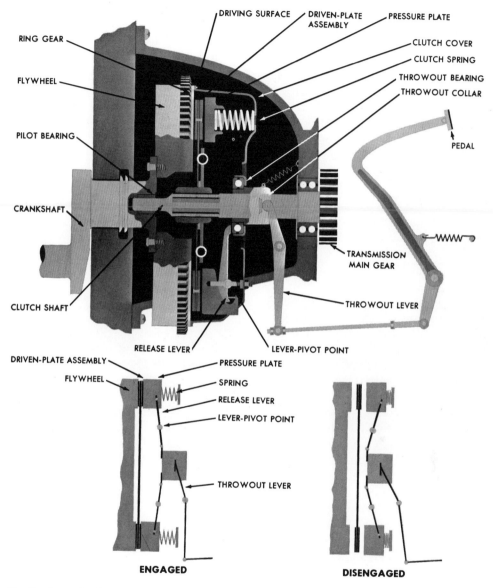

RING GEAR

FLYWHEEL

PILOT BEARING

CRANKSHAFT

CLUTCH SHAFT

DRIVING SURFACE

DRIVEN-PLATE ASSEMBLY

PRESSURE PLATE

CLUTCH COVER

CLUTCH SPRING

THROWOUT BEARING

THROWOUT COLLAR

PEDAL

TRANSMISSION MAIN GEAR

THROWOUT LEVER

RELEASE LEVER

LEVER-PIVOT POINT

DRIVEN-PLATE ASSEMBLY

FLYWHEEL

PRESSURE PLATE

SPRING

RELEASE LEVER

LEVER-PIVOT POINT

THROWOUT LEVER

ENGAGED

DISENGAGED

Single-plate clutch.

the transmission and pressure plate. When the clutch is engaged, the clutch disc is squeezed against the flywheel by means of a series of powerful springs. When the clutch is disengaged, a series of fingers or levers actuated by pressure on the clutch pedal move the pressure plate away from the clutch disc. In some cases a clutch driving plate is attached to the flat face of the flywheel to provide a seating surface for the clutch disc. In other cases the face of the flywheel is specially finished or treated to form the seating surface.

The clutch disc is a circular steel plate with facings of frictional material riveted or bonded to both sides. The facings are made from a variety of woven or molded materials, including those containing a large percentage of asbestos fiber, sintered metal, and ceramic compositions. The outer rim of the clutch disc, which carries the facings, is attached to a hub with a splined center, which engages the transmission input shaft. One of the most important factors in clutch design is the manner in which this clutch-disc hub is secured to the outer portion of the disc. A series of torsion damper springs are used to make this attachment. When torque is applied to the disc, the springs compress and absorb the sudden shock of engagement before the hub begins to turn. This both protects the facings and contributes to smooth operation of the clutch.

The pressure-plate assembly includes the plate, clutch cover, springs, and clutch release levers along with other components. The plate is a flat steel ring, held against the clutch disc by a series of springs interposed between the cover and plate. The cover is bolted to the flywheel and serves to enclose the pressure plate and the clutch disc. When the clutch is released, a series of clutch levers move the pressure plate against the clutch spring tension and away from the clutch disc. The clutch release levers have their fulcrums located on the clutch cover. One end of these levers is attached to the pressure plate and the other end is free to move. When the inner end of the levers is moved forward, the pressure plate is forced away from the clutch disc. A thrust-type clutch throwout bearing, which slides on the clutch shaft, is used on the clutch-pedal linkage to engage the levers.

Because the pressures exerted by the springs in the pressure-plate assembly must be very high in order to maintain adequate contact between the driving and driven clutch members, the manual pressure required on the clutch pedal can also be very high if some form of pedal assist is not provided. On some cars an over-center spring is incorporated into the pedal linkage to provide this assist. This over-center assist spring is so arranged that on one side of center, the spring holds the pedal in its normal position, and when the pedal is depressed, the action of the spring is reversed to aid the release levers in the clutch pressure-plate assembly in overcoming the pressure exerted by the pressure-plate springs. The midpoint in the action of the over-center assist spring is on center at the point where the throwout bearing engages the release levers.

The advent of very high-torque engines has made greater pressure between the clutch disc and pressure plate necessary in order that the full power of the engine can be transmitted to the balance of the driveline without slippage when the clutch is fully engaged. Over-center springs in the pedal linkage help overcome the stiff springs necessary for firm clutch engagement, but a simple and more effective solution is the semi-centrifugal clutch now used in modern high-powered cars.

In the modern semi-centrifugal clutch, flyweights on the pressure plate increase the pressure on the clutch disc as the rotational speed of the clutch and flywheel combination increases. Centrifugal force acting on these flyweights can exert enormous pressure between the driven and driving members at very high rotational speeds. At low speeds, or at the initial shifting into low gear, this centrifugal force has a minimal effect. With a semi-centrifugal clutch, lower spring pressures may be used in the pressure plate assembly to reduce the effort required on the pedal to disengage the clutch. At high speeds, the centrifugal clutch still requires very high pressures on the clutch pedal to effect disengagement, but it is hardly any worse than a clutch which depends on very stiff springs for positive engagement. The advantage of the semi-centrifugal clutch is that the driver is not obliged to contend with high pedal pressures when moving the car along in heavy stop-and-go traffic.

Slippage in a clutch cannot be tolerated at high speeds if the power output of the engine is to be fully utilized. But at low speeds, as has been stated previously, a certain amount of slippage is both necessary and desirable. This becomes most apparent when starting a car from rest. The rear axle and wheels must be set in motion progressively; they cannot suddenly be rotated at even the reduced revolutions produced by low gear. The frictional contact provided by the clutch should be increased gradually in order that the balance of the driveline and wheels can accelerate smoothly.

While a lot of engineering know-how has been incorporated into clutches, the driver is still important. The driver should "slip" the clutch, particularly on take-off. If he does not feel out the action of the clutch with his foot, power will be applied to the drive train in a sudden jolt. In a car of moderate power output the engine will probably stall.

Clutch Linkage

There are only two types of clutch linkage used in most modern cars: mechanical and hydraulic. Occasionally a car will be equipped with a pull-cable linkage, but this is rare. The mechanical linkage is a series of rods that connect the overhead pedal assembly to the clutch throwout-bearing arm. Usually there will be an idler arm in the system, for the sake of routing ease, and occasionally this arm will have different-length levers as part of the overall clutch-pedal-linkage pressure ratio. The only real point of wear in a mechanical system is where this idler shaft connects to frame and engine. There will be balls and sockets at each end, which should always be lubricated (see Chapter 15). Should these points of pressure wear, the shaft will probably need replacement, as well as one or both balls. The linkage will seldom need anything other than adjustment at the throwout arm to compensate for wear of the clutch-disc facing material. However, keep in mind that a fraction of disc wear will show up as considerable travel of the clutch pedal.

The hydraulic linkage includes a master cylinder connected directly to the clutch pedal, and a slave cylinder that connects to the throwout arm. There are seldom any problems with a hydraulic linkage, and the least expensive repair is replacement of either cylinder should it begin to leak. Adjustment

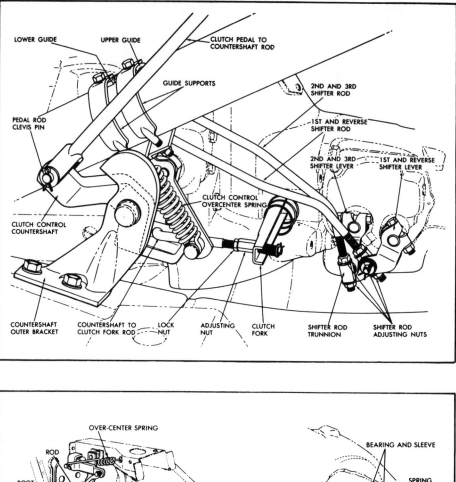

LOWER GUIDE UPPER GUIDE CLUTCH PEDAL TO COUNTERSHAFT ROD

GUIDE SUPPORTS

2ND AND 3RD SHIFTER ROD

1ST AND REVERSE SHIFTER ROD

PEDAL ROD CLEVIS PIN

2ND AND 3RD SHIFTER LEVER   1ST AND REVERSE SHIFTER LEVER

CLUTCH CONTROL OVERCENTER SPRING

CLUTCH CONTROL COUNTERSHAFT

COUNTERSHAFT OUTER BRACKET   COUNTERSHAFT TO CLUTCH FORK ROD   LOCK NUT   ADJUSTING NUT   CLUTCH FORK   SHIFTER ROD TRUNNION   SHIFTER ROD ADJUSTING NUTS

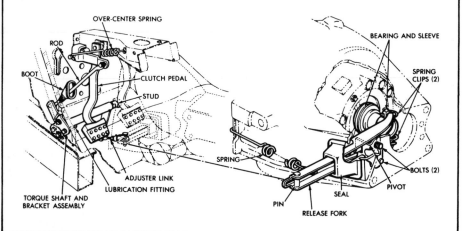

OVER-CENTER SPRING

ROD

BEARING AND SLEEVE

BOOT

SPRING CLIPS (2)

CLUTCH PEDAL

STUD

ADJUSTER LINK
LUBRICATION FITTING

SPRING

BOLTS (2)

PIVOT

TORQUE SHAFT AND BRACKET ASSEMBLY

PIN   SEAL

RELEASE FORK

Transmission linkage and clutch linkage for Pontiac (top) and Dodge show different methods of achieving the same results. The Pontiac shifting linkage is typical, with adjustment points at the transmission shifting levers. Clutch linkage for all cars with suspended pedals will include a countershaft (or torque shaft) that usually mounts between engine or transmission bellhousing and the frame.

When a transmission is being removed, the transmission crossmember (a) should be removed, then the transmission bolts (b) can be removed. The clutch inspection cover (c) should be removed and left off until the unit is again bolted to the engine block. Speedometer cable (d) and the shifting linkage (e) should be removed. Driveshaft must be disconnected at universal joint; transmission is then ready for removal.

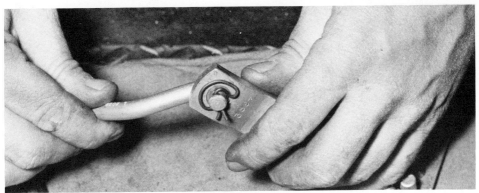

Transmission shifting linkage is often held to the shifting lever arms by a spring clip. This clip is designed to eliminate linkage rattle. Other designs use a cotter key or nylon bushing inserts.

for disc wear is achieved at the slave-cylinder actuating rod, the same as with a mechanical linkage.

The clutch is definitely a point of mechanical problems, especially with the smaller imported cars. While a typical clutch can be expected to give as many as 100,000 trouble-free miles, it is not uncommon for the clutch to wear out within 20,000 miles. Usually, the clutch will give other signs of maladjustment before it wears out completely, and you can save many thousands of miles on a clutch by learning how to diagnose potential trouble.

If the linkage is not adjusted properly, the clutch can be slipping, and this will quickly cause clutch failure. You can tell if the clutch is slipping simply by listening to the engine. If the engine revs up but the car doesn't seem to move faster, the clutch is slipping. If you smell an odor from the transmission area that smells like hot brakes, the clutch is slipping. A slipping clutch will ruin the pressure plate and flywheel also, so don't let such a situation go.

Look for the cause of clutch slip in the linkage between pedal and release fork. It may be out of adjustment. A misadjustment in any part of the linkage between pedal and pressure plate will try to hold the pressure plate from squeezing in fully against the clutch disc, thus causing the slip.

You can determine if the linkage is at fault by checking the amount of "play" (free pedal travel) at the clutch pedal. Using your fingers and holding a ruler next to the clutch pedal, depress the pedal. It should move very easily inward for only about 1 inch. This is designated "free play." After that it will seem to strike something and you will have to push much harder. The hard

point was where the throwout bearing and the clutch-release levers contacted. If you have 1 inch to $1\frac{1}{4}$ inch play, the slippage cause is probably in the clutch itself. If there is no play in the pedal, the trouble is most likely in the linkage. This is a quick adjustment. A mechanically operated linkage will have one or possibly two points at which the rods can be adjusted. The threaded adjustment rod(s) usually have locking nuts (or jam nuts) which must be loosened and the pivot point disconnected before the rod length may be adjusted. Make two turns on the free-travel adjustment, reconnect the clutch rod, and check pedal travel. Repeat this process until you have about 1 inch of pedal travel.

The adjustment of a hydraulic clutch is the same process, with the adjusting link between the slave cylinder and the clutch fork. However, before adjusting a hydraulic clutch, check to see if the fluid is full and "bleed" the line to remove any air. Air in the system will prevent the clutch from operating correctly and smoothly.

Clutch Disc and Pressure Plate

If you're sure linkage is not at fault, the cause of slippage may be inside the clutch. The most likely trouble is oil or grease on the friction disc. It can come from the transmission by way of a leaky input shaft seal, the pilot bearing, or throwout bearing. Oil can also come from a leaking rear main bearing seal, but this oil is usually deflected by the engine side of the flywheel.

Slip can also be caused by broken springs behind the pressure plate. Some bellhousings have an inspection plate which can be removed for a visual check to determine clutch slippage. Another

286

possibility is that the friction material that is bonded or riveted to the disc has become loose or broken. In either case, the disc must be replaced.

The trouble is very easily recognized. No matter how slowly and carefully you release the clutch pedal, the clutch will engage with a hard jerk or a chattering—or maybe a series of smaller jerks. It's never smooth, and can sometimes be violent.

The first thing to check would be to see that the pedal linkage is not hanging up and then suddenly releasing, so that the clutch is engaged with a jerk even when you let the pedal out slowly.

Clutch chatter can also be caused by the disc binding on the input shaft, so that it cannot slide back and forth freely (even though it only has to move a few thousandths of an inch). This can be caused by dirt, rust, scratches, or corrosion on the splines which interfere with proper engagement and release.

Another important area of alignment for the input shaft, and thus the clutch disc, is the pilot bearing. The pilot bearing is located on the center line of the engine driveline and is mounted in the flywheel or in the end of the crankshaft. Since the tip of the transmission input shaft rides in the pilot bearing, clutch chatter can be caused when this bearing becomes worn and causes misalignment.

Always check engine and transmission mounts carefully. The retaining nuts or bolts must be tight and the rubber mounting pads in good condition. You will have to inspect the front engine-mount rubber carefully on all late-model cars, as the rubber is bonded to the bracket and it's sometimes difficult to tell if it's torn loose. A spongy feeling on the accelerator pedal when accelerating real hard can be your tip-off to a broken engine mount.

Sometimes the clutch friction disc will not be fully released from the pressure plate when you push the pedal to the floor. This will cause a clutch to drag and make the car want to "creep" when standing still—and you will grind the gears no matter how carefully you try to shift.

The most likely trouble here is nothing more than an adjustment in the external linkage between the pedal and clutch release fork. This adjustment is actually the reverse of the clutch-slip trouble we talked about earlier. In other words, the full travel of the pedal does not push the pressure plate far enough to release the disc fully. A quick linkage adjustment will usually take care of it. If this doesn't do it, the trouble is inside the clutch. Most likely it's a warped disc that's dragging, requiring replacement of the complete disc. Binding of the disc on the input shaft splines is a possibility, but misadjusted external linkage or a warped disc are the chief causes of clutch drag.

Overhauling a Clutch

Serious clutch troubles will require taking the clutch assembly out of the car. This is a big job, but not beyond the beginner who is willing to work.

Generally, there are two ways to remove a clutch assembly. The most accepted method is to remove the transmission and take the clutch assembly out of the bellhousing. On early Ford products (through 1948) the easy way is to pull the engine, if you have a hoist handy.

Clutch removal by pulling the transmission is the shortest and easiest way

Removal and installation of a clutch disc, clutch pressure plate, and flywheel will require these basic tools. The only one that may prove difficult for the home mechanic to find is the splined alignment shaft at the top center. Most transmission shops will have a used transmission input shaft in the surplus bin that can be cut off and used.

Once the bellhousing is removed, the clutch assembly looks like this. Loosen the bolts holding the dish-shaped pressure plate to the flywheel a few turns at a time, alternating around the plate circumference. This will eliminate chances of warping the plate housing, which is under spring pressure.

The transmission will be aligned with the cylinder block by dowel pins (arrows). After the bellhousing bolts are removed, gently pry the transmission and bellhousing away from the cylinder block until the pins are cleared. Clean these pins and their bellhousing holes before reassembly.

When the pressure plate is removed from the flywheel, the clutch disc will be free to fall out.

If the clutch material has been worn down to the rivet heads, the rivets may have worn grooves in the pressure plate face. The damaged plate face can sometimes be machined; if the damage is severe the pressure plate assembly should be replaced.

Pilot shaft is inserted through splined hub of clutch disc to show how it positions the disc against the flywheel. Clutch disc must be installed with the correct side toward flywheel; this side will normally be marked on the disc.

If the pressure plate has been damaged, the flywheel may also need repair.

The flywheel is held in place by several short bolts. It is imperative that these bolts be tightened to the manufacturer's specifications. Safety wire may also be used to keep the bolts from loosening.

With disc held in place by pilot shaft, install pressure plate by tightening bolts in alternating sequence, making sure to torque these bolts to the manufacturer's specifications. Pilot shaft will slip out of clutch disc. The disc is now aligned to receive the transmission input shaft.

for an experienced mechanic, but you'll never believe it if you do it yourself because of the many parts that must be disconnected.

On a car with an open driveline, start by disconnecting the universal joint(s) on the driveshaft and removing it. Use a plastic sandwich bag to cover the end of the transmission housing and secure it tightly with a large rubber band. This is to prevent the transmission oil from leaking out as well as to keep dirt from getting in. Disconnect the speedometer cable and transmission shift levers. If the car is equipped with overdrive, disconnect all wires. Do not attempt to disconnect the overdrive unit from the transmission. It doesn't come apart this way and must be removed as a complete unit. Disconnect the parking-brake cable, remove the rear transmission mounting bolts, and support the rear of the engine with a jack or blocks. Now remove the bolts that attach the transmission to the flywheel housing.

At this point you're ready to remove the transmission, but be careful—some transmissions weigh over 100 pounds, so it's best to have a friend to help you lift it out. The transmission must come straight back until the input shaft clears the clutch splines. Because of the transmission's weight and the way it's balanced, it's all too easy to have the splines bind in the disc, making removal difficult and possibly bending the clutch disc.

On some cars it will be possible to remove the bellhousing to completely expose the flywheel and clutch unit, or the bellhousing may be part of the transmission case. On others, you will have to be content with the removal of the lower half only, or an inspection cover. The lower-half type makes for slower work because you have to rotate the flywheel to expose each set of clutch mounting bolts. Then, when the last bolts are removed, the clutch must be slipped out the bottom.

Before removing the bellhousing, check to see if there are any brake or clutch linkage brackets that need to be disconnected. If you have a factory manual it will tell you exactly what needs to be disconnected. Also at this time, disconnect the clutch release fork. It's held in place with just a spring or snap-spring clip.

With the clutch and flywheel exposed, centerpunch a mark at the edge of the pressure-plate cover. Make another mark directly opposite on the edge of the flywheel. This must be done so that the pressure plate and flywheel will be assembled in exactly the same position, because they are balanced as a unit. If you don't do this, you won't know where to remount the pressure plate and your engine will be out of balance.

Now to remove the clutch, which is the same procedure for all types, early Ford or other. There are two correct ways to do it. The first way, and probably the best, is to use a steel bar (jack handle, etc.) to pry down each clutch release finger one at a time. As you do this, insert a large nut about ¼ inch in height between the release arm and the cover. This releases all the pressure from the pressure plate, and all the cover bolts may be removed quickly and in any order.

The second way—and this goes for all diaphragm-type clutches as well as the finger type—is to back off each clutch-cover bolt in order around the cover about one turn at a time. You must loosen the bolts evenly so as not to warp the pressure plate. At first they'll turn hard because of the spring pressure, but when they're about halfway out the release fingers will contact the cover and relieve the pressure.

Now that the clutch is out, inspect all the components. If the disc is oil-soaked, has a cracked or broken friction lining, has warped or loose rivets at the hub, or is worn down to the rivet heads (bonded lining less than $\frac{1}{32}$ inch thick on either side), then it must be replaced. Also check for broken springs. Springs loose enough to rattle will not cause noise when the car is operating. If the pressure plate was at fault, but if the lining is half worn, it is best to replace the disc anyway so you will get a new full-life span with the complete unit.

Check the pressure plate for scoring, burn marks (blue-colored spots), or ridges. Generally, pressure-plate re-surfacing is not recommended. However, minor burn marks and scratches can be removed with crocus cloth. If you don't see the problem right away—broken spring(s), warped or cracked facing, scoring, etc.—then the pressure plate should be taken to a good clutch-repair shop for checking. They'll check the finger-release height, operation, and run-out. Never try to adjust the fingers or dismantle the pressure plate yourself.

Examine the flywheel for scoring, burn marks, or deep ridges. If any of these problems exist, or if the surface is highly polished, then the flywheel must be resurfaced. Taking a light cut off the face will ensure like-new performance, and it's not expensive.

The clutch release bearing is pre-lubricated and should not be cleaned in solvent. Instead, wipe it clean and hold the bearing inner race and rotate the outer race while applying pressure to it. If the bearing rotation is rough or noisy, replace the bearing.

Most release-bearing failures are caused by improper clutch-pedal adjustments. If the clutch linkage does not have enough free travel, the release bearing will constantly touch the release fingers and will spin whenever the engine is running. Riding the clutch is also a cause of bearing failure. This constant turning heats up the bearing and burns out the lubrication, and shortly thereafter you have a bearing failure. Since this bearing is an inexpensive part, it should be replaced. This goes for the pilot-shaft bearing (ball bearing or bushing) too. You should check it for wear or roughness, but it's far easier and safer to replace it and forget it.

If the flywheel is off the engine, there is no problem knocking the pilot bearing out. But if the flywheel is still in place on the crankshaft, then the pilot bearing must be removed with a special puller. There are a number of ways to do this, but usually a slide-hammer puller is used. It has a hook on its end. The hook is inserted in the hole in the pilot bearing on one side of the bearing, and the slide hammer used to knock the bearing out. Of course this doesn't do the bearing much good, but you wouldn't take it out if you weren't going to replace it.

Clutch release bearings, called throw-out bearings, are usually pressed onto the bearing hub. The old bearing can be easily knocked off the hub and a new bearing tapped on with a hammer. However, many mechanics do not bother to do this. They buy the bearing and hub already assembled. It's a little more expensive that way, but it saves time and trouble.

Inspect the release-bearing hub for burns or scratches. The release bearing should slide freely. If you're in doubt or you feel a scratch, polish it out with crocus cloth. Coat the release-bearing hub with a thin coat of oil before re-assembling.

Check the disc on the splines of the input shaft. It must slide smoothly. If it doesn't, see what's wrong. Crocus cloth can be used to polish up the spline. Give the spline a very thin coat of oil before reassembly.

If the clutch disc was ruined because of an oil leak, you must determine the cause—engine or transmission—and get the leak repaired. If you don't, your new parts will last only a short time.

A greasy fingerprint on the flywheel, pressure-plate facing, or clutch disc can ruin a good clutch job. It can cause chatter. Clean the flywheel and pressure-plate faces just before reassembly.

The assembly process is the reverse of removal. Start by installing the flywheel and putting a thin coat of bearing lubricant inside the pilot bushing or bearing race.

To align the clutch disc you will need some kind of pilot shaft. There are special tools for this, but the most inexpensive way is to make a tool by cutting an input shaft off a junk transmission.

Hold the pressure plate and disc in close location and push the alignment shaft through the disc spline and into the pilot bearing. Line up your center-punch marks and start bolting up the pressure plate, using the same procedure you followed during removal.

Both the flywheel and the clutch bolts must be torqued to factory specifications. Once the pressure plate is torqued down, remove the spacers and pull out the alignment shaft.

Lubricate the clutch-release fork at the pivot points and then complete the assembly (see Chapter 15). Remember, you'll need help installing the transmis-sion, and you must be extra careful not to bend the disc and ruin your good clutch job.

MANUAL TRANSMISSION

There are several parts of an automobile that will always wear to some degree, and will eventually wear out. The brakes are one example. The standard (or manual) transmission is another, but for a completely different reason. While the brakes wear because of direct friction, the standard transmission wears primarily because of load variations. And while brakes can be expected to register a specified amount of wear in a given period, the manual transmission may fail at any time and under any particular condition. Fortunately, standard transmission repairs are of the simple remove-and-replace variety and within the scope of the home mechanic.

The transmission is nothing more than a mechanical torque multiplier. If you want to move a big rock, you get a long lever and move the fulcrum close to the rock. Now consider the teeth of meshing gears as the fulcrum. The gear with the smaller diameter has the advantage of rotational leverage, and since it will turn faster than the big gear, the engine can run at high rpm where greater torque is developed.

Gearing of both the transmission and the final-drive assembly determines vehicle performance. To this end, a truck may have a very high numerical transmission and rear-end combination, the better to move heavy loads. The racing car may have lower numerical gear ratios, since the engine is kept running near maximum power range at all times. To clear up a bit of confusion, low numerical numbers (those numbers closer to 1) are generally referred to as being high gearing. High numerical numbers mean low gear ratios. The lower the gear ratio, therefore, the greater the torque multiplication between crankshaft rpm and driveshaft or axle rpm.

The principle of gear or rotational torque multiplication has been around for many centuries. Until the automobile created such a widespread demand for special gear boxes, however, the sliding-gear type of multiplier was of little necessity. The changes in the very few years since cars became common are readily apparent—the Model A and a modern Ford are proof of that advancement.

How a Manual Transmission Works

Before any kind of detailed work is undertaken on a manual transmission, it is best to understand just how the pieces function, at least in general.

In the typical standard transmission, there are two shafts involved, the "clutch" and the "drive" (which may be called the same unit for brevity), and the "counter." Somewhere near the rear or side of both shafts will be a third shaft and an idler gear, with the sole purpose of giving the transmission ability to reverse direction between the input shaft (clutch) and the output shaft (drive). The same general design holds true throughout the industry; only the details of operation are different, and then but slightly.

When the transmission is in neutral, the clutch shaft turns the counter shaft via gears which are always connected. However, none of the gears on the counter shaft in turn are meshing with gears on the driveshaft; thus the output shaft is not turning. The input shaft and

output shaft are on the same centerline, but are not directly connected.

When the transmission is shifted into reverse, one of the two sliding gears on the output shaft is slid to the rear, engaging the reverse idler gear. Thus, the clutch shaft may be turning to the left. If the counter shaft were to connect directly to the output shaft gear (as it does in all forward gears), the output shaft would continue to rotate in the direction of the input shaft. The reverse idler keeps this from happening.

If the sliding reverse-low gear is moved on the output shaft, it will mesh with a small-diameter gear on the counter shaft. Since this gear is smaller than the one on the output shaft, low gear is the result.

In second-gear position, the low-reverse sliding gear is moved to the midway neutral position on the output shaft, and the front sliding gear is moved to the rear (or forward, depending on design). This causes it to mesh with a slightly larger-diameter gear on the counter shaft, thus effectively reducing the amount of leverage between the engine and the rear end.

In the high-gear position, the second gear is slid forward on the output shaft. The front portion of the second-high gliding gear is machined (splined) to accept matching splines on the rear of the clutch shaft. Thus when the two mate, the input and output shaft are turning in a locked position, or a direct 1:1 gear ratio. The counter shaft is still turning, but it connects to no output shaft gears.

Refinements to this basic approach have been mainly in designing helical (slanted) gears to reduce noise and gain gear-tooth strength, and in synchronizing clutch action. The mechanic is primarily

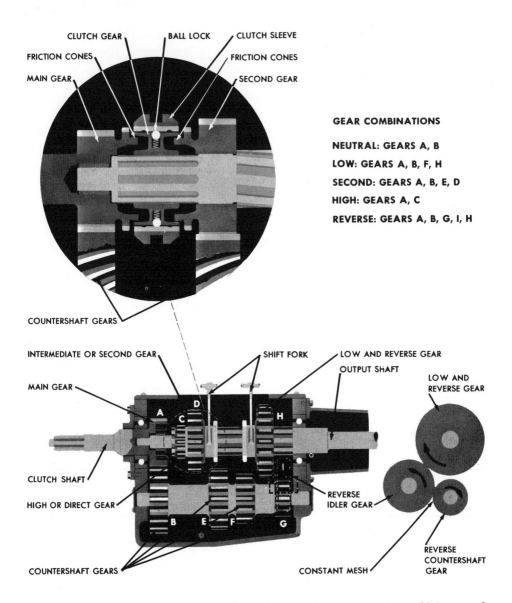

GEAR COMBINATIONS

NEUTRAL: GEARS A, B
LOW: GEARS A, B, F, H
SECOND: GEARS A, B, E, D
HIGH: GEARS A, C
REVERSE: GEARS A, B, G, I, H

Mechanical three-speed transmission. This unit furnishes three forward speeds and one reverse speed. Gears A and B are always in mesh and the countershaft must therefore always revolve when the clutch shaft revolves. However, if no other countershaft gear is in mesh with its proper main shaft gear (or with the reverse idler gear) the countershaft merely rotates idly. Under these conditions, gear C would have to be meshed with the internal portion of gear A in order to cause rotation of the main shaft (high gear or high speed). Simple locking devices are used in sliding-gear transmissions to maintain the various gear positions until a change is intentionally made by the operator. (Mobil Oil Corp.)

These are the many parts that go into a
Chrysler four-speed manual transmission.
An exploded view like this from a service
manual can be of great help when trying
to disassemble, reassemble a transmission.

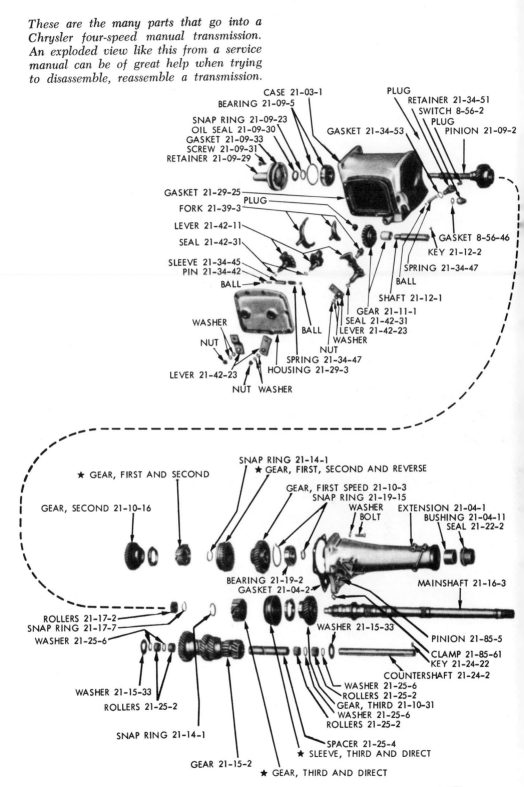

Manual transmission gears stack snugly into a Chrysler four-speed case. In recent years the emphasis on performance has greatly improved the reliability of manual gearboxes.

Compare this Ford overdrive transmission with the Chrysler four-speed and note how the overdrive planetary gears take up room in the tailshaft housing that is quite spacious in the Chrysler model. When an OD unit is defective, it is usually best left to a professional for repair, but a home mechanic can do any of the main box repairs as well as anyone.

American overdrive three-speed transmission is much smaller than similar English gearbox with OD. As a rule, American boxes are stronger than imports.

concerned with synchronization, as it is the culprit in so many manual-transmission overhauls. The synchronizing clutch is a drum or sleeve that slides on the output in conjunction with the sliding gear(s). Until recently, synchronizers were not included on the low gear, and on the older "crash" gearboxes they were not included on any gear.

When the gearshift lever is moved, the synchronizer drum starts sliding first. The movement is very slight until the sliding gear itself starts to move, but it is just enough movement for the bronze tapered cones at either side of the synchronizer sleeve to barely touch the gear being engaged. When they do touch, they act as clutches, starting the output shaft to change speeds to the new gear position before the appropriate gear teeth are in actual contact. All this is done to get the two different rotational speeds nearer each other, and effectively "soften" the shifting load. "Double-clutching" does the same thing, but not nearly so well.

Disassembling a Manual Transmission

There is nothing secret about how a transmission works, and that's why repairs are so easy to handle. However, before tearing into the gearbox be advised that there are certain tools which are essential to efficient work. First of

It may be less expensive to pick up a used transmission from the wrecking yard. Unless the yard operator can guarantee internal condition, always remove cover and inspect visible gears and shifting synchronizers. If there is any doubt, always reject the box.

all, a good set of expander pliers will undoubtedly be needed to remove the several snap rings. Bearing pullers or graduated diameter punches are essential, and even a dial indicator will come in handy. All these may be purchased, of course, or rented.

From the foregoing brief transmission engineering course, it is obvious that wear within the transmission will come at three basic points: the synchronizer clutch, gear teeth, and bearings. Metal fatigue and shaft or gearbox-housing failure are usually the result of an outside influence, like too many hard "drag-racing" shifts in which clumsy clutch-pedal/throttle feet don't coordinate. Lack of lubrication can be a cause of transmission failure, but this is not a common ailment.

Because the transmission gears are literally immersed in lubricant, the early part of the repair will of necessity be dirty. Working in a large drip pan or some kind of shallow tub will confine the oil and make subsequent clean-up much easier. Do not drain the transmission lubricant before initial disassembly, as much may be learned from that oil.

During initial inspection, remove the

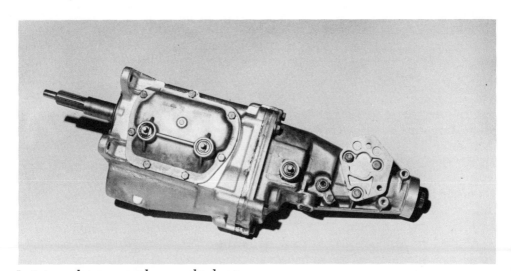

Just to make any gearbox overhaul more pleasant, start by thoroughly cleaning the exterior, draining all grease from insides. This is a GM four-speed.

And this is the same gearbox with all the parts removed. It doesn't seem possible all these parts can be stuffed inside the housing; certainly there is little room to spare. If you end up with one piece left over from an overhaul, better start again.

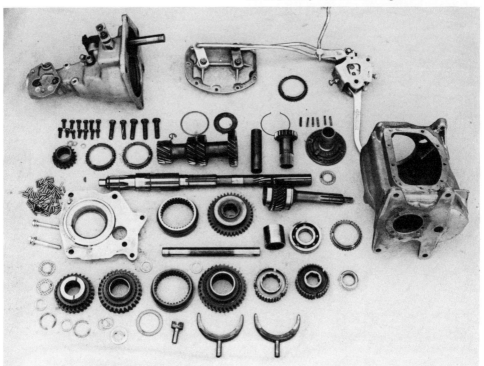

top cover plate, if the gearbox has one, or the shifting-lever cover. Do not jostle the transmission too much as it is being removed from the vehicle, as small particles of metal, such as chips from broken gears, will wash around and become lodged in bearings, etc. After the cover plate is removed, feel in the bottom of the case for these pieces of metal. They are not uncommon, and will give some clue about transmission failure. The synchronizer clutches are sure to wear, resulting in fine particles of brass in the case sump.

All the lubricant may then be dumped in the pan, and the gearbox can be given a cursory cleaning if desired. Disassembly of the component parts comes next, but careful inspection at this point can save much labor. While broken gears are not uncommon within a standard transmission, excessively worn synchronizers are perhaps the greatest enemy to smooth transmission operation. Be-

cause of them, the transmission will not stay in second gear, or it will not shift smoothly without clashing gears, etc. Now is the time to determine just how far disassembly must go to effect a repair.

If gear teeth are involved, very carefully go over each gear. It is possible for several teeth to be broken on the output shaft, but with no damage to the counter shaft. If this is true, and none of the counter-shaft gear teeth have been gouged or chipped, then nothing more than the output shaft assembly need be repaired. If, however, there is the slightest indication of harm to counter-shaft gears, replacement is in order. Trying to make do with gears that have been damaged is only asking for another repair job.

Because the synchronizers are constantly subjected to friction, they should be replaced in practically every repair job.

Remove all the shifting cover bolts. In all reassembly, follow torque specification from service manual. If no specs are available, just remember to snug the bolts, do not overtighten. Inspect the shifter housing cover around the levers for cracks; replace the cover if large cracks are visible.

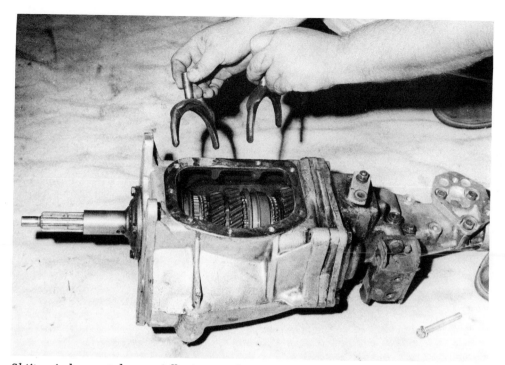

Shifter forks must be carefully inspected. Cracks, excessive wear of yokes or stub shafts mean replacement is necessary. These can be bent from abusive shifting.

Three-speed is disassembled in basically the same way as this four-speed, but four-speed has reverse gear in tailshaft housing of some manual boxes. Drive out a locating pin as shown to release shifting lever.

Inspect the mating gears for nicks, worn edges. Small brass gears are synchronizers and excessive wear here will result in clashing gears when shifting. They should always be replaced if the gear train is fully disassembled just as a matter of insurance.

Since there are so many different manual-transmission designs, it would be impossible to cover each one within these pages. You should certainly try to get the shop manual for the car you are working on. But here we will concentrate on a simple variety of three-speed and four-speed, covering each separately. In the three-speed category, we will work with the transmission common to Chevrolets, the transmission utilized in the typical small V8 combination.

After the side cover is removed from this three-speed, the extension housing (sometimes called the tailshaft housing) is unbolted from the rear of the case. Low-reverse gear can then be slid rearward off the clutch sleeve and taken

Tailhousing is removed to show reverse gear on tailshaft.

out through the side cover opening, followed by the clutch from the clutch gear. The pilot rollers are taken from the clutch gear, then the clutch gear bearing retainer is removed and the input shaft moved as far forward in the case as possible.

This allows the cluster gear (countershaft gears) to be removed by knocking out the counter shaft with a dummy shaft. When the counter-shaft gears are then lowered to the bottom of the case, remove the snap ring around the outside of the clutch-gear bearing. This ring keeps the input shaft (clutch gear)

Cluster idler gears are now removed from case by sliding shaft forward or aft (depending on design). Inspect this shaft for wear and replace if there is even a small sign of wear.

Reverse idler gear is free to be taken from case now. Note how splines on tailshaft are twisted, caused by rough shifting. Entire tailshaft must be replaced when this happens.

Input shaft will be located in front of housing by bearing held in place by some kind of ring locator. Here it is a snap ring.

 303

Entire mainshaft (which may or may not be part of tailshaft) is now removed. Note exactly how gears are in the case that might fall loose at this time, and reassemble in the same way when gear tower is being reinstalled.

Snap rings of various sizes will be used to hold gears on main shaft. It may help to make a sketch of how everything comes apart to aid reassembly if no manual is available.

All the sliding gears will come over main shaft in one direction or the other. Inspect each and lay aside in order. If in doubt as to condition, consult parts man at dealer.

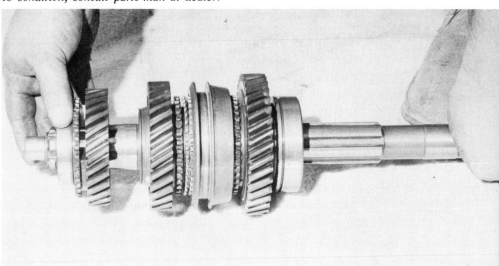

from sliding back into the case during operation. After it is removed, the clutch gear and bearing are tapped back through the case and removed through the output shaft opening. The counter-shaft (cluster) gear is taken out through the output shaft opening.

The reverse idler is next to be removed. Drive the idler-shaft lock pin into the shaft, then drive the idler-gear shaft out of the case. Be careful not to rotate the idler shaft during this operation, as the lock pin can drop down and damage the thrust washers during removal. The main case is now empty and may be cleaned. Check for burrs or chips on any of the bearing surfaces and smooth with a file.

The extension housing still includes the output shaft (main shaft) and gears. Expand the bearing snap ring at the front of the housing and tap the shaft forward through the case. The speedometer drive gear is taken off the shaft, followed by the bearing. This is held in place by a snap ring and must be pressed off. The washer and second gear are then removable.

Inspecting and Reassembling

Now starts the job of inspect, replace the bad parts, and reassemble. Starting with the output shaft, check the shaft for straightness. The bearing surface must be perfect, with no indication of localized overheating caused by poor lubrication. Of special importance is the splined area at the rear of the shaft, which can twist. If the splines show the slightest evidence of twist, the shaft should be replaced. A good test for spline straightness is to slide the U-joint slip yoke onto the shaft. It should slip easily along the splines.

Always replace transmission bearings if there is the slightest doubt of condition. Bearing condition is difficult to assess, but new replacements can be an inexpensive insurance policy, particularly if there were any traces of metal in the oil.

To assemble the output-shaft components, first lubricate the second-gear bore and then slide it onto the shaft. Having an exploded view of the particular transmission will be of invaluable help during reassembly; if this is not available, you'll have to remember exactly how everything came apart. In the case of our typical transmission, the bearing is reinstalled on the shaft with the groove on the bearing outside diameter toward the gear (forward). Snap rings have a tendency to lose tension, so

Use new seals to rebuild the housing; some form of gasket sealant is also a good choice.

 305

install new ones. In this case, the snap ring is placed on the shaft behind the bearing with a maximum .004 inch of end play between bearing and ring. The speedometer drive gear is pressed in place with the chamfered inside diameter toward the gear (forward).

The output shaft is then ready for reassembly in the extension housing, which is merely a reversal of disassembly. The extension housing should be inspected for cracks, which are possible and common on transmissions given harsh treatment. The housing can be checked for bearing-bore alignment, and the front mating face checked for runout via the dial indicator. As a rule, however, if the transmission has seen nothing more than normal use, the housing will be OK. Check the bearing bores for nicks and burrs, which must be removed. After the output shaft is reassembled, the rear grease seal must be installed per manufacturer's instructions. This seal often has two lips, one facing to the rear and the other forward. The lip facing forward must be folded into correct position with a thin tool, such as a feeler-gauge blade, or the seal will not work properly.

If the input shaft (clutch gear) is damaged, it is usually necessary to install a new bearing also. To do this, remove the bearing retainer nut and oil slinger, then set the gear and bearing in the transmission case. Place the snap ring on the bearing OD and tap the shaft rearward. This will press the bearing from the shaft, and then the bearing can be tapped from the housing with a mallet.

The new input-shaft assembly has the bearing slid in place with the snap-ring groove forward (away from gears). The retainer nut (don't forget the oil slinger) will pull the bearing into place, so tighten the nut until the bearing is seated against the gear.

Use caution when tightening the nut. It should definitely be tight against the inner race of the bearing, but not so tight that it swells the race and causes the bearing to bind. After tightening the nut, test the bearing by turning it with your hand. The bearing should turn just as freely as when it was off the shaft. If there is some sort of locking arrangement for the nut, it must be used. In this case, a centerpunch forces a bit of the nut material into a depression in the shaft.

Since the synchronizer assembly or at least the cones will probably need replacement, the low-reverse sliding gear is first taken from the clutch. Different makes of transmissions use different types of synchronizer assemblies. In this case, the synchronizer ring in the clutch should be turned until the ring-retainer ends can be seen through the slot in the sleeve. Snap-ring pliers are inserted in the slot and the ring is expanded so the synchronized ring can be removed. If these rings are damaged in any way, they must be replaced. As a rule, any wear or looseness (rocking,

Broken synchronizer ring is result of harsh shifting.

Small thrust washers at various places in the transmission must absolutely be replaced; this one is at rear of cluster and rides between it and housing.

etc.) will mean replacement of both ring(s) and clutch sleeve. The unit is reassembled in reverse order, but make sure synchronizer rings are free to turn easily. If they seem stuck, chances are the snap ring is not seated correctly.

All thrust washers should be inspected and replaced if they are worn, which is probable. If the reverse idler gear is good, it may then be reassembled in the case. To do this, put the gear in the case with the thrust washers at the rear, then drive the idler shaft back in place. The lock-pin hole is at an angle, so make sure the case and shaft pin holes align. This lock pin should be removed from the shaft prior to reassembly. It must drive into place with slight force, or otherwise it can fall out later. Permatex No. 2 can be used as a lock, and the case hole may be peened slightly. The expansion plug is then installed in the case to prevent oil from leaking around the idler shaft.

The cluster (counter-shaft) gears are either good or bad. There is seldom a

maybe. If the gear teeth are broken, replacement is obvious. Not so easily spotted, however, are teeth just beginning to wear. Look for signs of uneven tooth mesh, flaking of the tooth groove, etc. If there is any sign of wear, replacement is advisable.

Install the bearings and thrust washers on either end of the gear assembly, holding them in place with heavy grease. Set the gear in the case and then turn full attention to the input shaft.

Put heavy grease in the output (main-shaft) pilot hole in the rear of the input shaft. Where the input and output shafts mate there are a number of small roller bearings (two different sizes). If any show signs of wear they should be replaced. Install the larger bearings first; they will stay in place with the heavy grease. Next install the washer with the small inside diameter which corresponds to the small stub on the front of the output shaft. The larger-inside-diameter washer follows, and then the group of smaller roller bearings. Remember, this is the order for the common Chevrolet transmission; other manual transmissions will differ.

The input shaft (clutch gear) can now be installed in the case, inserting it from inside. Tap the bearing until the snap-ring retainer groove is outside the front of the case, install the snap ring, and tap the shaft rearward. The bearing retainer is then bolted over the shaft and to the face of the transmission. Make sure the oil slot in the retainer lines up with the oil slot in the case, and the gasket fits correctly. As the retainer bolts in this and most manual transmissions extend into the case, they should be coated with Permatex to keep oil from seeping by the threads. Follow torque specifications exactly; in this case, the bolts are tightened to 12-15 ft./lbs.

The counter-shaft gears are now aligned with the case holes and the gear shaft. It is sometimes difficult to keep the cluster bearings and thrust washers in place during assembly, so they may be installed on a dummy shaft that has been cut off to equal the assembled length. When the final shaft is driven into the case and gear assembly, it will push the dummy forward and the bearings/washers will remain aligned on the new shaft. This shaft must be replaced exactly like it was originally. For the Chevrolet transmission under discussion, the flat on the end of the shaft must be horizontal and toward the bottom of the case. When the shaft is driven in flush with the back of the case, the extension housing will then fit correctly.

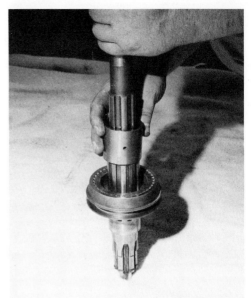

Shifting collar and internal synchronizer is removed. Excessive wear in collar where shifting forks fit signals replacement.

The low-reverse gear is installed on the clutch sleeve, and the assembly worked into the case through the side cover. The synchronizing ring lug is aligned with the slot in the clutch sleeve. The output shaft/extension housing is then slipped into place, with a gasket between the two housings. The synchronizer lug is aligned with the output-shaft slot so that the lugs slide in the slots on the gear, and then the output shaft is pushed into the clutch sleeve. The housings must fit perfectly. Never try to pull them together with bolt force, because the problem is in the gear assembly somewhere. The extension-housing bolts are torqued to 40-45 ft.-lbs.

If you find small parts like these somewhere, compare to see if any seem broken or deformed and replace as necessary. It helps to use tape to hold these small parts together until reassembly.

A direct indication of transmission use and wear is the amount of wear in the shifting mechanism. If the sliding gears are worn where the shifting fork rides, the gear assembly must be replaced. If the shifting forks are worn or bent, they must also be replaced.

Damage to the shifting mechanism is a direct result of two problems: harsh treatment and excessive use. The latter

Needle bearings inside cluster must be inspected for wear. Replace by coating inside of gear housing with heavy grease, fit the bearings and then fit shaft. Go slowly and carefully here to make sure no bearing drops out.

Measure distance of speedometer gear from housing in disassembly, replace it at same measurement on tailshaft.

cannot be helped, the former can. Inspect the shifting-mechanism cover plate carefully, looking especially for cracks around the shift-lever bosses. Aluminum cover plates are particularly susceptible to damage. Worn bushings should be replaced, and often the shift lever itself will wear. It will need replacement.

Position the gears in the case in neutral. Place the shifting mechanism in the same location and assemble the cover plate. The gears should shift to all positions smoothly. Fill the transmission with lubricant, and it is ready for the car. One note of caution: If the manual shifting rods are not adjusted properly, or if the clutch mechanism is not adjusted, the transmission can be damaged.

There are a number of four-speed transmissions in use, all relatively similar. However, some do not have full synchromesh shifting characteristics. For the sake of repair, this is not vital. The four-speed transmission is repaired in the same manner as the three-speed, with the exception that some four-speeds locate the reverse-gear mechanism in the extension housing.

Diagnosing Manual-Transmission Problems

The internal problem of any manual transmission may often be diagnosed without removing a single bolt. The clue may be a growl, or a hum, or a physical characteristic of the unit, such as jumping out of gear. In some cases,

 309

particularly with some four-speeds, this jumping out of gear may be the result of excessive end play between input-output shafts and housing.

Transmission noise in neutral:
1. Insufficient lubricant
2. Excessive end play in counter-shaft gears, reverse idler gear, or input shaft
3. Input-shaft gear worn or broken
4. Misalignment between engine and transmission
5. Excessive counter-shaft gear wear
6. Wear in reverse or idler gears
7. Counter-shaft bearings worn
8. Reverse idler bearings worn
9. Counter shaft bent
10. Pilot-shaft bearings worn or broken.

Transmission noise in gear (previous possibilities plus the following):
1. Rear output-shaft bearing worn or broken
2. Sliding gears worn or broken
3. Excessive end play in output shaft
4. Speedometer gears worn excessively

Transmission slips out of high gear:
1. Misalignment between engine and transmission (a frequent cause)
2. Input-shaft gear teeth worn or broken
3. Input-shaft bearing worn
4. Shifting linkage out of adjustment
5. Worn parts in shifting cover plate

Transmission slips out of second gear:
1. Worn or broken teeth
2. Worn bearings
3. Worn synchronizers
4. Shifting linkage out of adjustment
5. Worn parts in cover plate
6. Excessive end play in output or counter gear shafts

Transmission slips out of low or reverse gear:
1. Worn or broken gears
2. Worn bearings
3. Output shaft splines worn or twisted
4. Excessive end play in output, counter gear, idler shafts
5. Worn parts in shifting cover plate
6. Shifting linkage out of adjustment

Transmission hard to shift:
1. Clutch not releasing fully
2. Twisted or burred output shaft splines
3. Worn synchronizers
4. Shifting forks bent
5. Shifting linkage out of adjustment

The noises a transmission makes directly reflect what is happening inside. If the gears clash when being engaged, the synchronizers are worn. If the noise is of the low-growl variety, excessive wear can be expected in the bearings or between gear teeth. If the noise is a definite clunk-clunk, a gear is broken. In any case repair is unavoidable.

Lubrication of Manual Transmission

The kind of lubrication used in the transmission is important, too (see Chapter 15). Since the gears run in oil at all times, the case is oil-tight, and keeping it this way is imperative to long transmission life. It is normal to use SAE 80 or 90 weight oil in a manual transmission, and it should never be filled above the fill hole in the side of the case. Sometimes the gears act as a pump to create pressure inside the case; therefore a vent may be placed somewhere on the top of the case.

Transmission-oil leaks can have a number of causes:

1. Damaged oil seals
2. Damaged oil slingers
3. Bad or missing gaskets
4. Bolts loose or missing
5. Vent plugged
6. Oil level too high
7. Wrong or poor-quality lubricant (excessive foaming)

AUTOMATIC TRANSMISSION

Any kind of repair or overhaul of an automatic transmission might seem too complicated for the home mechanic, but this is hardly the case. The automatic transmission is nothing but a standard transmission and clutch assembly with the parts rearranged, and a fluid coupling or torque converter added. You can do your own work on an automatic, if you will purchase a repair manual for your specific car and follow the directions explicitly. To give you an idea of how easy an automatic is to work on, a transmission specialist can usually completely disassemble and reassemble an automatic (after it is taken from the car) in less than one hour! Generally, an automatic does not break. Parts wear out, so repair is usually a matter of removing and replacing parts.

The idea of an automatic transmission for cars is not new, though it has taken designers and engineers three decades of concentrated development to create the efficient device we know today. The Hydra-Matic transmission first appeared on luxury General Motors cars before World War II, though car buyers did not become really interested in automatics until about 1950.

By 1952 the Hydra-Matic was improved to include the now-famous Dual-Range feature in drive position. Meanwhile, the Buick division of GM was concentrating on their Dynaflow turbine automatic; Chrysler Corp. was hard at work on their own type of automatic; and Ford was developing an automatic in anticipation of their forthcoming ohv V8 engine. (The V8 engine was not necessary to an effective automatic transmission, but it did serve to speed up the development process.)

Automatic-transmission development progressed at a rather sedate rate through most of the 1950s, until drag racing became popular. Engineers had been experimenting with such things as sprag clutches and torque converters for several years, but it took the heavy demands of ¼-mile acceleration contests to get their designs developed quickly. Chrysler Corp. was first on the road with a really suitable three-speed automatic incorporating the torque converter. Their TorqueFlite had been around for several years, initially in a cast-iron housing. In the late 1950s the assembly was redesigned and placed in a light-weight aluminum housing, making it more than competitive with the manual-shift four-speeds.

About the same time, several hotrod speed shops had been achieving excellent results with highly modified Dual-Range Hydra-Matic transmissions. Obviously if an automatic could be made to handle the nearly 1000 horsepower that a racing engine developed, it could chop valuable moments from a drag car's elapsed time.

General Motors and Ford were not as attuned to the demands of drag-strip racing as Chrysler Corp., but as soon as owners of such marques began adapting the Chrysler TF behind Chevy and Ford engines, the engineers started burning midnight oil. They had the units under development—all that was needed now was production. The result of all this

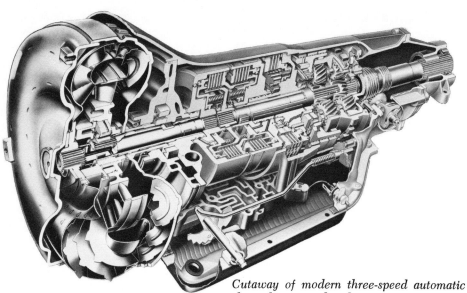

Cutaway of modern three-speed automatic shows how complex the torque converter is (home mechanic should never mess with the converter—take it to a professional for appraisal) and how tightly the various clutch housings fit inside the gearbox. As a rule, the home mechanic should not attempt an automatic overhaul until he has some experience.

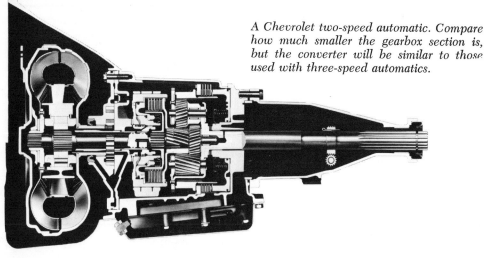

A Chevrolet two-speed automatic. Compare how much smaller the gearbox section is, but the converter will be similar to those used with three-speed automatics.

concentrated effort was a wealth of top-quality automatic transmissions. The modern automatic is a three-speed assembly using a torque converter, usually weighing under 200 pounds and refined to take tremendous punishment without failure.

How an Automatic Transmission Works

The home mechanic faces an automatic-transmission repair with some trepidation, simply because he does not fully understand the inner workings of the magic box. Whether the design is an early Hydro, a two-speed, a Dynaflow, or a modern three-speed, the same basic principles are involved.

In essence, all automatics currently popular include one or more sets of planetary gears, one or more fluid couplings or a torque converter, and control valves to direct hydraulic fluid. The control systems may vary con-

Planetary gear. This illustrates the structural principles of a planetary gear. The number of planet gears is usually a minimum of two, a maximum of four.

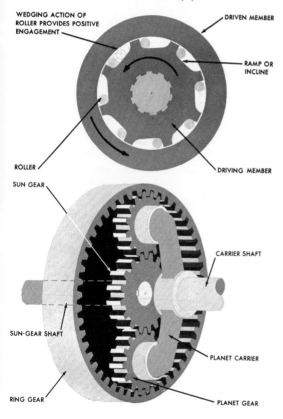

WEDGING ACTION OF ROLLER PROVIDES POSITIVE ENGAGEMENT

DRIVEN MEMBER

RAMP OR INCLINE

ROLLER

DRIVING MEMBER

SUN GEAR

CARRIER SHAFT

SUN-GEAR SHAFT

PLANET CARRIER

RING GEAR

PLANET GEAR

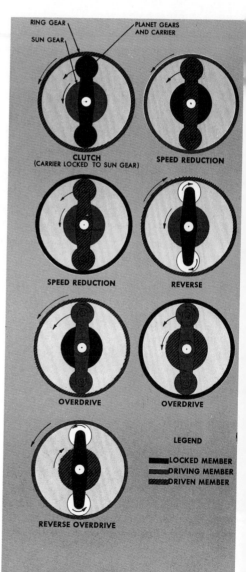

RING GEAR

PLANET GEARS AND CARRIER

SUN GEAR

CLUTCH
(CARRIER LOCKED TO SUN GEAR)

SPEED REDUCTION

SPEED REDUCTION

REVERSE

OVERDRIVE

OVERDRIVE

REVERSE OVERDRIVE

LEGEND

LOCKED MEMBER
DRIVING MEMBER
DRIVEN MEMBER

siderably, since an automatic transmission may be controlled manually by the driver (shifting lever), hydraulically by throttle movement, by engine vacuum, by speed-sensitive governors, or by an electrical device. And, two or three different types of controls might be included on any one transmission.

The biggest difference between automatics is the type of connection between engine and transmission. The Hydra-Matic of earlier days used a fluid coupling, while the later transmissions rely on a torque converter. The advantage of a torque converter is simple: through ingenious routing of fluid, considerable torque multiplication can be gained when a car needs it most—at standstill and during the first few moments of movement.

Within either the simple fluid coupling or the torque converter, a pump located near the center of the revolving wheels distributes oil outward through vanes. As the engine rpm drops below a certain point near idle, this hydraulic pressure is not enough to overcome the static weight of the vehicle. However, as engine rpm increases, the hydraulic pressure is not enough to overcome the static weight of the vehicle. However, as engine rpm increases, the hydraulic pressure also goes up. The oil thrown across reaction vanes then begins to turn the transmission smoothly, with a certain amount of slippage. At high engine and hydraulic-pump rpm, the driving and driven members of the coupling or converter are operating at a near 1:1 lockup ratio.

From the driven member of the converter or coupling, power is transferred through a shaft to clutch/drum assemblies inside the transmission housing. These clutches are similar to the single large clutch common to the standard

transmission in that they function solely on the principle of friction. Planetary gear sets are connected to the clutch packs, producing the final gear ratios that exit through the transmission output shaft.

Of all the workings inside an automatic transmission, the amateur would have most difficulty with the valve-control body. For this reason, it is advisable to purchase a new valve body should one be damaged. There is very little choice with the torque converter; repair must be left to the professional shop equipped with special tools.

We cannot cover the specifics of repair on each and every automatic transmission in current use; it would take the entire length of this book. Instead, we will concentrate on a single typical example, in this case the common cast-iron-case two-speed Chevrolet Powerglide.

Because each transmission design has peculiarities all its own, no extensive repair should be contemplated without the aid of a specific transmission shop manual. These manuals are available through new-car dealers at reasonable prices and are an invaluable guide for overhaul assistance. Special tools are sometimes required for work on a particular section of the assembly, but they can be rented or purchased. An alternative to this is to have a professional mechanic disassemble and assemble the parts that require specific tools.

The cast-iron Powerglide transmission was introduced to the Chevrolet line in 1950 and remained the mainstay of the marque until 1963, when it was replaced by an aluminum-case Powerglide. The latter made use of the best features of both the early Powerglide and the Turboglide. The earliest design (1950-1952) did not have an automatic shift,

314

and the converter was quite complicated. In 1953 an automatic shift was placed in the drive range and the torque converter was simplified. While there have been many running changes in this basic transmission, the repair procedures remain generally the same.

The Powerglide transmission features a torque converter that multiplies engine torque by changing fluid velocity into power. This conversion provides an infinite number of gear ratios up to 2.1:1, making it well suited for all sizes of engines. The Powerglide converter consists of three elements: a pump, mounted in a housing, driven by the rim which is bolted to the flywheel; a turbine which is fluid-driven by the pump and attached through a hub to the transmission input shaft; and a stator, mounted on an overrunning clutch on a stator support. Oil under pressure is supplied to the converter, thus preventing bubbles and aiding cooling.

The pump, or driving member, is designed with 31 curved blades placed radially on the inside of a housing which is engine-driven. An inner ring reinforces the blades and forms the desired path for the oil. As the pump rotates, fluid is thrown through the curved fluid passages in the turbine. The turbine is the driven (output) member of the converter and is mounted by splines to the input shaft. The design is similar to the pump, except it has 33 blades curved in the opposite direction to the pump blades. Oil thrown from the pump blades hits the turbine blades and causes the turbine to rotate, in turn rotating the transmission input shaft.

The stator is mounted through a free wheeling clutch to a stator hub splined to the stator support, which is stationary with the transmission case. The stator is a reactionary member which gets oil

from the turbine and changes its flow back to the direction of pump rotation. This helps the pump do its job without hydraulic interference.

All automatic transmissions take advantage of the planetary-gear system, since this provides constant gear mesh and takes up very little space. The planetary unit and clutch of the Powerglide is a complete unit within itself, containing a hydraulic-clutch assembly and planetary gearset to give drive, reverse, and emergency low, plus neutral. The hydraulic-clutch assembly is built into a clutch drum, which includes a clutch piston, clutch spring, and piston seals. There are nine clutch plates. Five of them are steel externally splined to a clutch flange; the remaining four plates are steel, faced on both sides with a combination friction material of paper and cork. These four plates are internally splined to the clutch hub, which is in turn splined to the input shaft. All these parts are kept inside the drum by a clutch flange, flange retainer, and retainer ring. The clutch flange is splined to a low sun gear.

When oil pressure is applied to the clutch piston, the clutch plates are pressed together, connecting the clutch drum to the clutch hub and the input shaft. This engagement of the clutch causes the low sun gear to rotate with the input shaft. When oil pressure to the clutch is released, the clutch spring returns the piston to free the clutch plates, disengaging the clutch.

The outer diameter of the clutch drum is used for low-range band application. When the band stops the drum from moving, the low sun gear is also stationary.

The planetary unit consists of the reverse sun gear, low sun gear, short and long pinions, a reverse ring gear and drum, and a planet carrier. In the planet carrier assembly, there are two sun gears—the reverse sun gear and the low sun gear. The reverse sun gear is splined to the input shaft, and always turns with it. The low sun gear may revolve freely until the low band or the clutch is applied.

The reverse sun gear is in mesh with three long pinions, and the long pinions are in mesh with three short pinions. The short pinions are in mesh with the low sun gear and reverse ring gear. Both the long and short pinions are mounted on, and revolve about, planet pinion pins solidly fastened to the planet carrier (which is part of the output shaft). The reverse sun gear and short pinions always rotate in the same direction. Band or clutch application determines whether the output shaft rotates in a forward or reverse direction.

The transmission functions rely primarily on hydraulic fluid. To this end, two oil-circulating pumps of the internal-external gear type are incorporated in the transmission, the front pump driven by the engine and the rear pump driven by the output shaft. The control-valve body regulates the flow of oil and directs it to the proper place as dictated by the positioning of the control lever.

Overhauling an Automatic Transmission

Removal of any automatic transmission from the vehicle starts with preparation. That is, no bolt should be loosened until all the dirt and grease from around the filler tube has been cleaned off, the electrical wires tagged and removed, oil cooler lines removed and taped shut, and the transmission sump drained. Cleanliness is an absolute must when working with automatics! Steam-clean the complete transmission

if it needs it. When cleaning interior parts, never wipe solvent from a part with a rag, as this will invariably leave lint. The tiniest particle of foreign material can clog the hydraulic system, leading to an early and untimely transmission demise. Use air to blow parts dry.

Each and every automatic transmission must be disassembled in a 1-2-3 order; thus the need for a service manual as mentioned above. In all cases, the torque converter or fluid coupling should be carefully removed and drained of fluid if possible (some converters are sealed). If the converter has been damaged—an assessment that should be left up to a professional—it should always be replaced. Often the converter or coupling will be misaligned, and the pump or pump drive will show obvious wear on the shaft or shaft support. If such a misalignment shows up, it is imperative that the converter, crankshaft flange, and engine/transmission mating surfaces be carefully checked for run-out with a dial indicator.

If there is any indication of excessive wear in the oil pan—that is, traces of metal and fiber; you can rub them up with the finger from the pan surface—the converter will need cleaning (see Chapter 15). If a transmission has failed because of excessive clutch wear, or because of wear in any of the metal parts, the particles will mix thoroughly with the oil. Even if the converter is drained, these particles remain to flush out into the rebuilt transmission, leading to another possible failure.

There is nothing the amateur mechanic can do about rebuilding a converter or fluid coupling, and unless the shop is equipped with the proper tools even the professional will not attempt these repairs. Under no condition should the

The worst enemy of an automatic transmission is excessive heat. Keep a close check on the automatic transfluid, and when it loses its distinctive odor it is probably time for a change. Any time the transmission is overheated, as when pulling a heavy load up a mountain grade, it is possible the fluid will fail.

It is necessary to check the transmission pickup screen on occasion. If the screen is dirty it should be cleaned, and if it doesn't seem to clean well, replace it. The screen is shown here immediately in the center of the valve assembly which has been exposed by removing the pan.

nonprofessional cut apart a sealed converter and attempt repairs. During operation, the converter is subjected to tremendous hydraulic pressures, enough literally to explode an improperly repaired or rewelded unit.

If the converter looks good and it seems likely that it may be reused, it should nevertheless be inspected carefully with a dial indicator. The fluid couplings common to Hydra-Matics of the older type are separated, leaving the torus cover and the flywheel. Both torus and flywheel should be checked for run-out before being considered for reuse.

Quite often the front pump will fail on the automatic, but when this happens the primary cause for failure can usually be traced to poor lubrication or misalignment. Anytime the pump must be replaced, the cause must be found or it will fail again.

If the pump and/or converter fail, it is possible for the input shaft to be damaged. Each bearing race should be checked with a micrometer and the entire shaft checked for run-out. The output shaft should be inspected the same way.

It is in the clutch pack that the general wear shows up, and this is where the average mechanic must do the most parts replacement. This wear is normal, although it can be controlled to some extent by maintenance and careful parts selection. The automatic transmission is designed to transfer some tremendous torque loads, and it must do it smoothly. This means that some form of friction device must absorb the load gradually, making the transfer without harsh engagement. This very requirement of smoothness means the slippage rate must be relatively high, a rate controlled by the coefficient of friction of the clutch plates, and the hydraulic pressure actuating them.

In the Powerglide transmission there are five steel plates and four composition plates. Were this same transmission beefed up to handle extremely heavy-duty chores, it would have perhaps seven to nine steel plates and six to eight friction discs. The hydraulic pressure would also be increased to make the application more positive, and the clutch hub and drum would be drilled to increase the supply of cooling oil across the clutch pack. All this would create an assembly very positive in action, but not entirely desirable for "smooth" street driving.

Therefore, the factory has produced a clutch assembly that is a good compromise, but cannot be expected to operate in abnormal conditions. If the transmission fluid is allowed to get too hot (towing a trailer, etc.) and is not changed, the clutch pack will show immediate signs of wear. The composition will begin to burn and chip from the steel core, and the steel plates will immediately run too hot and warp. Wear accelerates at an alarming pace from this point.

When the clutch pack is being repaired—and it should be considered an essential replacement with any transmission overhaul—both the hub and drum must be inspected for the slightest sign of wear. Nicks and burrs on any of the machined surfaces should be filed smooth and all oil transfer holes blown clear. Any face where a thrust washer or bushing has been riding should be inspected and repaired by machining if worn. Caution: Do not machine any part of an automatic transmission more than a very few thousandths, and then only after referring to an appropriate

The home mechanic can remove the valve body in a full unit as shown. If there are some mechanical linkages involved, note how they connect; do not force anything loose.

Screen on bottom of the valve body is clear in this case. Often on a car that has not been taken care of, the sludge will clog the entire screen.

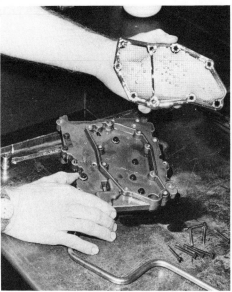

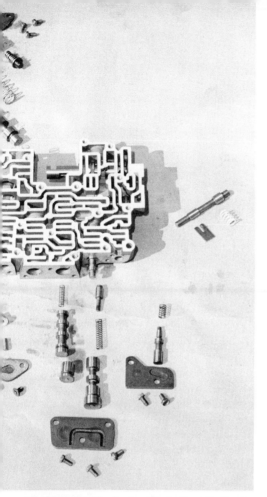

first contacting a specialized automatic-transmission shop for instructions.

It is likely the bands will need replacement. However, the servos do not necessarily need repair. O-rings generally need replacement, and all servo cylinders and cylinder bores should be carefully inspected for wear (much as engine cylinders). The slightest nick or burr will cause a servo to work poorly, or not work at all. Bad O-rings can sometimes have the same effect.

The planetary gears and planet carrier assembly normally will not be broken unless the transmission has been treated harshly. However, wear is possible, so inspect the planet pinions, pinion needle bearings, pinion thrust washers, reverse sun gear, and/or reverse-sun-gear thrust washer. All this can be done with a feeler gauge. Do not reinstall a bad planetary gearset!

A typical shift improver kit will usually include a modified plate, which controls the passage of fluid to operate the various clutch packs.

If the valve body is plugged with foreign material, the various valves and springs can be removed for cleaning; but make sure everything goes back exactly where it came from. Should a valve body be in bad shape, it is probably best to install a new one. It is also possible to get shift improver kits or complete high-performance valve bodies for replacement.

unit-repair manual. Size and thickness of the metal parts is critical.

When new clutch pieces are installed in the hub/drum, they should be of original-equipment quality or better. Do not attempt to modify any part of an automatic for high performance without

Although the transmission case does not normally fail, it can, so inspect it carefully for the smallest of cracks. Pay particular attention to the new aluminum cases, and keep in mind that an improperly installed converter (loose, misaligned, etc.) will tear an aluminum case apart in seconds. The tailshaft housing (output shaft) is also a point where cracks can originate.

Reassembly of the transmission is done with normal transmission fluid as a lubricant. It is absolutely imperative to follow the assembly instructions verbatim, making each and every clearance check recommended. The difference of .005 inch in a single clearance may cause the transmission to work poorly, or not work at all. Remember that the transmission builds up very high pressures during operation, so all gaskets must be sealed correctly, with a compound if recommended. Each bolt should be torqued to specifications.

Diagnosing Automatic-Transmission Problems

It always helps to have some idea of the possible cause of transmission malfunction before you start looking.

Again, because of the great variety of automatic transmission designs, it is impossible to cover each and every unit. Every transmission service manual includes a troubleshooting index and should be consulted for individual diagnosis. However, the following list of problems is representative of what can occur with the automatic (in this case, the Chevrolet Powerglide).

Transmission fluid needs topping-up frequently:

1. Transmission housing side cover and/or pan leaking
2. Valve body or servo cover leaking
3. Tailshaft extension leaking
4. Oil-cooler connections leaking
5. Filler-pipe connection leaking
6. Front or rear seal leaking

Oil forced out filler pipe:
1. Oil level too high; aeration and foaming caused by planet carrier running in oil
2. Split in suction pipe permitting aeration of oil
3. Damaged suction-pipe seal, permitting aeration of oil
4. Ears on suction-pipe retainer bent, preventing seal from seating
5. Bore for suction pipe in housing too deep, preventing compression of the seal
6. Sand hole in suction bore in case
7. Sand hole in suction cavity in valve body
8. Water in oil

Difficulty in shifting from drive to low and vice-versa:
This trouble can be caused by an improperly drilled high clutch feed orifice in the valve body. Oil restriction at this orifice would result in slow application of the clutch with the selector in drive range.

Slipping and chatter in lower range:
This can be caused by poor ring fit or a broken ring on the low servo piston. This allows oil to leak into the clutch apply circuit in greater volume than the high clutch orifice can handle, resulting in sufficient pressure being built up to partially apply the clutch at the same time the low band is being applied.

High clutch failures (burned plates):
This can usually be traced directly to improper hydraulic pressures, and is caused by the valve body. Sometimes, however, a servo ring may be leaking. Check the valve body for porosity or sand holes, or a damaged gasket.

More Automatic Troubleshooting

Troubleshooting procedure applies to the newer Powerglide transmission, but is indicative of steps necessary to isolate problems in any modern American automatic transmission.

No drive in any position:
1. Low oil level
2. Clogged oil suction screen
3. Defective pressure-regulator valve
4. Front pump defective
5. Input shaft broken
6. Front pump priming valve stuck

Engine speed flares on standstill starts but acceleration lags:
1. Low oil level
2. Clogged oil suction screen
3. Improper band adjustment
4. Servo apply passage blocked
5. Servo piston ring broken or leaking
6. Band facing worn
7. Low band apply linkage disengaged or broken
8. Converter stator not holding.

Engine speed flares on upshifts:
1. Low oil level
2. Improper band adjustment
3. Clogged oil suction screen
4. High clutch partially applied, blocked feed orifice
5. High clutch plates worn
6. High clutch seals worn (leak)
7. High clutch piston hung up
8. High clutch drum relief ball not sealing

9. Vacuum modulator line plugged

Transmission will not upshift:
1. Stuck low-drive valve
2. Defective governor
3. No rear pump output caused by stuck priming valve
4. Sheared drive pin
5. Defective pump
6. Throttle valve stuck or out of adjustment
7. Manual valve lever out of adjustment

Upshifts harsh:
1. Incorrect carburetor-to-transmission rod adjustment
2. Improper low-band adjustment
3. Vacuum modulator line broken or disconnected
4. Vacuum modulator diaphragm leaking
5. Vacuum modulator valve stuck
6. Hydraulic modulator valve stuck

Closed-throttle downshifts harsh (coasting):
1. Improper band adjustment
2. High engine idle speed
3. Downshift timing valve malfunctioning
4. High mainline pressure (check for broken or disconnected vacuum modulator line; ruptured modulator diaphragm; sticking hydraulic modulator valve, pressure regulator valve, or vacuum modulator valve)

No downshift:
1. Sticking low-drive shift valve
2. Low-drive shift plug stuck
3. High governor pressure
4. Low throttle valve pressure

Clutch plates burned:
1. Low band adjusting screw backed off more than specified

2. Improper order of clutch plate assembly
3. Extended operation with low oil level
4. Clutch drum relief ball stuck
5. Abnormally high-speed upshift caused by improper governor action or transmission operated at high speed in manual low

Car creeps excessively in drive:
1. Incorrect manual valve lever adjustment
2. Reverse clutch piston stuck
3. Reverse clutch plates worn out
4. Reverse clutch leaking excessively
5. Blocked reverse clutch apply orifice

Wrong shift points:
1. Incorrectly adjusted carburetor-to-transmission linkage

2. Incorrectly adjusted throttle valve
3. Governor defective
4. Rear pump priming valve stuck

Unable to push start:
1. Rear pump drive gear not engaged with drive pin in output shaft
2. Drive pin sheared
3. Rear pump priming valve not sealing

There is nothing super-secret about an automatic transmission, and once inside of the gearbox, the average amateur mechanic (with the right degree of self-confidence fortified by the appropriate shop manual) usually finds the operation quite simple to understand. You can save yourself as much as $200 by doing your own removal and overhaul.

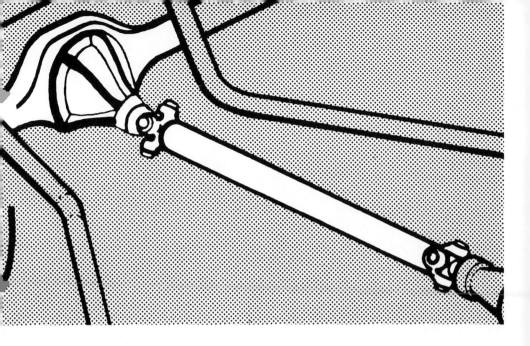

12 final drive

You CAN HAVE all the horsepower in the world, but if that power doesn't get to the road smoothly and efficiently, the car will be miserable to drive. Whether you have a 500-horsepower muscle car or a 40-horsepower VW, the amount of power you actually put on the pavement determines exactly how well the car performs, whether this performance is in the form of speed and passing power or gasoline mileage. Fortunately, the final drive (that portion of the drive train from the transmission tailshaft to the wheels) does not normally give trouble. At the same time, the car owner who cares about getting the best results for his money will observe careful final-drive maintenance programs, and he'll be able to effect most repairs without calling on the professional mechanic.

DRIVESHAFT AND UNIVERSAL JOINTS

Although universal joints seem to last forever, they are under tremendous loads in any car, and they must receive periodic maintenance or they will fail (see Chapter 15). The U-joint is an articulated device that allows for variations in the alignment of driveshaft between rear-end third member and transmission output shaft. Because the rear end will swing through a converging arc, there must also be some method of allowing the driveshaft to shorten and lengthen during operation. This may be taken care of by a sliding, splined yoke on the transmission output shaft, or in the case of some cars, a sealed ball-and-socket U-joint.

Universal joints either are prelubri-

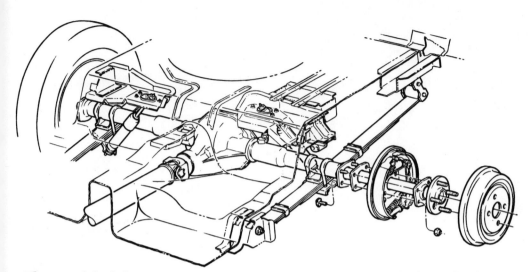

The typical final drive unit consists of the driveshaft, differential, axle housings and shafts, and perhaps the drums. The home mechanic can do much of the rearend work at home, including replacing gaskets that might leak between brake backing plates and axle housings or broken axle shafts. With some experience, the home mechanic can remove the differential and make minor repairs, although most of the actual gear setting should be left to a professional with tools.

cated and sealed at the factory or will have a lubrication fitting and should be lubed every time the chassis is greased. If you're using a grease gun at home, the idea is to force in new lube until you see grease just start to ooze out around the U-joint bearing caps. If this grease looks rusty, chances are good the bearing has already worn to the replacement stage and you shouldn't delay replacement any longer than necessary. If the bearing won't take any grease, it is also probably on the verge of failure. You can't do anything about the sealed bearings, except wait until they fail.

When a universal joint just starts to fail, there may be a slight clicking when the driveline is loaded and unloaded, sometimes accompanied by a slight squeaking noise. This clicking will often get louder until it becomes a loud clunk, at which time the driveline can fall out

on any revolution. If there is no sound, but you suspect a bad U-joint, place a finger near each bearing cup in turn, and twist the driveshaft each way. This slight loading/unloading will show up as a noticeable sloppy feel at a worn bearing.

You might run across a two-piece driveline in some cars and many trucks. These lines use three universal joints, and the end of one shaft will be supported by a bearing bolted directly to the frame. This extra support bearing is almost always lubed when the car is serviced, but a frustrating problem can arise at this point. Should you be experiencing an unusual speed-related vibration problem with the car, and you have made the usual checks—front-end alignment, wheel balance, engine flywheel/vibration damner balance—to no avail, suspect this bearing. Sometimes

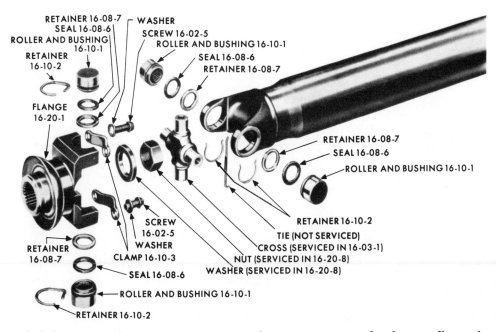

RETAINER 16-08-7
SEAL 16-08-6
ROLLER AND BUSHING 16-10-1
RETAINER 16-10-2
FLANGE 16-20-1

WASHER
SCREW 16-02-5
ROLLER AND BUSHING 16-10-1
SEAL 16-08-6
RETAINER 16-08-7

RETAINER 16-08-7
SEAL 16-08-6
ROLLER AND BUSHING 16-10-1

SCREW 16-02-5
WASHER
CLAMP 16-10-3
RETAINER 16-08-7
SEAL 16-08-6
ROLLER AND BUSHING 16-10-1
RETAINER 16-10-2

RETAINER 16-10-2
TIE (NOT SERVICED)
CROSS (SERVICED IN 16-03-1)
NUT (SERVICED IN 16-20-8)
WASHER (SERVICED IN 16-20-8)

Exploded view of a Chrysler rear end, showing relationship of the various final drive components. The clearance between gears is extremely important; outer wheel bearings can often give trouble. Home mechanic can remove axles, but usually needs a machine shop service to remove and replace bearings. (Illustrations courtesy Petersen Publishing Co.)

the bearing will wear just enough to allow driveshaft wobble, which will produce a vibration very much like a wheel-balance job that is almost, but not quite, good. At the same time, it is possible for the driveshaft itself to give a balance problem, especially if you have run over an obstacle that could have bent the shaft ever so slightly. Most better machine shops in larger towns now have dynamic balancing equipment that can balance shafts for under $10.

On the subject of driveshaft design, unless the shaft has been damaged, it should never give trouble. But if the shaft has ever been damaged and repaired, it is possible the repair was not done correctly. The relationship of either shaft end yoke may vary from car to car, and the engineers did this for a reason. If you suspect the driveshaft

may be modified or incorrectly repaired in any way, the cheap insurance is to install a good used one.

Driveshaft Removal and Replacement

Since most late-model cars use the open-type driveshaft, which has exposed driveshaft and universal joints, removal is easy. There will be a cross-shaped shaft inside the bearing cups at either end of the drive shaft. This is called the trunnion, and it is usually the piece that wears out. When you install a new U-joint, you will include this cross-shaft along with four needle-bearing cups. The cups fit in holes at either driveshaft end, and in corresponding holes in both the companion flange (the yoke that fits the rear-end third member) and the

An example of closed driveshaft, bottom, and open driveshaft, both Chevrolet. Most cars since 1955 have used open driveshaft, which makes servicing rear end or transmission easier.

splined yoke that connects to the transmission. In this respect, most U-joint designs are the same. However, how the joints are held to both driveshaft and yokes will vary. Some are press fits with circle-clip retainers, others have bolt retainers.

The rear U-joint is made so the bearing bosses on the rear yoke are split, enabling the joint to be taken apart. The bearings are secured to the yoke by U-bolts, by some kind of casting with cap screws, or by just a strap of steel with clamps or bolts. This design is necessary in order to get the driveshaft out of the car. Split the rear yoke-bearing retainer, and the U-joint will come apart so the driveshaft will drop down at the rear. Be careful that you don't damage the trunnion and needle bearings. The needle bearings should be taped to protect them until reassembly.

After you get the rear U-joint split and the back of the driveshaft dropped, the shaft can be removed by pulling it back until the splines in the front slip joint slide apart. This distance might be 3 to 4 inches.

Installing a driveshaft is the reverse of the above. The tough part is holding the shaft up while you connect the U-joint.

Servicing Universal Joints

In recent years, car manufacturers haven't been recommending any regular service work on U-joints other than periodic lubrication through a grease fitting. But a few years ago they used to suggest taking them apart and cleaning and lubricating them every two years. If you want to do this on your car you will need some information on assembly and disassembly.

On a typical conventional trunnion-type joint you have needle bearings on each end of the trunnion where it pivots in the two yokes. It's a bit of a trick to get these bearings out and the joint apart. You will note that the bearing cups are retained in the outer ends of the yokes by clip rings in a groove. When these clip rings are removed, the bearings will not slip out easily. The rings can be removed by pinching the ends together with needle-nose pliers. Unfortunately the bearings don't just drop out at this point and take a little urging.

Set the joint up in a vise or on a support of some kind that is open below the bearing hole in one end of the yoke (there are four of these ends in all). Then take a punch and gently tap the opposite bearing cup inward with a hammer. This will push the trunnion through the yoke far enough so the bearing cup will drop out of the other end. You have to repeat this the other way, then on the two bearings on the other yoke.

Another approach is to use a punch and tap on the center of the trunnion (at the cross) until the bearings drop out. Just tap easy, not too hard. Be careful not to damage the bearing bores in the yokes or the surface on the trunnion. And it's a good idea to cover the bearing cups with tape to prevent damage.

Servicing this conventional trunnion-yoke joint is simple. First clean everything carefully with solvent, including the grooves for seals and rings, then inspect everything. There shouldn't be any excessive wear in the yoke bores or on the bearing surfaces on the ends of the trunnion arms. The needle bearings should look good, with no looseness in their cups and no obvious wear, galling, or broken needles. Replace the bearing cups anyway if you have the U-joint apart. Also be sure to replace the seal rings and retainers.

After everything is clean and ready for reassembly, put a small amount of chassis grease in the bearing cup. This will be retained by the seal and retainer, and you should have adequate lubrication for at least two years.

Now you're ready to reassemble. This procedure is pretty much the reverse of what you've done. Modern U-joints have seal and retainer rings on the inner ends of the bearing cups, which go between the cup and a shoulder on the trunnion arm. These will have to be assembled before the bearing cup. A standard procedure is to put the seal and retainer rings on the trunnion, then tap the bearing cups into the yoke bores part way, alternating each end so that the trunnion journal can be slipped up inside the bearing. You can readily see the easiest way with your particular joint design. Just be very careful when tapping these bearings into place that nothing gets damaged. It's a ticklish job. Also be sure the little C-shaped clip rings are snug in their grooves, and not bent or damaged in any way.

The U-joints in the front end of torque-tube drives are generally of this trunnion-yoke type, with minor variations, so the servicing procedure would be about the same as above.

REAR END

The rear end on most modern American cars is a very strong assembly. It got that way because of heavy vehicles and high-horsepower engines, not because of any engineering desire for a

Not a common item would be this Dana two-speed rear axle. Such "exotic" rear ends should be left to service by professional.

never-fail system. Fortunately, while Detroit is no longer in the horsepower race, the manufacturers have already geared up for producing heavy-duty rear-end units, and these designs will stay even though engine power is way down.

While you probably won't experience severe problems with the rear end, unless you are unduly harsh on the components with "drag" starts and tough, off-road use, the various rear-end parts will wear until repair is needed. As a rule, a modern car's rear end will give over 150,000 trouble-free miles, but you should be able to handle a repair anyway. Some of the work you'll be able to do at home, such as tearing the rear end apart and reassembling it, but other functions must be left to a profesional with the right equipment for certain tasks, such as pressing on axle bearings and pre-loading third-member gears (differential assembly gears).

The rear end assembly must do but one basic job: transmit engine torque to the rear wheels. How it does this job depends entirely on assembly design and driving requirements. Essentially, the rear end is one cone-shaped "pinion" gear aligned with the driveline that turns a "ring" gear attached to the axles. However, the rear wheels are often not turning at the same rate, so some kind of "differential" gearing is necessary between one axle and the other. The ring gear is bolted to a housing. Each axle shaft end enters this housing and connects to a beveled side gear, and each side gear in turn is linked to the ring gear by other beveled gears, forming a planetary-gear linkage. All this allows one wheel to turn faster than the other, but torque can still be fed to each wheel.

The problem with such a conventional rear end is that engine torque is split between each wheel in proportion to its lack of resistance; if one gets on slick water or ice and can spin freely, it will get all the engine torque and the other wheel will get none. Limited-slip rear-end assemblies were invented to overcome this problem. These designs have special clutches between the slide gears and the ring-gear housing so the housing can be "locked up" when only one wheel

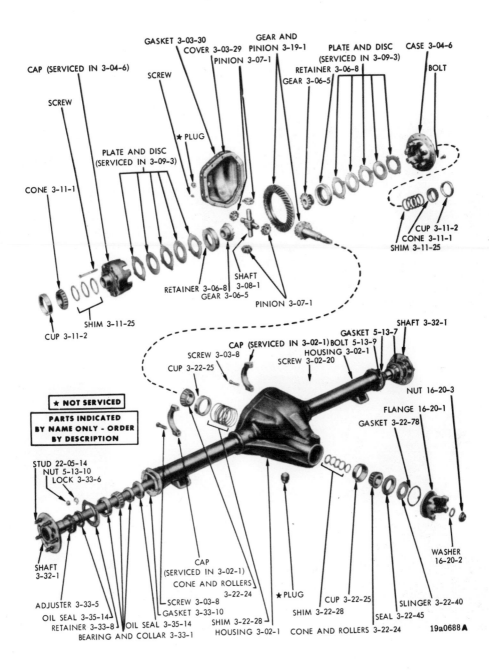

CAP (SERVICED IN 3-04-6)
SCREW
CONE 3-11-1
PLATE AND DISC (SERVICED IN 3-09-3)
CUP 3-11-2
SHIM 3-11-25

GASKET 3-03-30
COVER 3-03-29
PINION 3-07-1
SCREW
★ PLUG

GEAR AND PINION 3-19-1
PLATE AND DISC (SERVICED IN 3-09-3)
RETAINER 3-06-8
GEAR 3-06-5
CASE 3-04-6
BOLT

CUP 3-11-2
CONE 3-11-1
SHIM 3-11-25

RETAINER 3-06-8
GEAR 3-06-5
SHAFT 3-08-1
PINION 3-07-1

SHAFT 3-32-1
GASKET 5-13-7
CAP (SERVICED IN 3-02-1) BOLT 5-13-9
SCREW 3-03-8
HOUSING 3-02-1
CUP 3-22-25
SCREW 3-02-20

NUT 16-20-3
FLANGE 16-20-1
GASKET 3-22-78

★ NOT SERVICED
PARTS INDICATED BY NAME ONLY - ORDER BY DESCRIPTION

STUD 22-05-14
NUT 5-13-10
LOCK 3-33-6

SHAFT 3-32-1

ADJUSTER 3-33-5
OIL SEAL 3-35-14
RETAINER 3-33-8
OIL SEAL 3-35-14
BEARING AND COLLAR 3-33-1

CAP (SERVICED IN 3-02-1)
CONE AND ROLLERS 3-22-24
SCREW 3-03-8
GASKET 3-33-10
SHIM 3-22-28
HOUSING 3-02-1

★ PLUG
SHIM 3-22-28
CUP 3-22-25
CONE AND ROLLERS 3-22-24

WASHER 16-20-2
SLINGER 3-22-40
SEAL 3-22-45

19a0688A

Exploded view of Chrysler universal joint. Failure of a U-joint can usually be traced to lack of lubrication and excessive wear will be on the tie ends or the bearings. The home mechanic can replace U-joints at home using a vise. Retainers are removed first, must not be left out when new joint is fitted. (Courtesy Chrysler Corporation)

Special tube tool goes where ring gear and differential gears would normally be. Mechanic here is checking clearance between end of pinion shaft and substitute rear end. These are the tools a home mechanic would not likely have.

The bearing carriers are torqued to specifications before the ring gear clearance is checked.

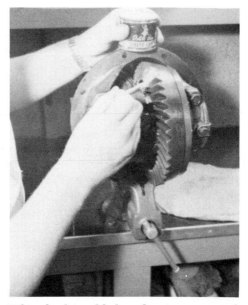

The pinion will be preloaded to a certain amount of pounds indicated in the particular car's service manual. This is vital if the rear end is to operate satisfactorily. Most home mechanics remove the differential assembly and take it to a professional for this part of the checking/rebuilding.

White lead is added to the ring gear teeth and the gear rotated several revolutions. By checking where ring gear/pinion gear teeth mesh the mechanic can tell what kind of adjustment is necessary. If these teeth are not set just right, rear gears can whine and/or wear out rapidly.

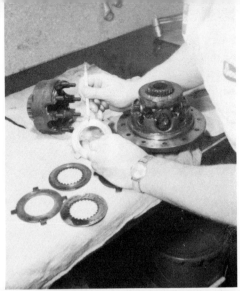

A dial indicator is used to check run-out of the ring gear carrier assembly.

Pro should be left with limited slip differential, as he will check the internal components for wear and replace what is needed. These clutches are worn and need replacement.

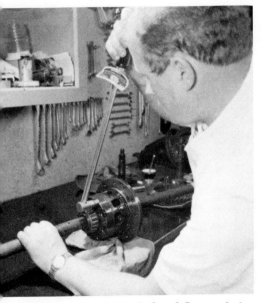

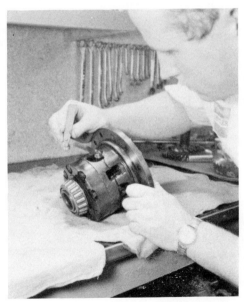

This unit is a limited slip differential, but has all the parts typical to the regular rear end. Ring gear fits around collar to right of torque wrench. It is vital that all rear end bolts be secured to specified torque readings.

During reassembly, the limited slip is checked for recommended clearances with a feeler gauge.

spins. If you have such a rear end and it needs servicing. you should take the entire ring-gear housing to a professional. Be sure and explain the type of driving requirements you have (towing a trailer or boat, off-road driving, lots of foul-weather driving, and so on), as the clutch packs can be adjusted to give exactly the kind of rear-wheel control you require (see Chapter 15).

Rear Axle

Most rear-axle trouble shows up as unusual noise from the axle; usually either gear noise in the ring and pinion or bearing noise in the axle housing.

Gear noise is a high-pitched whine that tends to "cycle"; it gets louder and softer, sometimes higher and lower, in a rhythmic pattern. The noise is more pronounced at certain car speeds than others, and it might almost disappear at some speeds. You have to drive the car up and down the speed range on a smooth road to find it, checking under "pull" and "coast" conditions.

Bearing noise is entirely different. It is a lower-pitched whine or growl that remains quite steady, and tends to be louder when accelerating under load than when coasting. Usually the trouble will be in the wheel bearings at the outer ends of the axle.

There's a chance the bad bearing could be one of the differential side bearings or the pinion bearing in the nose of the axle center section. In this case the whine would be higher-pitched (because of the higher shaft speed) but would tend to remain steady. Also it would be louder under power. Bearing trouble in the axle center section is much less likely than in the wheel bearings.

There are other possible axle troubles. A broken axle shaft is clear enough. The car won't move with a conventional differential, though it will move slightly under half power with a limited-slip. A bad grease seal gets oil all over everything. Main grease seals are at the nose of the center section, at the pinion housing (just behind the rear U-joint), and at the wheel bearings. Usually it's the wheel-bearing seals, as they are subjected to more stress forces under driving loads. Broken gear teeth in the differential are not common, but easy enough to detect. There will be a clunking feel at each revolution.

There have been many complaints by some new car owners the past few years about outer-axle-bearing failures on brand-new cars. Often during shipment the cars are tied securely to the trailer or rail car. The axle bearing is free to jiggle thousands of times in a very limited space, resulting in just enough wear to cause bearings to sound the alarm immediately. Some new-car dealers make it a practice to change these bearings routinely before releasing the car, and other dealers ignore the problem.

The simplest axle repair is to pull the axle shafts and wheel bearings, to replace either a broken shaft, a wheel bearing, or an outer grease seal. This may take some special tools, and you may have to have the bearing replaced at a garage. But you can pull the shafts, bearings, and seals on most late model American cars with just a slide-hammer axle puller and ordinary hand tools, which can be rented, borrowed, or bought at a reasonable price.

Jack up the rear end and remove the wheel lug nuts and the wheel. The brake drum is retained by these same nuts, and you can pull this off after the wheel. When the drum is off, it will expose a flange on the end of the axle shaft (forged as part of the axle)

Should wheel lug nut studs become worn they can be hammered or pressed out and new studs installed.

be put back in exactly the same place. Refer to a Chevrolet repair manual for specifics.

You may need an axle-puller. This is a device that has a bracket on one end that attaches to the studs on the axle flange. There's a weight that slides back and forth on a rod attached to the bracket, and you can hammer this against the stop to pull the axle shaft and bearing out of the axle housing. Work the shaft out slowly so the jarring won't damage the bearings. You can buy one of these axle-pullers for your particular car, or universal types are available at any rental yard.

After the axle shaft and bearing are out, inspect them for wear, corrosion, and cracks. You can tell a bad bearing very easily. It will feel sloppy or rough; that is, the outer race will be loose on the balls. Sometimes the balls are pitted and galled, and the central ball cage may be loose. Replace the bearing if you have any doubts at all, as they aren't expensive. However, it does take a special tool and sometimes a press to remove the bearing and replace it, so you'll probably need to have this done at a shop.

If you're replacing an outer grease seal, it can be done without removing the bearing. There are different types and designs of seals, and sometimes there are two or three on both sides of the inner race bearing and a ring around the outside. Usually these rubber seals can be pried off with a screwdriver. This will damage them beyond repair, but you will always be replacing them anyway. Sometimes seals can be put back without special tools, or with a makeshift drift or collar. Just be careful not to damage the seal surface putting it back on the bearing. And always replace the seal with the open edge or

that has studs spaced around it for the lug nuts. This is what you pull out of the axle housing; the shaft bearings and seals will come with it. But before it will come out you have to go behind the flange and remove the small bolts that hold on the axle-bearing retainer plate and brake backing plate (which holds the shoes and cylinders). Remove these bolts and remove the retainer plate. New Chevrolet products do not use this retaining flange. Instead, a common pin through side gears inside the differential housing must be removed, then clips holding the axle side gears may be removed and the axles are then free to be pulled out. It should be stressed that when the initial pin is removed, small shims between each side gear and the housing can be dislocated. These are part of getting gear clearance just right in a rear end, and thus they must flange facing the lubricant. If you put it on backward, it will leak.

After everything is cleaned and lightly lubricated with chassis grease you're ready to put the axle shaft back in. Run the shaft clear into the housing until you can feel it strike the differential side-gear bearing or shaft. This will have splines that must fit the splines on the end of the axle shaft. Feel around with the shaft until the end slides into the splines. You can't see anything. Just work it around until it slips in.

Then drive the bearing into the outer axle housing with the axle-puller working it in reverse as a drive hammer. Or you can do it with a heavy hammer on the face of the axle flange. When the bearing is seated in the axle housing, replace the bearing retainer plate, brake drum, wheel, and lug nuts.

Differential

There are two general types of rear axle third member designs on modern American cars. The most common has the main axle and differential housing like a large banjo in the center, with tubes tapering off on each side for the axle shafts. The banjo is closed at the back, and the gears and differential are in a cast-iron "carrier" that bolts to the front of the banjo. You can get to the gears by unbolting the carrier and pulling it out.

In the other layout, the carrier housing is much larger and contains the entire differential. The side axle tube housings may be pressed into this carrier casting, and it's closed at the back by a stamped cover that bolts on. This design is used for late Chevrolets, small Chrysler models, and others. It has the advantage of keeping all parts in more rigid alignment, but it's harder to work on the

gears and seals. In both cases, when removing the carrier you must disconnect the rear U-joint, drop the driveshaft, and pull axle shafts from the outer ends of the axle housing.

Any center-section service will be quite a bit easier on axles with removable carrier. Just unbolt the carrier from the banjo housing and pull it out. All gear adjustments can be made right on the carrier assembly. With the "integral"-type axle (late Chevrolets and others) you either have to pull the entire axle out of the car to work on it, or put the car up on a hoist and work from underneath. The latter is not so easy, but can be done for minor jobs like replacing the front pinion oil seal. It takes very special tools to do almost any center-section work on any car, and adjusting axle gear lash to reduce noise is a very complex job that takes professional knowhow. So you'll have to decide how far you want to go yourself for center-section work.

Rear-end gear adjustments are critical for low axle noise. For instance, gear lash—the distance a tooth on the ring or

Rear end gear ratios are direct result of combination of different pinions (gears on shafts) and ring gears. The smaller the ring gear the lower the ratio, numerically, but the "higher" the ratio.

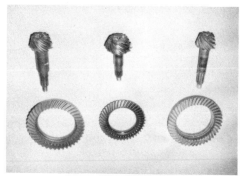

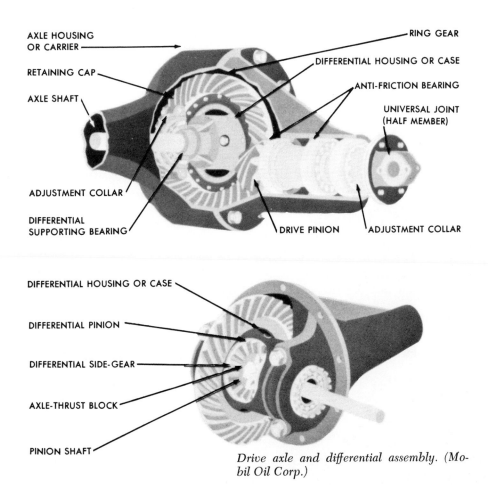

AXLE HOUSING OR CARRIER

RETAINING CAP

AXLE SHAFT

ADJUSTMENT COLLAR

DIFFERENTIAL SUPPORTING BEARING

RING GEAR

DIFFERENTIAL HOUSING OR CASE

ANTI-FRICTION BEARING

UNIVERSAL JOINT (HALF MEMBER)

DRIVE PINION

ADJUSTMENT COLLAR

DIFFERENTIAL HOUSING OR CASE

DIFFERENTIAL PINION

DIFFERENTIAL SIDE-GEAR

AXLE-THRUST BLOCK

PINION SHAFT

Drive axle and differential assembly. (Mobil Oil Corp.)

pinion can be moved back and forth before contacting the next tooth—must be held generally between .004 and .008 inch. Lash is adjusted by shim spacers on the pinion stem and at the differential side bearings. These adjustments move the pinion gear back and forth and the ring gear from side to side.

You can save plenty of money by removing your own replaceable carrier assembly (on nine out of ten cars) and taking it into the shop for work. Then you won't pay labor for removing this from the axle. You can tell whether your gears need adjustment by gear whine on the road. A quick inspection of the ring

Often the rear end gear ratio is stamped on the differential housing.

 335

and pinion-gear teeth can tell a lot about gear lash. If adjustment is right, the wear pattern (where it is shiny and smooth) should be right in the middle of the tooth face. This is both across the tooth and up and down on the tooth. Right in the middle. If there is a wear spot at one end of one tooth and at the other end of a mating tooth, or if the wear spots are high up on the tooth or low down, or if they are egg-shaped and slightly off-center or slightly tilted, you can be sure your gear adjustment needs attention.

Rear-axle gear ratio has a huge effect on the performance of a car. This ratio determines how fast the engine turns in relation to rear-wheel rotation, or car speed. With a 3.55:1 ratio, for instance, the driveshaft would turn 3.55 times for each full turn of the rear wheels (in high gear).

It's important for you to know your car's axle gear ratio. In most cases you will have a pretty good idea by the standard ratio that is supposed to be in that model, from the factory catalog. If you bought the car new, there may be a listing of the ratio on the invoice or price sticker. Also, on assembly-line cars there is always a mark or number stamped on the differential housing that indicates the ratio that was put in that axle at the factory, and whether it's a standard differential or limited-slip. Unfortunately, each company uses its own code of numbers or letters to indicate these ratios. There would be no way you could interpret them without consulting the shop manual for your model.

Gear ratios do get switched around from time to time—and you may still not be sure of the ratio in your car. Then you will have to measure it. Make a chalk mark horizontally at some point

on the driveshaft and a vertical mark on the outside edge of the tire. Jack up the rear end and put the transmission in neutral. Now turn the driveshaft slowly, accurately counting the revolutions, and have someone tell you when the rear tire has made exactly one full revolution.

You can't get an exact measure of the ratio this way, because it's hard to determine accurately the degrees of rotation of the driveshaft when the wheel has made its full turn. But you can tell the difference between the various ratios that are available for your model in the catalog. Let's say the catalog lists optional ratios of 3.08, 3.36, 3.55, and 3.70 for your car model. You could tell the difference between these. The 3.08 ratio would be just a shade more than three turns of the driveshaft. The 3.36 gears would be about another third of a turn, and the 3.70 gears another three-quarters of a turn.

Something that is quite often overlooked in final-drive maintenance is use of correct lubricant. If you have a limited-slip differential, it is essential to use lubricant recommended for that assembly. Rear-end gears and bearings do get hot, very hot; they are the items that quite often fail and put racing cars out of action. Some NASCAR-type "stock" racing cars even use oil coolers for rear-end lubricant. It is imperative that any vent tube on the rear-end housing be kept open to vent housing pressure to atmosphere. If this is not done, lubricant will eventually be forced out a gasket sealing surface.

It is also possible for the rear-end housing to sag, which will often show up as uneven wear on the inside edges of both rear tires and unusually rapid outer-axle-bearing wear. Special supports are made for practically all American car rear ends, and are available through most dealers and frame/front-end shops. If a rear-end housing has sagged, it must be straightened by a professional, and a support strap is then definitely recommended.

As you can see, final drive repair is not a frequent occurrence, but when it does happen, you will be able to do just so much of the work. Some professional help is probably going to be needed. Nevertheless, you can save a lot of money by getting everything down to the essentials, and that's reason enough to learn what makes the final drive tick.

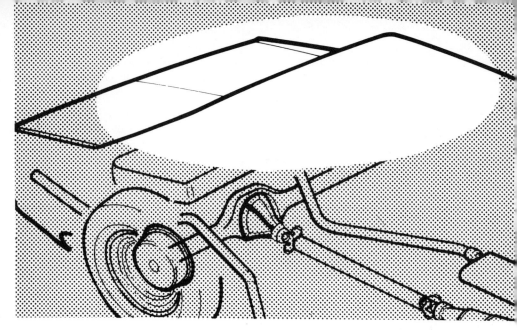

13 sheet metal and fiberglass

No MATTER HOW utilitarian the automobile may be, its value is often more than utilitarian to the owner—especially if it is brand-new, with shiny chrome and paint. The owner seems to take extra pride in his vehicle up until the time of that first minor accident. Then, when a parking-lot blunder leaves a small dent in a door or fender, the metallic innocence seems to be violated, and the car is just another car.

The first accident is usually a small one, and the cost of sheet-metal repair seems outrageously high for such a minor problem. If the owner has $100-deductible insurance, chances are good the small dent will go unrepaired, to be joined by another and yet another small dent. Economically, it may not make sense to keep the body panels flawless. But in fact, nothing keeps a new car new quite as well as a new look. Fortunately, sheet metal repairs are not at all difficult, especially those that might fall in the category of minor collision damage. A very few special tools are required, but these are quite inexpensive.

CHARACTERISTICS OF SHEET METAL

It would be unwise to contemplate sheet-metal repair without a fundamental understanding of the medium to be worked. You must have certain basic information about steel and know how to apply this to various aspects of the job at hand.

Because of the requirements of forming and later use, the sheet metal used in a car body is of low-carbon steel. If a higher-carbon metal were used, the parts might resist certain impacts better, but the panels would be very hard to form at the factory and extremely difficult to repair in the field. Special car bodies have been made from rather exotic steel and other metals through the years, usually as a publicity stunt or as part of a research program, but ordinary mild steel remains the leader in automotive body construction. The strength that the mild steel lacks itself can be achieved designing panels with extra reinforcements, a strong shape, or more metal thickness.

The foundry must produce a product that can be formed and welded, will have adequate strength, and will meet surface-texture requirements. These properties can be covered by three terms: plasticity, work hardening, and elasticity.

Plasticity permits a shape change when enough force is applied. In the beginning, the metal is a large flat sheet that becomes a fender or a hood or a top panel. When the flat sheet is modified by the press, the change is called plastic deformation. The amount of deformation possible without breaking is relative to the metal hardness. This plastic deformation occurs under both tension and compression. Deformation under tension is called ductility, and deformation under compressive force is called malleability. The end result of tension deformation is stretching, and the result of pressure deformation is upsetting.

Work hardening is a phenomenon associated with cold-working. When metal is bent, stretched, upset, or changed in shape at a temperature less than red heat, the process is called cold-working. That is, plastic deformation takes place without the use of heat. Of course, how much a piece of metal can be worked cold has a limit, beyond which it will break. As the metal is worked toward this limit, it becomes harder, with an increase in strength and stiffness. This is called work hardening. The effects of work hardening can be

seen by bending a flat piece of sheet metal double without creasing the bend, then flattening the metal out again. Instead of flattening completely, the original bend remains, and two new ones are added, one on either side of the first. This is because the metal stretches at the first bend and becomes work-hardened, and thus stronger than the rest of the metal. Some work hardness will be found in all body panels, caused by the original press forming. When a panel has been damaged, additional hardness will occur, and still more hardening will accompany the straightening process.

Elasticity of sheet metal is the ability of the metal to regain its original shape after deflection. When a panel is warped slightly, it may spring back into original shape when the restraining force is removed. This is elasticity. Of course, the harder the steel the greater the elasticity, which means elasticity will increase as work hardening increases. When the metal has been bent to the point where it will not spring back completely to the original shape, it has reached the elastic limit, or the yield point. When a damaged fender is removed from a car, both the fender and the inner splash panel will have a tendency to spring back toward their original shape slightly. All sheet steel will retain some spring-back no matter how badly damaged. This is of significance to the body repairman, since a badly "waved" panel may return to normal shape when a single, simple buckled spot is removed —the buckled spot was holding the panel out of shape.

When a body panel is made in a press, or die, residual stresses are left in the panel. That is, there will be areas of stress that remain in the panel. If you cut through the edge of a hood panel the two pieces will pull apart slightly; the residual stress from the original stamping causes this. Such stresses will usually be greater the more complicated the panel shape. Thus, when a panel is repaired, it will probably be restored to a state of minor tension.

Crowns

All body panels have some curvature, and this is called the crown. There are four basic qualifications: the low crown (low curvature), high crown (high curvature), combination high and low crown, and reverse crown.

Panels with low crowns have very little curvature, and consequently very little load-carrying ability. The roof panel is a good example, with slight curves at the edges and a midsection that is nearly flat. At the extreme edges near the drip molding, the top panel will usually curve sharply with a high crown.

A high crown is often considered a shape that curves sharply in all directions. Such surfaces are quite common on older cars, and will usually resist deformation well. Such a high-crown area would be the top and front portions of a fender, the body roll at the rear of the top, and so on. Obviously, a high-crown area is very strong in itself and will not need reinforcements as will the low-crown panel.

The combination high-crown and low-crown panel, which is very common to the modern car—examples are fenders and door panels—provides a very strong structure. A door panel is usually much stronger than a roof panel.

The reverse crown shows up in the complicated areas of design, as an inside curve on a hood or fender. A typical example of an inside curve or reverse crown would be the tail-light area of a Corvair, where the metal is "pooched" out to accept the tail light assembly. These are usually concentrated areas of very high strength, which is why damage to such an area is usually severe but localized. To the body man, such damage usually means use of some kind of filler.

When the metal of a high-crown area is struck, the metal can always be expected to push outward from the point of impact. When a low-crown area is struck, the metal will tend to pull inward. A combination panel will include both outward and inward forces.

TYPES OF DAMAGE

When a collision occurs, damage will be dependent upon the area affected and the force of the collision. The damage can be separated into five types: displaced areas, simple bends, rolled buckles, upsets, and stretches.

A displaced area is a part of the metal that's been moved but not damaged. If a door panel is smacked sharply, for instance, the entire panel may buckle inward. But there will be actual damage only around the edges of the larger buckle. If the panel is lightly pushed from the back, it may snap back into place, and repair is needed only around the small buckles, or edges. If a fender is hit slightly near the headlight, it may cause slight waves down the side of the fender toward the door. There may be a small buckle in the fender somewhere that is holding the metal down. If the fender is pushed or pulled in a reverse direction from the impact, the displaced metal reverts to original shape and only the small buckled places need repair.

Whenever collision occurs, there is usually some form of simple bending involved. In the above case, if the fender is struck hard enough, the small buckled area may turn into a simple bend, where the metal makes a kind of S-shape as it is forced out of place. As the severity of the simple bend increases it becomes a rolled buckle. In the simple bend, the outside of the bend includes metal under tension and the inside of the bend metal under compression. This is in a very small area, since sheet metal is so thin, but there is a distortion of the metal involved.

In the rolled buckle, the S-shape of the bend is pronounced, with the metal trying to tuck under itself. Such damage is not unusual in front or rear end collisions, and indicates a rather severe impact. For the mechanic, such a buckle indicates a considerable amount of metal work, starting with pulling or pushing the panel back into some semblance of its proper shape and then working the buckled area carefully with hand tools.

An upset in metal happens when opposing forces push against an area of metal, causing it to yield. Because of this yield, the surface areas of the metal will be reduced and the thickness increased. An upset area will tend to gather the surrounding metal. Upsets do not occur often in automobile bodies. However, a very small upset can cause the panel to react strangely, sometimes even as though the panel had been stretched. Unless the metal shows signs of having been worked before, chances are the panel has an upset area somewhere.

Stretching is the result of tension rather than pressure, as in upsetting. Stretching is typical of the gouge type of damage. When a car bumper rakes down a door panel, it will probably cause a gouge in the panel. This is stretched metal, and the repair procedure is usually to fill the gouge, as there is seldom a raised bump anywhere near. A false stretch can result from a nearby upset, but it usually takes an expert to see this.

DIAGNOSIS AND DISASSEMBLING

When deciding what kind of repair procedure to follow, the body man must determine the angle of impact; the speed of the impact object; the size, rigidity, and weight of the impact object; and the construction of the damaged panel. Trying to visualize how the metal folded during the impact is the first step, since applying an opposite force will pull much of the damage out.

The impact angle will be either a direct or a glancing blow with a resulting effect on all the other areas of the car. A big impact on the front end can cause misalignment at the rear of the body, and so on. If the impact angle is not too great, much of the impact force will be absorbed by the panel. If the angle is high, the impact energy may be diverted, leaving small damage. In some cases, the impact object may be sharp, driving some of the metal before it. This pushes the metal up in front of the object and stretches it behind. A typical sideswipe causes this kind of damage, and is difficult to repair.

It is vital to understand that the time a repairman spends trying to repair or modify a piece of body sheet metal will cost you money. An untrained metal man can spend three hours repairing a dent a good metal man could fix in half an hour. Learning to assess the damage is important and not too difficult. A few

The dings in this Camaro front end don't look bad, and they really aren't, although to have them fixed in a body shop will be expensive. There is nothing here that the very inexperienced home mechanic cannot straighten except for the bumper.

Even as bad as this front end collision appears, it is primarily a matter of R and R (remove and replace) of the sheet metal. Front suspension has been damaged, so that part of the repair will be sent out to a professional.

minutes spent looking at a crumpled fender may save many hours of labor later on.

One typical consideration is determining how much of a crumpled front end must be removed for a straightening operation. The body teardown takes time too, but it is often easier to straighten a particular panel, perhaps an inner splash panel, if it is removed from the vehicle, and sometimes the removal of an adjacent panel makes repair of a specific panel easier and faster.

As a general rule, a large amount of damage to the front end means that most of the front end should be disassembled. If the impact has been severe, chances are that the frame has been damaged, as well as parts of the body farther back, such as a doorpost or cowl section. However, if one fender is in relatively good shape, it need not be removed unless extensive frame repair on that side is necessary.

When you take the body parts apart, save all the nuts and bolts, as well as small brackets. These parts are seldom included on replacement panels, and they are difficult to obtain separately.

The front sheet metal can sometimes be removed from the chassis as a unit, by removing bolts down either cowl and one or two bolts holding the radiator-core support to the frame. When the electrical wiring and radiator hoses have been disconnected, the front fenders, grille, radiator, and core support can be detached as a single piece. Nothing else on the body is so easily removed. The door and deck lid are removable at the hinges.

Automobile bodies are welded together in giant jigs at the factory, with the outer panels welded or crimped in place over supporting framework. The top panel and drip molding are spot-welded in place, the cowl section may be a separate unit, the quarter panels

This is how the front of a car looks with the grille and bumper removed. Many minor accidents only bend these items, and good used pieces can be purchased from a wrecking yard at much under new unit price.

Unit body construction has basic "frame" built into the body structure. Any extensive damage here (especially to the front end) usually requires cutting away the bad areas and replacing with new or good used pieces. Repairs on a unit-construction car that is badly crunched should not be attempted by the neophyte without some professional advice.

are spot-welded at the door posts and deck lid opening, and so on.

Frame Damage

Anytime a vehicle is damaged, it is possible that the frame or frame structure has also been damaged. While some of the damage may be obvious, misalignment can be present without being seen.

Frame checking is usually done at three stages: in assessing how much damage is involved, during the repair, and as a final repair check. The frame can be considered in three parts—front, center, and rear. The front is from the firewall forward, the center portion is the passenger compartment, and the rear is what is left.

Frame damage can run the gamut from twisting, to collapse of one section, to slight misalignment. In all cases where frame damage is suspected, the mechanic should entrust the vehicle to a frame shop for repair. Such shops are completely equipped with the necessary gauges and equipment to check and repair the frame. Major repair of

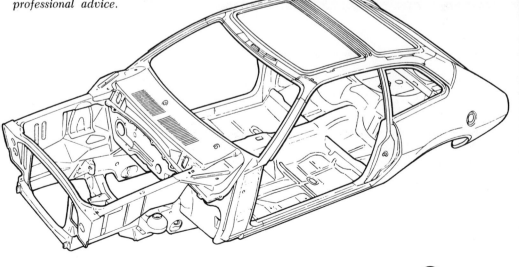

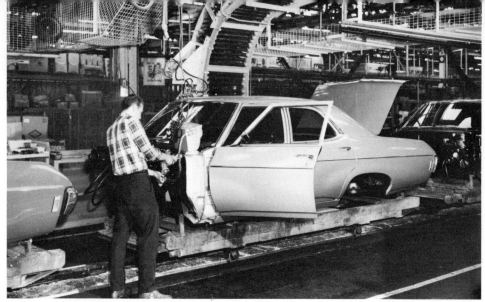

This is an "ordinary" car body getting all the component pieces before it arrives at place on assembly line where chassis is mated.

Entire sheet metal from car with frame will come off the car as single unit (here it is shown being lowered in place); often a replacement from wrecking yard can be purchased in this complete manner.

the frame is not a back-yard project. It is possible to replace small front-frame extensions, called frame horns, but nothing larger should be attempted in the home garage.

However, it is possible to save considerable money on a frame repair by removing all sheet metal that might be in the way. If the frame shop does not have to spend time just getting to the job, they will charge much less.

PANEL REPAIR

An important tool for body repair is the body jack. It exerts a steady pressure—a very high pressure—that can restore buckled metal to near factory-fresh shape quickly. The average home mechanic won't want to buy anything as specialized as a body jack with all the attendant pieces, but such units can be borrowed or rented.

If a dent is banged out with a hammer, the metal will tend to be upset. A similar effect will occur when you push a dent out with a hydraulic jack. It is usually easy to push a crumpled fender back into some semblance of shape, but getting really good results may be impossible because of the excess force of the jack. In areas where the primary concern is alignment, such as door posts, the pushing method of jack use is acceptable if done correctly.

Pulling the wrinkles from a piece of sheet metal is better than pushing. This is particularly true if the section has a low-crown configuration, such as a top or quarter panel. When tension is applied to the panel, the dented area is pulled to shape rather than pushed. Pushing or driving a dent tends to concentrate the force in small areas, with a resulting upset in the metal. This means the upset areas must then be taken out if the final

First part of any repair is to push major damage out with a hydraulic jack. A mechanical screw jack can be substituted.

job is to be a success. By pulling the metal straight, there are no upset areas, thus less work.

Positioning the Body Jack

Learning where to attach jack points for pulling a dent from sheet metal is a matter of knowing the proper leverage angles, lift reaction, work hardening of the damaged place, variations of the surface crown, and alignment with the panel crown. Attachment of the jack ends should be done so that the most leverage is applied directly to the bent area. As an example, it is not too difficult to begin to straighten a steel bar that has been bent double by simply pulling the ends apart. But as the ends are pulled farther apart and the bar becomes more nearly straight, more effort is required to continue straightening it. The leverage has decreased.

At the same time, lift reaction enters the picture. For every action there is an equal and opposite reaction. When a jack is attached on either side of a dent, there is an action to pull the dent up and a reaction through the jack to force the metal downward at the attachment points. This reaction force will cease when the dent is pulled out, although the jack can still be bumped to increase tension on the metal being straightened. When looking for attachment points for securing a jack in tension-straightening, these points should be strong. The edges of the door or fender would be good examples.

When a panel has been crumpled from collision, the area most affected will have been work-hardened because of upset of the metal. When tension is applied to pull the metal back into a rough shape, as much of the area as possible should be worked out with hand tools before the tension is released. The reason is simple enough—any work done to the metal will tend to stretch it back to the original shape.

Areas of high-crown or combination-crown design are a little harder to repair than those of simple low-crown design, but the jacks can still be used effectively. The key is to go slowly at first. In fact, this should be a maxim in any jack work. Proceed with caution, as it is easy to overdo a good thing.

Hand Tools

Hand tools used to straighten sheet metal accomplish the job in one or more of the following ways: by striking a direct blow on the metal surface, as resistance to a direct blow struck on the opposite side of the metal, and as a lever prying against the surface. This means hammers, dolly blocks, spoons, body spoons, pry tools, and caulking tools. Unfortunately, none of these tools

Basic tools for sheet metal work are inexpensive, can usually be purchased used from a professional.

is automatic. Using each requires some degree of skill, and the body man must practice before learning to strike a blind dolly or slap a spoon just right.

Hammers come in a variety of styles, sizes, and combinations. There are many small manufacturers of body tools, but most auto-parts stores carry a reasonable supply, as do the larger mail-order houses. This is especially true of hammers.

The large, flat face of a body hammer spreads the hammer-blow force over a fairly large area of the metal surface. This is essential when working with sheet metal. A good metal man will wince if he sees metal being struck with a ball-peen hammer. It is difficult for the beginner to strike a hidden dolly (one that is being held behind the panel) accurately, so the large, flat-body hammer face reduces the chance of a miss. The best hammers have a dead-flat spot in the center of the head, blending into a slight curved edge to prevent making sharp edges.

The home mechanic may need only

two body hammers. Each will have a flat-surfaced head on one end, but another surface on the other. The combination hammer is the most common, and may include a slightly smaller, more rounded head, or a picking end. The rounded head is great for working out raised sections of metal without a backup dolly, and the picking head is used to raise stubborn low spots.

Dolly blocks come in every possible shape and size, but the most common are the general-purpose, low-crown general-purpose; heel, and toe. The general-purpose dolly is often nicknamed the railroad dolly because it is shaped something like a piece of railroad track, with a variety of curves. The low-crown general-purpose dolly has a flatter main working face, better suited to working flatter panels. When working in narrow confines, the heel and toe dollies are useful because they are thinner. These dollies have sharp edges for working flanges.

A dolly can be used as a handleless hammer. Watch a good body man at work and note how he will strike a low dent from the back with a dolly during the hammer-and-dolly phase. This raises a low spot so the hammer work will be effective as the dent is being raised. A dolly is not an anvil. That is, it is not intended as a place to smash the sheet metal. Instead, it serves to raise metal with its working face, whether by being struck directly by the hammer or from a nearby blow. The correct dolly will weigh about three times as much as the hammer, and when used by a good body man, the dolly-hammer combination is hard to beat for near-perfect surface finishing.

A spoon is a bar of steel, forged flatter and thinner on one or both ends. It may be bent in a number of shapes, with the forged end serving as a working face to use against the metal. A spoon can serve as a means of spreading the force of a hammer blow over a large area, as a dolly block where access to the inner face of the panel is limited, and as a prying or driving tool.

Rough Shaping

The initial step of any body repair after disassembly of damaged pieces is roughing the metal into shape. This first step will be followed by hammer-and-dolly work and the finishing part of the repair and is usually included with roughing, but it is so full of tricks that we have treated it separately.

Repair of sheet metal is something like building a house, in that each step builds upon those taken previously, with a mistake made at first likely to be magnified several times at the finish. With automotive bodies, roughing means bringing the particular piece of sheet metal back into the proper general contour, including supporting members and reinforcements. When a panel is being roughed into shape, it may have force applied by using a hammer and dolly, by pushing with a jack, or by pulling with a jack. Sometimes a combination of these methods will be required.

The vital importance of initial roughing cannot be overemphasized, since the newcomer to bodywork will have less tendency to make mistakes if the roughing is reasonably successful. The first is always to pull if possible, and never push or hammer major damage unless absolutely necessary.

Hand-Tool Techniques

Once the rough shape has been attained and the panel at least looks like part of an automobile, the second and third phases of repair start. This begins with the hammer and dolly, two hand tools that can easily be misused if the workman is not careful. While the dolly can be used as a hammer, it is primarily used in conjunction with a hammer in both the hammer-on and hammer-off methods.

When the neophyte begins to learn metal work, the hammer-on method seems the most difficult. This entails placing the dolly behind the panel and striking it through the metal. It is difficult at first, but can be mastered with brief experience. It is advisable to practice hammer and dolly coordination on a piece of scrap metal before attempting an actual repair.

At first the force of the hammer blow on the dolly is not nearly as important as hitting the dolly. It is important to learn to make the hammer hit with just the right amount of force, time after time. Further, the hammer is allowed to "bounce back." That is, the dolly should remain in constant contact with metal, with the hammer rebounding from the blow. You can expect to make mistakes with the hammer and dolly at first: the hammer will strike the metal, and the dolly will bounce away and then restrike the backside of the metal. The dolly bounces away slightly even when the hammer is used properly, but it will not be a pronounced "limp-wrist" bounce.

The hammer-on technique is especially effective for raising a low point in metal, as the hammer first tends to flatten the metal being struck. This is followed by the reaction of the dolly as it slightly rebounds from the hammer blow. If the hand holding the dolly increases its pressure, then the tendency of the dolly to raise the low spot also increases.

It is advisable to use the hammer-on technique sparingly until you know just about how much the metal can be expected to "stretch" during the operation. It is not entirely correct to say the metal stretches during hammer-on work, but this is the common body-shop term. At any rate, too much use of the hammer-on technique will cause the beginner to end up with too much metal in the right places.

In the hammer-off technique, the dolly is placed next to the hammer blow, not directly under it. Learning the hammer-off style is easy after learning the hammer-on. The spot struck by the hammer drives the metal down, since it is not being supported by the dolly. Movement of the metal transfers the hammer-blow force to the dolly, making it rebound the same as with the hammer-on technique. The effect is to drive the low spot up (from dolly force) and the high spot down (from hammer force) with a single hammer blow.

When using the hammer-off technique, the hammer blow should always be on the high metal adjacent to the low spot, never anywhere else. Learning to "see" with the palm of the hand is part of metal-work skill, and feeling to locate the low and high parts of the damage becomes a natural reaction. The dolly should be of the high-crown type or the portion used should have minimum contact with the metal, and hammer blow should be just enough. Too much hammer effort will cause more damage. Normally the dolly would be about a quarter of an inch away from the hammer blow, depending upon the "springiness" of the metal.

The spoons are used differently than dollies. They are really methods of spreading out the force of the hammer blow. They are used to straighten long, smooth buckles. A high-crown or combination panel needs a very low-crown or flat spoon, and a low-crown panel needs a high-crown spoon. This is because high-crowned panels are stiff and need lots of force spread over quite an area for straightening purposes. The low-crown buckle has springy metal on either side, so the force should be concentrated directly on the buckle.

When using a spoon, place the center directly over the area to be worked, then strike with a ball-peen or similar hammer. Never use the body hammer. Grip the spoon only lightly to allow the spoon face to conform to the panel. If the spoon is gripped too tightly the hammer-blow force will be transferred to an edge, causing damaging marks at that point. Move the spoon over the entire buckled area, striking it with the hammer as it is placed in a new spot, starting as far from the main damage as there is sign of distortion. A common mistake is trying to use the spoon on too sharp a buckle. If this is the case, the area must be roughed into near shape and then finished off with the spoon.

The body spoon is used like a dolly, held behind the metal being hammered. It is really just a form of dolly for getting into very tight places or for prying, and should not be used as a dolly substitute if a dolly can be used. The body spoon can be left in the toolbox until the hammer and dolly are mastered.

Another tool the beginner should understand, but does not necessarily need at first, is the pry bar. A pry tool is used when the damaged area cannot be reached from the inside, such as the lower portion of a door panel. A prying tool is usually considered a kind of last resort, because the surface will always be roughened. When using a pry bar, avoid too much force; it is better to work up the area with a series of low force pries than with a single pry that may raise a bump. The problem with the bump distortion is that it may grind down too thin (or even clear through). Go slow with pry tools!

Correcting Low Areas

After the hand tools have been used to straighten a damaged section, the metal must be finished preparatory to painting. In bodywork, metal finishing means restoration of final surface smoothness after straightening has been carried as far as practical. This means that areas which are still too low (or too high) can be picked up or lowered as necessary.

The file and disc sander are the two prime tools of metal finishing. The beginner should become thoroughly familiar with the file first, since it does not work as fast as the sander, and consequently will not make as big mistakes.

Body files are usually fitted with flat, 14-inch blades. Wooden file holders are preferable. Metal file holders are available, some allowing adjustable blade surface. The beginner who expects to do a good deal of bodywork should equip himself with files of various shapes that will conform to the sometimes odd curves he will be working.

When a file is used correctly, the many cutting blades down its length remove minor surface irregularities. When a file is drawn over a freshly straightened surface, the blades will cut on the high or level spots and leave the low spots untouched. So the file becomes a sort of tattletale straightedge.

The file should always be moved in

Although a file can be used to remove paint, the grinder is faster. Here a minor ding in front fender has been roughed back into shape, grinding disc held almost flat to show up low spots that must be worked out (low spots still have paint).

A body pick hammer is being used from inside the fender to raise low spots; small pick dolly on outside keeps metal from deforming. This takes a bit of practice, but pick dolly keeps amateur from making bad mistakes.

the general direction of the flattest crown of the panel in order to show up the greatest imperfection in the panel. At the same time, the file must be shifted to one side slightly during the stroke to get maximum area coverage. During the filing stroke, the area covered will not be as long as the file, usually, but several inches wide. At the same time, the blade is curved very slightly so that the stroke starts with the front of the blade in metal contact and ends with the rear.

After the file has been passed over a straightened area, any excessively high spots will show up as sharp cuts by the file and should be worked more. Usually, however, the appearance will be of low spots spread throughout the filed area. These spots can be lifted with any blunt-ended tool, but the best is the pick hammer. Here is where the home body man can do an excellent job—or

get into serious trouble and ruin a panel.

It is very difficult to "hit where you look" when learning to pick up low spots. The pick hammer is being driven toward the user and is out of sight behind the panel, and the normal error is to hit below the desired spot and often off to the left side. Learning to use a pick hammer is a matter of practice. The way to begin is to have the hammer into view at first, then move it up to about where the low spot should be. A good way to keep the hammer working in the same spot is to rest the arm on some solid nearby piece of metal, which will keep the hammer from wandering during use.

Start with a gentle tap to the metal and see where the blow lands. It may be difficult to locate this spot at first, so lay your flattened hand against the metal as a guide. The small bump can usually

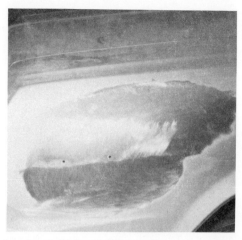

After a small area is raised by picking, it can be checked with a body file. The beginner should use file, as it is slower and will not grind away too much metal should a mistake be made.

After all the low spots have been picked up and filed smooth, the metal is straight. If there are some tough spots that cannot be raised, they can be filled with plastic filler at this point.

be felt and the pick adjusted to hit the low spots. Low spots will be high spots on the inside of the panel, so the pick head can be rubbed against the metal to locate the spot if your touch is sensitive enough. As with the pry bar, go easy and slow with the pick hammer, as too much metal can be hammered up.

Use a blunt pick unless the area to be lifted is very small, then a sharp pick may be desired. In any case, it is possible to create a pick dolly which will limit metal displacement. After the area has been picked up lightly, use the file again. Repeat the pick-and-file operation until the damaged surface is smooth.

Sanding

The disc sander is one of the most versatile of power tools and fills the need for a lightweight, heavy-duty grinder on the toughest of jobs. Good used sanders can often be purchased at very low prices from a body shop with newer equipment. Often broken sanders require only minor repairs, and can be bought at bargain prices.

The sanding discs are fiber discs coated on one side with an abrasive grit, usually an aluminum oxide. The grit size is identified by number. Disc size refers to the disc diameter; 7 and 9⅛ inches are the common sizes, and smaller discs are made by cutting down the larger ones.

Grit size is designated by a number, such as #34, #36, etc. These discs are available in open- or closed-coat types. The open-coat discs are commonly used as paint removers. The closed-coat discs have a heavier layer of abrasive for heavy-duty use in metal grinding. The open- and closed-coat discs are available in glue bonding only, and the resin-bonded discs come in a single style.

 351

Grit size varies with how the disc will be used. Coarse grit is used for paint removal and coarse cutting. A #24 disc is most commonly used as an all-round grit since it will cut paint and finish off the metal smoothly. A #36 grit is better for finishing.

Professional body men use the disc sander as a file substitute, but the beginner should use it only to finish off the rough file marks. It takes some practice to use a disc sander properly on sheet metal.

When using the sander in place of a file, the disc is run across the surface at such an angle that the grit swirl marks will bridge across the low spots. This allows the low spots to stand out as with the file. The sander is moved back and forth across the panel, following the flat direction of the panel as with the file. The sander is held so that the disc approaches the metal at an angle, and pressure is applied to cause the disc pad to flex slightly. This will produce the best cutting action but the sander motor will not be loaded so much that it will slow down. During the side-to-side strokes, the sander is tilted first to one side and then to the other. That is, when going toward the right, the left side of the disc is working; when moving back to the left, the sander is twisted slightly and the right side of the disc is working. Moving the sander this way will cause a criss-cross pattern which will show the low spots better.

If there has been considerable metal work in an area, it is advisable to go over the area with a file after the sander has been used. This is a final check for low spots.

After the area is smooth, a #50 or #60 disc can be installed on the sander and the metal buffed. While when sanding you follow the flattest plane of the panel, usually lengthwise with the car, the buffing is done across the greatest crown, usually up and down. The sander is not tilted on the edge quite so much, so that a much larger part of the pad contacts the metal surface during a stroke. The final buffing cuts down the deeper scratches of coarse discs or a file and is a preliminary to painting.

When using the sander around a reverse-crown area, it is advisable to cut the disc into a "star" shape. A round disc edge will have a tendency to dig into the reverse crown, while the floppier corners of a star-shaped disc will follow the crown contour. A disc may have any number of points, depending upon how severe the reverse crown is—the more severe the crown, the more points on the disc.

Never use the disc sander without some kind of eye protection. Although the flow of particles may be away from the face, they can glance off other surfaces and can cause serious eye damage. The disc can cut a nasty wound in a leg or arm too. Be especially careful when resting the sander on your leg during work; the disc can wind up loose clothing such as coveralls.

Planning a Repair

There is much that can be learned about a damaged panel during initial inspection, and the following hints apply to all types of collision damage. First, locate the point, or points, of initial impact. Then decide if there are two or more points of impact. If so, are they equal or is there a significant major impact point with others secondary? How are the secondary areas of impact related to each other, and will repair of any area be related to the others?

Should any specific area be repaired first? When looking at collision damage, categorize the type of damage involved (buckles, displaced metal, etc.) and then decide how each will be best repaired.

Obviously you can't proceed with the repair plan without some kind of organization, something a beginner soon learns. The best procedure is to decide where to start, and whether the repair should be roughed out by driving, pushing, or pulling. You must anticipate what the panel or area will look like after the initial roughing, and which panel should be repaired next. After you have some kind of organized plan, doing the job is much less of a problem.

The beginning body man, whether he plans on making a simple repair or an extensive modification, invariably is surprised by the size of the job after his initial glow of enthusiasm subsides. It is one thing to dream of restoring a damaged car, and quite another to do the work successfully. Still, because bodywork is a step-by-step proposition, whether straightening a fender or a grille, the average person can expect to achieve at last acceptable results if he plans well and takes time with the work.

The beginner can even repair a very badly wrecked vehicle if he has the patience to stick with the job. There are no particular areas he cannot do, at least reasonably well, but it is certainly helpful to have some practice before doing a major repair job.

REPLACING BODY PARTS

If a panel is badly damaged, it may be quicker and easier to replace it than to beat out all the dents, even though a replacement panel will cost much more

This rear fender could be repaired, but it will prove easier and faster to replace the entire unit.

than a few hours of your own labor. Whether you repair or replace will depend on whether you have a surplus of cash or a surplus of energy.

Practically every portion of a car body is available in replacement form from the manufacturer, but the exterior panels are normally the only units replaced. Such external sheet metal may include the front fenders, hood and deck-lid panels, quarter panels, door panels, top panel, and rocker panels. All these units are available directly from the factory and are listed in collision manuals.

It depends largely upon the factory as to how the various panels are attached to the substructure, but as a rule large panels that can easily distort from heat, such as the top, are spot-welded. Areas that are not easily distorted, or where stress may be concentrated, such as quarter panels, are usually fusion-welded in several related seams. Fender panels are bolt-on and require no welding. There may be a combination of welding methods involved, such as the quarter panel, which is fusion-welded where it

 353

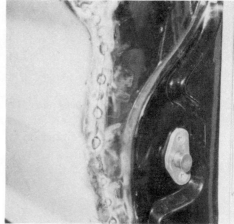

Entire damaged panel can be cut away with torch or handsaw and snips. Any damage to inner panels can usually be worked out with hammer and dolly.

Panel is mated to original doorpost facing with brazing tack welds. Rivets could also be used.

Note how far into the body flooring it was necessary to cut in order to remove all the bent metal. New replacement piece was taken from another wreck, is welded or brazed in place.

meets the top panel and spot-welded along the door post and deck opening.

If a panel is to be replaced, or even if a partial panel replacement is required, the general area must be roughed into alignment before the panel is removed. Panels may be removed in several ways.

If spot welding is involved, each spot may be drilled. A ¼-inch drill bit is normally big enough for this job, but there will be many welds to break loose. The area near a fusion weld may be cut away with a torch if distortion can be limited and there is no danger of fire (inside a door, inside the headline, etc.), but the best tool for cutting large areas of sheet metal is the panel cutter.

Panel cutters (chisels) were usually moved by a well-placed hammer blow until recent years, when the air chisel became common. Such chisels are great time-savers, and produce little panel distortion, so they are considered indispensable by any professional shop. The home craftsman can still do a good job with the older-type cutters, especially if they are kept sharp.

When a fusion weld is to be parted, it is wise to cut below the weld—that is, toward the damaged panel, about one inch. This is particularly true if a torch is used. The final trim up to the original weld is made with a pair of right- or left-hand aircraft-type tin snips. If the

Area where new piece of replacement metal can lap over original metal is a good place to run a line of blind rivets. Lap seam is then filled with plastic.

The new rear fender panel now ready for primer and final paint.

After attaching new panel to original door-post facing, fiberglass filler is used and it is nearly impossible to detect where work was done.

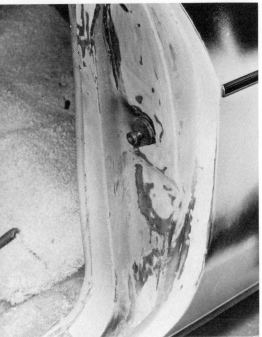

replacemeent panel is new there may be a lapping lip where fusion welds are required, but not always. If the replacement panel has been cut from another car, the area near the fusion weld must be trimmed to fit the vehicle being repaired. In the case of a partial replacement, this trimming must be careful and precise.

Rust Damage

Collision damage is not the only reason a panel might need replacement. Rust can cause damage too. Rust is particularly prevalent in areas where salt is used to control snow on the streets, and it attacks new cars as well as slowly nibbling on older vehicles. Such attacks are generally limited to areas where the salt slush can gather, as on lower-door panels, rocker panels, and the skirts for both front and rear fenders. In any of these cases, a partial panel may be considered the best replacement.

To understand how a partial panel

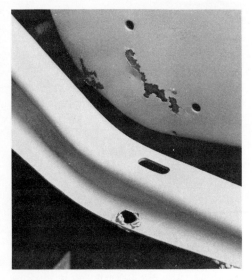

Rust is always a problem with older cars and trucks. The area can be repaired by inserting a new section of metal (difficult), use of body solder (not so difficult) or use of plastic filler (easy).

Welding can be farmed out to a professional.

An alternative to welding is the pop or blind rivet for any kind of panel repair. This alternative has become popular with professional metal men, since it reduces chances of distortion and makes the repair job considerably faster. For the panel just mentioned to be riveted into place, make the panel to be inserted about ½ inch larger than the section cut from the original fender. Drill holes around the panel edge and insert rivets, then hammer the rivet edge down and fill, usually with plastic filler. Obviously this is not the finest method of repair, but where quality may be sacrificed for speed, it works.

Replacement of a rocker panel is relatively simple, since it entails drilling spot welds and either riveting or brazing the new panel into place. In the case

might be repaired, assume a late-model car has a large rust area (or critical damage) in the panel between the wheel opening and rear bumper. As a guide, mark off the area that must be cut out and carefully inspect the remaining part of the panel for damage or distortion. Measure to the chalked lines from nearby reference points (molding, door, deck opening, etc.) and transfer these measurements to the replacement panel. This second panel is usually part of a larger panel that was purchased at a wrecking yard.

Cut the replacement section from the second panel, making the edges as straight as possible. Place this piece against the original panel and scribe a mark around the edge. Cut away the fender along the scribe lines. Straighten the edges of both pieces (the original fender and replacemeent panel), then butt-weld the new panel into place.

After all the rusted area is cleaned with wire brush in drill motor, plastic filler is applied. If rusted area has to have secondary backing it would be best to bond fiberglass cloth to area, then finish off with filler.

Essential to any body work is the "blind" rivet tool. This tool can be substituted for a welding torch in majority of rebuilding jobs.

of a small gouge or rust damage to a rocker, it is better to fill than replace, as far as time goes.

Quarter Panels

Replacement of a quarter panel may be easier than repair, especially for the beginner. The panel will usually be riveted along the door post and at the deck opening flange, with a fusion weld where it mates to the top (this may be a lapped spot seam, also). The method of replacing such a panel depends largely upon the damage involved. A good example would be the quarter panel on a 1957 Chevrolet station wagon. If the panel has been hit in the tail-light area, it will have been severely damaged. Removal is accomplished by drilling the spot welds along the door post and the the tailgate opening. This particular car has a chrome molding between the quarter window and the quarter panel. Remove the molding and cut the damaged panel off at the bottom edge of this molding line, either with a

panel cutter or by the torch/tin-snip method.

The replacement panel should be trimmed just above the molding line. A small, vertical slot (the width of the molding) is cut at the panel's forward end where it joins the door post, and a similar slot at the rear end where the panel joins the tailgate flange. In this way, the replacement panel may be slid up under the molding line of the original body. This is to keep water from running down between the panels where they lap.

Now align the molding clip holes in both panels and the replacement panel at both the door post and tailgate flange. When the panel is zeroed in, drill holes down the molding line and use rivets to make the connection. Spot-braze or weld the door post and tailgate flange. When the molding is replaced it will cover the rivets, while the spot welds can be finished with a grinder and filled if desired (remember, plastic filler will not take a good bite over brass).

On sedans, replacement of the quarter panel is a bit more difficult, because the panel does not usually have a chrome molding between the top and quarter panels. Furthermore, the two panels are usually factory-welded with the seam running into the rear-window lip. This means removal for panel replacement.

However, most professionals don't wish to take so much time. Therefore the panels are removed as with the station wagon, but the seam cut is made near the original weld to a point just outboard of the rear window. Here the cut skirts the window opening until it meets a line from the deck-opening flange. A butt weld may be used where the two panels meet, but more common is a lap joint with rivets and plastic filler.

Doors

Other than the front fenders and quarter panels, the doors receive more panel replacement than any part of the car. Damage is usually due to collision. Rust is a reason on older cars, but usually only because the water drain holes have become plugged. When rust has taken the door panel, chances are good that the lower part of the reinforcing substructure is also badly rusted.

A door may receive a full or partial panel replacement, depending upon the damage. If the lower part of the door has a severe gouge or is rusted away, replacing the panel below the chrome molding (if one is used) may be all that is necessary. If there is no molding to hide the rivets, it is wise to replace the entire panel, since welding and

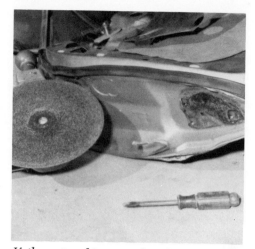

If the outer skin on a door has been damaged beyond repair, the skin can only be removed by grinding along the edge as shown. A new panel can be purchased from dealer, and edges folded over with body hammer and block of wood.

Some car doors have hinge pins that are removable, others rely on the entire hinge being removed. If the door is badly damaged, it is often easier to remove it and do basic reshaping on bench, then refit it for alignment checks.

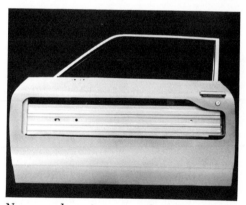

New cars have inner guard. If this is bent, it will require a lot of effort to straighten. A used complete door might be less expensive than effort needed to straighten bent door.

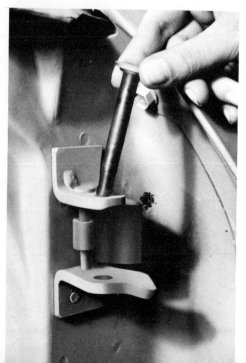

working the middle of a low-crown panel is a considerable job.

Late-model cars usually have a window-opening structure separate from the panel, which means replacement panels come only to the window. Earlier cars had panels which carried through to the window-opening edges. This means earlier doors will need to be cut and welded somewhere near the top of the door panel in a high-crown area, usually just below the window (chrome trim at this point was common). Incidentally, deck-lid and hood panels are crimped to the substructure much the same as doors, so replacement would be similar. However, before a door, hood, or deck-lid panel is replaced, the cost of a good used item should definitely be considered.

BODY FILLERS

Body fillers, whether plastic or lead, are perhaps the most abused of all repair materials. It is easy for a beginner to form the unsatisfactory habit of filling a low spot when very little effort would be required to straighten the damage. In many cases, it would be much faster to repair the metal, and save the added cost of the filler. Excessive use of filler breeds poor work traits and, usually, poor workmanship.

Plastic and lead fillers are an essential part of body repair, but their use should be limited. When fillers are used they must be applied with care. Experience comes with use, and the more experience a body man has, the less flller he uses.

Lead solder has been used in basic automobile construction for decades, and will undoubtedly continue to be used for many years to come. Plastic fillers are relatively new, and while they do some jobs quite well, they are not to be considered a total replacement for lead.

Practically all automobile bodies use lead to some degree during the intital construction, usually at the visible points of panel mating—where the top panel mates with the quarter panels, where the deck-lid skirt panels mate with the quarter panels, on the cowl panels, and so on. However, the amount of lead used is very small, and it's sometimes necessary for the repairman to melt this lead when replacing the panel. Lead work should be left to a professional.

Plastic

Plastic and fiberglass repair procedures are often mistaken for one and the same thing, but they are not. The so-called plastic filler is basically a substitute for lead, while the fiberglass repair is primarily for fiberglass surfaces, but may be used on sheet metal. Fiberglass is almost always used only as a repair of a rust-rotted area that could otherwise be repaired only by panel replacement or patching.

There have been tremendous efforts to create a true no-heat filler that will work as well as lead. While a perfect plastic filler has yet to be found, the product of today is vastly improved over that of a few short years ago. Today, plastic can be relied upon to give a good, hard finish that will not shrink or crack with age, yet will adhere to the metal even under the most extreme temperature conditions.

There are many companies making plastic fillers. Prices range from very low to quite high, and about the only guideline for the beginner is to use the filler that the majority of local body men use. A plastic filler usually takes about 30 minutes to harden. It takes less skill to apply a plastic filler, but the dust created from grinding some plastics can injure the lungs. By and large, the plastic filler has a definite place in auto body repair.

Because the metal cannot be worked after a plastic filler has been used, it is imperative that all high spots be driven

Plastic filler is inexpensive, and can be used by the least experienced mechanic. It is wise to practice on a piece of metal before doing first job, however.

The heavy-duty professional body grinder is often available in used condition for a bargain price, but if one is not available . . .

. . . then air or small electric hand grinder will do.

down before the application of plastics. The area to be filled must be cleaned of rust, paint and welding scale. Grind the metal with a #24 open-coat disc to give a rough metal surface for good plastic "bite," then wipe away any oil or waxes that might prevent a good bond. Clean an area larger than that to be repaired, with the surrounding paint featheredged before the repair is started. This will allow the filler to spread into the surrounding metal to ensure the necessary buildup. Do not spread the filler over any paint, as it will probably peel later on. To cut down on the labor involved, do not fill more than is absolutely necessary.

Plastic fillers include a resin base and a catalyst. Unmixed, the two agents remain pliable indefinitely, but once the catalyst is added to the resin, the mixture will harden in a matter of minutes. It is possible to control the hardening time somewhat by the amount of catalyst (hardener) added, but the best course is to follow mixing instructions on the containers.

The most common type of plastic filler kit includes a specific amount of resin (usually contained in quart cans) and a small tube of liquid hardener. Normally, no more than two small drops of hardener are required for a golf-ball-size hunk of resin. Any type of plastic filler must be thoroughly mixed. The mixture should be kept free of any contaminants. A piece of safety glass is a good mixing board, easy to clean and store. Cardboard will work in a pinch.

Never mix more plastic than immediately needed, even if the fill will require several coats. The filler on the panel and that on the mixing board will harden at the same rate, so the unused portion is useless once it has been mixed.

Plastics can be applied with a wide putty knife, a rubber squeegee, or practically any kind of flexible straightedge. The rubber squeegee is perhaps the easiest to use, since it will tend to follow body contours and leave a smooth finish.

As soon as the plastic is completely mixed, it should be applied to the work area. Apply the mixture onto the area with a downward-sideways motion to force out any air bubbles. These bubbles must not be left in the work, as they will shrink or burst later after the paint is applied. At the same time, this pressure will cause the plastic to gain maximum bond with the roughened metal.

If the area to be filled is more than ¼ inch deep, successive filling is necessary, with each coat allowed to dry before the next is applied. Such a deep fill might be a gouge, in which case the deepest part of the fill would receive the plastic first. No plastic would be feathered to the edges; instead the feathering would be done on the last coat.

If too much hardener is used, or if the material stands too long before it is applied, it will tend to roll up and pull loose from the metal. Don't bother going further; mix a new batch and start again.

Finishing plastic can be either very easy or extremely difficult, depending upon how long it is allowed to set before the finishing process is started. Often you will see a car with a gouge obviously filled by the car owner with plastic. Usually the owner has applied the filler rather roughly and apparently waited until the plastic has become very hard before attempting to file or sand it smooth. By then, it required a very sharp file, a disc sander, and lots of elbow grease. He had none of these.

A regular body file is not used to work plastic. The type of file used is referred to as a cheese grater, a kind of file used in woodworking. Blades for these files are available in a variety of sizes, as with normal lead files, for unusual contours. Special holders are also available, although the blade can be used without a holder.

Plastic fillers set up hard because of chemical interaction, thus they do not "dry" in the normal sense of the word. However, they are affected by high temperatures, so they will harden faster on a very hot day. To speed this hardening, lamps used for paint drying can be directed on the mixture. At any rate, it is best to begin working the material while it is still "soft." This can be determined by touching the surface lightly with the grater. When it is just right to work, the plastic will peel through the grater openings in long strings.

Work the area with the grater and a very light touch, shaping carefully until the filler is almost down to the desired height. Let the plastic harden for a while longer, then finish it off with a long, flat block and #180 grit sandpaper. Coarser paper will tend to leave scratches. The long sandpaper "file" will smooth the filled spot into the surrounding area just as the lead file does. Finally, finish the area for painting with a rubber sanding block and #220 grit sandpaper.

If the plastic is allowed to become too hard, it must be worked out just as lead with a regular metal file and/or a disc sander. The beginner will find the file as necessary here as with lead, since the filler can be cut down too low. If you use a sander, you will need a respirator or some kind of nose protection to protect your lungs against the plastic dust.

Plastic fillers should not be used as a substitute for poor body repair, no matter

 361

Number 220 sandpaper is used to sand rough file marks smooth on metal. The edges of the paint are feathered smooth so there will not be a ridge showing when area is spot painted.

This fender is now ready for painting. In a body shop, the repair would cost about $55.

how easy they are to apply. Using too much plastic filler is just asking for trouble.

Plastic should never be used where the body is liable to flex or where strength is required, just as lead should never be used to bridge a gap that should have been welded. Nor is plastic acceptable as an edge. If an area must be filled out to an exposed edge or lip, lead should be used at the edge, then the plastic added. The lead won't be as strong as sheet metal, but it won't chip like plastic.

In areas where there are extreme temperature fluctuations during short periods of time, plastic fillers have been known to give problems. If this is the case, local body men will have found which plastics should be utilized.

Apply a primer-surfacer that is recommended for plastic, as some paint compounds have a bad effect on fillers. The auto-parts store specializing in paints will know what compounds will work. Should problems occur after the paint

is applied, it will be because of poor filler application (surface not clean, etc.) or because the paint is reacting to the filler.

Fiberglass

Fiberglass has been called the wonder product of our age, and rightly so. A few ounces of resin and several yards of matte will make practically any type of shape possible, for nearly any purpose. There are fiberglass cars, fiberglass boats, even fiberglass houses, and the future possibilities appear limitless. Advances in this amazing construction medium have piled one upon the other during the past two decades.

Fiberglass can easily be likened to concrete, a material well suited to molding but not exceptionally strong in itself. However, with the addition of steel reinforcements, concrete becomes the basis for fantastic architectural schemes. So with fiberglass.

By itself, resin is easily formed but has little strength. This is the job of

362

glass-fiber reinforcements, which are available as interwoven blankets or as matted blankets (the latter formed by pressing individual filaments together with a weak binder). There is no use working with fiberglass unless you understand what it is.

Synthetic resins come in a number of forms, including phenolics, acrylics, epoxies, ureas, and polyesters. The auto industry has chosen polyesters because they are easy to use and control and are inexpensive as well.

Resins of polyester are a heavy liquid, weighing about 9 pounds per gallon and ranging in viscosity between water-thin and molasses-thick (between 75 and 70,000 centi poises). Mechanics use a cps of about 700, since this is the easiest to work with and easily saturates both fiberglass matte and cloth.

It is the property of curing itself, or hardening, that makes resin so desirable as a binder with fiberglass filaments as

Fiberglass filler can be mixed on anything, but a piece of glass works best of all. Application can be with a putty knife or rubber applicator sold at parts supply store. If the cavity to be filled is deep, it is best to make several thin layers, letting each harden before next is applied.

Before the filler has set extremely hard it is rather easy to shape with a "cheese grater" file. As the filler hardens, test it with file, and when filler files easy, it is just right. But grater is for rough shaping only.

If the filler sets up hard before it can be shaped with a cheese grater, the easiest way to work it then is with a disc sander. A block sander with some number 80-grit sandpaper can be used, but it will be slow.

Note how the filler on this door blends into the metal. If the filler edge peels up slightly, the filler should be dug out, the metal cleaned again, and the area refilled. If the job isn't right at this point, it never will be.

This car was sideswiped; the area has now been filled with plastic and is ready for priming. Simple jobs like this can be done by anyone with a very few hand tools.

If a very large area has been filled with plastic, it is advisable to use a big, flat sanding tool to get the surface even.

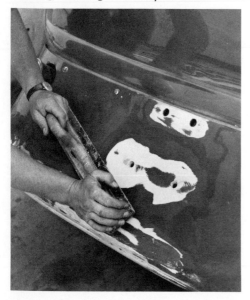

the core strength material. For resin to harden, it must have a catalyst added and then must be heated to 200° F. for approximately two hours. However, if the heat is not added, the combination of resin and catalyst can last for several days before the catalyst begins to cause internal heat and subsequent hardening. This chemical heat, called exothermic heat, will turn the liquid into a solid—a characteristic that hobbyists use in plastic crafts.

Exothermic heat cures the resin just as the external heat will, but at a much slower rate—far too slow for the auto repairman. Since a big heating oven is not available, and long natural curing time is unsatisfactory, an accelerator is added. This accelerator serves to "kick" the catalyst in a much shorter time, causing the exothermic heat to intensify.

Thus the mechanic can vary the time it takes resin to "kick" simply by the catalyst/accelerator combination he uses. However, the resin will harden much faster in a large mass (due to the exothermic heat involved) than when spread thin. That's why resin must be mixed in relatively small batches to avoid unnecessary waste.

Two types of fiberglass are used in body manufacture and repair: woven cloth and matte. Woven cloth is practically the same as any other woven material, but the texture of the weave, which means the amount of glass contained in a particular square inch of cloth, has a direct bearing on the cloth strength.

Matte is designed to give thickness to a laminate, and consequent strength, at a reasonable price. It is not as strong as cloth, but is ideal for use as a thickness agent in conjunction with resin and cloth, reducing the cost over several layers of cloth. The glass fibers are laid so they run in one direction. A sheet is then laid against another with fibers running 90 degrees opposite; thus a kind of laminate plywood effect is obtained, ensuring very good strength.

Check with any body shop and chances are you'll find only one or two metal men thoroughly familiar with fiberglass repairs. It is a profitable repair business, but because of the products involved, it is not integrated into the overall metal-repair trade as it should be. Part of this problem stems from the fact that fiberglass can irritate the skin. This irritation can be circumvented by using a protective cream on the hands, or rubber gloves. Wear long-sleeved shirts, button the collar, and use a respirator if necessary. Fiberglass dust kicked up by a disc grinder may irritate the nostrils.

Resin mixtures should be used in well-ventilated areas, since they give off toxic fumes. These resins will tend to accumulate on tools, shoes, clothing, practically everything—so the resin should be cleaned while it is still soft. Lacquer thinner is an excellent cleaning agent.

Repairing Fiberglass Body Parts

Repair of fiberglass parts will follow the same general scheme (even a metal panel that is heavily rusted may be repaired much the same way). To repair large or small holes, first remove the damaged material and bevel the edges to about 20 degrees. Grind off the paint and gel coat to reach the raw fiberglass. This should be done on both sides for maximum bond strength.

Special fiberglass repair kits are available for this type of work, and may be used on either steel or fiberglass. In the case of steel, however, an epoxy resin must be used rather than polyester, as polyester will not adhere well to metal. The epoxy kit can be used for both metal and glass.

This is interior view of front end of older Corvette with a cracked front end. Section of fiberglass cloth is being applied to gain necessary strength over cracked area. Most fiberglass repair kits include excellent instructions.

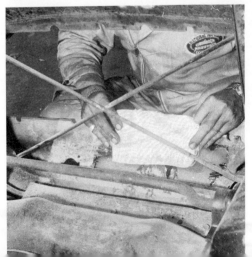

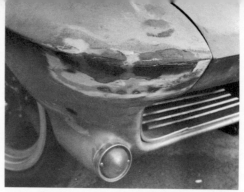

After fiberglass matte and/or cloth are added to break, exterior can be filled with ordinary plastic filler and sanded smooth.

After fiberglass cloth and/or matte are applied, resin is brushed on to bond fiberglass to original surface. This same technique can be used on front or backside of sheet metal for repairing holes/rusted areas.

Cut two pieces of matte so they will extend past the hole edges about 2 inches. Mix the resin and catalyst (hardener) per the container directions, then spread the resin through the fiberglass. You can make yourself a handy non-stick work area with a polyethylene sheet (suit bags from the cleaner's work well). Coat both inner and outer surfaces of the hole with resin mixture; then when this mix is tacky, apply the saturated matte to both the inner and outer surfaces. Press the two patches together, working out any air bubbles, which should leave a saucerlike depression where the hole was.

Allow the repair to cure. Since this is a chemical action, as soon as the surface is hard, it is hard clear through. The curing can be speeded up by raising the temperature, easy enough to do by placing heat lamps about 18 inches from the work. After the spot is cured, grind the surface smooth and fill the remaining low spot(s) with plastic filler from the kit. If additional coats of resin are necessary, sand lightly between coats.

Repairing Metal with Fiberglass

Repairing sheet metal with glass kits is slightly different but easy. First, clean the metal to bare surface with a #16 or #24 grind disc, to at least 6 inches beyond the area being repaired. Indent the area to be repaired, making a sunken lip about two inches wide beyond the damaged area. Cut a piece of matte the same size as the surface being repaired; then a piece of cloth the same size. Several pieces of matte may be needed to fill the indentation. Brush the resin mixture on the clean metal surface and saturate the matte and cloth, allowing all components to become tacky.

Apply the matte and cloth patches, pressing the laminations down tightly with a polyethylene bag to produce a tight bond (the cloth is to the outside). After the material has cured, sand and file the surface and fill with plastic filler if necessary.

ALIGNING BODY PARTS

There are two kinds of alignment involved in automotive body work: alignment of the basic substructure and alignment of the various panels, both stationary and opening. When some kind of repair is undertaken, if the reinforcement structure is not exactly perfect, the external panels cannot hope to align. Fortunately, alignment of the substructure can be accomplished by the beginner with a minimum of tools. The secret is measurement.

It is possible for a panel to be completely out of alignment without a visible sign of damage. The quickest way to tell, of course, is to look for hidden damage. A slight unnatural kink somewhere in the frame may lead to an entire front or rear body section being out of alignment. The best way to check for this misalignment is with a measuring tape. If a car has had a severe impact, misalignment can be expected. Always check and recheck with the tape measure. If the frame is out of alignment, it should be trusted to someone with all the necessary corrective equipment. However, merely straightening the frame will not straighten the body.

Following work on a major collision, it is necessary to check openings with tape measure to get correct alignment. Measure diagonally.

Measuring for Misalignment

It doesn't matter whether the car has a unit-body construction or a separate frame; body measurements are taken in the same places. Usually, any deviation from standard in these measurements will show that the substructure needs repair, and the measurements are really just comparisons, since an automobile is basically symmetrical. These comparisons are usually of the diagonal type, normally called X-checks, and will include the four general body sections. These are the front section, from the front door forward; the center section, which includes the small area from the front door to the rear door; the rear section, from the rear door to the trunk; and the trunk, or deck section.

The front section is usually checked first at the immediate forward part of the passenger compartment—that is, from the door-hinge posts to the windshield pillars. All measurements must be made from the same point on both sides, which will give results within extremely close tolerances. The farther apart the points being measured, the more accurate the check.

The measurement from the bottom edge of the left door opening to the top edge of the right opening should be the same as that from bottom right to top left. If there is a slight variation, measure again, and perhaps a third or fourth time. If there is a significant difference in the two measurements, it means the top of the body has been slanted to one side, typical of a rollover accident.

It is obvious that this same kind of diagonal measurement can be used for checking all aspects of the car, from frame to body substructure to individual panel openings. Once a starting point has been established, and all other sections have been checked for alignment, then each section also can be checked against the other.

This type of checking is just a variation of the individual section checking, in that a specific point is selected on opposite sides. This might be the top of the windshield pillar, as when checking the front section, or the lower rear corner of a rear door opening. This measurement should be the same as opposite measurements, and will normally be in alignment if the individual sections are all right, When measurements are taken between sections, it is wise to double-check your work by taking measurements for several different points of reference.

It is not uncommon for the individual sections to be well out of alignment. For instance, a quartering accident to a front fender might include serious damage to the door post. Obviously, this post must be returned to its original position before the door, front fender, inner panels, etc. can be replaced. This reinforcing substructure can often be either pulled or pushed back into shape, but if it's badly damaged, it will probably need at least partial replacement.

As a rule, a front or rear collision does not produce great problems in substructure realignment, but a rollover or a side collision does. When a vehicle rolls it is common for the entire top substructure to collapse toward the side away from the direction of roll. If the roll is not severe, the reinforcing structure can be pushed back into place. In this case, the substructure can be realigned and a new top panel installed. However, if the substructure is severely bent, a new top including reinforcement is usually installed. This is the common

method of repair on modern cars, since it is fairly easy to cut the original top off at the windshield pillars and across the rear panel and weld on a replacement purchased at a local wrecking yard. From a cost standpoint, this procedure is perhaps the most economical. However, when such a new top is installed, diagonal alignment measurements are imperative.

Rear-end damage is more likely to crumple a substructure than a front collision, but here again, the entire reinforcement area can be pieced in from another vehicle as long as the measurements are accurate.

Aligning Front and Rear Openings

Alignment of the vehicle extremities, the front and rear ends, is usually a matter of making the hood and deck lid fit. But before these panels can even be tried for a fitting, the openings must be made as nearly symmetrical as possible. Fortunately, there are built-in guides that make the job easier, especially at the front end.

The deck area is the harder of the two to align, since the quarter panels are welded to mating panels and X-checking is necessary to get good results. When there is major rear-end damage, it is necessary to work from a straight frame. This is essential. Once the frame is straight, it is possible to push or pull the crumpled metal back into place until the trunk flooring again aligns with the frame.

Working from frame/flooring reference points, the inner body structures are straightened until the deck-lid opening checks out perfectly by the X-reference. If the deck lid has not been damaged, it should then fit the opening. If the lid must be straightened, it must be repaired to fit the opening. Finally, if the panels surrounding the opening are straightened, a considerable amount of measuring will be required when getting the damaged rear end back into shape.

The front end is not nearly so difficult, since the entire front-end assembly is bolted on. The fenders are attached with several bolts into the cowl structure, and the radiator-core support bolts to the frame. If these bolts are removed, all the sheet metal ahead of the cowl, with the exception of the hood, can be lifted off. Cars with unit construction do not disassemble in this manner, since the front fenders and inner fender panels form part of the frame/body unit. However, some cars use unit construction for the main body with a subframe bolting to the firewall. This is common on recent Chrysler Corp. products, with the front sheet metal being removable.

As the front sheet metal is not very rigid, a quartering front collision will tend to collapse the assembly, leaving the opposite fender virtually undamaged. Impact force is transferred to a much greater degree by unit-construction bodies, but still the tendency is for damage to be relatively local.

Because front-end pieces are so easy to remove and replace, replacement with used parts may be the most economical course. In any case, when a front end is being worked on, it must be returned to perfect alignment or the hood will never fit properly.

The front fenders, inner panels, and grille assembly all bolt in place (except in unit construction, in which the fenders and grille only are removable), thus alignment is primarily a matter of making the bolt holes line up. While it is possible to have the entire section out of alignment and still have all the bolt holes align, this would be rare. The holes serve as reference points only, however; final alignment is determined by the X-check method.

Quite often a front-end collision will cause little visible damage, but the entire panel will be driven out of alignment by the force of impact. A good example would be a fender hit almost head-on near the headlight. The fender may apparently sustain little damage, but the impact can drive the entire fender rearward. The obvious checks would include the area around the door to see if the original clearance has been impaired.

You can make very slight changes in hood-opening size, because the grillework and inner-panel bolt holes are elongated, but this should not be considered a substitute for proper repair. As a rule, if the core-support panels and the grille assembly do not fit well, realignment is in order. As with most other parts of the body, the flooring or frame provides the basis for most X-checking measurements in the front sheet-metal section.

Aligning the Hood and Fenders

Any damage to a hood that is repairable will require constant checking, both against itself and against the fender/grille opening. The hood can be checked for correct dimensions with the same X-check procedure of diagonal measurements, but twist or contour damage can only be checked relative to the fenders. At the same time, a new or replacement hood may need minor "tweaking" to fit either a repaired or undamaged front end.

Hoods are normally held in place by spring-loaded hinges at the rear and a spring-loaded latch at the front. The hinges hold the hood open, but can also be designed to pull the rear of the hood downward when the hood is closed. In this way the hood is always "loaded" while in a closed position. Small rubber or lubricant-impregnated fabric buttons along the fenders, cowl, and grille form vibration dampeners between the hood and the surrounding panels. Most automobile body-opening panels (doors, hood, deck lid) flow into the surrounding panels in a smooth contour. For this reason, the slightest bit of misalignment in any of these panels will stand out. In virtually all cases, the opening panels must be flush with the surrounding panels. There is a considerable amount of built-in adjustment in the hinges to make a hood fit, but only one or two are generally involved during the adjustment process.

Finding that the hood doesn't fit is no difficult chore. Making it fit is where it gets to be difficult. If the problem lies in the hood opening, it will usually be necessary to shift the fenders and/or the front-end sheet metal/grille to get the right opening.

If a particular fender is too high, too low, too far aft, or too far forward, all the attaching bolts should be loosened and the fender shifted by use of a long lever (a 2 × 4 makes an excellent bar). In the case of fore/aft movement, a hydraulic jack will do the trick.

The inner panels between the fenders and adjacent to the radiator-core support are called the front-end sheet metal. If the hood opening is too narrow at the front of the hood, loosen the front-end sheet metal bolts at the fender, jack the fenders apart, and add shims between the radiator-core support and the

fenders until the correct fit is obtained. The hood strainer may bolt to the grille, the front-end sheet metal, or both, and then can be shimmed to fit correctly.

Hood hinges can be a bag of snakes to the beginner, but they are a delight to the professional, since they allow the hood to be adjusted fore and aft, either corner in or out, and up or down. When a hood has been removed from the hinges, the lock washers usually leave a visible mark on the hinge. Better yet is to scribe around the hinge and the attaching bolts before the hood is removed.

To shift the hood to the front or back, slightly loosen the bolts. The bolts should be left barely tight, because otherwise the hood can shift on loose hinges as it is raised in order to get at the bolts for tightening. If the hood is adjusted to the rear, make sure the

Hood hinge is where all adjustments are made to get hood to fit opening tightly. Sometimes moving rear of hinge upward will make hood go downward. Always make a scribe mark to give yourself an idea where starting point was. A little bit of movement is all that's needed.

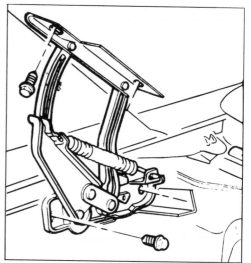

safety latch will still catch when the primary latch is released.

It is possible to raise or lower the hood corners (assuming all other points of alignment are OK) by bending the hood hinge plate on the cowl. Bend toward the cowl to raise a corner (move it away from the fender/cowl), or bend away from the cowl to bring the corner nearer the fender. On later-model cars, there are various hinge adjustments. On Fisher bodies, for instance, the hood rear height is adjusted by special washers between the hinge and hood. Here are some more hints for Fisher body hoods:

If the hood flutters, there is not enough tension, so add special washers between the hood and the hinges at the front hinge bolts. As with many modern cars, hood height at the front is determined by adjustable rubber bumpers, but the latch must be adjusted.

Most cars have similar adjustments at the hinges for both fore-and-aft and up-and-down alignment. In addition, the latching mechanism can be moved both fore and aft and sideways to compensate for alignment shifting. It is easiest to adjust this latching mechanism by loosening the bolts slightly (the latch may be on the hood or on the strainer), then closing the hood securely. Carefully open the hood and tighten the bolts. If the mechanism has been bent during a collision, realignment is a matter of minor metal shaping, then following the above indicated course.

Most modern hoods (on cars produced during the last two decades) must rest securely on the rubber bumpers provided. The bumpers help to keep the unit in tension, remove flutter, and dampen vibration. In some cases these rubber bumpers are adjustable and should be adjusted up snug to the hood.

If the bumpers are not adjustable, the hood should rest on them perfectly (also see Chapter 15).

Aligning the Deck Lid

Like doors and hoods, deck lids should fit closely and securely. However, achieving and maintaining deck-lid alignment can be difficult because there are only three points of minor adjustment—the two hinges and the latch. Yet the deck lid must fit as tightly against the sealing rubber as possible in order to keep out water and dust.

The deck lid is aligned when it fits the body all the way around, and not until. Usually the lid is in alignment if the gap between the lid and body/fender panels is the same all the way around, but this doesn't mean the lid is sealing. First chalk the body-flange edge (or the lid, whichever is the case) that comes into contact with the rubber weather strip. When the deck lid is closed this chalk will be transferred to the weather strip at all the points of

Measure diagonally across deck lid opening when repairing rear of car to see when the opening is true.

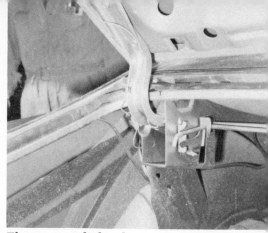

If sides of deck lid need to fit tighter, block of wood is positioned in center, sides pressed down lightly. Work slowly at this point, checking until fit is attained.

There is very little adjustment room at the deck lid hinge.

If one side of deck lid is high, wood block is placed on low side, high side bent downward.

If lid has a sway, block is set midway down the side.

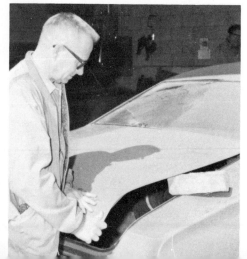

contact. Where the chalk line doesn't show, the lid is not sealing. Check for nonsealing several times before making any corrective action, and make sure the sealing rubber is in good condition and in the correct place. If the lid is not sealing along most of the bottom edge, it can be drawn tighter with the latch, or by loosening the hinge bolts and sliding it forward or lowering it slightly.

As previously mentioned, it is imperative that the deck lid opening be in perfect alignment or the lid cannot be expected to fit. This does not hold true if the lid alone is damaged, but usually rear-end damage includes both lid and quarter panel/fender. If the deck lid is severely damaged, replace it with a used unit and align the opening to fit the replacement lid.

If the deck lid seems to be twisted on the hinges—that is, one side seals but the other does not—the lid can probably be twisted by hand to fit. Open the lid and place something like a rubber mallet between the body and the lid on the side that is sealing correctly. Push downward on the opposite side, but do not use excessive force. After a few test "heaves," check the lid for a fit, then repeat if necessary. This is for a minor misalignment only.

Matching the deck lid to surrounding panel contour is the big problem if collision damage has occurred. These places of contour misalignment will be around the lid perimeter, and unless the deck lid has been worked, chances are the opening is out of alignment. If the deck lid opens and closes correctly, but the contour between the lid and top panel is off, the panel must be raised or lowered to fit. This panel will usually be too low, and can be jacked up with light pressure from a hydraulic jack, placed between the hinges.

Along the quarter panels/fenders, chances are the body flange will be too high. If so, tap with a mallet on or very near the flange to bring it into alignment. If this area is too low, use the hydraulic jack. Making the lower edge of the lid fit is a matter of either hammering the lower body panel out or bending the lid. If the lid is not sealing tightly at the latch, adjust the latch. If the center part still does not seal, place a piece of 2×4 (or two rubber mallets) at either side and push forward along the lid center. If one corner is high, place the mallet under the opposite corner and push down on the offending corner. If both corners are high, place the mallet under the middle and apply equal pressure to both corners.

Making a deck lid fit, especially the modern lids with such large expanses of low-crown metal, is a matter of patience and working with just small areas at a time. The key is to keep watching the crack between the lid perimeter and the surrounding panels, keeping it as equal as possible.

Aligning Doors

Perhaps the most perplexing panels to keep in alignment are the doors, since they can become misaligned through use and age as well as from damage. Even if the beginner is not an accomplished metal man, he can adjust the various openings and panels, which will be especially helpful when working on door alignment.

A door is out of alignment when the contours do not match the surrounding panels and when the door itself is not exactly centered in the door opening. Remember, contours and centering closely control how the door seals, which is particularly critical on late-model cars.

If there has been extensive damage to a door or door area, chances are the opening itself will have sustained some damage, and must therefore be carefully X-checked. At the same time, distortion of the door opening can be caused by frame misalignment, body twist, and other seemingly unrelated factors. If damage is involved, the opening must be X-checked to make sure it is ready for door alignment.

A damaged door can be out of shape in many different ways, enough to cause frustration and hours of seemingly pointless labor in trying to get true alignment. Obviously, the door must be returned to the correct shape or it isn't likely to align with the opening.

The surface contour of the door in all directions must match that of the surrounding panels. The opening gap around the door perimeter should be uniform. Sometimes there may be a slightly larger gap on one side, but this should also be uniform throughout its length. An unequal gap is unusual, however, since factories have specialists who do nothing except align doors in the openings.

While making the visual alignment check, look at the scuff plate to see if the door is dragging (sagging). Open and close the door slowly and note whether the door raises or lowers as it latches. If there is an up or down movement, the door is out of alignment and is being centered by the dovetail.

There are two specific controls that keep a door in position when closed: the striker plate and the dovetail. The striker plate is the latch, and the dovetail limits up-and-down movement of the closed door. The dovetail function may be assumed by an integral assembly of the latch mechanism, but sometimes must be included to keep the door from jiggling up and down on the hinges.

Striker plates can be adjusted over a relatively wide range, but before any adjustments are made the striker should be replaced if worn. A little wear is no problem, but excessive wear, which is visually apparent, or sloppiness in parts (such as rotary latch) means replacement. If the door won't close or fits too loosely, the striker needs adjustment. The striker can usually be moved at an angle (cocked), which should be avoided.

Types of strikers will vary from year to year within a given model car, but generally speaking the same design principles hold within a certain line. For instance, all General Motors Fisher-body strikers are similar, but different from Ford or Chrysler strikers.

If a Fisher-body striker is to be removed, mark the original location with a pencil. When the striker is replaced, make sure caulking compound is applied around the striker-plate bolts and around

Door can also be adjusted with a block of wood; sometimes a slight hump can be taken out with hammer and block as shown.

the outer edge of the striker back face. This is to eliminate squeaking. It also tends to keep the striker plate from sliding out of adjustment.

Now try the door and see if it closes properly. If spacers are required to shim the striker so the lock extension will engage the striker notch, first add some caulking compound to the striker where the lock extension engages. Close the door to make an impression in the compound, then measure this compound thickness. If the distance from the striker teeth to the rear edge of the clay depression is less than $1\frac{1}{32}$ inch, spacers and different-length attaching screws will be needed.

Ford strikers are adjusted differently. The striker pin may be moved laterally and vertically, as well as fore and aft. As with all cars, the striker is not an adjustment to cure door sag. With the Fisher-type striker, there is a measurable tolerance between striker and lock that should be checked. To get this, coat the striker stub with some dark grease, then shut the door. The lock clips should close over the striker stub with a tolerance between stub cheek and clip of between $\frac{2}{32}$ inch minimum and $\frac{5}{32}$ inch maximum.

On Chrysler products, the striker-plate top surface should be parallel with the door-latch bottom. The striker plate is in position when there is a very slight lift to the door as it is closed (which will prevent door noise). The latch can be adjusted with shims between it and the pillar—shims of $\frac{1}{32}$ and $\frac{1}{16}$ inch thickness that bring the latch closer to the door. To check for the door seal, move a piece of paper at 6- to 8-inch intervals around the door opening as the door is closed. If the paper can be removed with no drag, the door is not sealing and the striker should be moved inward. If the striker adjustment will not ensure sealing, the hinges must be adjusted.

The dovetail is not to correct door sag either, but it will allow slight movement of the door up or down for adjustment. The dovetail on older cars will probably be very worn and should be replaced (also see Chapter 15).

There is considerable adjustment possible at the hinges, but no hinge work should be attempted without making sure this is where the problem lies. This is especially important on older cars, which do not have hinge adjustment in the fore/aft plane. Such hinges have to be spread or closed. If there is a sag, the usual remedy is to spread the lower hinge slightly, which moves the door bottom closer to the pillar. Sometimes the upper hinge must also be closed to correct sag.

A hinge can be spread by placing some kind of interference between the leaves. There are fiber blocks available that can be stuck to the leaves, but most body men rely on the trusty hammer or screwdriver handle. First the handle is placed between the opened hinge leaves, then the door is pushed toward the closed position. When the handle is tight in the hinge, the door is forced toward the car (sometimes it will close if the interference is slight). Make all forceful spreading adjustments in small increments to keep from spreading the hinge too far. After each adjustment, check the door for proper fit. Proceed slowly!

If the top hinge must be closed, the hinge has to be removed. If the door has been damaged and the hinge bent, the distortion will be apparent. Repair is a matter of squeezing the hinge leaves together in a large vise.

If the car has adjustable hinges, as most modern cars do, close alignment is possible with very little labor. Remove the striker and dovetail assembly so they do not interfere with how the door actually hangs in the opening. The major difference between different makes of cars is whether the hinge adjustment is made at the door or the pillar, but in all cases, the door can be adjusted up or down, in or out, or fore and aft.

There is a big difference among the Big Three in how hinges are made, but they all perform the same service. And in all cases, adjustment is a matter of slightly loosening the bolts. This will allow the door to be forced into a new position. If the bolts are too loose the door will slide all over the place, making it difficult to control.

If proper door alignment cannot be achieved by adjusting the hinges or the striker-plate assembly, the trouble lies either in the door body opening or the

 375

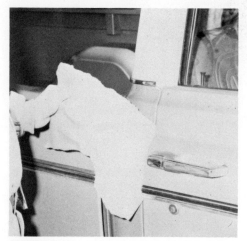

To check fit of doors and deck lid against rubber wind lacing, place piece of paper in opening. If paper can be slid out easily, lid or door aren't fitting tight enough to keep out wind, water.

door contour. If the door contour is not correct, it could require special tools in severe cases, or nothing more than a knee and two hands in others. If the door is not contoured enough (bowed), the top and bottom must be bent inward while the middle is kept stationary. On older cars with a strong framework around the windows, this can only be accomplished with what is known as a single or double door-bar tool. Most shops have these tools. On late-model cars, the window framework (if there is any) is very light and can be bent by placing a knee against the door center and pulling or pushing. As in hinge spreading, use force gently.

Body and fender repairs, as well as any degree of painting, are more a matter of thoughtful planning than of any special degree of skill. The home mechanic may not be able to accomplish major body repairs, but if he does nothing more than take care of the day-to-day dings a car is likely to receive, he will have saved hundreds of dollars over the lifetime of his vehicle.

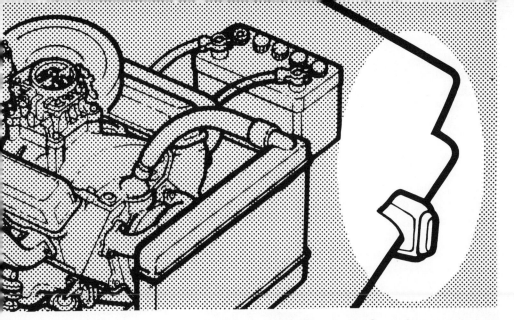

14 paint and chrome

NOTHING SO ESTABLISHES the value of an automobile as exterior appearance. While this may not provide an accurate evaluation of vehicle condition, it is nevertheless the vital first impression. Generally speaking, however, a car with first-rate paint and chrome will have been maintained well and will thus be in good mechanical shape too. So this is one area in which home repair shows immediate results for minimal expense and labor.

The best single bit of advice for care of any car exterior is never to let the paint or chrome deteriorate in the first place. Modern paints are far superior to the older enamels and lacquers, especially in their resistence to breakdown from exposure to chemicals and sunlight. A great deal of experimentation by the auto companies has produced a metal covering that is long-lasting, yet resilient and inexpensive to apply. The acrylics that are used on practically all new cars are especially easy to apply at home, with minor touch-up fast and simple. There is some current experimentation with new urethane paints, and should these become feasible on a production basis, automobile paint will then become almost a plastic coating impervious to everything but severe fracture.

Let's start with the care of paint and chrome trim first, and then get into repairs of both you can do at home.

MAINTAINING PAINT

Wax is the best friend a car ever had. Although you can't see it, paint is a very porous medium that does not entirely seal off the exterior. If you were to look at paint, or even chrome, under a magnifying glass, you'd see millions of tiny craters in the finish, and each of these cavities will capture and hold debris and chemicals that will eventually destroy the finish. (Urethane paints do not have these openings.)

If the paint luster is good (no fading), clean the car thoroughly with soap and water, then rinse several times with water. Be sure no soap is left on the finish. Use a chamois or lint-free towel to dry the finish, then move the car to a shaded, but warm, area for waxing.

If the paint does not seem to be in good condition, chances are that the outermost layer has oxidized to some degree. Cars more than ten years old may have a severe oxidation problem (Volkswagens, and some other imports, are especially prone to this form of paint breakdown). Never apply wax directly over an oxidized paint, and although some waxes are advertised as being dual-purpose (that is, they are both a wax and a polish), such a product will not do the quality job you're looking for. Road tar should be removed before the paint is polished. Most auto-parts stores sell tar remover, or you can use kerosene. Whatever you use, wipe the area dry.

Polishing

Polish is not the same thing as wax! A polish is nothing more than a mild rubbing compound and does the same job on automobile finishes as a gritty cleanser does in a dirty kitchen sink. The polish is a fine abrasive in solution, and the purpose is to clean the paint in preparation for waxing. It is not an end in itself, and if you do not put a protective coating on a just-polished paint surface, it will oxidize again almost immediately. Most polishes will work on any paint, either lacquer or enamel. Just remember to apply the polish when the car is parked in the shade, and if the day is very hot, polish only a panel at a time.

Some polishes are allowed to dry before the surface is wiped clean, others may be removed while still wet. In either case, if the panel looks streaked after the polish job, do the panel again. The following wax will not remove the streaks; it is only to provide a smooth, protective coating for the finish. You may polish a car with an electric buffer if you desire. A small sheepskin buffing head is available at auto-parts stores for an electric drill, and this combination will make short work of polishing. But there are some pointers you should not overlook.

Any kind of buffing of a painted finish will rely on a cutting compound, thus the buffing is roughly the same as sanding the finish with a very fine sandpaper. When a new paint job is applied to a car, the professional will often "rub the finish out," using a special lacquer or enamel rubbing compound. Since commercial polish is just a thinner version of this same compound, you can rub through the paint by pushing on the electric buffer too hard, or staying in one place too long. The secret of doing a good job with the electric buffer is to thin the polish ever so slightly with water, then run the buffing head over the panel lightly with only slight pressure. Keep the buffer moving. If you've done a good job, a kind of swirl pattern will be left on the panel. This is buffing-compound residue and wipes clean with a rag.

Whether you're doing the polishing by hand or with a buffer, you'll note that the rag or buffing head turns the same color as the paint. You're actually removing a thin film of paint. Make sure your rag or buffing head is free from any grit that might scratch the paint deeply (clean the buffing head by running a screwdriver across the surface lightly while the head is spinning. This fluffs up the wool again).

After you have polished the car, you can wipe it clean and apply the wax, or you can do a super job and rinse the car again. This will get all the compound off and clean the porous paint surface again.

Touching Up

If there are nicks in the paint, such as those made by small rocks striking the leading edges of fender and hood, now is the time to make a touch-up. You can buy touch-up paint in stock factory colors at most new-car dealerships and auto-parts stores. If a small brush is not included with the paint, use the frayed stem of a paper match as an applicator. Daub the chipped area with unthinned paint. It will look slightly brighter than the surrounding surface until it dries, and it will probably have a slightly rounded appearance at first. Once the touch-up dries, however, it will be very hard to detect. Such paint is usually fast-drying, but it is best not to apply wax for at least four hours, and a full day would be better.

Waxing

As mentioned, wax is nothing more than a protective coating. It will not restore luster to paint, it will not hide scratches, and it will not last forever. The finest waxes are those that contain a great amount of carnuba. These are usually the more expensive brands, and invariably they are more difficult to apply. But they will do a far better job, and they will last longer than less expensive waxes. There has been a great deal of research done in waxes the past decade, especially in the area of application, so that a modern wax is nowhere near as difficult to apply as a good wax of ten years ago.

Follow the container directions explicitly. Apply the wax to a warm (not hot) surface, in the shade, and rub it to a luster with a lint-free towel. You aren't likely to get too much wax on the surface, so if you want to do the wax job twice for extra protection, go ahead. Let the wax set up on the surface before you move the car into hot sunlight. From then on, it is just a matter of keeping the surface washed with clear water and dried with a chamois. How long the wax stays on the surface will depend on whether the car is garaged or left outdoors, the weather conditions, how often you must rinse the surface, and so on. In smoggy Los Angeles, where smog drop-out is murder on paint, I expect a good wax job to last from one to two months. Of course, the subsequent waxings are easier because I don't have to polish the paint and do all the hard preparation again. Custom-car and antique finishes need a good waxing only about twice a year, because I keep these cars garaged.

Incidentally, if you have a convertible with a plastic rear window, the wax will fill all the small scratches that such windows inevitably acquire, and you can see through the plastic almost as though it were new.

While you're waxing, don't forget the door jambs, trunk interior, and all the metal pieces inside the car. And finally, lay an extra good coat on all bright trim.

MAINTAINING CHROME

While some cars use stainless-steel and aluminum brightwork for trim, chrome plating is still the predominant type of trim on American cars. It requires special care. The word "chrome" is something of an incorrect label, since the real plating is primarily nickel, and the quality of a chrome-plating job is in direct proportion to the amount of nickel used in the process. You may have noticed some car bumpers seem to be especially prone to a light form of rusting. These bumpers invariably are replacements that have been put on the car following a wreck, and the cause is poor nickel plating by a bumper exchange trying to save on the expensive base plating material.

Chrome plating begins with the initial polishing job. If the piece of metal has been polished well, no scratches will show up in the finished product. The metal is chemically cleaned, then it is given a good coat of copper, followed by the nickel plating. The chrome plating is a very thin coating that is really just a surface coating for the nickel. The chrome is very, very thin, and will scratch. This is where home maintenance comes in.

When the outer protective coating of chrome is scratched, the plated surface will be attacked rapidly by rust. It is good practice to periodically inspect all chrome-plated parts on the car. When a scratch is discovered, any rust should be removed with a chemical. The metal conditioner used on bare metal prior to painting is good. It is available from any store that sells automotive paint. Through the years there have been several "chrome-plating" products sold, but none of these are good. The only way to get real chrome plating is by going through the entire plating process. Once the scratched area is free of rust, cover the scratch with some form of clear paint, such as clear fingernail polish.

This will hold for quite a long time, and will make the scratch quite unnoticeable. Most important, the paint seals the scratch so moisture and rust will not attack.

Never use a coarse paint-rubbing compound on chrome or aluminum trim, as the abrasives in the compound will leave bad scratches on the trim. You can buy a very fine abrasive just for chrome and aluminum. There are some chemical cleaners available, and these all work well. Following the cleaning of chrome and aluminum, apply a good coat of wax. If the car is to be stored for several months, it is wise to coat all trim, inside and out, with a silicone spray. This is a very effective deterrent to rust, though it is not as good as wax when the car is in daily use.

REPAIRING CHROME

Repairing damaged chrome is deceptively easy, and a bit of time taken with a piece of trim will save a great deal of money. Brightwork is usually applied to only two gauges of metal, the very heavy bumper, and the lightweight grille/body trim pieces. It is possible to remove slight dings in a bumper, but the bumper must almost always be removed from the car to do a good job.

Until about ten years ago, bumper material was quite thick. The modern bumper is thinner (an obvious saving in production cost) and will pick up minor dents that older bumpers would not have sustained. But because the material is thinner, it is also necessary to back it up with something firm when removing the dent. A block of wood, covered with a piece of carpet, makes an ideal straightening block. Lay the bumper face down on the block and strike the dent from the bumper backside. A medium-size ball-peen hammer will work. Don't use too many hammer blows, as this will often distort the metal and leave a multitude of small bumps where the dent once was. A leather or plastic mallet is better than a hammer, but a rubber hammer is useless.

A common accident is striking some fixed object with the end of a bumper, causing the end to bend rearward. Before removing the bumper, try straightening it on the car. Turn the front wheels so the bumper edge will just hook a solid object (tree trunks work great) and then use vehicle power to pull the major kink from the bumper. You can't get it all, so the remainder must be removed after the bumper is taken from the car.

Other trim, such as side pieces and grille sections, are highly susceptible to damage, and unless you are careful your repair efforts can make a bad situation worse. When straightening a piece of thin-guage plated metal (or aluminum), you must use a block of wood as backing. Rather than striking the metal directly with a lightweight hammer, form a piece of wood into the shape of the metal being repaired and use this as a striking set. Work very slowly, since the thin metal will distort easily and there is no way to shrink plated metal to the original shape without destroying the plating. It is possible to return badly bent pieces of trim to original shape, if you are willing to be patient and work slowly. If the piece of trim has been torn, careful use of a gas torch and brass will repair the tear without ruining the plating. Nearly any professional welding shop can do this type of work, and the cost is minimal.

APPLYING NEW PAINT

Paint work is where any home mechanic can really learn some tricks. Fortunately, practically any kind of paint repair short of a complete paint job is possible in the home garage, and you don't have to be an experienced painter to do the work. But before you tackle any painting job, you should be familiar with the medium in which you will work.

Types of Paint

Automobile paints are separated into three basic categories: lacquer, enamel, and the acrylics. There are also epoxies and urethanes, but they are still too new to be of much interest to the average car owner, although they are finding great popularity among race-car and custom-car enthusiasts.

Essentially, any paint is a mixture of pigments (for color) and some kind of binder that is used merely to keep the pigments together. The pigments are usually made from inorganic matter and can be mixed with practically any substance. The quality of a paint, therefore, is determined by the type of pigments and binder used. Virtually all automotive paints are of excellent quality, with only a small variation in price between brand names. Thinner, which is essential to automobile painting, is really the paint base and makes the drying possible. Paint viscosity is also effected by thinner, making the paint thin enough to flow through the paint gun, and wet enough to go smoothly on the vehicle surface.

Enamel paint is the most difficult to apply, except for the new epoxies and urethanes, but it requires the least amount of preparation time. Enamel is very tough, resistant to the wear associated with everyday driving, and retains a high degree of resiliency for years. A good enamel paint job is distinguished by the high gloss, almost as though the surface were plastic, or wet. This comes from a varnish used in the mixture by the paint manufacturer. Varnish comes from a solution of resins mixed with alcohol, turpentine, or amyl acetate. Enamel paint requires the use of enamel thinner, which is not as "hot" as lacquer thinner. A number of automobile manufacturers continue to use enamel as a production-line finish for their cars, although acrylic enamel is fast becoming the favorite. Baked-on enamel is not common these days. This is merely a process of heating the just-painted surface with heat lamps to speed up the enamel drying time.

Enamel does not dry as rapidly or as thoroughly as either an acrylic enamel or lacquer. A kind of surface glaze will occur with enamel within several hours after application, but the paint will still be "soft" for several days after it is sprayed. It never does completely dry, one of the reasons it is not as prone to cracking and chipping as lacquer.

Acrylic paint, either lacquer or enamel, is like lacquer in that it dries rapidly. Acrylic is a plastic-base paint (lacquer is cotton-base) and undergoes a chemical change as the paint dries and unites with oxygen in the air. In this respect, acrylic is similar to epoxy and urethane paints. Acrylic is not sprayed the same as lacquer or enamel, and must not be applied in a single, heavy coat (which prevents thorough drying).

Lacquer paint is made from cellulose, resins, and lac. Lac is a sticky substance deposited by insects on trees of southeastern Asia. In this form, lac is brittle. It is made elastic by the addition of plasticizers. Lacquer is often used in custom-car painting, but the traditional cellulose form is fast losing favor to acrylic lacquer, which is much easier to work with.

These, then, are the basic forms of automobile paint. There are variations of these basic paints that have become common words in automobile showrooms—names such as "Metalflake," "candy apple," "metallic," and so on. Such seemingly exotic materials are merely additions to the paint to produce a striking appearance, and have nothing to do with the basic paint itself. For instance, Metalflake is a trade name for microscopic chips of aluminum foil. When these chips are applied in a paint coat, they catch and reflect sunlight at different angles for a sparkling appearance. The so-called candy paints are really translucents, or light toner coats of paint applied over a reflective base of gold, silver, or copper powder. Metallics are basic paints mixed with aluminum powders.

Primers

Never apply a paint color directly to bare, unprepared metal or fiberglass. Paint color should be applied only over a suitable primer/surfacer; enamel may be used over a lacquer or acrylic primer, but lacquer paint should never be used over an enamel primer. Acrylic paints should always be used only over acrylic primer.

The objective of any primer is to form a bond between the bare metal surface and the subsequent paint. At the same time, primer can smooth scratches in the metal. After the primer is applied, it can be sanded until smooth (if the primer is sanded through to bare metal, more primer should be applied) to hide scratches which would otherwise show in the final color paint. Certain metals, such as aluminum, require a special primer; in the case of aluminum a zinc chromate is used.

If a fast repair job is being done, it is best to use an acrylic lacquer primer and color paint. If there is time available, primer can be allowed to dry for two or three days to allow for whatever minute shrinkage might occur, and then the color paint is applied.

Glazing compound, or putty, should never be used as a major filler. If putty is applied in a thick patch, it will invariably fall out after a few months because it shrinks or because it has a different expansion rate than the metal. Putty is to be used like a thick primer, only for small surface imperfections that would normally show up in the finished paint job. When buying a glazing compound, always specify a nonshrinking brand. Apply this putty sparingly, and then block-sand it for a smooth, professional finish.

You may want to follow the instructions below for doing an entire paint job, but more likely you will be concerned with painting only a small area where some metal repair has been done, or perhaps a full panel that has been severely chipped from parking-lot battles. In either case, a good paint job starts with good surface preparation.

Sanding

The real secret of a good paint job is the sanding. Water sanding is the fastest, cleanest, and easiest method. Obviously, it's wise to pick a place that drains well for your sanding location. The residue from sanding actually acts as a mild

Sandpaper for automotive use comes in either dry or wet-dry types. Only use dry paper for very heavy cutting; use the wet-dry combination paper with water for most sanding jobs. 220-grit is good for initial fast cutting, then switch to 320-grit or 400-grit for another good sanding before spraying on final primer/sealer or color paint.

stain, which discolors driveway concrete if left standing.

If possible, use a hose for water supply, with a bare trickle available at all times. If this is impractical, a bucket of water and a sponge will suffice. Thoroughly wet the surface before you start, and if possible, do the sanding in the shade, if for no other reason than comfort. Another hint: Figure on getting wet, for you certainly will before you're through.

Hold the hose in one hand, keeping the end connection from making new scratches, and sand with the other. Direct the flow of water on the work area as needed, which means a fine film of water at all times. You can't get too much water as far as sanding is concerned, but the more water you use, the wetter you become. When you're getting just enough water, the paper will glide without grabbing, but will have enough drag to tell you it's cutting.

If a bucket and sponge are used, you'll have to squeeze the sponge regularly to keep the water flowing, which means you'll use up the water supply rapidly. You can hold some of the moisture longer by adding a cake of Lava soap to the materials, working up a good lather, and spreading it over the sanding area.

The sanding pattern is extremely important, and can have a drastic effect upon the finished job. Always go in one direction as much as possible, preferably lengthwise with the panel (much like the grain in wood), and never, never sand in circles. On many panels, such as the top near the windshield, the lengthwise direction will not get around the windows well, so the direction must be changed to fit the circumference, but

The use of a rubber sanding "block" keeps the paper from rubbing tips of fingers raw, but hand-held paper is needed for getting around tight spots. Always sand in fore/ aft direction; never sand in a circle as the circle lines will show through final paint job.

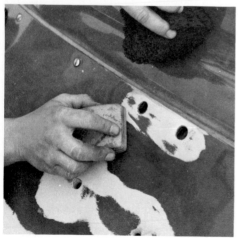

the pattern here will be a straight, criss-cross effect.

The sandpaper may be used either by itself or with a semi-flexible sanding block. The block is very good for large panels, but the hand conforms better to curves. If a sanding block is used, tear strips from the sheet just wide enough for the block. Use #220-, #280- or #320-grit paper for pre-primer sanding. If hand-held, the paper is torn differently. The 9x11-inch sheet is turned on its side, folded together, and torn down the center. Each piece is then triple-folded, leaving one face toward the paint, one toward the hand, and one folded between the two.

When sanding by hand, keep the entire hand in contact with the surface, not just the finger tips or side of the palm. However, for specific areas, these two pressure points may be used.

After the entire area has been sanded, let it dry and check to make sure every inch has been covered. Any missed streaks or corners must be touched up.

With the biggest part of the surface sanded, attention can be directed toward the repaired areas, scratches, and chips. Getting these places featheredged properly is vital. This point cannot be overstressed.

After the initial fast cut, switch to #320-grit sandpaper and the block, plus water, and repeat. The idea is to feather the break between paint and metal over a wide area. There will be at least two layers of paint showing, the color coat and the primer/surfacer. However, on older cars the number can be as high as eight or nine layers. The wider the band of each paint layer showing, the better the featheredging job! A 1-inch band means a much better job than a ¼-inch band. Finally, sand the featheredged

Electric or air powered sanders (called Jitterbugs) are often used by professionals for quick featheredging of paint, but it is necessary to follow with hand-held paper to remove tiny circles left by power sander. It is very difficult to sand entire car with power sander and get decent paint results.

After an area has been sanded, fill small imperfections with body putty. This is not a fiberglass (plastic) filler, however, so don't use it on larger areas. Usually, this type of putty is for filling tiny rock chips and the like. After it has dried thoroughly (usually 3–4 hours), it can be wet or dry sanded and primer/surfacer applied. Always get a nonshrinking putty.

area in the direction of the overall panel sanding job.

Scratches are easy to remove if they are only one paint coat thick. Just a little more localized pressure on the paper will do the job, but the "trough" should be feathered as much as possible. The little, minute rock chips along the car's front and around the wheel openings are harder to remove, and because of their sheer number, it's best to use a block or electric/air jitterbug. Incidentally, you can rent one of these handy gadgets. When the rock chips are really numerous and deep, resort to an initial attack with #100-grit paper, then follow up with the finer grits before priming. When this happens, the entire color coat area is usually removed, but the effort is necessary.

Chips on the rest of the car, such as around exposed hinges or door openings, are really the hardest of all to featheredge, mainly because their size means the featheredging will leave a sort of smooth crater. Although the paint may be thin, the crater will really show up (even if properly featheredged) in the finished job if you're not careful. The best technique when fixing up chipped places is to make the featheredged area several times bigger than the size of the chipped area. If there were several coats of paint on the car, the crater might best be filled with a thin coat of putty after the primer is applied. The important point is to make a chip crater as smooth as possible, flowing gradually into surrounding paint.

Be careful when sanding next to chrome, aluminum or glass, as the paper will cut these surfaces quickly. Next to chrome, slide the index finger or little finger off the paper and use it as a guide. The same goes for the other materials, too. With a block, just be careful.

The edges of all opening panels should be block-sanded to bare metal. This won't be hard, as the paint here is usually very thin at best. This procedure will eliminate a large percentage of edge chips, and will keep the new paint's thickness at these points to a minimum, which cuts down on the chances of future chips.

The door jambs and door edges should be washed clean of all accumulated dirt and grease, then thoroughly sanded with both paper and #00 steel wool. The steel wool gets down in all the little irregularities the paper can't reach, ensuring that the final paint will bond securely.

If a spot has been worked, sand the bare area well with #220-grit so grinder scratches are no longer noticeable to the touch. The jitterbug also can be used here. Don't use rough paper, and don't lay on the pressure. Be careful—lead and fiberglass will scratch before the surrounding metal will.

Should the fiberglass area have what appear to be blisters, some further repair is in order. This sometimes happens, so just peel out the air-bubble blister with a knife blade and patch it with more glass or resin.

Special attention must be paid to a repaired area before primer/surfacer is applied. If lead was used, wash the entire area thoroughly with properly diluted MetalPrep, which removes the inherent acid and grease. Wash away the MetalPrep residue with water. With both fiberglass- and lead-repaired areas,

clean thoroughly with grease and wax remover (even though they've been well sanded), then spot with a good coat of primer.

Paint Guns

At this stage of the game, you'll want a compressor handy, which can be rented along with the paint gun. You'll only need it for a day (actually much less). The compressor should be able to maintain a steady 80 pounds pressure, which is more than enough for painting.

Build up a tank pressure, drain the tank of any oil or water (the renter will show you how), then blow all the dirt and sanding residue from the car. Be especially careful to get all the little pieces of stuff that get in the cracks around windows, windshield, hood, hinges, etc. Use a lint-free rag or tack cloth as you go along to clean the surface as well as all chrome and glass areas.

When the car is clean, tape off the trim, glass, and interior. Since the prime/surfacer will be either lacquer or acrylic, you don't have to worry about spray sticking to everything.

For automobile refinishing, two types of paint guns are common, one having the gun (mixer) and the paint container (cup) integral, the other having the container separated from the gun by an extra hose. These types are further divided into bleeder and nonbleeder, external-mix and internal-mix, and pressure-, gravity-, suction-feed guns.

The bleeder-type gun is more common in the very inexpensive lines, and is designed without an air valve. The air passes through the gun at all times, which keeps the air pressure from building up in the hose. There are no air-pressure control devices involved, so the

As part of the taping-off procedure, be sure to open doors, deck lid, hood, and tape off rubber insulation strips. Clean grooves around openings with sandpaper or steel wool, wipe the area with lacquer thinner to remove any grease, then apply the tape. Cover inside of trunk, driving compartment, engine with newspapers to protect from overspray.

To make masking job easier, lay roll of paper or newspaper on flat surface and lap masking tape over the edge, then lift the paper and tape to attach where needed.

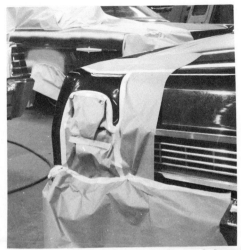

To get excellent taping results and limit amount of paint sprayed on chrome trim, etc., run piece of tape over trim; add tape and paper in second operation. Never sand basic paint before taping, though primer can be sanded. Always check for tape peeling back off surface before shooting paint.

gun is used with small low-pressure compressors. More suitable to automobile painting is the nonbleeder design, which has an air valve to shut off the air as the trigger is released. With such a gun you can control both the air and the paint flow by trigger manipulation.

The internal-mixing spray gun mixes the air and paint inside the cap, but this design also is not well suited to automobile work. Better is the external-mix gun, which mixes and atomizes the air and paint just outside the cap. A suction-feed gun uses the force of a stream of compressed air to cause a vacuum, which causes the paint to push out of the container. The fluid tip extends slightly beyond the air cap on this design. Practically all paint shops use this type of gun. If the fluid tip is flush with the air cap, chances are the gun is

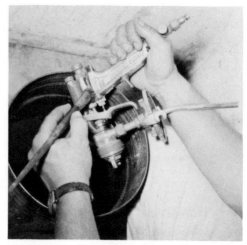

It is wise to clean the paint gun before doing any work, especially if the gun is borrowed or has been allowed to set idle for a long period. Do not dip the spray head in thinner; just clean the places that can be reached and make sure nozzle head is clear.

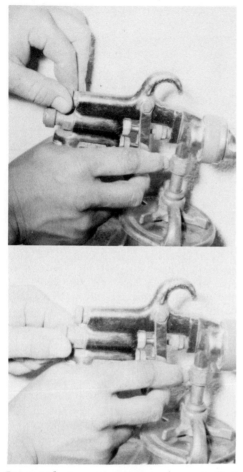

Paint and air spray mixture are controlled on most paint guns by two knobs at back of head assembly. Lower knob adjusts amount of air. When adjustment is correct, spray fan is about ten inches wide ten inches from head nozzle.

of the pressure-feed type, commonly used on automotive assembly lines, in which the paint is forced to the gun by air pressure in the container attached to the spray gun.

The air cap is located at the extreme tip of the paint gun, with a knurled face so it can be gripped and removed by hand. Such a cap may have one to four orifices for air, which is directed into the paint stream to atomize the mixture. Heavy materials will atomize better with multiple-orifice caps.

It is imperative to keep all spray-painting equipment as clean as possible, so that means cleaning the gun after each and every use. If the gun isn't cleaned, the paint will dry in those difficult-to-clean nozzles. When cleaning the suction-feed gun, loosen the cup and hold the gun handle over it with the siphon tube inside the container. Unscrew the air cap several turns, then cover the cap with a rag and pull the trigger. Air pressure will be diverted through the fluid passages and will force any paint in the gun back into the cup.

Empty the cup and clean it thoroughly with thinner, then pour a small amount of thinner into the cup. Spray this solvent through the gun to flush the

If the gun seems to clog up while spraying, the siphon tubes can be backflushed by holding rag tightly over head nozzle and pulling trigger. This will also blow breather hole in top of can lid open, so watch for any spatter. Keep the breather hole punched clear of drying paint.

It is essential that all paint be strained as it is being poured into the gun cup. Thinner can be added in cup, if not previously added in larger can.

fluid passages. Keep a small can of solvent handy for gun cleaning. Wipe the gun housing with a soaked rag or a bristle brush, preferably the latter.

The air cap should be removed and cleaned by soaking it in clean thinner. Dry the cap with compressed air. If the small holes are plugged, soak the cap longer, then open the holes with a toothpick or broomstraw. Do not use a metal object, as this may enlarge the orifices.

Priming

When the entire car is taped, and the spray gun ready to fire, mix up the primer/surfacer. Always remember that neither lacquer nor acrylic will go over enamel in color-coat form! The only time this can be done is over a baked-enamel job where the paint is dry clear through. Even baked enamel from local shops is likely to blister when covered with the hotter paints. This applies only to the color coats, and not to the primer, which will cover the surface with no adverse effects.

No matter what kind of paint will be finally used—enamel, lacquer, or acrylic —use a multi-purpose primer with the appropriate thinner. Mix according to the directions on the can, which is usually about two parts thinner to one part primer, then stir thoroughly. For primer, a good all-round spray-gun head will do, something like a #30 on the DeVibliss and #362 on the Binks. Adjust the gun so that the spray fan is about 8 inches wide, 12 inches from the gun head. If the fan is too wide, there will be a thin spot in the middle, and if it's too narrow the pattern will appear as a tight band. The fan adjustment is the top knob above the handle. The second knob is for material adjustment.

The paint gun is held in this fashion. If it is tipped in any direction so that nozzle is not "flat" with surface being sprayed, the spray will be uneven. Practice spraying thinner on garage door before starting to paint.

If the paint gun drips around cup/lid connection, wrap a rag around the area as shown to prevent drips onto the surface being sprayed.

Make several practice passes on a piece of cardboard, with the compressor setting at 60 pounds constant. If you use the DeVilbiss, keep the gun 8 to 12 inches away from the surface; if you use the Binks, make it 10 to 12 inches. Notice that when the paint-gun trigger is first depressed there is a moment when only air comes out, quickly followed by the paint. Practice making a smooth pass, keeping the gun at a constant distance from the surface until the pass (which will average about 2 feet per swing) is completed. Start the pass on one side, swing horizontally to the other limit, raise or lower the gun nearly a fan width, and go back. The gun should be kept parallel to the surface, so that one end of the fan isn't closer than the other.

If the paint is going on correctly, it will appear smooth and wet for just a bit after application. If it looks grainy (as if full of sand), the paint is too thick or you're holding the gun too far away from the surface. If the paint runs (you won't need anybody to show you what this is!), it is too thin or you are holding the gun too close to the surface. If the patch alternates dry-wet-dry, or wet-runny-wet, your pass is not constant.

Plan your time so that you're through spraying with at least two hours of sunlight left, and when the temperature is at least 60° or above. If you are spraying in winter or inside when it's raining, use special thinner (the paint store will tell you).

Next, use the wax-and-grease-remover solution again, even in the tiniest cracks. This is vital, for any foreign substance will invariably ruin an otherwise perfect paint job. Just the marks left by your fingers will leave dark splotches under the final color. When washing the car

All bare metal must be cleaned with a special cleaner to remove grease and foreign materials, then primer/surfacer is sprayed on.

If the spray pattern leaves a vacant spot in the middle, as shown on practice board, adjust the knob on the head. Each painter has his own special adjustment, so the amateur should play around a bit here before starting to spray the car.

with the cleaning solution, always use clean, lint-free rags (don't use shop towels, as they often are cleaned with low-grade solvents that will interfere with good paint adhesion). It's wise to use a special cleanser always, but in a pinch you can use lacquer thinner, applied with a very wet rag and immediately wiped off with a dry rag. Don't wait even a minute if you use thinner, as it is "hot" and will quickly soften the primer surface and may cause other damage below.

Finish Painting

The car is now ready for the final color, and this is the precise time most amateur painters get the jitters. It's also the time when one step must follow the other in rapid succession, so it's well to have the procedures well established in your mind.

What you do from now on depends a

This happens if you get too close with the spray gun. Keep the gun 8–12 inches from the surface. If the paint seems to go on dry and "grainy," the gun is being held too far away.

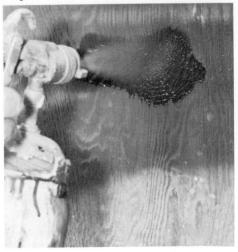

lot upon the paint you're using—the type, not the brand. Lacquer is the easiest to spray for the novice, followed by acrylic, then enamel. Lacquer and acrylic dry much faster, compensating for many errors in application.

Before ever blowing color at the waiting car, test the pattern again. Start by opening the gun up by turning the spreader adjustment (top thumb screw above the handle) all the way out, and backing off the fluid screw (right beneath the spreader adjustment) until the first thread shows. Adjust the air-pressure regulator to give a constant 40 pounds pressure for lacquer and acrylics, or 60 pounds pressure for enamel. Hold the gun 6 or 8 inches from the test surface, parallel to the surface, and give the trigger one full pull, then release it again.

The resulting pattern of paints should be uniform throughout, with fine atomization and no distortion. If something

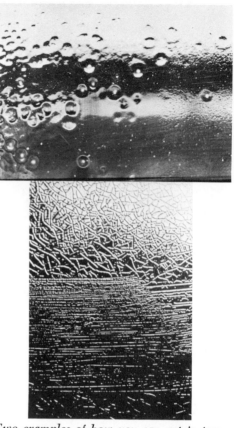

Two examples of how you can get in trouble. In the one case, the paint "checks" because two different types of paint and/or thinner have been mixed (lacquer and enamel). Always check with the paint store to see what kind of paint is needed. The cratering effect can be caused by oil on the metal surface, water in the paint.

It is possible to paint something quite well with pressurized can paints; the ideal distance is about the width of spread fingers as shown. Never mix this type of paint with type shot through spray gun.

is wrong with the pattern, it will make the painting process exceptionally difficult for a nonprofessional.

The color coat is sprayed exactly like the primer/surfacer. However, some extra preparation might be needed if lacquer or acrylic is being applied over enamel. Just as a precaution, if the old paint is enamel, spray on a coat of Du-Pont #22 sealer, which will keep the enamel from raising due to the hot

Always peel tape back over itself and away from the adjoining paint. Peel slowly. This will keep the tape from lifting paint that has not yet adhered completely to under-base.

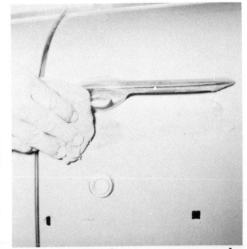

If the paint is a lacquer type, it can be rubbed out for luster. Use rubbing compound and rag for hand-rubbing around areas that can't be reached by power buffer.

lacquer thinner. If you're not sure, you can spray a test patch first, but a sealer is the best bet.

All the previous work will come to naught if the final-color spraying is done haphazardly. Before actually spraying any paint, practice the proper spraying swing.

The single biggest problem the amateur faces is stroke inconsistency. The paint must overlap everywhere, otherwise it will appear streaked when it dries. It might be advisable for the neophyte to make horizontal strokes on the panel first, followed by vertical strokes (the gun laid on its side to keep the fan pattern right), and finished by criss-cross strokes. The idea is to get the same amount of paint everywhere.

If lacquer is being used, you can paint merrily on your way. However, acrylic must be allowed to "flash"—that is, surface-harden—before the next coat is applied. Following the enamel procedure works well with acrylic. Enamel, being a very slow dryer, cannot be applied all at once. The first time apply a very light, or tack, coat. This will become sticky in a few minutes and helps make subsequent spraying easier by increasing

Power buffer with good sheepskin head requires very light touch to keep from rubbing through paint. Tip buffer head slightly. Final buffing with corn starch gives final sheen.

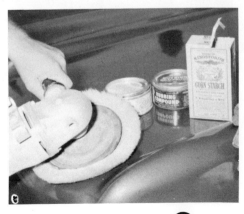

adhesion. The second coat of enamel is sprayed normally, but the amateur should never try to get all the paint in one pass.

A note about enamel and moisture. Moisture and paint just don't mix, so if you wash the floor to keep the dust down, let it dry before painting. This also might be a good time to discuss temperature and paint. The temperatures shouldn't be under 60° or over 100°F. when you paint the car, otherwise special steps are required. Remember, this is the temperature of the metal. If you're painting lacquer or acrylic out in

Nicks can be repaired with tiny brush or frayed end of paper matchstick. It usually takes two or three layers to get good matching coverage.

You're not likely to have a fine paint booth at home, but you can get the car ready for the final color coating and deliver it to a good paint shop. This way you will have saved considerably on cost of total paint job. Lacquer paints can be sprayed without benefit of booth, but they won't be dust free.

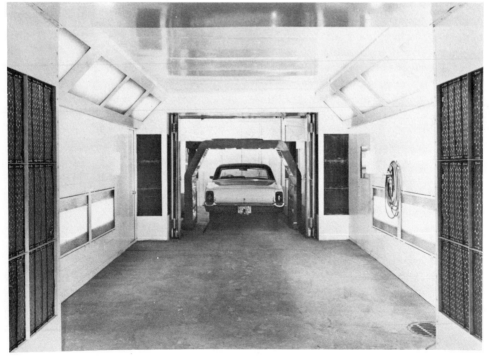

The final care of any paint job rests with good periodic cleaning with cold water and chamois, use of mild polishing compound to cut hazing, excellent coverage with premium wax. Just driving car through automatic car wash with hot wax is not enough.

the back yard, that hot sun can get the body sizzling.

Special additives are available to control the drying time, such as DuPont #3656 (rather than normal 366/g) for acrylic, which will slow down drying if the temperature is too hot. If you are painting when it's wet or cold, the color can "blush"—that is, moisture gets trapped in the paint—so a slower-acting thinner or special retarder might be needed. The local paint salesman will guide you here. At all times, follow the mixture directions of the manfacturer!

A note about the spraying environment. It is often possible to rent the facilities of a paint shop over the weekend, thereby gaining the equipment and paint booth. However, the only real requirement is that enamel should be painted in a dust-free atmosphere. A fly walking across the surface makes a mess. Don't spray enamel inside your family garage, unless you don't mind an overspray on everything. Enamel overspray will stay, while lacquer and acrylic will dust off or wash away. Lacquer and acrylic can be sprayed quite well outdoors.

Although the enamel job can be done all in one spraying, lacquer and acrylic require more elapsed time for the best results. If you have the time, spray the latter in several good coats, then allow to dry for a couple of days. Water-sand with #600-grit sandpaper, then spray with several more coats. Whereas enamel doesn't require any special after-spray attention, lacquer and acrylic must be color sanded with #600-grit paper before final rubbing out.

In case you have ended up with some sags (runs), which is easy to do if you've used enamel, very lightly water-sand the run ridges after the paint has set at least two weeks, then lightly fog the area with new paint.

15 lubrication maintenance

PRACTICALLY EVERYTHING that has to do with a modern machine, including the automobile, relies to a great extent on friction. Whether it is the use of friction to do a job, such as tires against the pavement or brake shoes against a drum, or the reduction of friction with good lubrication, the idea is to control friction. In neither case—desired or undesired—can we completely modify friction. Rather, we learn how to live with it. Because the automobile is so very dependent on friction in either function, it is necessary to understand the value of periodic vehicle maintenance if we are to get our money's worth from any car.

Anytime we talk about lubrication and an automobile, we are concerned not with the problem of making friction do a job (such as we might with the clutch disc), but rather with how we can control the friction in the various component parts. In one place, we may be content with merely using a dab of grease for several years, while at other places we might need to give the part almost monthly attention. This is something each car owner can do, no matter how little he knows about automobiles, and it is something that will invariably ensure his car against premature failure. The automobile that has been maintained with a good lubrication schedule will ordinarily last many thousands of miles longer than the vehicle that gets only occasional maintenance. Combine good lubrication attention with good attention to the engine tune and the paint, and you can be assured of prime transportation long beyond the "normal" life of a given vehicle.

Automotive lubrication may be considered either "liquid" or "solid," although neither description is precise; as lubricants. Obviously, these latter are not lubricants in the normal sense of the word, but they do require periodic checks and thus fall into the lubrication maintenance schedule.

These items should be checked every time you fill the gas tank. While you may leave this procedure to the station attendant, it may prove worthwhile for you to do the actual checking yourself. Frequently attendants do not check all the underhood items unless specifically requested to do so, and if you get in the habit of doing this small job you will have a first-hand knowledge of what is happening to the car. Checking the coolant may seem a useless chore (see Chapter 10). Yet if you look at it each time you get gas, which means every 300 miles or so, you may pick up some early signs of engine trouble and be able to prevent larger problems at a future date —bubbles or foam in the water that would indicate a blown head gasket, for instance.

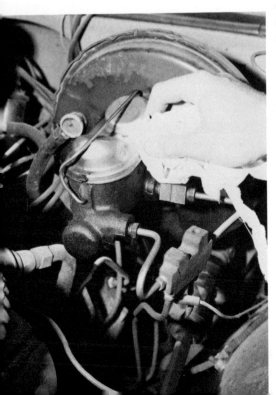

The battery should also be inspected for fluid level. But don't just pull off one cap and look inside, assuming all the chambers will be the same. In Chapter 8 you have found that the battery stores energy, and unless each cell is full of water and capable of taking a full electrical charge, the unit can be expected to fail soon. It is a good idea to wipe the battery top clean every time it is inspected, and if there is any residual acid buildup this should be removed with soda and water. To keep this residual controlled, and to help maintain a good connection at the battery poles, spray the area with a good silicone treatment, such as WD 40. The battery water level can decrease rapidly during hot weather, or if the electrical system is subjected to an abnormally high load for a length of time, such as on a long trip with the air conditioner working.

It is not necessary to check the hydraulic fluid level every time you gas up, but you should give the system a brief visual inspection. If there are any hydraulic leaks, you'll note them quickly addition it is common to think of the radiator coolant, battery water, and power steering/hydraulic brake cylinder fluid as wet spots on the brake backing plates, or as wet "runs" on the master cylinder housing (see Chapter 2). If the brakes seem to be "lower" than normal—that is, the brake pedal seems to depress more than usual to get braking—first

Part of lubrication maintenance is checking on fluids. Always clean the master cylinder thoroughly before opening it to check fluid level; add only the fluid recommended for your particular car. Wipe off any spilled fluid, as it will remove paint.

suspect low brake fluid in the master cylinder. Check the fluid at this time, or check it every time the engine oil is changed. A note on checking the fluid: Always clean the area around the cylinder housing thoroughly with a rag before removing the cylinder cap, and be especially careful not to get dirt in the fluid during checking or refill.

Often overlooked for service is the power steering pump reservoir (see Chapter 3). This pump is usually on the left (driver's) side of the engine, and may be well down inside the compartment. It may have other accessories mounted over it, making it somewhat difficult to reach. Some PS pumps will have a reservoir as part of the pump housing, usually with a dipstick as part of the cap. Other pumps may have the reservoir mounted remote, often on the fender splash apron. If there is no dipstick, the reservoir is normally filled to near the top edge. Use only power steering oil for this system. Should the oil already in the system appear unusually dirty, chances are good it has become contaminated. Drain the oil (usually by removing the hose which exits the pump housing at the lowest point), and put in new oil. Should this oil also become contaminated soon, the reservoir cap may not be sealing properly, or the pump may be on the verge of failure.

Check all the drive belts, and make sure they are in tension according to the manufacturer's specifications. It is impossible to define the exact tension limits in this book, since they vary so widely; however, if the belt has more than 1/2-inch play midway between two pulleys it is probably too loose. Never take a chance on a belt that looks frayed. Replace it immediately. It is also a good practice to carry a spare belt for water pump and generator/alternator. Should

Check power steering reservoir fluid level and keep this level topped off for best results. If fluid seems discolored, drain and refill the system.

you ever be caught without a spare it is possible to jury-rig an emergency belt from a piece of rope. This is a poor repair at best, and the engine rpm must be kept very low while you limp into a station.

Another underhood fluid check should be the automatic transmission. This is too often left to chance. Rather than checking it only when the engine oil is changed, check the automatic transmission fluid at least every 1000 miles—at every gas stop is even better. This becomes especially critical if you are towing a trailer or subjecting the transmission to adverse heat conditions. Check the automatic when the fluid has warmed up, with the shifter in one of the drive

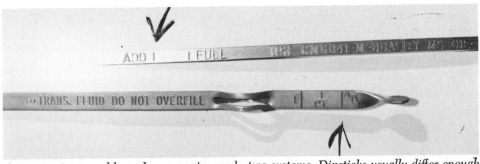

Arrows point to add marks on engine and automatic transmission dipsticks. Transmissions is usually marked in pints, engine in quarts. Never mix the types of oil for these two systems. Dipsticks usually differ enough so that they cannot be switched accidentally.

positions. This causes the pump to pull fluid into the valve body (see Chapter 11), and if the oil level is low it will show immediately. Use only a premium quality automatic transmission fluid (ATF). Every time you check the transmission fluid level, smell the fluid. If it has a pungent odor, it is probably all right. When the fluid has been subjected to excessive heat and has "broken down" it will lose the odor. Under such conditions, say towing a trailer up a long desert grade, it may be best to change the fluid whether the odor has been lost or not.

Finally, check the engine oil level. If the engine has just been shut off and the dipstick shows the level to be about one-half quart low, the oil level will be fine. By the time the oil flows back into the oil pan from all the galleries, the level will be up (see Chapter 9). However, if the dipstick shows the oil to be one or more quarts low, you should add oil. Some dipsticks will have two level indications marked; one for a low reading (which is usually one quart low), and another which says "add," which usually indicates two quarts low. Never drive the car if the engine oil is two or more quarts low. On occasion, an engine will

come along that seems to "kick out" the top quart of oil, and consistently run one quart low. You may continue to run this one quart low, but keep a very close check on the oil pressure and the oil level if this condition prevails.

Now, let's assume you have been taking good care of your car, and you are about to take a vacation, driving from your Ohio home to California via Glacier National Park in Montana. The driving conditions you'll encounter will put your car through just about every type of torture the automobile can expect. With this in mind, you can perform your own lubrication at home so that the car is in top shape throughout the trip.

Run the car onto a hard surface, one that is level and dirt free. Jack up the front of the vehicle and install jackstands under the frame. If you have an extra pair of jackstands, do the same to the rear. The car doesn't have to be very high—just enough to clear the tires.

If you haven't warmed the engine previous to this, do so now. In fact, since you are also going to check the transmission and rear-end lubricants, it is a good idea to start your lube maintenance only after you've driven the car for five miles or so.

 399

Drain the engine oil. An adjustable wrench will provide the correct size. You won't have a great amount of room beneath the car to maneuver, so make it easier by first laying down a section of plastic. You can slide around on this, and should you spill water or oil on the driveway the plastic will protect your clothing. Use whatever is handy to catch the draining oil; anything from milk cartons to a dishpan. Unless you've done this before, however, get a pan big enough to hold all the engine oil, which is anywhere from four to six quarts.

Position the pan so it is to the rear of the drain plug, because the oil will tend to squirt out in a strong stream at first. Remember, too, that the oil will be hot, hot enough to scald your hand. Loosen the plug with the adjustable wrench, then take it out with your fingers. Work with your hand coming in from the side of the oil pan. While the oil is draining, you will be able to check other parts.

Since this is going to be a long trip, check the front wheel bearing lubrication (see Chapter 1). No need to remove the wheel; just take off the hub cap and the drum dust cover. Remove the cotter pin that prevents the spindle nut from backing off prematurely, and remove the spindle nut. If the front wheel bearings have been packed recently, the grease will appear almost new. If the grease seems thin or runny, you should repack the bearings. Pull the wheel drum assembly from the spindle. Remove the outer bearing. Chances are good that the lubricant has not failed to the point where the inner bearing and seal must be also removed. Use your finger or any handy object to remove as much of the original grease from the hub inner section as possible. If this grease also looks black and thin, you should probably knock out the grease seal and remove the rear bearing. Don't expect to save this seal for reuse, so pry it out with a screwdriver if necessary. Do not scratch the seal or bearing seat.

Wash the bearings in a clean solvent. Although it is nice to force new grease into the bearing retainers with the compression device most gas stations have, you can get the job done at home by liberally coating the bearing with grease, then rotating each roller bearing to make sure it is coated. Put on a lot of grease and you can't go wrong. Install the inner bearing (it will only go in one way) and tap new grease seals in place. Place about one tablespoon of grease inside the hub; if you put in too much grease here it will tend to work out around the seal. Put the wheel drum back on the spindle, and slide the outer bearing in place. There will be a thick washer that fits between the outer bearing and the retaining nut; make sure this is installed!

Pull the retaining nut down taut, and rotate the wheel. You can tell by "feel" when the nut gets too tight, but it is best to follow the manufacturer's recommendations on spindle nut tightness for your particular car. These specifications vary from car to car, and they should be followed. If you don't have the specs handy, ask the local gas station attendant how tight your particular front wheel bearings should be. As a general rule, you want the tapered roller bearings to be just tight enough to give minimum friction between roller and bearing race, but not loose enough so you can feel "slop" in the bearing. If for some reason the dust cap has been damaged, get a new one; dirt inside the wheel bearings will destroy bearings immediately.

One final note on front wheel bearing lubrication. There is a difference in the kind of bearing grease used in new and old cars. Always tell the parts store exactly what kind of car you are working on, and they will give you the correct type of grease.

By now, the engine oil should have thoroughly drained. Before replacing the drain plug, run your finger into the plug hole and feel for any residue on the pan bottom. If there is any, it will come off on your finger; if you see a lot of silver particles in the residue, you might suspect abnormal bearing wear. If the residue is just black and sludgy, it is normal. Feel in the drain pan for particles of metal. If you find what really is metal (rather than flakes of carbon from the combustion chamber, or corrosion residue from the inside walls of the cylinder block), take the piece(s) to a mechanic. It might be part of a small gear tooth, or part of a broken ring. Replace the drain plug snugly, but don't overtighten it.

Now move the drain pan below the oil filter and remove the filter. Some filters are of the "spin-on" type, while others are cannister design. The former will be self-contained, while the latter will be a filter inside a metal container. If you have the cannister design, remove the center bolt holding the can to the engine block. When you have loosened the bolt, oil may start to drain around the bolt. Remove the bolt completely and the cannister will fall into the drain pan. Of importance here is to check the sealing gasket that fits around the upper lip of the cannister, where it mates with the engine. Your new filter element will include this gasket.

Remove the cannister and bolt, and clean them thoroughly in solvent. Wipe the residual oil from around the engine block, being especially careful to clean the area where the sealing gasket fits. Install the new element in the cannister, and place the gasket on the block sealing surface. This gasket may be difficult to hold in place while getting the cannister snug; make sure it is in correct position before tightening the cannister bolt. Don't overtighten the cannister bolt, just bring it up snug. After you refill the engine with oil, run the engine for ten minutes and recheck to make sure oil is not leaking out around the cannister seal. If it is, tighten the bolt slightly. If this doesn't stop the leak, your gasket isn't in place correctly and you'll have to loosen the bolt to adjust the gasket.

The spin-on filter may be removed with giant "water pump" pliers. But since you aren't likely to have such a tool, the best bet is to purchase a low-cost filter "wrench" at a parts store. This is really just a band that tightens around the filter body so you can remove and replace the filter. This type of filter usually has the sealing gasket built into the filter top, and all you have to do is clean the block area before installing the new filter. Check for filter leaks after running the engine ten minutes, as with the cannister type filter.

Should you decide to change from the cannister type filter to the spin-on type (the latter is definitely easier to change at home), you can buy a special adapter plate at the auto parts store. This plate is simple to install, and comes with complete instructions.

While the car is up on jackstands, you can do a complete lubrication job on all the grease fittings, as well as check the condition of universal joints and transmission rear end grease. You can also adjust the brakes.

If the automatic transmission fluid

needs changing (changing ATF once a year is not a bad idea, more often if it fails due to heat), the transmission pan may or may not have to be removed. Some auto transmissions have a drain plug in the pan, others do not. In either case, it is good maintenance to go ahead and drop the pan. Just remove all the bolts around the pan and it will come off. Have the drain pan handy, because there will be several quarts of oil to run out. Not all the oil will drain, however, since some ATF will be in the torque converter (see Chapter 11). Check the oil residue in the bottom of the pan; if there are any silver particles, again suspect wear somewhere. In this case, it is most probably the torque converter pump. If the transmission has been acting up lately, and if there is a significant amount of silver particles, you had better see a transmission expert before starting that trip. But chances are you will find no indications of excessive wear in the transmission oil pan. There may be flecks of a fibrous material; these will be particles from the clutch discs inside the transmission, and unless the pieces are big they will be of no concern. If the transmission is severely overheated, however, these discs will be the first to fail.

With the pan removed, inspect the filter screen. If this screen seems to be plugged, it should be removed and very thoroughly cleaned. Restriction of oil flow at this point cuts down on the amount of oil available to the transmission for shifting gears, lubricating and cooling parts, etc. If the pump screen appears okay, clean the pan and replace it. Use a new pan gasket if you have one handy, if not use one of the new silicone cements (such as Gel-Gasket from Permatex). This product will form a gasket; just don't make the bolts too tight until

the cement has had a chance to harden into rubber, then torque the bolts to recommendation.

Some torque converters are sealed, others are not. To find out what you have, remove the converter inspection plate. This will be a small plate that bolts to the transmission bellhousing face (front end). It will be directly behind where the oil pan meets the engine block, and is usually held in place by from four to six bolts. When the plate is removed, rotate the torque converter (spin the engine with the starter). If there is a plug in the converter, it will be readily apparent; remove the plug and the converter will drain. Replace the plug and the inspection plate, and refill the transmission. If the converter has been drained, the transmission will take the full amount of oil. If the converter has not been drained, add a quart of ATF at a time, checking the transmission dipstick to make sure the unit is not overfilled. Do not overfill!

To check the lubricant in a standard transmission, note that on the transmission main body there will be one or two plugs. These threaded plugs usually have square heads. If there is a plug in the bottom of the case, it is for draining the unit. The plug about halfway up the case side is for filling the unit, and for checking the fluid level. Remove this plug. The transmission grease (grease is not the correct term, since it is really just a heavy weight of oil) should be level with this hole. Too much lubricant and there is not enough room for air in the transmission, forcing oil out around the seals.

If the transmission fluid seems low, curl a finger into the hole. If the finger tip does not touch fluid (the vehicle should be level for this check, one reason

Use a good white grease on all points of movement of the body parts. Brake lube works well for the hood latch mechanism.

with a lubrication grease nipple, or they may be sealed. It is easy enough to tell if a U-joint is getting good lubrication if it has a grease fitting—merely squirt grease in the nipple and if grease runs out around the edge of the U-joint, it is getting lube. If one of the bearing cups does not show grease, it may be plugged and suspectible to failure. If the joint is lube-sealed, however, you can't tell whether or not it is okay. You can disassemble the U-joint and insert grease into each cup, then reassemble the unit. Or, you can do what most home mechanics are doing; you can keep a close watch for the tattletale trace of dry powder (usually a black or dark red) that shows up around the lip of a cup that has run dry. At this point, replacement of the U-joint is almost imperative.

The rear end assembly uses the same oil, 90-pound grease, that the standard transmission uses. Usually, the access to a rear end is much greater than to the

for using jackstands at the rear as well as at the front), additional oil must be added. This will normally be 90-pound transmission "grease," and it is available at the auto parts store in plastic bottles. Getting the oil into the standard transmission is usually difficult without a special "grease gun;" this too is available at the parts store.

While at the transmission, it is also advisable to lubricate the shifting arms and clutch throwout linkage. Use a good white grease, perhaps the same used for lubrication where brake shoes touch the backing plates. Apply this grease to the shifting linkage friction points, and to the clutch linkage (especially where the clutch linkage touches the throwout fork). Note that late model automobiles often use nylon bushings where the linkage connects. These bushings are very durable, but if one should show signs of wear, it can be replaced at minimal cost.

Check the driveshaft for unnecessary "sloppiness." Note from Chapter 12 that driveline universal joints may be fitted

Depending on your model car, rear end housing may have a drain plug in lower portion or on side of housing (may be at rear as shown, or in front part of the gear housing). This opening is used to fill and to check fluid level. Special suction pump gun for removing and filling lubricants in rear end is available at parts house.

transmission, and you can pour oil directly from the container into the rear end. Check the end lube level by removing the plug and keeping the lube level with the plug hole. Should you experience unusually hot weather, a heavyweight rear end and transmission oil is available, but this should be drained prior to cold weather. A special note on rear end and transmission lubricants: If you have a limited-slip type differential, it may need a special lubricant. If this lubricant is not used, the rear end may tend to "lock up" on turns and in general act unruly. Special lubricants for limited-slip rear ends are available at the parts store.

It is also desirable to change transmission and rear end lubricants because they do "wear out." This may be at recommended mileages, but a rule of thumb is to change it yearly. The special suction type grease gun that parts stores sell for transmission and rear end servicing can be used to suck the old lube out, and to put the new lube in. On occasion, a transmission will leak between two cast iron mating surfaces. In this event, you can seal the leak by wiping the metal dry and spreading a layer of silicone rubber cement across the joint. This is an easy way to stop an annoying oil stain on the driveway. This type of remedy does not work where oil is seeping around a rubber seal, however. In this case, which usually shows up at the rear of the transmission or the front of the rear end gear assembly, the solution is normally a new seal.

You will want to purchase a grease gun and a good supply of chassis grease. But before you start pumping grease to the chassis, it is advisable to study the suspension points for awhile, so that you will not overlook a grease zerk (fitting).

Grease guns available from parts stores will do an excellent home lube job. Force in grease until old grease is seen squeezing out from bearing or bushing. If the grease seems to flow through with no effort, the bearing or bushing may be failing and should be replaced.

As a rule, you can expect to find a grease fitting at any point on the suspension where the suspension moves against another piece of metal. This is not always true, however, as some new cars are beginning to use nylon bushings and bearing surfaces, which do not need lubrication.

Use a screwdriver to pry away accumulated grease and dirt, especially around pivot points at the front end A-arms. If the car uses a beam axle, there will usually be two grease fittings at the king pin boss, one above and one below the spindle. If the car uses A-arms, there may be fittings on the upper ball joints, as well as one or two fittings on the spindle boss. Clean each of these fittings with a rag, wiping the fitting free of dirt and used grease.

Some new cars have "long-life" fittings, where the parts are sealed for several years and many thousands of miles. Some modern ball joints are of this type. In this case, there will be a threaded hole where you might expect to find a grease fitting. Leave greasing this part to the service station.

Once in awhile, you will find a fitting that has "frozen up" and will not accept grease. In this case, remove the fitting

Replace fittings with factory types only. If a particular fitting, if curved, could be better serviced at home, install the new fitting but make sure it will not interfere with movement of the suspension member.

and soak it in solvent. If this does not free the internal valve, install a new fitting. It is also possible to find a broken fitting, in which case only a new fitting will work.

Install one of the grease cartridges in the grease gun. The nose of the gun will "snap" over the grease fitting, then all you do is pump the handle. As new grease goes into the fitting, old grease (which may be "broken down" or contaminated) will be forced out around the bushing, bearing, or rubber seal. Force just a bit of this "old" grease out of the area, then wipe the excess off. Wipe each fitting clear of grease to prevent dirt building up at the inlet, dirt that can later be forced into the bearing surface.

Some of the fittings will seem very difficult to get to; in this case the solution is usually turning the steering wheel, or jacking up the wheel slightly. Do not overlook a single fitting! There will be fittings on the steering linkage, on the shifting linkage (usually at the steering mast), on the clutch linkage,

Always clean off all grease fittings with a rag before attempting to force grease into the fitting. The fitting must be replaced if it will not accept grease.

Spray all rubber isolated parts of the suspension system to eliminate annoying squeaks and to increase rubber life. Silicone works well here.

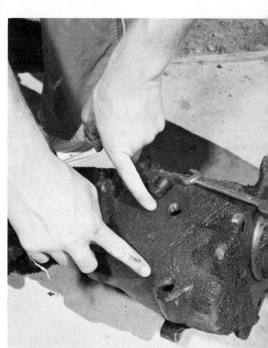

Transmission drain hole is at bottom of the case on standard transmissions; the hole about half-way up the case side is for filling with oil. Check to see that oil is level with fill hole. Drain old oil in transmission once a year.

on the brake/clutch arms if the car is an older one, (most late-model cars have "hanging pedals," with no grease fittings), perhaps at the universal joints, rarely on the outer ends of each rear axle housing (to grease the bearings), and on both ends of semielliptic springs (at the front pivot and rear shackle points). If it moves, it gets grease!

You're still not through under the car, so don't remove those jackstands yet. It is also advisable to lubricate places that do not have grease fittings. At any point where rubber touches metal, squirt on some silicone spray, such as WD-40 or Ruglide. This will keep the rubber from squeaking. Lube the shock absorber ends, rear spring front and rear pivot points, and even the spring leaves. Now you can let the car down off the jacks.

If you haven't done so already, fill the engine and automatic transmission with oil. Use the kind of engine oil you anticipate buying throughout the trip. Never mix an engine oil unless absolutely necessary. Under no conditions should

you mix different weights of oil. Decide what kind of driving you are going to be doing, and add an oil for that temperature. For our trip through the West, one of the heavier oils would be good because of the hot desert temperatures and high mountain passes. By the time the trip is over the car will have covered at least 5000 miles and it will be time for another oil change, anyway.

Start the engine, and note that the oil pressure gauge or light shows there is oil pressure. Let the engine idle for awhile so you can check for filter leaks. While the engine is running, squirt some of the WD-40 on the carburetor linkage (this includes the firewall linkage pivot as well). Some distributors will have a small oiling neck to lubricate the shaft; use a fine machine-type oil for this. Older cars with generators usually had two oiling points, one at the front, the other at the rear of the generator. Use the same machine oil for these points. Older cars often had a grease fitting on the water pump; if so, make sure this fitting is lubed. Do not overlube this area, as it will merely force grease into the water.

It is possible the air cleaner will need lubricating, too. Many cars use a paper filter air cleaner element, but there are a few that still use the oil-wetted element, and some new cleaners with a polyurethane element. Both of these types need to be cleaned in solvent. The polyurthane element should be squeezed dry and soaked in 30-weight oil before replacement; the wire mesh type should have 30-weight oil squirted on it liberally and allowed to drip "dry" before replacement. While cleaning with the solvent, also clean the breather cap wire mesh.

Use a dab of white grease on the hood latch mechanism and the hood hinges, and you are through in that area. Now you can start on the "insides."

The speedometer cable should be serviced periodically. Disconnect the cable at the speedometer head, and pull the drive cable from the housing. Wipe the cable clean; if the old lubricant is dried or hard, clean the cable with solvent. Coat the cable with speedometer lube, and reinsert it in the housing. You may have to spin it slightly to get it to seat in the lower drive gear. Wipe away excess lubricant and attach the housing to the speedometer head.

Pull out all the control knobs, clean the shanks with a rag, and spray with WD-40. Squirt WD-40 on the seat track mechanisms and on all door hinges. It

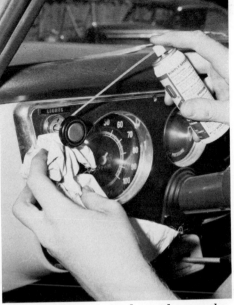

Clean the shafts of switches with a rag, then spray on a thin coat of silicone, such as WD-40.

Sticking doors may only need a light coat of lube to free them. Lubriplate and Door-Ease are types of nonstaining lubricants for the door locks.

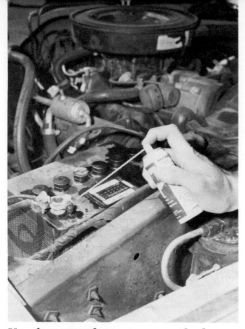

Use the same silicone spray on the battery terminals to reduce buildup of corrosive acids.

Spray all points of the carburetor linkage with silicone at every lube job. Linkage becomes stiff with buildup of grease; clean it thoroughly every time carburetor is overhauled.

may take several applications before the hinges work freely. Spray the ends of all control cables—where the cables operate heater flaps, vents, etc.

There is a special lubricant for the door latch mechanism, called Lubriplate. Use solvent to clean off all old grease and apply the new grease liberally. Apply this grease to the striker plate, the dovetail, and any place where the door may seem to "ride" on the latching assembly.

If the sun visors seems to be stiff, pull the visor off the suport shaft. Clean the shaft and relubricate with ordinary bath soap. If the visor is still too stiff, remove the soap and use WD-40. If the visor is too loose after cleaning the shaft, and tends to fall free, bend the shaft slightly to increase interference with the visor.

You can lubricate the window glass by squirting a light coating of dry graphite on the window channels. Use the same graphite in the door locks and deck lid lock. With this, you have completed your pretrip lubrication. Subsequent lubes will not require as extensive a coverage as this one, which we might call a 6000-mile checkup. If you have most of the equipment and material you need, you can do this entire job in the driveway in about four hours, and you will save yourself a handy sum of money in the process. By purchasing your oils and greases at a discount store, you can expect to save 30–50 percent on materials alone.

Excellent lubrication maintenance may be as near as your driveway!